# OF BENS, GLENS AND RAMBLING AULD MEN

# OF BENS, GLENS

## AND

## RAMBLING AULD MEN

ROBERT SCOTT

AND

GORDON NICOL

Matador
9 Priory Business Park,
Wistow Road, Kibworth Beauchamp,
Leicestershire. LE8 0RX
Tel: (+44) 116 279 2299
Email: books@troubador.co.uk
Web: www.troubador.co.uk/matador

ISBN 978 1784623 739

British Library Cataloguing in Publication Data.
A catalogue record for this book is available from the British Library.

Printed and bound by CPI Group (UK) Ltd, Croydon, CR0 4YY
Typeset by Troubador Publishing Ltd, Leicester, UK

**Matador** is an imprint of Troubador Publishing Ltd

To all those who love our Scottish hills


'*Every ramble was a radiant adventure in a new-created world*'
Edward A. Armstrong


'*I'm chained to the work-bench on Monday*
*But I'm out on the high crag on a Sunday*'
Adapted from song by Ewan MacColl


'*Things are done when men and mountains meet*
*Things that are not done by crowds jostling in the street*'
*William Blake*

# Contents

# Introduction

While the title of this book, *Of Bens, Glens and Rambling Auld Men,* gives a broad hint of its contents, the authors felt that a few words on how this book originated and what it is about would be of interest to our readers.

Bob Scott and Gordon Nicol first met in the early 1950's; in those now vastly remote austere post-war years when war-time rationing and terrible shortages were still the norm; when almost the entire country was a (blessedly?) car-less and phone-less place. United in their deep love of their wild Scottish land they soon became great friends and fine novice climbing companions. Weekend after weekend in summer heat and in the depths of winter they, just the two of them, or sometimes with other equally keen new-found friends, camped and bothied; hiked, hill-walked, rock-climbed and braved the steep snow and ice slopes.

They became members of one of Glasgow's best climbing clubs, the Lomond Mountaineering Club. The club's hired-for-the-weekend bus introduced their bodies and minds to exciting new places: Glencoe, Ben Nevis, the Cairngorms. Gordon's instinctive rock-climbing skills brought him to the notice of this club's other keen young rock-climbers and he soon became one of a team of six who were known as 'The Lomond's young rock-tigers.' This group fairly quickly raised their rock-climbing standards, ticking off ascents of some of the exciting new routes being put up in the 1950's, mainly by their Glasgow rivals of the famous Creag Dhu Mountaineering Club.

Bob, wisely knowing his limitations, was well content to climb much less severe, but still exhilarating thrilling routes like the grand auld Cobbler's 'Nimlin's Direct'. Despite their very different grades of rock-climbing skills Bob and Gordon still often met, often stayed in bothies, often enjoyed long, strenuous, hill-walking days. Increasingly they both agreed on one thing:

they would, they had to, get out of Glasgow, not just for weekends, but forever, and the sooner the better.

The two of them did eventually get out of the city, but in very different ways. Bob became a warden at a Scottish Youth hostel near Lochinver. Then he was offered the job of being a trainee ghillie and gamekeeper on Assynt Estate. He eagerly accepted this most unexpected wondrous offer, and so for some thirty years the hills, heather moors, rivers and lochs of Assynt were his workplace.

Gordon completed an engineering apprenticeship and joined the Merchant Navy as an Engineering Officer. At the age of 33 he switched careers, studied at Glasgow University and became a teacher. He taught English in various countries abroad before settling with his wife in Brunei, where they stayed for some thirty years. Whilst there, Gordon became fascinated by the tropical rainforest and took up 'hashing', a sport which involves running through the jungle. This would take place once per week and in his time in Brunei he amassed nearly 1200 runs. Being in Asia, he took the opportunity to go trekking in the Himalayas, a wonderful experience for any lover of mountains.

For about forty years Bob and Gordon completely lost touch with one another; neither knew if the other was alive or dead.

Then, out of the blue, Bob – now living in his Pitlochry retirement flat – received a phone call from Gordon who, while holidaying in Assynt, had obtained his address through the local bookshop owner who sold Bob's books. These long parted old friends spoke to each other as if they'd only been a few months apart.

They met up. They were soon engrossed in blethering of their old, well remembered, post-war climbing years. 'We should put all these grand memories in a book,' Bob suggested. 'Aye, and do it now while we clearly remember them,' Gordon agreed, 'Before we get too damned senile!' Bob smiled.

So here is that book, and we sincerely hope that our readers will find our tales about our old climbing and rambling days interesting and, hopefully, entertaining.

# PART ONE

# Well Met at Crianlarich

Once more I, Bob, was part of that cheery crowd of keen young hikers and climbers who thronged Glasgow's Buchanan Street Bus Station most Saturday mornings. But this time there was a difference – a considerable difference. I was on my own.

The friend who had shared a few previous hiking and hill-walking weekends with me had fallen by the wayside. He had never been as keen as me to be out and about rambling over our wonderful Scottish countryside. He was never possessed by such deep feelings as I was inarticulately consumed by as I gloried at being amongst my native hills, wooded glens and entrancing lochs. While I had thrilled at climbing Ben Lomond for the first time, he had moaned at its weary steepness and when drizzling mist obscured the summit view he was all for hurrying home while I insisted we wait for the mist to clear; as it almost magically, soon did.

And then that friend had been seduced by chess. We had light-heartedly played many casual games but he now got really serious. He became a member of a chess club. Now with eager excitement he played chess every weekend instead of going out on our hills.

So I took my lone seat on that happy, crowded MacBrayne's Oban-bound bus that would drop me off at Crianlarich. This was a place I had not stayed at before, and I looked forward to spending a night in the Youth Hostel then possibly climbing its nearby mountain, Ben More. As it was not far short of 4,000 ft. this would be the highest mountain I had ever climbed and would be, after Ben Lomond, my second 'Munro'.

As I stared out at all the enticing passing West Highland scenery and listened to the animated happy voices of other, more experienced climbers in the throbbing, mile-devouring bus I wondered if it would be foolish for me to climb this unknown Ben More by myself. Would it perhaps be better for me to go on some easier lower hike? I decided I would wait until tomorrow morning to make up my mind. I would see what the weather was like. And perhaps I would learn about Ben More from other climbers in the Youth Hostel.

When I got out of the bus at Crianlarich I was surprised to see how small the place was. It was hardly a village, was barely a hamlet. There seemed to be nothing but the hotel and a small railway station. And yet all over the countryside signposts pointed to Crianlarich as if it was some great important place.

Seeing me stare around in some bemusement at the quaint reality of this misleading place, one of the other climbers waiting to retrieve his rucksack from the bus's crowded luggage compartment grinned at me, 'There's not much to see, is there?'

'No,' I said, 'I thought it would be a much bigger village than this.'

'Is this your first time in Crianlarich?'

'Aye, it is. Have you been here before?'

'Aye I have, many times.'

'Are you staying at the Youth Hostel?'

'Och no, I stay with two climbing friends at a bothy along the road. We've used it often.' He smiled, 'It's much better, more free and easy about how you come and go than the strictly regulated hostel. And its simple cosy comforts are better than a hostel's stuffy atmosphere. Have you ever stayed in a bothy?'

'No, I haven't. I'm quite a novice at this hiking and climbing game.'

As we retrieved our bulky rucksacks and heaved them on our backs my new companion joined the two friends who were to share the bothy with him. After speaking with them he turned to me as I started walking away. 'As you're on your own, why don't you walk with us? We'll pass the hostel on our way to our bothy.'

'Oh, yes, I'll be glad of your company.'

One of his friends grinned, 'We will grant you the great privilege of joining our elite company.'

Laughing with the others, I said, 'Thank you. I'm sure I'll enjoy your company very much.'

He smiled and bowed. He seemed a real 'character.' Of sturdy middle height his broad face beamed and his chin sported a neatly trimmed beard. He wore a pair of tweed breeks that seemed a cross between climbing-breeches and gamekeeper's bulky plus-fours. Later that day I learned that his name was Dave Martin and, as he proudly told me, he had his own well known doss – 'Martin's Doss' – high up on the Cobbler's slopes. He seemed the oldest of these three friends.

The second of my new friends was taller and slimmer. He expressed his welcome in a quieter, more polite and gentlemanly, but no less sincere manner. 'Yes, my dear fellow, walk along with us. It's much more pleasant to be in happy convivial company, is it not?'

'Oh, yes, it certainly is. Thank you. Thank you very much. It's very good of you to invite me to accompany you.'

'Oh, my dear fellow, I'm sure we will enjoy your company too.'

I was secretly amused by his use of that expression 'my dear fellow;' it was an amazingly posh English phrase to come from a Glaswegian who, as I later learned worked as a skilled mechanic in a Western S.M.T. bus maintenance workshop. I also learned his name was Lawrie Travers. Despite his rather unusual genteel manners there was no suggestion of anything really 'pansy' or sissy about him. As I again later learned, he was a keen and hardy climber and camper on Scotland's summer and winter hills.

The third of the group was also the tallest and bulkiest of the three. I guessed his age to be about twenty three years, a couple of years younger than me. Like me he was more or less a novice at this climbing game and, again like me, he was keen to get away every weekend to learn more of our Scottish hills and to test his skills on easier rock faces and on winter's challenging and ever changing snow and ice. He, too, had been in the R.A.F. He had served at the time of National Service in the Air Force Police, while I had served in the immediate post-war years in clerical and some low grade intelligence work. His name was George Morrice, but because of his bulky size he genially answered to the name of 'Podge'.

I walked by Podge's side while Dave and Lawrie followed behind us. We enlivened our way with animated talk and carefree laughter. Glowing with the easy freedom and deep camaraderie of the climbing and hiking fraternity, by the time we got near Crianlarich Youth Hostel I felt as if I'd known those new friends for ages. They seemed to feel the same, for as I prepared to leave them and go to the hostel, Podge said, 'It's a pity we have to part here.'

'Yes, my dear fellow, it is a real shame,' Lawrie agreed.

'Why don't you come along with us to our bothy?' asked Dave.

'Aye, why don't you?' Podge urged. 'There's plenty room and it's really quite cosy and couthie. The farmer who owns it allows us to bring friends to it.'

I was excited by the prospect of using a climber's bothy and of sharing it with my great new friends.

'Have you got a sleeping-bag?' Podge asked.

'Oh yes, I've got old ex-army sleeping-bag. It's not great but it should be warm enough at this time of year. I've got plenty food but no primus stove to cook it. I was going to use the hostel's cooking stove.'

'Och, with our three primuses we'll cook your food as well as our own. That's no problem. Come on, Bob, be our guest, then tomorrow we'll all climb Ben More together.'

This further enticement of climbing my second 'Munro' with these more experienced friends decided me. 'Thanks, Podge. Thank you all. I really look forward to sharing your accommodation and your hill with you.'

And so the four of us walked past the hostel and headed for that alluring bothy that nestled at the foot of Ben More.

Our pleasant walk through early May's smiling sunshine brought us to Ben More farm and to the old stable behind it which was where we would stay. While Dave went to let the farmer know of our arrival, we three others went direct to the stable where Lawrie led the way past the disused horse stalls and up steep wooden steps to the hay-loft above. This clean and tidy loft was brightened by sunshine that eagerly peered through its skylights. Countless dust motes danced in this slanting light and its warmth teased out subtle hints of mellow hay meadows from this cosy old place.

'Well,' Podge asked me, 'how do you like it? Does it meet with your approval?'

'Oh, it's great! I'm really looking forward to staying here.'

Like the experienced old bothy-user that he was, Lawrie quickly staked his rightful claim to the best, most draught free corner of the loft by spreading his sleeping-bag there. He smiled 'Well, that's my familiar place secured, and old Dave will take the equally fine place near me as usual. So just you, my dear fellow, choose a good place near young Podge.'

Smiling, I did as instructed.

Dave now arrived, 'I told the farmer we had a new friend with us this weekend, so that's all right.' He smiled at me, 'The farmer and his wife are fine people. You'll probably meet them later on.'

As I unrolled my old ex-army sleeping-bag it looked really shabby compared to the apparently quite new and much better and warmer looking sleeping-bags the other three had spread out. I grinned at Podge, 'My tatty auld bag's kind of outclassed by yours. I hope you won't drum me out of the bothy for letting your standards down.'

Podge laughed, 'Och no, Bob. We won't turn you out. Your sleeping-bag's fine. At least it's fine for summer time, but if you're going to be using places like this in the winter you'll need to get a better one, like ours.' He pointed out his new sleeping-bag's many merits. 'It's a Black's Icelandic. It's stuffed with the down of eider ducks. It's very warm, very light and not too bulky. It's the best bag I've ever had.'

'Yes, my dear fellow,' Lawrie said, 'these Icelandic sleeping-bags are really great. You should get one if you're going to take up winter climbing and bothying, as we hope you will. They've only recently become available at Black's Glasgow shop. They're the first post-war luxury we three have indulged in.'

'Aye,' Dave agreed, 'they're splendid bags. I had to cut down on my smoking and boozing for a while to save enough to buy mine, but those sacrifices were well worth while when I revelled in its snug warmth when camping or bothying in the coldest weather.'

Black's Mountaineering Shop was at this time the only such shop in Glasgow. Its only competitors were rather shabby shops selling ex-army clothes and gear. This old military stuff was attractively cheap. However, I made up my mind I'd sooner or later manage to afford one of those much more expensive Icelandic bags. I would also need to buy a small primus stove. Then, hopefully with these new friends, I too, would be all set to be comfortable in the rigours of even the coldest weather.

Strong tea was quickly brewed. Four steaming mugs were handed around. These mugs were soon drained and some bread, cheese and biscuits were hastily consumed, for the afternoon sunshine, gaily slanting through the bothy's skylights, seemed to reprehend us for being indoors when the great outdoors was so near to hand.

Soon we were climbing that great green slope that rose directly from our bothy's door. 'It's a pity it's too late to climb the Ben today,' Lawrie said. 'We must hope the weather will be just as good tomorrow.'

We went across a wide glen then started climbing the sheep-dotted grass lush ridge that rose to Stob Garbh's Munro summit. Even though I was a beginner, I knew of Munro's list of all Scottish mountains over 3000ft. high. But in these easy-going post-war years there was no desperate rush to climb and tick off every Munro. The term, 'Munro-bagger', had not yet been invented.

When we reached the top of Stob Garbh sooner than expected, we decided to push on to the 300ft higher nearby peak of Cruach Ardrain. As the four of us stood on this second summit Podge grinned at Dave and Lawrie and said, 'Well Bob's easily passed his test, hasn't he?'

'What test was that?' I laughed.

'Oh, my dear fellow,' Lawrie said, 'we wanted to make sure you were fit enough to keep up with us more experienced climbers when we were out on the hills together.'

'Aye,' Dave laughed, 'and you've passed that test with flying colours. At times it was me who was having some trouble keeping up with you.'

Later, after enjoying our evening meal, we again left the bothy and climbed, not another summit, but a nearby grassy knoll where Podge tried to capture the glorious sunset with his insatiable camera while Lawrie, Dave and I sat and let the beauty of the blushing Western sky awe us to contemplative silence.

When darkening dusk started swallowing up the last lingering remnants of evening's 'Shepherd's Delight' we returned to our bothy, and soon we were all in our sleeping-bags, not to sleep but, by the light of flickering candles, cosily drink more tea. Then came wisely moderate drams, and, enthralled, I listened to happy tales that told me more about my grand new companions.

Dave told the best, most amusing tales. Obviously he revelled in the role of being a 'character'. He proudly told of how by himself he'd built up the rock walls of 'Martin's Doss' under the rather doubtful shelter of a rocky overhang high up on Arrochar's triple-peaked beguiling hill, The Cobbler. In his younger days he'd happily stravaiged around his special hill, his burly body draped in a jaunty kilt and his head crowned with a Glengarry bonnet. When he met any young lady climbers unencumbered with male escorts, he never failed to invite them to come and share the comforts and delights of his very own 'eagle high' doss with him.

When Dave came to the most interesting part of his romantic tale,

Lawrie laughed, 'Oh but, my dear fellow, we know that very few of these innocent young ladies took you up on your kind offer.'

Dave gave a rueful grin, 'Och aye, perhaps that's true.' Then with a remembering gleam in his eyes he insisted, 'But, damn it, Lawrie, some did, some most assuredly did!'

I was surprised and rather disappointed to learn that this fine vivid 'character', who was also into folk-singing and reciting 'Eskimo Nell' type poems, worked as a warehouseman in a Glasgow wholesale ironmongers. I had expected something much more exotic.

I also found it hard to envisage Lawrie Travers at his work when, dressed in an oily boiler-suit, he as a skilled mechanic, repaired broken-down buses of Western Scottish Motor Transport's extensive fleet. With his natural genteel politeness I had expected that 'dear fellow' to be a teller in a bank or in some such neat, clean, office occupation, complete with a correct tie.

Ironically it was Podge, who with his height and well muscled width would not be out of place labouring at a building site, whose occupation had some connection with the graphic arts. He was a printer, trained also in silk-screen printing and photography.

As for myself, there was nothing in the least exotic about the various office jobs I had had in the last few years. I had a vague unsettled feeling and, like Mr. Micawber, felt sure that something better was bound to turn up soon.

Eventually when the tea, the whisky and the tales were done we blew out the candles and settled down to sleep.

Dawn's gentle cloudless brightness gave promise of another perfect day. It lured us to leave our sleeping-bag's cosy comfort with eager haste.

After a quick unshaven wash at our bothy's outdoor standpipe we savoured the fresh morning air before the appetising scent of crisp frying bacon drew us inside. Then, after eagerly demolishing our fried ham, scrambled eggs and brown bread, the four of us started lacing up our climbing boots.

As we left the bothy we were delighted to receive a lively, friendly, not too noisy welcome from three lovely black and white collies. As we petted these welcoming dogs their master, the Ben More sheep farmer who owned the bothy, arrived. We received as warm, if not so openly demonstrative, a welcome from him as we had got from his three collies. Lawrie Travers, always the correct gentleman, formally introduced me to him, 'Mr.

Cameron, this is our new climbing friend, Mr. Robert Scott. This is his first time at your bothy.'

As the sturdy farmer's powerful hand gripped mine his weather-tanned face broke into a broad smile, 'Welcome to Ben More Farm, Robert. Or is it, Bob? Guid auld Lawrie is always sae damn formal.'

I returned his friendly smile, 'Oh aye, my friends call me Bob.'

'Good. That's settled then. An' my name is Andy.'

'Those are great, really friendly collies you've got. That's not all that usual with working farm dogs, is it?'

'No, it's not. Far too many of them are real unfriendly brutes, real ankle-nipping sly bastards.' Andy's face again broke into a broad smile, 'Och, but a friendly farmer, like me, always haes guid-natured dogs!'

After some pleasant minutes of cheery talk Andy laughed and said, 'Ah well, I canna stand here blethering a' day. I'll need tae go an' look at the lambs. An' you lads better get away tae your Ben.'

We took his advice and started on that long, steep, green slope that led to Ben More's waiting summit. Even I, with my limited experience and quiet excitement at now climbing my highest 'Munro' could not help feeling that there was nothing very grand about this mountain. Its grassy slope seemed to crawl its featureless way endlessly upwards in a way that made what should be joyous climbing into something of a weary, never ending slog. Of course I kept those treacherous thoughts well hidden.

As we gained higher ground our leisurely halts got more frequent and more pleasant as the May sunshine got ever brighter and many distant views were more clearly revealed. My earlier foolish feelings of having some disappointment with this hill now completely vanished.

As Podge again got busy with his expert camera he smiled at me, 'Well, Bob, it's now well worth the weary long climb, isn't it?'

Ashamed of my unworthy secret earlier thoughts about Ben More's weary featurelessness, I replied with smiling haste, 'Oh aye, Podge. It's well worth the effort. It's great for me to be climbing this hill with the three of you. I'm now really enjoying it.' Oh damn, I thought, I should have left out that '*now*'. But Podge did not seem to notice it.

Comfortably stretched on the verdant grass enjoying the warming sun, Dave told an amusing nostalgic tale of a hot summer day when he'd been carefree swimming nude in a high remote, Highland loch with, as he thought, no other humans anywhere nearby. He vividly described his shock, not so much at the sudden arrival of three middle-aged lady climbers, but at their unexpected reaction to seeing him nude. Instead of modestly retreating with maidenly screeches they'd brought out cameras and with mocking laughter, while standing by his discarded clothes, captured this unique Highland scene.

Lawrie laughed, 'Oh, Dave, trust you to get into scrapes like that.'

Refreshed by our rest and our laughter we made for Ben More's summit with renewed eagerness.

Soon we stood beside the summit cairn and, searching in every direction, gathered in every view. The jagged peaks of Glencoe snarled in the West, while to the East there rose shapely Ben Lawers, and, much nearer, more modest Ben Vorlich graced the view beyond the Braes of Balquidder.

Once our admiring eyes and Podge's recording camera had drunk their fill we pushed on for our next peak. We dropped down the hollow then climbed the ridge that joined Ben More to its near neighbour, Stobinian.

After admiring more views, resting and eating, we made our leisurely return down the wide, sheep-dotted, lamb-bouncing glen that swept all the way to our bothy and Ben More Farm's back door. There, gleaming in the afternoon sunshine like a guiding beacon, we saw what seemed a jolly Dinky Toy but was actually Andy Cameron's bright red tractor.

Soon three primuses again hiss and glow their cheery message as they heat our eagerly looked forward to evening meal. Unfortunately this dinner cannot be such a wisely civilized leisurely affair as was last night's meal, for all four of us are all too well aware that we have still to pack our sleeping-bags and other gear into rucksacks then hike back to Crianlarich in time to catch MacBrayne's evening bus back to Glasgow.

The chattering reminiscing pleasure of this return journey is slightly dampened by the knowledge that a return to work awaits us all tomorrow morning. However I am greatly cheered as Podge says, and Lawrie and Dave wholeheartedly agree, 'We must keep in touch, exchange addresses and arrange to meet again for other climbing weekends together.'

'Oh yes, that'll be great, really great. 'Thank you Podge, thank you all. I'll buy my own primus stove this week and I'll save up to buy myself a Black's Icelandic sleeping-bag soon, definitely before the autumn and the colder weather.'

All too soon that most reliable bus delivered us punctually on time at Buchanan Street Bus Station. As we shook hands before scattering to catch corporation trams, buses or the subway to our homes in various parts of the sprawling city I said, 'I'm really delighted that you think me a good enough hill-walker and companion to join your 'elite' weekend company.'

'Oh you are one, my dear fellow, you most assuredly are,' Lawrie said. 'We definitely will stay in touch and, I'm sure, enjoy many climbing, camping and bothying weekends together.'

★ ★ ★

And we did. As members of Glasgow's Lomond Mountaineering Club we shared many summer and winter climbing weekends throughout most of the 1950's. And the more we got to know one another the greater true friends we all became.

# My Unique First Weekend

After another week of six a.m. rises followed by an hour's journey by subway and smoke-filled, steamed-up-windowed-bus into the confines of the factory in Dalmuir, the week-end had arrived at last.

I, Gordon, meet up with Matt, Jimmy, Gus and Bill and we have many a good old laugh. Maybe have a couple of half bottles of VP wine, British, sherry-style, cheap, tastes terrible but does the trick. Certainly helps us produce witty chat-up lines to the passing girls, not that it ever had any positive results, but the intention was there.

Saturday, look forward to the football. I played in the works team, in Dunbartonshire Amateur League, third division, which meant a bus journey down to the Dumbarton area of Clydeside for yet another time that week. Enjoyed it though and my father approved despite being, maybe even because of him being, a considerably better footballer in his day than me.

Often, when I got back home on a Saturday evening from the football, my mates had already sloped off to the dancing, the Locarno or the Palais, always a last minute decision, leaving me at a proverbial 'loose' end. Hang about the café, sometimes passing the time of day with a fellow straggler. Once even going to the 'dugs' the greyhound racing at White City which provided a big surprise to my 'treacherous' mates on the Sunday when I produced an impressive £4 .15 winnings. 'The milk-shakes are on me!'

Our Sundays usually consisted of walking around Bellahouston Park seeing if any passing lassies were even remotely interested in us. The evening was a walk along Paisley Road West as far as the 'Halfway,' (between Glasgow and Paisley) calling in to various cafés on the way to see if any lassies were remotely interested, etc. We'd end up standing in the doorway of the Bank of Scotland in Gower Street discussing life as we knew it, our lack of success with lassies and once, how having a bit more cash, would change it all for us.

Jokingly, I said, 'Money, you want money? Come in and get some.' I took out my house Yale key, inserted it into the lock in the door and turned it. There was a click as the lock opened. Astonishment all round. Now what would we have done if the bank door had had only one lock I'm not sure, but for a moment...

Our final words on a Sunday night were always, 'Right another one over, never mind it'll soon be Friday and the week-end'll be here again.'

Two weeks later the three of us, Matt, Jimmy and I gazed out the window of the Alexander's bus. It was Friday evening and we had passed through (the second time for me that day), Partick, Clydebank and Dalmuir. After Garelochead, the bus now laboured up the twisting Whistlefield Brae on its way to Arrochar, our destination, new names, new places and a huge change from our normal week-end routine.

At Jimmy's suggestion we had decided to escape the smog and the grime of the city, cobbling together some week-ending gear, to experience for ourselves, The Great Outdoors. Under severe warnings of, 'No mess now, don't break anything or you'll pay for it and especially, don't upset the locals,' we were heading for Jimmy's parents wee but and ben, a small wooden hut that they used for the odd week-end away.

Now, with Millets ex-army rucksacks and 'dixies,' rectangular steel cooking pans with fold-away handles, which had the considerable advantage that you could eat from them after cooking, we headed into the great unknown, for a couple of days which would change the three of us in very different ways.

When we reached Arrochar, Jimmy, who knew the village, said, 'Right, we get off here and the first thing we do is sink a pint or two at Ross's Hotel. It used to be a Temperance hotel, no alcohol allowed, but things have changed, they've now got a licence so we'll be O.K.'

Being the end of the week and pay day, the bar was packed, heavin' is the word often used to describe the scene which greeted us. Forestry and Hydro workers working on the local schemes, Royal Navy submariners from Faslane, farmers, shepherds, and a few hikers and climbers, jam-packed around the bar. And, apart from one bar-maid, evidently very popular, hectically serving and fending off the almost constant advances, no women. This might have explained the speed and enthusiasm with which beer and whisky were being consumed, no distractions to the sole purpose of the evening just drinking, roaring and laughing, with the noise and heat soaring out into the Argyll air.

When we eventually got served, Jimmy shouted, 'Come on, there's a room through the back, it might be quieter there.'

It only took us three squeezing in to make the back room equally heavin' but at least it was marginally homelier with a roaring fire burning away in the grate, not that warmth was necessary amongst that crowd. With a couple of extremely difficult sorties through for more drinks, Matt then decided a visit to the toilet was imperative. Turning to a huge bearded figure next to him he shouted above the clamour, 'Can you tell me where the toilet is please?'

'The toilet, och, it's through behind the bar, but your best way is oot that window over there, you'd probably pish yerself before you got there trying to get through that mob.' Matt looked kind of shocked as he stammered his thanks to his informant then turned to us saying, 'Did you hear what he said, the window, d'you think he means I've to pee out of the window?'

Now the poor lad wasn't the brightest bulb in the packet so, roaring with laughter, we suggested, 'Well, maybe you should do as the man tells you, don't fancy saying no to someone that big, and besides there's no women here, so on you go.'

Muttering, 'OK, fair enough, I'll no' be long,' he squeezed his way through the crush to the half-open window, stood there a moment, his hands in front of him when a roar from the giant had his head jerking round in horror.

'Hey you, ya silly bugger, stop that. I meant you to climb out the window to get to the toilet, not bloody pee out it. Now get out that window smart like, before I flatten ye. Ye'll be getting Ross's a bad name.'

One or two were giving us curious looks at the big man's outburst, in fact more glowering than curiosity, accompanied by some very uncomplimentary remarks, causing us to consider our immediate options. 'Let's exit via the window, get a carry-out and escape while we can, I don't fancy our chances here the longer the night goes on,' was my suggestion, swiftly taken up by my mates as one after the other tumbled out the window to the safety of the darkness.

On the walk to the Succouth road, where the hut was situated, Matt was very quiet. 'Cheer up Matt, it wasn't really your fault, we thought that's what he meant as well, we weren't having you on, honestly.'

'Bastards, miserable, miserable bastards,' was the reply, repeated all the way down the road and round the end of the loch.

In the sanctuary of the cabin we had a quick look round, bunk beds, a table and four chairs, a sink, and a two-ring cooker fuelled by Calor gas. Luxury compared to later weekend accommodation I would have, caves, shelters under overhanging boulders, sheep fanks, disused byres, decrepit barns and run-down shooting lodges, all collectively known as 'dosses.' But their time will come.

Peckish after our pints and escape from possible harm, we got out our table-ware and provisions for the meal. The former consisted of our ex-army dixies. The latter was two tins of Heinz sausage and baked beans, half a dozen eggs, and a packet of tea. 'Hey Matt did you bring anything?'

'Sure did,' was the reply. He reached into his rucksack and with a flourish, produced a tin of Bird's Custard Powder. 'Found it in a cupboard at home and thought, great, that'll go down well.' A loud groan went up.

'That's not going to keep us going for long. And besides, we need milk, which we haven't got. Och, we'll need to go into the village tomorrow and buy bread or rolls or something,' said Jimmy in an exasperated voice. It was decided to keep the eggs for breakfast so all our cooking expertise was brought to bear on opening the cans and heating the contents, what could be simpler?

Sitting back, drinking our cans of beer we laughed and jeered at Matt's story of how his dyslexia had got him thrown out of a music shop in Glasgow. Apparently he had been browsing through the music books at the counter and asked an assistant, 'Does this teach you how to play the drums?' referring to a song sheet he was holding, entitled, 'You too, can be a Dreamer.'

'Right you, out, don't try taking the mickey out of me, you waster. Go on out, and don't come back,' came the reply, from the irate assistant.

'No sense of humour,' said Matt to us, 'Just because I'm no' very good at reading, I thought that's what it said,'

'What's that smell? Christ the beans. Quick get them off. Now look what you've done, you and your stories you've burnt the bloody dinner.'

'It wasn't my fault, I was only passing the time 'til it was ready, besides, you lot never listen to me half the time anyway.'

We made the best of it, dividing it up. One third each. One third just about OK, one third distinctly barbecued flavoured and one-third burnt to a frazzle. Guess who got what? Our weekend adventure was well under way.

About ten-thirty the following morning we were startled by a heavy knock on the wooden door. It was the local policeman, 'Good morning lads, I'm afraid there's been an accident up the hill. Somebody's fallen. Can you give us a hand to go up and help?' Now none of us had any experience of any hills other than in Bellahouston Park, so there was a moment's hesitation as we let the request sink in. Then Matt, trusty Matt, spoke up, 'When you say "up the hill" how far up the hill do you mean?' The policeman reddening slightly, glared at him and shouted, 'It doesn't matter how far up it bloody well is. ARE YOU COMING?' In those days you didn't question the police and "give us a hand" meant, "get your arses moving right away", so Jimmy and I hastily stammered, 'Sure constable, give us a us a minute to get our boots on and we'll be right with you.'

'Good, that's better,' was the reply. 'Be at the police station in ten minutes.'

The rescue party of ten; seven locals and us three novices wound its way up the steep slopes above Loch Long to reach the Hydro track which traverses the hill to join the foaming Buttermilk burn. At the dam, the stretcher was laid down as we paused to catch our breath. Above us reared the outline of the three peaks of Ben Arthur with 'The Cobbler', crouching over his work-bench on the Central peak, frowning down as if to say, 'You've been warned, don't meddle with me.' Looking up, I shivered slightly as I remembered the sombre nature of our incursion into his territory. The locals, who knew each other well, were chatting amongst themselves. Angus, a forestry worker pointed up the hill and asked the policeman, 'Where did the daft bugger fall, Ian. Have you any idea?'

'Well it was supposed to be on the South Peak, but I don't know where exactly. Any ideas, Willie, this is your land, what do you think?'

The person addressed was Willie Paterson the owner of Succouth farm and of the sheep we encountered on the way up, which at first approached us recognising him, and then scampered off seeing too many unfamiliar faces. I later learned that this enlightened farmer allowed his old barn to be used as a climber's bothy. I used it often and got to know its resident rats quite well.

'We'd best go up into the coire then cut across to that gap in the ridge. We should be able to see right round the base of the peak from there,' replied the farmer, nodding in the direction of the summit ridge.

As we got nearer to the cliffs I began to wonder at the scale: the size, the verticality, and dramatic outlines of the dark grey rock towering above us. Surely, people didn't climb up these faces and if they did why? Puzzled, my unspoken questions were answered as Angus burst out, 'Bloody mad, coming up here with their ropes and everything. Risking their lives and ours too scrabbling about up here. Should be banned the lot of them.'

'Come, come, Angus, they're not doing any harm really and besides, nobody forced you to come up here. I can understand them needing tae get oot o' the city and on tae our braw hills.'

'Och I ken you've to be up here, it's your livelihood Willie, but no these fools. I could be sitting doon with the paper and a cup of tea at hame right now if it wasnae for them.'

We pushed on further up the hill and just below the gap Willie had mentioned, two figures appeared waving their arms. 'Over here,' they shouted. By the time we had reached the ridge one had gone down the gully and was standing looking down at the jumble of rocks beneath him. The other, obviously distressed said, 'He's gone! He's dead! He fell from up there,' pointing upwards to the jagged summit of the South peak. 'We weren't even climbing, just going up the tourist path and Neil tried to get out of the way of someone coming down. He lost his balance and fell. It's terrible, terrible. What are we going to say to his parents? He graduated as a doctor only last week.' As he began shaking and sobbing, the second policeman put his hand on his shoulder and murmured, 'There now, it's one of these things that's a horrible accident. It can't really be explained. How about your pal, is he all right down there? I think we'd better go down to him.'

The tragic victim was lying on his back. His friends had tied a sweater, now blood-soaked, round his head, covering up his face. The rescue party had gone very quiet. None of us had suspected on the way up that the accident was going to turn out to be fatal.

Ian looked round at us all and said quietly, 'It's a terrible business but we'd better get moving.' Angus, the forestry worker, who was slowly shaking his head, muttered in a low voice, 'Right then, come on let's get the poor wee lad down the hill.'

The stretcher, like a sledge on runners, slid over the clumps of heather as we made our way down the Rest and be Thankful side of the hill, that being a more direct route to the ambulance waiting at the roadside. My eyes kept being drawn to the chilling sight of the sweater-clad head rocking from side to side as we bumped down the slopes. How suddenly a life can be over. Here was this young man, happy last night celebrating his graduation, looking forward to his day on the hill with friends and now lifeless, shaking his head grotesquely, as if to say, 'If only I hadn't stepped to the side.'

Back at the hut our week-end kind of petered out. What to make of all this? Matt joined me on another couple of trips to the hills but gave it up after we spent a very cold night under the Narnain Boulder on the Cobbler. Both of us lay shuddering and shivering in our sleeping-bags: army blankets folded in two and crudely sewn up. Our 'mattress' was a couple of corrugated iron sheets which effectively, though in total discomfort, kept us off the pool of water on the floor of the 'doss'.

Jimmy met a girl, fell in love and got married all in about three months, shortly afterwards disappearing from the scene.

And me; that first week-end of mine which ended so tragically, unexpectedly ignited a spark. Something caught. Something about the freedom, the dramatic scenery, the adventure, and, I suppose, above all, the total involvement. When you step on to a mountain you cannot be unaware of your surroundings, you become part of them. I had found something which had occupied every minute of the time I was there. For the rest of my life I knew that my thoughts would never be far from the mountains, their mystery, familiarity, beauty and harshness, and the companionship of those who shared these same feelings.

# We Meet at 'Greasy Eats'

The correct name of that wee cafe near Glasgow's Buchanan Street bus station was, as it proudly announced above its welcoming door, 'Easy Eats', but for all its regular users it was, and would ever be, fondly known as 'Greasy Eats'.

Its unofficial name was perhaps more true than its correct name, for its most popular speciality was its large, hot, heavy and greasy Scotch Mutton Pies. These favourite Glasgow pies were most generously laden with minced mutton, and both that meat and the enclosing thick pastry almost swam in a sea of greasy gravy.

Yes, these pies were dripping with grease all right but really tasty, and in that unenlightened post-war time, even most doctors were unaware of cholesterol's great dangers.

Of course there were no such sissy things as paper napkins; that delicious grease was licked from slippery fingers by keen drooling tongues. In these austere car-less and phone-less years 'Greasy Eats' was the favourite place for young (and some not so young) Glasgow climbers and hikers to meet on Friday evenings to arrange their climbing or hiking weekends.

On his first bothying weekend at Crianlarich's Ben More farm, Bob Scott had been told about this cafe, so here he was sitting at a table with one of his new-found climbing friends, Lawrie Travers. The wee cafe was, noisily, gregariously crowded. A large ex-U.S. Army juke-box dominated one wall and glaringly displayed and blared out its wares.

In these pre-pop music days the 'Old Groaner', Bing Crosby, ruled the roost in that juke box. He was being increasingly challenged by the rising young star, Frank Sinatra, while The Andrews Sisters still eagerly shrilled their patriotic wartime songs. But what was often played to the loudest laughing approval, was, The Ink Spots wonderful version of, *Cocktails for Two,* complete with hilarious sound-effects.

In the midst of their keen discussion of this weekend's plans Lawrie and Bob noticed a slim young man standing by himself and rather uncertainly looking around the crowded cafe. The only empty chairs were the two at their table. Taking pity on the seemingly rather confused lad, Lawrie with his usual gentle kindness called, 'Why don't you sit here with us? These chairs are not taken.'

With smiling thanks the lad took up that thoughtful offer. Under Lawrie's guiding politeness their three names were quickly, properly exchanged. The newcomer's name was Gordon Nicol. He soon revealed that he too was keen to get away to climb some hills this weekend. He would prefer to be with others, but if necessary was prepared to go by himself.

'And, my dear fellow, do you have much experience of weekending, climbing and bothying?' Lawrie asked.

'Oh no, I've not had much experience. Last weekend I went with some friends to Arrochar intending to climb the 'The Cobbler'.

'A climber fell to his death from the South Peak last Saturday, didn't he?' Bob asked. 'Did you see anything of that sad accident, Gordon?'

'No, I didn't see him fall, but I later helped to carry the body down from the hill.' He then provided a sombre but vivid account of the day's traumatic events.

When he had finished, Lawrie said, 'I've helped carry down dead climbers too. It's an unpleasant, but necessary task. Oh, my dear young fellow, it is good that that poor climber's death has not put you off still wanting to go climbing our fine Scottish hills.'

'Oh no, it hasn't. It was a bit of a shock. But being on a real hill for the first time showed me something else. It showed me the kind of place I want to spend more time in, in the future. Seeing and learning more about the mountains.'

Bob smiled at this new young friend, 'Oh, Gordon, you seem as keen as me. Like you, I haven't vast experience, but I intend to get away most weekends and rapidly reduce my shameful ignorance of our grand wee country's many hills and its more challenging higher Bens,'

'My dear fellow, why don't you come along with us this weekend?' Lawrie suggested. 'Our other climbing friends, Podge and Auld Dave, are coming with us to Ben Alder Cottage. We haven't been there before, but it's supposed to be a fine large bothy, so there should be plenty room for us all.'

Although rather wary of Lawrie's extreme politeness and his use of that strange, definitely un-Glasgow, expression, "my dear fellow", Gordon quickly agreed to his suggestion.

Details of where and when they were to meet the next morning were soon arranged.

As these three new friends walked along together over rain-glittered Glasgow pavements their senses were suddenly assaulted then helplessly seduced by a fish and chips shop's alluring scents. Despite the large mutton pie each had eaten at 'Greasy Eats', none could resist this promise of an extra, almost, exotic, feast. Each bought a generously heaped sixpence worth of lovely fat chips.

Neatly held in their newspaper wrappings, well doused with strong vinegar and thickly sprinkled with coarse salt, these chips had a taste that was something special. Many hoary auld Glesca worthies vehemently declared it was the strong vinegar soaking into the newspaper and mingling with printers' black ink that gave these chips their unique flavour.

When all chips were eaten and papers rolled up and put into a nearby bin, vinegary fingers were again licked. Lawrie displayed his fastidiousness as he finished off this action by then drying his fingers on a clean linen hankie.

These friends now parted and each made his own way homeward.

# At Ben Alder Cottage

**H**aving a compartment to themselves on the 5.46 am steam train from Glasgow's Queen Street Station to Fort William the five of them had ample room to sprawl in comfort and enjoy the journey's hours of pleasant leisure before they arrived at their destination, Corrour station. At that remote wee railway station set amongst the road-less and almost house-less desolate peaty miles between Rannoch Moor and Loch Treig, their relaxing journey would end and their strenuous hiking trip would begin.

When the train's guard came to inspect their tickets all five noted his smart new British Railways uniform. They also noted the conspicuous blank space on his jacket where the brand-new British Rail emblem should have been. Obviously he had not yet received it. These navy blue uniforms of the recently nationalized British Rail system were gradually replacing the old, fondly remembered, uniforms of the great auld L.M.S. (London, Midland & Scottish) railway line that had served this West Highland route so well.

So, too, the old L.M.S. signs at all the railway stations were being removed and being replaced with bright new British Rail signs. At some of the small stations the new replacement signs had not yet arrived and blank spaces sadly stared as they awaited their brave new emblems.

For Bob Scott and Podge Morrice those blank spaces at these stations and the guard's new uniform brought back vivid memories. They had both served in the R.A.F. in the devastated, defeated, but still arrogant Germany after the end of the war, and they well remembered all those blank spaces on almost every still reasonably intact large German building where, carved in granite, boastful Nazi Swastikas had defiantly glared. All these evil Nazi symbols had been removed by order of the victorious Allies. So had all the Swastikas been removed (often most reluctantly) by German soldiers from their uniforms.

As the emblem-less railway guard returned the inspected tickets to him, good old Dave Martin grinned, 'Och, now that this railway company is nationalized, is now British Rail and belongs to us, the Great British Public, surely we who own it should travel on it free.'

The guard laughed, 'Och man, your weekend excursion tickets are cheap enough as it is.' Still laughing, he raised his clenched right hand in mock communist salute, 'Aye, but I agree; come the red revolution and all railway journeys will be free!'

As he joined in the hearty laughter, the newcomer in the party, Gordon, the youngest of this happy group of keen hill-walkers and climbers gasped, 'Oh but surely if all railway journeys are free there won't be any need for ticket inspectors. You will lose your job.'

Some hours later the five stood on the modest wee platform at Corrour Station and watched their departing train scrawl its jaunty signature of white steam and dark smoke across this wild, remote, almost uninhabited landscape. They found it easy to imagine they were stranded on part of the Trans-Siberian railway. Some large old snow patches forlornly lingered, tenaciously clinging to the Northern Corries of the highest, most distant hills added to this odd impression.

Dave Martin voiced their thoughts, 'It's just as well we're tackling this trek to Ben Alder Cottage now, near the end o' May, rather than in mid-winter.'

The four others whole-heartedly agreed. Like auld Dave, they had thought of the four fit young climbers, who had died of exposure on this route in December, 1951.

They heaved on their heavy rucksacks and eagerly started out for that remote climbers' bothy by the shores of Loch Ericht which none of them had visited before.

The first miles along the track by Loch Ossian were easy and gave pleasing views. The hazy May sunshine was not hot enough to cause them discomfort. Once they passed the attractive wooded grounds of Corrour Lodge the way got rougher with a rather indistinct path leading steadily upwards by the side of a large Highland burn which, despite its un-flooded mid-May state, hurried in a wild impetuous rush and drained the glen shown on their old faithful O.S. one inch to one mile map as Uisge Labhair.

As they neared the top of the glen all haze burned away. The afternoon sunshine gloriously glowed. They stopped, eased off burdensome rucksacks, threw off surplus sweaty clothes, scooped pleasant cool refreshment from the amber burn then sprawled at blissful rest.

As they lay and let the welcome sunshine glow on their upturned faces they washed down some tasty light snacks with more of the golden nectar from the fast flowing burn. Their leisurely hedonistic pleasure was strangely subtly marred by unbidden thoughts that instantly came to all five of them. Sad thoughts of those four other young Glasgow men who, like them, had loved their Scottish hills and had savagely died somewhere about here amongst those ever indifferent hills.

'Those four members of the Glencoe Mountaineering Club who perished while making for Ben Alder Cottage that December must have died somewhere round about here, mustn't they?' Bob asked auld Dave.

'Aye, they did. I believe they all collapsed and died in the deep snow in this glen before they reached the Bealach that leads over to the safety of Ben Alder Cottage.'

'Aye,' Lawrie agreed, 'they were out here in the December darkness when they were caught by that winter's fiercest blizzard.'

'But the young woman with them survived didn't she?' Gordon asked.

'Aye, she did. Somehow she managed to plough back down through the deep soft snow in the darkness and in the face of that fierce blizzard to Corrour Lodge where she raised the alarm and got shelter.'

Gordon said, 'Survival of the fittest, eh? Perhaps it's proof that females are the toughest of the species.'

'Aye, it certainly looked like it,' Lawrie admitted. 'But perhaps the four men had taken too many drams on the long train journey to Corrour Station. It was at Hogmanay, remember. And what made it more devastating for that surviving young woman was that one of the men who died was her husband, and they had only been married for four months or so.'

For some moments sad thoughts silenced them all. Then, giving his usual impish grin, Dave heaved himself to his feet and ordered, 'Come on, let's hae nae mair o' this dull care. The last thing these four dead lads would want would be for their deaths to cast a pall over other Scottish climbers. Come on, let's get cracking!'

Leaving the company of the glen's lively wee burn they climbed the steepish rough heathery slope to the top of Bealach Cumhann from where the ground gently sloped right down to the very door of their eagerly sought loch-side destination.

Ben Alder Cottage lived up to its attractive name and its reputation as a fine climbers' wilderness bothy. They soon had their sleeping-bags spread out to claim the best places in this empty hut's largest, most comfortable room. They dumped their food on the large, candle-wax greasy table then had a quick brew up.

Wisely making the most of this glorious lingering day they sat outside, eagerly gulping their reviving tea and with perhaps even more keenness, drank in the surrounding beauty.

Almost from the bothy door Loch Ericht stretched out its widest bay while it kept its many much narrower Northern miles modestly concealed. Early evening's welcome breeze gaily danced a merry glitter over the loch's tiny waves and all this gleaming beauty decided these five healthily hungry men to delay their keenly anticipated evening meal until they had collected some firewood. At this time of year when, here in the Highlands, there is little real darkness a bothy fire was not needed for its re-assuring heat, but when ample firewood was to hand, a cheerful convivial fire was too good a treat to do without.

So with effortless ease they crossed over a wide expanse of smooth gravel and jutting stones where two wee, and sometimes fierce-flowing, burns met, but were now, thanks to the sun-blessed rainless month of May, almost dried out. This crossing would be quite a different story when Loch Ericht's wild lusty October trout were spawning in that flooded gravel.

They hurry along the bay's rugged shore to where a scattered forest of auld Scots Pines raggedly clad this wild land. They discover a grim battlefield of winter-assaulted trees. Still this sad harvest of defeated pines will be put to good use in the flaming warmth and glowing pleasure of Ben Alder bothy's hospitable inviting gregarious fireplace.

Soon all gathered firewood was neatly heaped and five wee primus stoves were comradely alight and crooning the cosy bothy room with their cheery murmurs. Generous rashers of prime bacon also blessed this room with their irresistible mouth-watering sizzling. Determined not to be left out of this chorus of jovial sounds five hungry rebellious male bellies added their discordant music of rumbustious rumbles.

With what uninhibited gusto these five male appetites, fuelled by healthy exercise and fresh Highland air, made all this generously heaped, but perhaps not quite gourmet food disappear.

Then came that equal, or some might say, even greater pleasure, of sipping their wisely modest drams while sitting replete, comfortably in a comradely group around their wood-heaped bothy fire. All five feel something of true ancient gregarious Pagan pleasure from being part of such a happy gathering.

Auld Dave re-told his oft-told stories while Gordon and Bob, hearing some of them for the first time, gazed wide eyed and wondered if some of his tall tales might even be true. Unnoticed time rapidly passed. The bothy fire's Scots Pine branches gave out their resinous incense of smoky pleasure that lulled them all into drowsy dreaming.

Then Podge suddenly leapt to his feet and, in a commanding voice stated, 'It's time we all got to sleep. Remember we have to be up real early tomorrow morning to do all the things we've planned.'

★ ★ ★

Another of May's seemingly endless perfect early dawns slid its gleaming beams across Loch Ericht and, peering into their East-facing room, cheerily woke them all from their deep untroubled sleep on the bothy's hard wooden floor.

Soon five primus stoves were again purring their promise of further culinary pleasures. Breakfast's golden treasure of ample scrambled eggs and noisy sizzling, heavenly scented, extra tasty bacon sure lived up to that purring promise.

It was a notable pleasure too for them to climb the steep heather slope directly behind the bothy without being burdened with heavy rucksacks. They left the bulk of their gear here to be collected later when they returned from climbing Ben Alder. This lack of bulky rucksack's constraining weight made this carefree climb seem almost effortless.

But they did not go directly to that distant hill. Under Podge's keen guidance they made for, and at last found a historic place, shown on most modern maps as Prince Charlie's Cave, but in Seton Gordon's expert books, more correctly known as Cluny's Cage.

It was here that after the disaster of Culloden, clan chief Cluny

MacPherson brought Bonnie Prince Charlie to hide from his searching murderous enemies and restore his strength in the comparative comfort of this well-prepared and provisioned refuge.

They all – even Podge, that avid reader of Seton Gordon's great books on Highland nature, history and legends – were deeply disappointed by this place. They saw no trace of the timber walls and roof that had once been the quite commodious place's main chamber. The actual 'cave' seemed little more than a large rock overhang. At least there was what looked like a natural old cooking hearth with what might be the remains of peat smoke stains on a rocky chimney.

'Are you sure this really is Cluny's Cage?' Dave asked. Hiding his own disappointment at this eagerly looked forward to place's meagre remains, Podge defiantly replied, 'Oh aye, I'm sure it is! This is the exact place shown in Seton Gordon's book.'

After taking his inevitable photos Podge said in what was more an order than a suggestion, 'Come on, we better get going!' Then, eagerly striding out, he led the way towards Ben Alder's Munro Summit.

From that central Highland mountain-top they were rewarded with glorious, cloud-clear views of impressive hills in every direction: beyond the haggard peaks of Rannoch Moor rose Ben Nevis and many-peaked Glencoe; in the East was that pure pyramidal peak, Schiehallion. To the South was higher, but less distinctive Ben Lawers.

After his struggle to keep up with Podge's killing pace auld Dave delighted to sit at restful ease while his younger friend rather belatedly contritely said, 'I'm sorry, Dave, you should have told me to ease-off a bit on that climb. You did real well to keep up with the four of us.'

Obviously pleased with this genuine praise, Dave pulled his enlarged belly in, puffed out his proud barrel-chest, and jovially grinned, 'Och, I can keep up wi' the fittest youngster onie day!' And the amazing thing was that this immodest boast usually proved to be true.

Being downhill all the way, the return journey to Ben Alder Cottage was much quicker and easier. So these five wee primus stoves were soon again purring their cheery message as all remaining eatables became an odd, high-heaped potpourri of heated food which gave out a quaint, surprisingly attractive aroma and, even more amazingly, turned out to be quite delicious. Greedily tucking-in, all agreed it was much better to carry this surplus food in their always ready bellies on the remaining miles they still had to hike rather than in their heavy rucksacks

It was a delight to stride through sunny heather glades and then enjoy the auld Scots Pines pleasant dappled shade before they stravaiged along by Loch Ericht's lower Southerly shore and then left it to climb a modest ridge and pass two lonely wee lochs. This would be the final stretch of the weekend hike that would end at isolated Rannoch Railway Station

Although they had wisely kept up a good steady pace, they were later than they had planned to arrive at the station and had only ten minutes to spare before their Sunday evening train (one of the few that ran on this disapproved of West Highland route on the sacrosanct Sabbath) came heretically screaming in with clouds of defiant hissing steam and squeals of braking wheels.

The train guard from the previous day was again on duty. As he inspected their tickets he asked, 'Well, lads, did you have a good weekend?'

Auld Dave answered for all, 'Och aye, we had a good weekend.' Then four sun-flushed, pleasure beaming, well contented faces nodded their confirming approval as Dave resolutely declared, 'No, in fact we've *not* had a *good* weekend – we've actually had a bloody *Great Weekend!*'

This was true. Oh, they had done nothing very special; had not climbed any severe rock routes; had not covered an exceptional number of rugged Highland miles; but yes, nevertheless, this had truly been a Great Weekend with really Great Friends!

# A Ten Penny Weekend

'Oh of course I'd love to come away with you this weekend,' Gordon said. 'It would be great to scramble over the Cobbler's three fine peaks again and to get to know them much better. But I really can't afford to. I'm completely skint. I haven't enough to pay the return bus fare to Arrochar.'

'Oh I know that feeling well,' Bob said. 'I, too, am a bit short of ready cash. I could just about afford the Arrochar fare myself.'

'What about the pair of us trying hitch-hiking again?' Gordon suggested. 'It's always interesting to see where the hitching gets us to, isn't it?'

'Aye, perhaps,' was the unenthusiastic reply. He all too clearly remembered a recent hitch-hiking misadventure when, after forlornly thumbing for hours in pouring rain on the Loch Lomond road, they had got a lift to no further than Duck Bay, well South on this long loch they had hoped to pass en route to Crianlarich or any of the interesting places further North.

Gordon grinned, 'You don't seem too keen on the hitch-hiking, Bob. Do you have any other suggestions, modestly-priced suggestions of course?'

'Aye,' Bob laughed, 'as a matter of fact I have. I was just about to suggest it. Have you ever been on a Ten Penny Weekend??'

'No, I haven't. At least, not as far as I know. What exactly is it?'

'It's a country weekend that, thanks to the guid auld Glesca' Corporation trams, costs exactly ten pence for the return fares.'

'Really, that sounds too good to be true.'

'It is true I assure you. Have you ever been out to Glasgow's water reservoirs at Milngavie?'

'Milngavie, no, I haven't.' (Gordon, like Bob, pronounced this the correct Scottish way: "MULGUY") not as the Sassenachs say, "MIL-IN-GAVY".

'It's where Glasgow's water supply is filtered after rushing through a large underground aqueduct from Loch Katrine, that's Glasgow's main reservoir.'

Gordon grinned, 'Very good, that's all very interesting, but what's it to do with your 'Ten Penny Weekend?'

'It has everything to do with it. What is the furthest out place some Glasgow trams go to from the centre of the city?'

'Could it be Milngavie?' Gordon hazarded.

'Aye, you've guessed correct. Some trams go as far as the reservoirs. And the outward and return fares each cost five pence, hence the Ten Penny Weekend.'

'That sounds great. I could just about afford that. What will we do once we get there? Milngavie's like Bearsden, isn't it, very posh with expensive houses? Surely there won't be any climbers' bothies or rough dosses around there?'

'Och no, of course not, ultra posh and pretentious Milngavie's well known for being a place that's, "A' fur coats an auld patched knickers!" No we won't stay there. Following the track that runs all the way directly above the aqueduct from Milngavie to Loch Katrine we'll soon get into "God's Own Country" out by Bonnie Loch Lomond.'

'Sounds good, Bob. There'll be plenty of places to stay out there.'

'Och aye, there are. In fact parts of what's now the Queen Elizabeth Forest Park are almost littered with disused Nissen huts that are old ex-army or ex-forestry wartime billets.'

'That sounds great,' Gordon repeated. He drew out a handful of coins from a trouser pocket and as he sorted through them said, 'I should just about have enough spare cash for my subway fares to and from the city-centre where we've to catch the tram early on Saturday morning.'

So it was arranged, and so we did. After travelling from Govan Cross subway station Bob only had to wait a few minutes outside St Enoch Station until Gordon appeared from out of the reliable subway's underground lair. After walking the few yards to Argyll Street they had to wait some ten minutes for their tram. These were not quite idle wasted minutes for, even at this early Saturday morning's bright June hour, this, major city street was already busy with many rumbling and clanging trams. It was interesting to watch these vehicles painted in various hues, each colour proclaiming its own special route as they ceaselessly clattered to every corner of the sprawling city.

Time after time they tensed as yet another tram came hurtling westwards towards them, but time after time they were disappointed as the signs on the front showed their destination as 'Renfrew, via Govan', or 'Clydebank, via Partick'. After yet another disappointment Bob grinned, 'How would this dear auld city ever manage without its braw auld trams?'

At last they boarded a suitably coloured tram that appeared to be going to Milngavie. However, with snobbish disdain it failed to mention it went via Maryhill and its working class tenements!

As the swaggering tram gathered speed the two of them struggled their rucksack laden way up the curving steep iron steps and, as at this early hour on a Saturday morning the tram was almost empty, they chose to make their uneven way down the length of the top deck to pull open the sliding door that gave access to the cosy small annex right at the front, and directly above the unseen driver's head.

From their high vantage point they had fine views of the rapidly passing Glasgow scene. On the long gradual climb up Maryhill Road, Gordon with a laugh, said, 'Why are parts of Glasgow named after lassies? I've come from near Bella Houston and now we're at Mary Hill!'

Returning his laugh, Bob said, 'Aye, and now we're just approaching the home o' Glesca's own sodgers, the H.L.I.; the guid auld Highland Light Infantry at their historic Maryhill Barracks.'

As the tram trundled closely past those grim grey barracks with a bored looking sentry wearing a bright tartan kilt and white spats standing outside, the only spots of welcome colour, Bob asked, 'How do you fancy doing your National Service in the famous H.L.I.?'

'I don't fancy any regiment. I hope, and expect, that by the time I finish my engineering apprenticeship all this National Service nonsense will have ended.'

Quite amazingly quickly their speedy and violently shoogly tram was out in pleasant open countryside. Then more sedately, it passed through the prosperous leafy township of Milngavie, and there, with the June sunshine playing on its sparkling water, was the first of the Milngavie reservoirs and there too was our tram's, by now, remote from Glasgow, terminal.

Ignoring the unwelcome notice about 'No unauthorised entry', they went through an unlocked gate and started effortlessly hiking along the aqueduct covering track that came all the way from Loch Katrine to the reservoir. Gordon suddenly halted and pointed, 'What's that strange structure over there?'

'Oh that's Bennie's overhead railway, his unique Rail-plane. Do you want to go and have a closer look?'

'Aye, I sure do.'

A few minutes later they were standing staring up at that small section of railway track held high on steel girders and at the neat green carriage precariously perched there in such isolated splendour.

'It's more than just a railway carriage, isn't it?' Gordon said. 'There's a propeller at its streamlined front and rear. It must have an engine at both ends, mustn't it?'

'Oh aye,' Bob said, 'it has. Old Bennie copied that idea from the Glasgow trams that could be driven from either end and so didn't need a large circling track to turn round on at each terminal. I believe Glasgow Corporation was toying with the idea of erecting Bennie's overhead railway system in parts of the city in the late 1930's. But then of course the war put an end to that.'

'I'm surprised it survived the war,' Gordon said. 'You'd think these steel girders and that carriage would have been cut up for urgently needed wartime scrap metal, just as countless British gardens and parks had their iron railings taken to be melted down.'

'Aye, that surprises me too. I believe that, pre-war, there was much more of the overhead track, so most of it would have been taken for wartime scrap, but for some reason that piece and that unique carriage were spared.'

'Who was this "Old Bennie" who made this overhead railway?' Gordon asked.

'Och he was a well known wealthy Glasgow eccentric who owned a cinema and a lot of other property in the city. He lived in a large mansion in Mosspark. Seemingly when war broke out he erected his own one-off air-raid-shelter in his large garden. Made of galvanised metal and of pyramid shape it had a deep, water-filled ditch all around it. His idea was that Luftwaffe bombs would slide down the steep sides then be harmlessly drowned in the ditch.'

Gordon laughed, 'Aye I suppose that idea might be quite effective against

German incendiary bombs, but I wouldn't fancy being there when a high explosive landed on his hare-brained air-raid-shelter.'

We now continued on our happy way. After passing Strathblane and Killearn the track led well East of Drymen and into the pleasant, silent, long lonely miles of the vast Queen Elizabeth Forest Park. All day we only met two other hikers. Little did we think that in years to come, that unwelcoming Milngavie reservoir would be close to the start of Scotland's most popular long distance walk – the West Highland Way – and be trodden by many happy thousands every year.

This forest's pre-war trees had been ruthlessly felled by British and Canadian foresters to help meet our beleaguered country's desperate need for wartime timber, but now in these, thankfully victorious, post-war years this grim denuded area had been largely replanted. Mostly less than three years old, these vigorous small firs still allowed distant hills and attractive vistas to be seen beyond them. But we could not help wonder what this fine forest walk would be like in twenty years time. Would these present views be smothered under a dark canopy of formally regimented trees?

At last we left the main forest track and took a welcome lesser track that led directly to the West and with a fine view of the enticing, Beinn Bhreac.

Then, following an overgrown barely visible path, we reached a bush-invaded clearing and, by a clear, running burn, our doss for the night; an ex-wartime forestry Nissen hut. We were delighted that its remoteness had kept this Canadian forestry billet free from all vandalism. Its only graffiti were scribbled names, the Canadian maple leaf and a really attractive charcoal drawing of wolves, bears and a massively-horned caribou. It was furnished with four narrow beds, minus mattresses of course, a table and four wooden chairs. Standing in the middle of the hut was an iron stove with its smoke stack rising through the curving corrugated iron roof. This long lingering warm June evening had no need of the stove's promised heat, but we kept it in mind for possible future use in weekends in darker cooler times.

Our rather frugal evening meal reflected our rather straitened financial condition. Porridge, that great, cheap, filling and nutritious grand old stand-by, was the essential main-stay of not only our much needed late dinner but could, fulfilling its guid auld Scots tradition, form the warming bulk of tomorrow's early breakfast. And, again true to wise old tradition, our porridge was made of real, rough, natural oats and not of that other Scott's imposter, the oats that came out of cardboard packets. Some spam and beans completed our surprisingly filling dinner. Again reflecting our shortage of money, our only drink was hot, sweet, milk-less tea.

Pleasantly tired after the long day's hike, we soon relished the delight of each of us having our own real bed (even if it didn't have a mattress) to lure us into much needed sleep in our own secret, remote and comfortable forest bothy.

As arranged the previous night, we had to be up very shortly after June's bright dawn, for an even more strenuous day stretched before us if we were to climb Beinn Bhreac then get back to Milngavie to catch one of the last evening trams for the return five penny journey back to Glasgow.

★ ★ ★

The morning found us keenly striding along one of the numerous forest tracks that wound its way through this seeming endless maze of freshly-planted trees until at last we saw, with some surprise, a convenient wooden stile that made easy our escape over an enclosing high deer fence. Now out on the welcome openness of this bright heather moor we headed straight for Beinn Bhreac.

Surprisingly soon, spurred on by the eagerness of healthy youth, we reached the mini-mountain's modest summit. Although less than 2,000 ft high and constantly over-shadowed by its famous neighbour Ben Lomond, the wee hill held its own for unbeatable views of that straight chain of wooded islands that made this, the widest part of bonnie Loch Lomond, also the bonniest.

We sat and eagerly drank in the fabulous scene before us and no less eagerly devoured our precious bananas. Only recently returned, in very limited amounts, to British shops after six long war years of being completely unseen, we thought of this now commonplace fruit as being something rare and extremely exotic.

After that brief rest with its inspiring views and our unfamiliar pleasure in rare fruit, we hurried back down this splendid hill. Suddenly we disturbed a covey of red grouse that had been hidden in the thick heather. As they burst away in every direction they urgently called and demanded that we 'go-back, go-back, go-back.'

We laughed and shouted out, 'No, we're not going back!' Definitely not! We've got as much bloody right to be here as you have!' But, unfortunately, *we did* have to go back – back to dear, dreary old Glasgow.

As our late evening tram wildly shoogled and thundered its final return journey into town, Bob asked Gordon, 'Well, have you enjoyed your first Ten Penny Weekend?'

'Oh aye, of course I have. It's been great, really great! It's been much, much better than being stuck in the dismal misery of the dreary city. This weekend has been worth ten thousand pounds, rather than a mere Ten Pennies!'

# The Driver in the Pearl Necklace

Bob and I sat opposite each other on the bench seats just inside the platform of the Glasgow Corporation Drumchapel bus on a Friday evening. This was something we were becoming quite used to. Our choice of seats was for two reasons; it was handy for eying up the conductress, should she merit it, and secondly, we could keep an eye on our rucksacks stowed away in the compartment under the stairs. The conductress that night was pretty and we tried our usual chat up lines, failing miserably to impress her, so reluctantly we turned our attention instead to staring at our rucksacks. Not that anyone was likely to nick them, they were heavy enough to carry when walking never mind running away with.

'Right here we are,' said Bob, and with a, 'You've missed your chance, this is our stop,' to the conductress, we rose, dragged out our packs and got off at the junction of Great Western Road and the right turn where the bus goes off into the wilds of the Drumchapel housing scheme.

Hefting the packs onto our backs we gave the customary cheer and shout of, 'The weekend starts now,' startling a wee dog that was sauntering along the pavement, sniffing at the weeds, and we strode off in the direction of Arrochar, some thirty miles away.

About fifty yards along that route was the spot where, usually, our walking stopped and hitch-hiking began.

We had almost reached that point where fate would take over and a wait of ten minutes, an hour, two or more would elapse, before a kind truck or car driver would take pity on us and transport us to, or near to our destination.

Suddenly, with a swish of expensive tyres an apparition, wonderful to behold, drew up beside us. The engine purred like a contented cat, the gleaming black paintwork and its sheer size identified it as, the ultimate in motoring luxury, a Rolls Royce! Our first thoughts were, someone asking for directions, perhaps improbably looking for directions to Drumchapel! But then we hadn't even raised our thumbs, we hadn't even started hitching. We were very glad these first thoughts were quickly proved wrong. The window slid down at the touch of a button, even in these days long before electric windows were common, and an angel's voice (we imagined so, not having heard one before) drifted out, delivering these words. 'Would you two like a lift? I'm going to Inverary.'

In a kind of shock we managed to stammer out, 'Yes, please, that would be great,' though tongue-tied with shock and embarrassment, it came out more like, 'Es pls tha be grate.'

'Jump in then', replied the angel.

In our haste the two of us tried, shoving and pushing, to get in the same rear door, resulting in an awkward exchange.

'Go round the other side.'

'Get lost, you go round, I was here first,' until the thought hit us that this bickering might cause our dream lift to purr off into the night leaving us, still arguing, still stuck in Great Western Road.

Scurrying round, I opened the door and literally walked in and sat down. The space, the smell of leather seats the faint aroma of expensive perfume (we imagined again) wafting back from the front seat had us, in an instant, seriously questioning our socialist views and our dislike of the upper classes, even, yes even, whether or not this was all in fact happening and the driver really was an angel and we had been somehow run over by the departing Drumchapel bus.

'So, where are you two off to?' asked our dark haired chauffeur, and as she turned slightly towards us, we noticed as we pulled away from the kerb, the glint of a three-strand string of large pearls around her neck.

'Arrochar, or just beyond,' mumbled Bob, 'We're going climbing.'

'How interesting, something I've never tried, maybe some day I will. I love skiing though. Have you been to Courmayeur?' was the bell-like reply, upper class, but with a very slight American accent.

'No, the Whangie, Arrochar and the Campsies are the places where we generally end up at the weekend,' said Bob.

'Arrochar I know, pass through quite often, but I've never heard of, what was it, the Whangie? What an unusual name.'

Not as unusual as Courmayeur, we thought.

'And where will you spend the night, where will you intrepid adventurers sleep?'

Anxious to get in on the conversation I ventured, 'In a doss.' But, quickly realising the inadequacy of that answer, I added, 'A cave actually, up on the hill.'

'My goodness, a cave, how exciting, is it comfortable?'

'Yes, very cosy, provided you have the gear, groundsheet, sleeping-bags an' that.'

A pair of dark eyes appeared briefly in the rear view mirror. 'By the way, we haven't introduced ourselves, have we? I'm Margaret,' she said and her right hand, palm bent back, appeared over her shoulder. The two of us shot forward and stuck out our hands as if to take hers but, realising the incongruity of the situation, hastily withdrew, saying simultaneously, 'I'm Bob. 'I'm Gordon.'

'Hello there, Bob and Gordon.' Obviously she had sorted out our mixed mumblings. As the miles flew past, the conversation went back and forth, becoming more personal as the three in the Rolls shared more of the journey together. She was a good bit older than us, attractive and well groomed. The way she spoke, the car, and the fact that she was going to Inverary, gave us a clue to her identity, helped further by her next remark.

'You know if ten years ago someone had said that in future I would be married and living in a castle in Scotland and have four children, I wouldn't have believed them.' A mumble from the back seat,

'And do you regret this?'

'Oh no, I never regret anything what's the point in looking back, one can't reverse life and besides, I love doing things on the spur of the moment, especially something new.' Again there was that quick glance back at us.

'We were wondering, why did you stop and give us a lift? Though obviously we're very grateful you did.'

I frowned at Bob, thinking he had gone too far with this one, too bold.

'Oh, I don't, know, just felt like some company on the way and, I must say you two looked quite interesting the way you were dressed, the boots, rope, and everything. I could also see you were young and fit.' A pause and then, 'Oh dear, I'm sorry. I appear to have embarrassed you.'

'It's, erm, quite warm in the back, what with our gear and everything.'

'Feel free to take it off, though I sense that might cause you to blush even more. You know that reminds me of the time last summer when I was walking in the castle grounds and I stopped to admire some roses. One of our young gardeners was crouched down, pruning-shears in his hand, I spoke to him, something along the lines of, the roses are looking splendid, or suchlike, and that it must be his magic touch. He spun round, not having heard me coming and stuttered words like, pruning stimulating the plant growth or some such thing. I realised he was staring at me and his face had gone red. I asked him what was the matter and he apologised and turned away, muttering something. I stood there a moment, puzzled, what on earth was wrong, before I worked out what had happened. Do you know, the sun was shining behind me, showing the outline of my legs through my summer dress, and that was all it was, but somehow it seemed to cause him a great deal of discomfort, making him blush, much as you two are doing at this moment.'

We believe we both had the same mental picture of the scene she had just described, blotting out the gardener, of course, an image which indeed, did cause us some discomfort. Why tell us this? Was she leading us on? Not perhaps what you might expect from a lady of her class, on her own, in a car with two young strangers she'd just picked up. Unless? No, exciting though it was, we were too gauche, too inexperienced for this kind of adventure. Besides, a wrong move or in our case a clumsy wrong move might lead to execution or deportation or something. They might still have that for people like us who get involved with people like them. So we sat, rather silently now, as we passed through Arrochar and were approaching Ardgartan when Her Ladyship questioned us again.

'What will two you have to eat this evening, in the warmth and comfort of your wee cave, I wonder, will it be a can of beans or similar?'

The reply, when it came, had her gasping in surprise. Bob, whose aunt worked in one of the very few delicatessen shops existing in Glasgow at that austere time, had brought home a few goodies for his week-end in the hills, and he announced, 'Tonight, Madam, we're having frankfurters, gherkins and pumpernickel with a bottle of Riesling, and we would be greatly honoured if you would join us.' (He sounded as if he was getting the hang of it at last)

'Gosh that sounds wonderful. I'm very impressed, but reluctantly, I must decline. Unfortunately, I don't have my walking shoes with me.'

I thought to myself, I'll ask her as she's not far from home, to nip down, get her shoes and nip back up here again. Failing that, I'm sure we could carry her, like some kind of potentate, which in a sense she was, up the hill to the doss. Because of the sheer improbability of either of these options being accepted, I didn't even light-heartedly, think them worth suggesting.

A moment or two later we got out of the car at the foot of the Brack and she bade us farewell. 'Goodbye then. I hope we meet again. I find it quite lonely travelling on my own and I must say, I have enjoyed your company, bye, once again.'

'I really bloody hope we do,' we said to ourselves as the dream came to an end and our most exciting and luxurious lift ever, swept off into the night.

Later that evening as we lay back in our sleeping-bags in our wee cave above the Rest-and-Be-Thankful, sipping the last of the Riesling from enamel mugs, Bob turned to me and voiced my own precise thoughts,

'What do you think would have happened if that goddess had had her walking shoes with her?'

With a groan I replied, 'I know, it's almost too much to think about. I was just wondering if, at this moment, she's sitting down there in her big castle thinking, "I'll need to remember always to have a spare pair of shoes in the car, just in case." They lay in silence for a while going over in their minds the incredible events of the past few hours and then at last Bob sighed and said, 'Ah well, it's a funny old world, as they say, you don't know what's going to happen next. I mean we'll never meet her again, but just think about this. Who in the world d'you think is ever going to believe our story?'

Footnote

*A series of Polaroid photographs were used in evidence in the bitter and acrimonious divorce case between the Duke and Duchess of Argyll. They featured Margaret in her Art-Deco-style bathroom at her Upper Grosvenor Street London home dressed in nothing but her signature three-strand pearl necklace. More shockingly they showed her performing a sex-act on a naked man whose identity was concealed because his head was not captured within the frame.*

*The press had a field day and the Duchess's reputation was ruined, not only because of the Polaroid photos, but that she was accused of sleeping with eighty-eight men including two cabinet ministers and two members of the royal family, (and almost but not quite, two young Glasgow hitch-hikers ,much to their regret it must be said.)*

# Ah Ambrosia!

At almost exactly the same moment Gordon and I saw one another amongst the cheery bustling, rucksack-laden Saturday morning crowd thronging Glasgow's Buchanan Street Bus Station.

After exchanging welcoming waves we struggled through this youthfully animated crowd. We met and congratulated each other on arriving dead on time, then made our way to the waiting MacBrayne's Oban bus that would take us to Arrochar.

As we fitted our bulging rucksacks into the cavernous luggage compartment in the rear of the crowded bus we saw that some of the many rucksacks already there had climbing ropes neatly coiled around them. We were impressed. In fact we, as quite novice, but keen newcomers to this post-war Scottish outdoor weekend scene were more than impressed; we were awed to think that would be sharing this bus, and would perhaps even share the same Arrochar hills with these real rock-climbers. This being our third weekend visit to Arrochar and to that rugged, rocky, impressive, triple-peaked hill, The Cobbler, we were now fondly familiar with the route this distinctively liveried bus so regularly and so reliably took.

Passing through Clydebank we were again saddened to see all these empty shells of gutted tenements that stood like gaunt gravestones, stark evidence of the Luftwaffe's devastating Blitz. Going round Dumbarton's Castle-crowned Rock we were reminded of this area's long history of human conflict. After going through cheery Helensburgh we hurried to Rhu where there was further evidence of our own more recent war. Massive hangers dominated Rhu; they sheltered R.A.F. Costal Command aircraft while many other surplus Sutherland flying-boats floated and slowly rotted out in the bay. But when uncertain October sunshine brightly lit up these huge, four-engine flying-boats and a lively breeze had them rocking in the water, they seemed to come alive as if wishing to re-live the brave days when they had sunk deadly skulking German U-boats.

With practiced ease our expert driver steered us up the hilly road that ran along beside the long length of narrow, aptly named, Loch Long. Even at Arrochar there were more reminders of war as this was the location where the Royal Navy fired its latest torpedoes down its testing range.

There was much happy lively bustle as the crowd of climbers and hikers tumbled out of the bus and started sorting through the heap of unloaded rucksacks piled on the pavement. Then, finding their own, the heavy packs were swung up on to impatient, youthful, eager-to-get-going shoulders.

After striding around the end of Loch Long, we left the road and took the steep path up the hill towards The Cobbler. As with rhythmic steps and gasping breath we 'conquered' the hill's testing slope, Gordon grinned and asked, 'Have you remembered to bring your half of the tent with you, Bob?'

'Oh, aye, I have. But have you brought your half?'

'Och, aye, it's packed safe and sound in my rucksack.' Having borrowed this tent from a friend who could not get away this weekend, we were keen to use it, not in the comparative luxury of a well-organised camp-site, but perched high amongst these, hopefully not too windswept, enticing Arrochar Hills. Of course this small, two-man tent had been bought at an Army Surplus Supplies shop. In these early post-war years the only climbing clothes and gear available were ex-army issue. Boots were black, with steel studs, with leather so stiff that, even after being repeatedly dubbined, took months to break in and almost invariably caused blistered heels and toes; there were slick camouflaged rainproof capes that doubled as ground-sheets; there were strong sturdy ice-axes, their long, wooden shafts well preserved with linseed oil. And for Scotland's small band of intrepid skiers in these pre-ski-lift times there were only long, heavy wooden ex-army skis, some of which probably saw active war-time service in Norway, the winter Ardennes or in the bloodily savage Italian Alps.

To spread the burden of carrying this small, but quite heavy ex-army tent, Gordon and Bob had shared it among themselves. Gordon was carrying the actual tent while Bob had the rubberised groundsheet and the two wooden tent poles. With laughter we agreed it was as well we had both remembered to bring our half of the tent. Bob said, 'It wouldn't be very pleasant to sleep out with only the horizontal tent draped over us.'

'Aye,' agreed Gordon, 'or to have only that ground sheet propped up on shaky tent poles.'

Stopping for a much-needed rest, we carefully scanned The Cobbler's challenging peaks. Of these three steep rocky peaks we'd only climbed one, the Centre Peak, the Auld Cobbler himself, and that was a fine exhilarating rock-scramble with its thrilling struggle through 'the eye of the needle' then the daring stand on the steeply exposed final summit.

As we admiringly and rather enviously watched a group of the 'real' rock-climbers we had seen in the bus head for The Cobbler's aggressive, thrusting, steep-pointed South peak we wondered where they had bought their climbing ropes. Were they too, ex-army gear? Bob voiced both their thoughts, 'Do you think we'll ever go with ropes and do some real rock-climbing on the South, or even the frightening North peak?'

Gordon grinned, 'Och aye, I'm sure we will. I don't see any reason why we shouldn't, apart from not having a rope, do you?'

Bob hesitantly replied, 'Oh no, of course not. But we'll need to get some more experience out on the hills doing easier rock-scrambling before we get too ambitious on these higher, steeper, more dangerous rock faces.'

Gordon again grinned, 'Aye, I suppose you're right. But it must feel great to try and have a go at some of these more challenging routes.'

'Aye, it truly must, but in the meantime we better get cracking and get to where we've decided to pitch the tent.'

It was strange as we headed northward round below The Cobbler's North Peak to come across fresh man-made structures high amongst what had been wild, untamed wilderness. But at least it was good use of some of the many thousands of tons of war-surplus cement to turn it into concrete channels, tunnels and small dams to direct run-off water to Loch Sloy's large new Hydro-Electric development, part of the ambitious post-war scheme that was going to bring electricity to every home in the Highlands. It was even stranger to come across a narrow gauge railway line that sloped steeply down towards the distant road. A couple of heavy steel trucks were immobilized by many chains and padlocks. While, with his fresh acquired engineering skills keenly engaged, Gordon inspected these trucks and their strong restraints, Bob laughed, 'Och, surely these padlocks and chains must be to stop the trucks from being illicitly used by some of the Creagh Dhu Mountaineering Club!' It had to be said, this was based on their reputation, although, as far as we knew, we had never met any members of that famous (or infamous?) Glasgow Club, even us novices at the climbing game had heard plenty of stories of some of these characters' fantastic antics, including having used these now padlocked trucks to take breathlessly fast, recklessly dangerous, time-saving trips down this steep railway track.

Now in sight of Ben Ime, we chose a lush grassy spot beside a fast flowing burn to pitch our tent. Without too much trouble we got our two halves of the tent correctly fitted together.

Soon, in response to our keen hunger, our two primus stoves were brightly glowing and hissing their heart-warming story and we brought our little practised, and certainly not very sophisticated cooking skills into play. In these early post-war years of rationing our choice of food was rather limited, but at least we had many rashers of what promised to be succulent sizzling bacon, and with that great, never-failing standby, tins of baked beans, we made a real fine outdoor, cowboy-like meal. As an exciting experiment we were going to try to transmute an ex-wartime packet of dehydrated eggs into an appetising – or maybe appalling, dish of scrambled eggs. Then like a conjurer producing his latest wonder, Gordon delved into his rucksack and brought out a real marvel – a large tin of Ambrosia Creamed Rice. Reverently holding and keenly inspecting this apparition, Bob asked with awe, 'How did you manage to get this? I don't think I've seen a tin of creamed rice since before the war.'

Gordon grinned and explained, 'I got it as a special birthday present from my sister who works in the office of a large wholesale grocer. The first few cases of this are just coming on to the market. I hope you like rice, I brought as a special treat for us.'

'Oh aye, I love rice. I'm really looking forward to it.'

The bacon, as always, was crispy perfection; the gaudy yellow scrambled eggs, made from powder, were far from perfect, but were fine when heaped with baked beans. Now, as with eager anticipation, Bob watched Gordon open the tin of Ambrosia Creamed Rice, he laughed, 'God, wouldn't it be hellishly frustrating if you had brought that tin, but we had both forgotten to bring a tin opener?'

'Och, such a terrible disaster doesn't hear thinking about, does it? Anyway now that I have got the tin opener will you go and fetch water for the tea while I heat our special treat?'

At a leisurely pace Bob made his way to the nearby burn then stooped to fill the large ex-army tin dixie giving Gordon ample time to get the succulent rice heated, he took his time about getting back to the tent. For some pleasant minutes he stood and stared at Ben Ime, the hill they were going to climb in the morning. Although at over 3,000 feet high this hill was (unlike The Cobbler) a 'Munro', it had nothing like the rocky rugged appeal of the lower hill's triple peaks. Tomorrow's climb would be a straightforward hill-walk on a hill they would be climbing for the first time. It should be interesting, but hardly as exciting as the grand auld Cobbler always was.

Returning to the tent Bob carefully placed the dixie of water on one primus then sat beside Gordon and expectantly took his dixie of hot creamed rice from him. For some blissful time they ate this rare dish in silence. Then, with, his heaped spoon poised by his mouth, Bob said, 'Oh this rice is great, it's really delicious. And it's unusual having raisins in it, isn't it? I don't ever remember having them with rice before.'

Gordon grinned as he answered, 'Oh aye, it is most unusual to have raisins right enough. But as long as you're enjoying them that's all that matters.'

For a few more happy contented moments they ate in silence then Gordon again grinned, 'I don't seem to have many raisins in mine. You seem to have got the lion's share of them.'

'Aye, so I have. Do you want some of mine?'

No longer able to contain his merriment, Gordon, laughed, stammered and gasped, 'No …no… thank you, Bob. I wouldn't want to deprive you of them!'

Suspicious at his obvious amusement, Bob asked, 'Is there something about these raisins I don't know about?'

'Aye, aye, there is,' Gordon gasped, 'but as long as you enjoyed them everything's okay.'

Both our dixies were now empty with the last grains of rice scraped out. We threw them onto the lush green grass outside the tent .We would clean them later after we had our tea. Bob smiled, 'Well, Gordon, now we're finished perhaps you'll tell me your secret about the rice, those raisins.'

Struggling to control his mirth, Gordon nodded, 'Aye, right enough, Bob, I suppose you're entitled to know, as long as it doesn't spoil your digestion. Well, when I was pouring the rice into your Dixie outside the tent some of it spilled onto the grass, and so, not to waste this precious food I scraped it up and put it into your Dixie. I managed to get all the grass out but unfortunately I couldn't get all the rabbit droppings out of it before you returned.'

'So those "raisins" I enjoyed were really rabbit's shit?'

Again helpless with laughter, Gordon gasped, 'Aye, Bob, I'm afraid they were!'

Bob stared at him for a few thoughtful silent moments then, seeing the funny side of it, started laughing himself, 'Ach well I don't suppose these rabbit 'raisins' will do me any harm, will they? After all, as part of their unique digestive system, rabbits eat and re-digest their own droppings.'

'I know we don't have a lot of food Bob, but surely you're not going to try that as well. Or are you?' said Gordon with a splutter.

For a while our helpless, unrestrained laughter echoed and re-echoed around the nearby Arrochar Hills. At last Bob managed to say, 'Now, be sure to tell me if you see my ears and my front teeth getting longer and I start preferring lettuces and carrots to a feed of bacon, won't you?'

# Their First Joint Rock Climbs

This was what Gordon and Bob had often thought about, talked about, and sometimes even dreamt about: of doing their first rock climbs under the more experienced guidance of their new, and older climbing friends, Lawrie and Dave.

So here they were, the four of them, standing at the foot of the impressive steep South Peak of that grand wee hill, The Cobbler: that irresistible magnet that drew the best of Glasgow's foot-loose youth to its challenging rocky peaks.

Grand auld Dave Martin was really at home on The Cobbler's familiar slopes. He was justifiably proud of having his name marked on climbers' Cobbler maps. Although not now used so much, his own very special overhanging dry rock shelter, 'Martin's Doss,' held great memories for him; fine days of climbs in summer's heat and winter's cold.

From 'Martin's Doss' there were grand views over Loch Long and Arrochar to broad-shouldered Ben Lomond, but what glowed most vividly and clearly in Dave's memory were the – regrettably all too infrequent and therefore all the more precious – times when he'd had great erotic pleasure in his very own high Cobbler doss.

These memorable weekends were odd occasions when some very bold and adventurous young lady climbers had been strangely smitten by Dave's fierce burly appearance and his rather eccentric clothing of wild swinging kilt and jaunty beribboned Glengarry hat. Then they may have been enticed to share the night with him in the Spartan private doss and bestow their sexual favours on the hugely grateful 'owner' of the doss.

Today however Dave's less urgent, less passionate mission was to pass on something of his not very advanced, rock climbing skills to these keen young novice friends.

Lawrie too, although not having his name marked on any map, knew

The Cobbler well and with real deep pleasure had climbed many of its less demanding rock routes. Wisely knowing his limitations, he left the newer, ever more severe rock climbs to be the province of the wild men of the famous Creag Dhu climbing club.

'Well, my dear fellow, will I guide Bob up 'Nimlin's Direct' while you take Gordon up 'The Jughandle'? Lawrie asked Dave

'Oh aye, that sounds fine.' Dave smiled at young Gordon, 'Come on lad, take my rope out of your rucksack and get it tied on'

With keen tremulous fingers Gordon tied Dave's thick old hemp rope around his slim waist. He cast envious glances at the new white nylon rope of Lawrie's that Bob was eagerly tying around his equally slim waist.

Bob keenly looked on and silently admired the steady, cautious, sure way Lawrie climbed the start of this steep rock route.

Gordon gazed at Dave's not quite so sure and steady upwards rock climbing progress. Even to his novice eyes it seemed quite clear that Dave's rather laboured climbing owed much to the strength of his weight-lifter's arms as his groping hands reached up to each rock jughandle and hauled his rather bulky weight up to the next ledge.

After tying his rope to a secure rock belay Lawrie called on Bob to start upwards to him. Thinking his climbing was just as reliable as Lawrie's, and well aware of the safeguard of the tight rope that stretched up to that safe belay, Bob's nerves and senses wondrously thrilled to his new rock-climbing skill.

Gordon was equally happily, effortlessly, it seemed, moving up the 'very difficult' rock route. Impressed by Gordon's instinctive climbing skills, Dave said, 'I'll lead the next difficult pitch, and from there I'm sure you can safely lead right to the top of this climb.'

Lawrie, too, eventually let Bob lead once he'd proved his worth by the cautious ease with which he'd climbed the crux of this Nimlin's, Direct route.

Soon all four stood on the rocky summit of The Cobbler's South Peak. After shaking hands in congratulations they stared around and took in the surrounding views of this wild rugged Argyll land.

Lawrie smiling pointed to the South, 'That's "Argyll's Bowling Green" down there, you know.'

'Aye,' Bob laughed, 'I do know. I've read about that wild sea-girthed landscape in one of Seton Gordon's great books.'

Auld Dave grinned at Gordon then generously admitted, 'Oh, lad, I doot there's not very much more that Lawrie or I can teach you about rock-climbing. The way you flew up that, admittedly fairly easy route puts my rather laborious climbing technique in the shade. You are a real natural, instinctive rock-climber.'

'Yes, my dear fellow,' Lawrie agreed,' with more practice and experience you could well become a great climber.'

Although absolutely delighted with this unexpected praise Gordon laughed and said, 'Thanks, you're very kind, but I'm not going to be much of a climber with a hugely swollen head, am I?'

# Not Climbing Gardyloo Gully

Gordon and Bob left their Glen Nevis tent early on this bright, clear, mid-March morning. Down here in the narrow glen all other human life seemed still asleep; seemed to be drugged by the chill coolness of the mountain-enclosed wild place's fierce gripping shade.

With impatient haste they made for the vital wee footbridge that's set high and safe above the savage glen's fierce rushing river, that's so prone to sudden flooding. They hurried along not only to get their sleep-sluggish blood faster flowing but to climb out of the glen's chilling shade and into the sunlight where morning's glorious urgency was transforming towering Ben Nevis's higher snowy slopes all aglow with inviting sparkling brightness.

With minds bright and eager as is the morning's glowing show and with bodies that are alive with healthy youthful fitness they soon reach this steep slope's deeper snows. They pause, then sit and revel in this bright March morning's sparkling beauty while its sunshine warms them with its promise of soon approaching Spring.

Gordon grinned, 'It's really grand to get out of the glen's cold grip, isn't it?'

'Aye it is. It certainly is. It's great to see a bit of sunshine. I could stay here for hours.' Bob also smiled, 'Och, but I suppose we better push on. Aye, we better get going if we're going to realise our dream of climbing the Ben's challenging Gardyloo Gully today.'

They heave themselves to their feet and start climbing steadily but with a recently learned, well disciplined pace.

Despite the weary breaking of their boots through the knee-deep snow that covered the tourist path they were amazed how quickly they reached the mountain's half way point. From here all the thousands of Ben-climbing summer tourists followed this path up to the right where it led directly to the large, flattish, somewhat uninspiring summit. Bob and Gordon also intended to reach the summit, but not by the straightforward, regular tourist route. They aimed to climb up the steep snow and ice of the impressive Gardyloo Gully on the North-East face.

This gully, with all the other snow-packed gullies and their enclosing steep towering ice-plastered rock ridges join together to form a vast amphitheatre of snow, rock and ice that stretches for two curving miles and savagely thrusts up for two thousand awesome feet. This was this mountain's secret heart that stays unknown and unseen by the many thousands of summer tourists who wearily slog up the well-marked tourist path. But for every keen young aspiring climber once he's seen this savage challenging heart of Scotland's highest mountain the inspiring sight remains forever bright in his heart and mind.

And so it had been for Gordon and Bob as they hastened down the snowy slope that leads away from the mundane tourist path and curves round above the snow and ice covered half-way lochan. They felt keen anticipation pounding their hearts and stirring their blood as Ben Nevis's fabulous Shangri-la burst into vivid view.

Taking turn about to lead the way, they broke an easy trail through the soft deep snow that covers the gentle slope that leads towards the foot of those alluring steep and soaring gullies.

A bit below them they saw the Scottish Mountaineering Club's C.I.C. Ben Nevis hut. That grand shelter is rather more than a mere 'hut.' Its strong roof, thick stone walls and securely shuttered windows defiantly brave the worst weather the savage Highland winters can fling at them.

Gazing at the snow-smothered building, Gordon said, 'It would be grand to stay a weekend in the S.M.C. hut sometime, wouldn't it?'

'Aye, it would, 'Bob whole-heartedly agreed. 'From there we'd be perfectly placed to get quickly to the Ben's summer-bare steep rock ridges or its snow-packed winter gullies,'

'Is the hut kept for the exclusive use of well-to-do S.M.C members and other posh university types?'

'Yes, mostly it is, I believe, but not entirely. They do allow other bona fide Mountaineering Clubs to sometimes hire it, but only at times when it's in least demand from their own club members.'

'Ach well I hope we'll get to use it once we've become fully vetted members of the Lomonds, if they manage to hire it.'

'Aye, I hope so too.' Bob smiled, 'Or, as a last resort, we might try breaking into it. It wouldn't be the first time some climbers have made an illicit entry.'

'Wouldn't be the Creag Dhu, would it?

'You said it not me,' Bob replied.

Then, with ever-rising spirits they continued on into the base of the vast snowy amphitheatre and gazed with increasing awe at those high, seeming almost vertical, snow filled gullies, those smooth-toothed rock spikes. Recalling a guide book's well studied map, they put names to some of the gullies and ridges. That vast towering ridge can only be the Tower Ridge and over there under where the Ben's weather observatory used to be, obviously is Observatory Ridge. And lurking not quite in sight behind it is that steep gully they aim to 'conquer' today – Gardyloo Gully.

This gully, too, gained its name from The Ben's observatory and the small hotel that graced its flattish summit in earlier times. As all the rubbish and human waste from both these high, airy, remote buildings was dumped down that most convenient gully, the auld Edinburgh tenement warning cry of 'Gardyloo' as chamber pots were emptied out of high windows, was jovially shouted in un-needed airy warning.

They reached the foot of the gully which, seen face-on, really seemed completely vertical. Standing gazing upward they again felt awe – real, deep and almost intimidating awe, allied to, perhaps, a deep touch of fear! Their eyes met and they guessed each other's hidden feelings. Keeping these fears unsaid, they both had overwhelming emotions of reverence, dread and wonder at this challenging, mountainous savageness. Young, keen, but not yet very experienced on hard snow and ice climbs, they wondered, were they being foolhardy to take on such a severe climb?

Perhaps being a bit over-optimistic they decided to press on. They fasten on their borrowed crampons. These unfamiliar ex-army crampons feel awkward underfoot. They also are heavy, made of steel rather than today's much lighter aluminium. However they immediately prove their worth as they eagerly bite into the snow and re-assuringly grip into the increasingly steep snow slope.

They pause to tie on their rope. This heavy, thickish, hemp rope had been borrowed from an older climbing friend, good auld Dave Martin. Dave said he had got it from a prison warder friend who worked at

Glasgow's Barlinnie Prison. He claimed that the warder had 'borrowed' it from the heaps of spare rope that occupied the hangman's hut at the prison.

As he tightened the final knot at his rope-encircled waist Gordon grinned. 'I hope this rope from Barlinnie hasn't been used for its original intended purpose?'

Bob laughed, 'No, let's hope not. And let's also hope that that we don't find ourselves hanging from it near the top of this fierce-looking gully.'

He now led the way on this lower easier part of this dreamt of Gardyloo Gully while Gordon followed in his footsteps slightly below him. The, as yet un-needed rope, was held coiled in their hands and stretched between them like a hemp umbilical cord.

They now take turns to lead the way as with increasing skill and seeming effortless youthful keenness they use their grand old ex-army ice-axes to shovel through the top layer of soft snow then cut out secure flat footholds in the underlying harder snow. They made swift upward progress.

As the snowy slope got decidedly steeper their climbing became more cautious and slower, then Bob said, 'I think I better make a snow-belay here and wait and rest while you continue up as far as the rope will let you, then I'll climb up and join you.'

Gordon agreed and continued upwards while Bob thrust the point and long wooden shaft of his ice-axe deep into the snow, wound the rope secure around this safe belay then patiently and alertly waited. He saw three climbers, small dark mobile dots, on the long narrow ridge of Carn Mor Dearg that rose impressively across from Ben Nevis and, curving round to meet the higher Ben, helped neatly enclose this high amphitheatre of rock, ice and snow. He almost envied those distant climbers with their wonderland of bright sunshine and the glitter of sun-reflecting snow while he waited here in the North-facing gully's perpetual sun-less shade.

The sudden loud slithering sound of fast-moving snow above him instantly drew his mind from these distant figures to the urgent need to take action. He tightly gripped his belayed ice-axe with both hands, braced his feet, hunched his back and with tense dread awaited an avalanche attack.

With a palpable thud a large lump of soft snow hit his back then slid over his stooped shoulders. For long anxious moments he was further assaulted by powdery soft snow, more a choking mini-blizzard rather than a real engulfing avalanche.

As he straightened up and shook the clinging snow from his clothes he heard Gordon shouting, 'I'm sorry about that, Bob. Are you all right?'

'Och, I'm fine. Some damned cold wet snow down the back of my neck, that's all. What happened?'

'A big lump of that soft surface slithered away from me when I was cutting my next foothold.'

'Well I suggest you don't cut any more and don't climb any higher. I don't think these snow conditions are safe. I think that was a warning. If we go any higher and steeper we might easily get caught in a real avalanche.'

'Aye, that's exactly what I was thinking. If we're wise we should get out of this dangerous gully while we can. If any of our club's older, more experienced members were here with us today I'm sure that's what they'd advise.'

Gordon climbed down to Bob and they made their swift safe way down one at a time, then, on the easier lower slope, they descended together.

Once out of the gully and round by a protective rock buttress they halted. They grinned rather ruefully at each other. 'Not a very impressive climbing performance, eh?' Gordon said.

'No, perhaps not,' Bob agreed. 'But at least we've come out of that experience alive and well. And surely we've learned from it. We should be better able to judge snow conditions on future winter climbs.'

Gordon nodded, 'Aye, I think we were right to retreat defeated. There must have been a real risk of us being caught in a deadly avalanche.'

No sooner had he finished speaking than a strange sudden sound silenced them. It came from the gully they'd been precariously perched in only a few minutes ago. It sounded like an avalanche, but instead of the roar they might have expected it gave a strange loud hissing noise.

Remembering a head-raised hissing adder he'd encountered the previous August on the Campsies, Bob said, 'Christ, it sounds like 10,000 angry, snakes, doesn't it?'

★ ★ ★

The avalanche now came into view; a slithering, sliding, hissing mass of moving soft snow which, having swept down Gardyloo Gully, was now spreading and almost reluctantly slowing down.

As they watched the snowy mass fan out, and at last stop, Gordon smiled, 'Well, we showed good judgement there, getting out of the gully when we did.'

'Aye, 'Bob agreed, 'we certainly did. That's a lesson we'll always remember. Aye, by God, it wouldn't have been very nice stuck in the gully with that mass of snow coming sliding down towards us.'

'Aye, 'Gordon laughed, 'I think we might have been be shitting ourselves!'

'Och well,' replied Bob, 'if we had shit ourselves it would have been an appropriately named place for it. We'd merely be putting Gardyloo Gully to its original use!'

Uplifted by their happy survival they hurry back on those snow tracks they'd made earlier and in an amazingly short time they rejoice to reach the Ben's summit and its brilliant sunshine. They hurry to the snow-shrouded ruins of the old observatory then, with needful caution, try to see over the jutting frozen snow cornice that crowns the top of their Gardyloo Gully. The highest, steepest slopes of the gully are completely hidden by the cornice, but at its distant base they see the avalanche's deep snows fanned out on the surrounding smooth surface.

As, profoundly impressed, they gaze down at the debris, their unspoken thoughts are the same: How very easily our two bodies could have been deeply buried beneath that suffocating mass.

They turn away and start down the tourist route with a re-born youthful vigour, with blood in joyous pulsing flood, with sure-footed hurrying eagerness to reach their cosy tent and its stack of waiting food.

Despite their Gardyloo Gully failure this day's climbing is judged a success. The warmish sunshine is sheer bliss. They've learned new mountain wisdom: the need to be wary of soft snow lying on firm old snow. But above all they rejoice that they live to climb another day!

# Loch Katrine Bothy

The five of us were keenly looking forward to this weekend's journey of discovery to a bothy we had never used before, had never even heard of until a couple of weeks ago. We'd been told in strict confidence about this loch-side bothy by friends who'd recently secretly used it. Caution was necessary, for this was not a normal, open to all, climbers' bothy and the loch it nestled beside was not just any normal Highland loch, but was Loch Katrine, that large natural reservoir that supplied all of Glasgow's immense water needs through its underground aqueduct to Milngavie's storage reservoirs. There the loch's pure unpolluted water's natural softness was not insulted by having any chemicals added to spoil its purity. The only treatment it received was some filtering to ensure no tadpoles or any other wee beasties could wriggle into any of Glasgow's many sinks or its considerably fewer baths.

After getting off the bus at the pleasant wee town of Aberfoyle this Saturday morning, we set out hiking along the quiet road that led to the wooded beauty of little Loch Ard, its beauty greatly enhanced by the glowing russet glories of mid-October's autumnal wonder. From there we continue along to the almost as scenically attractive, Loch Chon. About halfway down this second loch we should, if our verbally given directions were correct, find a vague, little used path that meandered over a heathery ridge then dropped down towards an unfrequented part of Loch Katrine's southern shore.

We had no trouble finding the path and we quickly climbed the wide ridge of rough heather and smooth, sheep-nibbled grass.

Resting at the ridge's summit we sat and took in the surrounding views. Here in the heart of the rugged romantic Trossachs there was much to admire. Befittingly, the most famous mountain was the most prominent. Ben Lomond loomed in impressive square-shouldered majesty above its unseen loch. Due North we saw those familiar old friends, Ben More and Stobinian, while Ben Vorlich dominated beyond Bonnie Strathyre.

Much nearer, we were for the first time seeing the fully revealed curving beauty of Walter Scott's fabled Loch Katrine as it coyly tucked itself away amongst the Trossachs' surrounding hills and lonely glens. And down there, halfway along the loch's southern shore, was 'Royal Cottage', the place we'd been warned to keep well clear of. For, belying its modest name, that former shooting-lodge which had been visited by Queen Victoria, now had seemingly become something of a luxurious weekend retreat for privileged Glasgow Councillors connected with the numerous committees that kept an eye on the city's widespread water department.

'If that's Royal Cottage over there, where's our bothy then? I thought we'd see it from up here,' Margaret said.

'Aye,' her boy-friend, Podge agreed, 'it's supposed to be on the southern shore, too. I hope to God we've not been given wrong directions.'

'Well,' Dave said, 'it'll be hellish if we've been sent on a wild goose chase and end up with nae place to sleep tonight.'

Lawrie and Bob held a good old Ordnance Survey one inch to one mile map of Loch Lomond and the Trossachs between them. They had studied it methodically and were in complete agreement as to what it informed them. So with absolute confidence, Lawrie spoke up to dispel those disheartening doubts. 'Oh, my dear fellows, our bothy's there by the shore all right. It's just a little further east from here and it's hidden by that bulging steep ridge to our right. Once we walk over there we're bound to see it clearly below us.'

And we did. There it was exactly as shown on that reliable old map, nestling in a minor bay with its attendant burn flowing passed it.

'What's its name, again?' Dave asked 'I've forgotten it.'

Having memorised it from his recent study of the map, Bob replied with confidence, 'It's called Glasahoile.' He paused and smiled, 'But I don't guarantee that's its correct Gaelic pronunciation,'

As, to our shame, none of us were Gaelic speakers, no one ventured to correct his reading of this word, and neither did we have a clue about its meaning. This lack of Gaelic knowledge was quickly forgotten as we made our eager way along, then down that ridge. Soon we were passing the sheep-fanks and pens, the dipping pit and the clipping enclosure where, rising like hangman's scaffolds, reared the wooden structures where huge jute sacks would be suspended and stuffed with many freshly clipped, roughly rolled, fleeces. Obviously the shepherd's house that was also surrounded by many sheds, a stable and byre must have been at times a real bustling centre of activity. Now, like far too many Scottish hill farms and shepherds' isolated homes, it lay in sad decay.

There were some anxious moments as it almost seemed we were not going to get the securely closed front door open. Was it locked? Our friends had assured us this bothy was unlocked. But what if they had been seen using it and some disapproving shepherd, gamekeeper or, worst of all, an estate factor, had locked it to stop any further illegal weekend squatting in this private property?

The dark green front door was actually two doors of equal halves that met in the middle. With disciplined force Podge thrust his impressive bulk against one door while Dave with his weight-lifter's skill, insinuated his straining muscles against the other door. Screeching indignant protests as they scraped over the small hallway's solid stone floor, both doors suddenly ceased their useless struggle against those implacable forces and flew open. We now got in to inspect the bothy's treasures.

We were delighted with what we found. While one large bare room was missing much of its ceiling and most of the wooden stairs had gone, what had been the large kitchen was intact, was furnished with a large table and its six wooden chairs set in front of the undamaged window. Two old tattered and dusty armchairs invited restful ease at each side of the large, old-fashioned iron cooking range. There was ample room for our five sleeping-bags on the reasonably clean wooden floor at the far end of the room.

Candles were soon brightly flaring and primuses were glowing and hissing their cheery message of lots of food on the go. Two half bottles of whisky were produced, were with reminiscent smiles gently placed flat on the table. 'We don't want a repeat of yon terrible accident, do we?' Dave said. All too clearly we all remembered that horrible occasion when an upright half bottle had been knocked to a bothy's stone floor and had tragically smashed.

'Ah, this is real civilized luxury, isn't it?' Lawrie said as he sat and smoked a small cigar and drank a moderate dram after having finished his meal.

'Aye, right enough, it's great to sit around in an auld armchair in this braw kitchen in this freshly discovered bothy with grand auld pals,' Dave said as he deeply sucked and liberally puffed clouds of bluish smoke from his huge-bowled Meerschaum pipe.

Happy hours flew by unnoticed as old tales were once more re-told and nostalgic memories got a fresh airing. Eventually all candles were blown out and the five of us settled down to relaxing sleep in our cosy sleeping-bags while the sad old neglected house gave endless creaking complaints as it much more slowly settled to its own restless sleep.

As dawn ushered in the fresh day's Sabbath calm we got up and about, all eager to make the most of what promised to be a fine autumnal day.

In due course we set out to climb nearby Ben Venue. At slightly less than 2,400 ft. this was a modest wee hill, but it was one none of us had ever climbed. We did not head directly for the Ben, but made our way eastwards along the ridge above Loch Katrine towards the rugged rocky, and Scots Pines clad jagged steep cliffs above Ellen's Isle, near where the tourist steamer 'The Maid of the Loch' was snugly berthed. The rugged grandeur of this part of the loch was impressive. But it was not merely this we had come to see, we were, at Margaret and Podge's insistence, going to search for the romantic 'Goblin's Cave' that, according to the map and the writings of Walter Scott and the more recent Seton Gordon, was somewhere near here.

We spread about in search over this rough ground, but no one found anything that seemed like a true Goblin's Cave.

'Oh, Bob,' Lawrie said, 'Bob Scott, you my dear fellow, should feel at home in this place with all its many links to Sir Walter Scott's poems and novels.'

'Aye, I do,' Bob laughed. 'The whole of Loch Lomond and Trossachs districts are impregnated with that other Scott's romantic writings. It was here with his best-selling epic poems, then with his 'Waverley' novels that he first put the Trossachs on the tourists' map. In fact he more or less single-handedly created the entire Scottish tourist industry.'

'Aye, that's true,' Dave said, 'And that's why to the present day our tourism is still largely based on romantic notions about kilts, tartans and bagpipes, isn't it?'

'Och, but is there really anything terribly wrong with that?' Podge asked.

'After all that's what most tourists, especially foreign tourists want, isn't it?' Podge was a keen reader of books on Scottish history, legends and traditions. His favourite author was Seton Gordon. Anyway, our many historic and romantic auld Scottish castles are solidly real enough, aren't they?'

'Yes, they are,' Lawrie agreed. 'They're a damn sight more real and solid than this elusive Goblin's Cave anyway. What about heading for the equally real summit of Ben Venue now?'

We all agreed and set out with steady pace, went up the steep heather slope towards the modest wee Ben.

At the summit cairn we all admired the widely-spread Trossachs views while Podge recorded these fresh vistas with his ever ready camera. But we couldn't linger long. We had to drum up our meal at the bothy then make the long hike back to Aberfoyle in time for the evening bus back to Glasgow.

As we approached the bothy we were greeted by challenging barks from two large collies. Then a loud commanding male voice rang out, 'Come awa' in here, Glen, an' ye tae, Corrie.'

The owner of the voice and of the two dogs appeared from behind a shed with the obedient collies now peering out from behind his legs.

Lawrie, Dave and Bob approached the sturdy elderly shepherd with some unease. Would he be greatly annoyed by us using this derelict house as a climbers' bothy?

'So it's ye three lads who've been dossing in that auld hoose, is it?'

Dave and Bob stood silently and allowed Lawrie full scope to use his gentlemanly diplomatic skills on the shepherd who, judging by his tone of voice, did not seem much annoyed. 'Yes, we three, and another two friends who're coming down the hill a bit behind us, we all slept here last night.'

'An' hoo long dae ye intend tae stay in it?'

'Och, just the one night, we all have to go back to Glasgow tonight.'

'Ah well, in that case I suppose ye're daeing nae harm.' His broad face broke into a beaming smile. 'In fact, as far as I'm concerned, ye can stay as long as ye like. I don't have onything tae dae wi' this place noo!'

'Oh aren't you the sheep farmer or manager or shepherd for the place? There certainly seems to be an abundance of sheep all about here.'

'Aye, there are, there damn well are. In fact that's why I'm leaving my job as shepherd here by bonnie Loch Katrine.'

Podge and Margaret had arrived, had stood silently listening. Now

Margaret said, 'Why don't we all go in and get some tea, brewing? I could do with a good full mug of char.'

'Yes, of course, let's do that,' Lawrie said. He turned to the shepherd, 'Why don't you, my dear fellow, come in and have some tea with us?'

That sturdy down to earth shepherd seemed rather bemused by being addressed as "my dear fellow." He hoped there was nothing queer about this unusually genteel salutation. He had heard strange tales o' real peculiar goings-on in a' yon terrible sinful cities.

Guessing the reason for the shepherd's hesitation, Dave spoke up with a more homely invitation, 'Aye, come in wae us an' we'll see how much whisky we've got left. You'll take a dram, won't you?'

All hesitation vanished. 'Aye, man, a wee dram wad be very welcome. Thank you.'

Dave drained what little whisky was left in both half bottles into a glass and handed it to the shepherd with an apologetic smile. 'I'm afraid it is only a miserly "wee dram" right enough. That's all the whisky we've got left.'

'Och this is fine, man, just fine.' He raised the modest drink and gave the traditional toast, 'Slàinte Mhath.'

Soon we were all sitting around the table enjoying our freshly brewed tea. Lawrie handed the shepherd a chocolate biscuit and said, 'Let me introduce us all to you. I'm Lawrie, the couple there are Margaret and Podge; that auld rogue there is Dave, and this is Bob. We're all delighted to meet you, my dear fellow.'

The shepherd laughed, 'Och, man, I dinna ken aboot me being a "dear fellow", I'm just wan o' Jock Tamson's bairns, ye ken. My name's Donnie Gordon.'

'Being a Gordon, you'll come from up by Aberdeen, I expect,' Dave said.

'Aye, I'm frae near Aboyne in bonnie Deeside. Aye, an' that's where the wife an' me are returning tae in twa weeks time. I've got a job as head shepherd on a big farming an' sporting estate up there.'

'Don't you like living here beside romantic Loch Katrine?' Podge asked.

'Och aye, the wife an' me like here fine. I would stay on here shepherding if it wasnae for a' the terrible bosses I have tae try an' please.'

'Oh, and are your awful bosses snobbish English would be gentry trying to act like Highland Lairds?' Dave asked, his Scottish Nationalist blood, ready to rise in sympathetic protest.

Donnie laughed, 'Och no, Dave, my bosses are not English. Are definitely not real gentry, either, I'm sorry tae tell ye they're Scottish; actually Glasgow councillors a' puffed-up wi' their monstrous ignorant conceit. They, an' some Glasgow Corporation officials, are on the many grossly over-manned committees that run the city's Water Department.'

'Oh,' Dave said, his ever ready indignant protest deflated, 'I see. I can understand those Glasgow councillors and officials looking after Loch Katrine, Glasgow's main reservoir for all its water, but why do they boss you, a shepherd with nothing to do with the loch?'

'Aye weel, that's the reason I'm leaving this job. You see Glasgow Corporation not only own Loch Katrine, they also own thousands o' acres a' around the large loch. An' they graze hundreds o' sheep on this hilly land. I look after the cheviots from beyond Royal Cottage tae here at Glasahoile. The other shepherds an' me still use this hoose when we're dipping an' clipping the sheep an' when checking up on the wee lambs. So you lads...' he hesitated then smiled at Margaret, 'Oh, an' you tae, my bonnie lass, better no' use this bothy at thae times. In fact I'm sure the Glasgow Corporation Water Department officials an' a' thae officious councillors would ban you, an' any other hikers, frae using this hoose at any time.'

'Aye,' Dave laughed, 'I suppose they'd worry that we might pollute Loch Katrine's pure water by peeing in the burn that flows into it from here, eh?'

Donnie echoed Dave's laughter, then, agreed, 'Aye, that would be their excuse, right enough.'

'But, my dear fellow, you haven't told us exactly why you're leaving your shepherding job here beside Loch Katrine,' Lawrie said. 'It seems a jolly nice place to work.'

'Oh aye, it is. The hills an' the loch are real bonnie. Aye, an' the sheep an' lambs are fine tae. Oh but it's a' thae Glasgow councillors an' Water Department officials that are damn near impossible tae work wae. They a' live in Glasgow, are real born and bred city folk. They don't ken onything aboot country life an' work. Many o' them hardly know wan end o' a sheep frae the other. An' yet they come swannin' oot here many weekends, supposedly on official Water Department committee business, but in reality tae have a fine boozy time, wi' every luxury laid on at Glasgow rate payers expense, while they stay in Royal Cottage that's now as posh as the most expensive Highland hotel.'

'But Glasgow Corporation's Labour dominated isn't it?' Podge said. 'Are those some of the city's few Tory councillors going on these luxury weekend jaunts to Royal Cottage? Surely the Labour councillors wouldn't abuse their socialist principles by using tax-payers' money in this way?'

Donnie exploded into helpless laughter. Still broadly grinning, he apologised to Podge. 'Oh, I'm sorry, lad, I don't mean tae mock you. I'm afraid you're still a political innocent. Nearly a' thae Glasgow councillors who use – or misuse – Royal Cottage are Labour councillors. They're a' supposed tae be great Socialists, a' bred in the grand tradition o' the Red Clydesiders. But when on thae weekend jaunts up here they behave worse, far worse, than any o' the real gentry I've worked for on private estates. Aye, an' a' the shepherds, gamekeepers, an' other estate workers I've met working here a' say the same. Not many o' them stay here long. They a', like me, soon get sick tae death o' having stupid orders barked at them by thae ignorant councillors who so glaringly show their city ignorance o' country life and o' the ways an' needs o' sheep.'

Donnie paused and his audience, as if stunned by his revelations, sat in bewildered silence. Then the experienced shepherd, as if pleased to relieve his pent up feelings, continued his impassioned story, 'Aye, an' the wives o' thae Labour councillors are even worse. They're terrible upstart snobs who order the servants at Royal Cottage aboot wi' never a "please" or a "thank you". My ain wife worked for a bit as a part-time cook there, but she soon had enough, she left the job before I handed in my ain notice.'

Lawrie frowned then grinned, 'Oh those ignorant Labour councillors and their wives must be real obnoxious types, right enough. It's surely a sign of getting older (and wiser) when you become disillusioned with ideas and ideals, principles and people, you held dear in your youth.'

Bob nodded his wholehearted agreement. Although he was a few years younger than Lawrie, he too had experienced some disillusionment with politics and politicians. One of his first disappointments was with Glasgow's former Lord Provost, Tom Johnston. This happened after a young, passionately committed 'Red', Johnson had written a small book called, *Our Noble Families.* This book revealed the shameful histories of Scotland's 'great' families and exposed the vile truth about how they'd acquired their land, titles, and wealth. This book helped to persuade Scottish Labour Party members to vote for the nationalisation of almost all private Scottish land.

They were especially keen to take over the vast private sporting estates that dominated most of the Scottish Highlands.

But now young, passionate 'Red', Tom Johnston, has been transmuted into Sir Thomas Johnston, the noble knight in charge of Scotland's Hydro Electric Board. Now many of those greedy Highland landowners his book had exposed were being generously rewarded by him in compensation for their salmon fishing being disrupted by his Hydro schemes that were bringing electricity to every home in the Highlands.

The friendlier he became with these Highland lairds, the more he tried to forget he'd ever written that critical book in his misguided youth. It was rumoured that he went around second-hand bookshops searching for, buying, then destroying every copy he found!

Further disillusionment came later for Bob when that even more fervent Red Clydesider, Manny Shinwell, who'd passionately praised Lenin's Bolsheviks and who'd wanted to abolish all Royalty and the obscene House of Lords, progressed to become the genial 'Father of the House of Commons'. Then with inevitable hypocritical certainty, he evolved to become a noble of the realm, Lord Shinwell.

Donnie's voice broke into Bob's thoughts of his lost political innocence as he said, 'The more I learned o' thae councillors an' officials trying tae run the Glasgow Corporation sheep farms a' around Loch Katrine the ever more ridiculous and inefficient they proved tae be.' He grinned, 'Dae ye want tae ken the ridiculous order I received, the one that finally made me decide tae leave here?'

They unanimously did.

'Ah weel this wee, fat, pompous Glasgow councillor who seemed tae think he was an expert estate manger an' sheep farmer, came tae see me one Saturday when he an' his nagging wife were at Royal Cottage for a free weekend. He demanded tae ken why some fencing had not been completed. I told him I'd had tae leave the fencing when the first lambs were born. New lambs were being born every day, an' the bulk o' the ewes, were due tae give birth that coming week.

'That annoying wee councillor said, "Oh damn it, man, I want that fence finished now. You better get on with it."

'Aye, councillor', I said, 'and what aboot a' the lambs due this coming week?'

'That stumped him for a minute, then he said, "Just get on with the fencing next week and put the lambing off till the week after that."

'By God, that fair flummoxed me. Then I quietly suggested, "Och weel, councillor, you better go roon a' the pregnant ewes an' order them no' tae give birth until the week after next. I'll be interested tae ken how many obey you.""

Still chuckling over this recent experience, Donnie Gordon left us saying, 'Use the bothy as often as you like, lads, but in winter don't show any bright lights or you'll ha'e those bloody pompous councillors or officials, a' those expert sheep farmers frae Glasgow, coming tae investigate and then throw you a' oot into the snow.'

Heeding his advice, we used the bothy a few more times but always with dimmed lights in winter. We never met, never had any confrontations with pompous councillors or officious officials.

Nor did we ever find Walter Scott's damned elusive, or perhaps entirely imaginary, Goblin's Cave.

# Grand Wee Ben A'an

Although a mere 1,750 ft. high, and shown on their map to be little more than a small, insignificant, rocky knoll, still Gordon and Bob had been assured that wee Ben A'an, its name as small as its modest height, was a hill well worth seeing and climbing . It seemed it had some real, if short, climbing routes on its steep rock faces, and at least one of these rock climbs was intimidatingly graded, 'Very Severe'.

This testing climb had been first climbed and named by that great Glasgow climber, the shipyard employee, Jock Nimlin. He had first claimed this modest wee hill's new rock route in 1934. And Jock, truly amazingly daring, had climbed it solo, as he had the other two new rock routes he'd bravely pioneered here in these pre-war years.

The terrible world-wide Great Depression that followed on from the Wall Street Crash of 1929 was well into its devastating stride by 1934, so perhaps Jock named this 'Very Severe' climb with these very severe times in mind as he named it, 'The Rent'.

Many Clydeside shipyards were then closed down, many thousands of skilled workmen were unemployed and countless Glasgow tenement families were struggling to survive on the means-tested dole. But still their grasping landlords were insistently demanding full payment of their rents.

With personal experience of unemployment, possibly Jock found the grim attempt to pay the rent a more severe struggle than to complete this new rock route on grand wee Ben A'an. Or had he, with a rueful grin, named this very severe climb 'The Rent' as his auld patched breeks suffered the further indignity of another tearing rent from this violated wee hill's sharp, hard, revengeful rock?

Our thoughts bright with the knowledge that such a great climber as Jock Nimlin had not despised this modest wee hill, we set out to find and climb it with his example to inspire and guide us on this fine post-war June weekend. But neither Gordon nor Bob, as far as they knew, had any intention of climbing any of Jock's severe rock routes. Any daring climbing ambitions that swam, half formed, in Gordon's mind he, wisely, kept well hidden.

Wee Ben A'an rose neat and rocky steep in the very heart of The Trossachs, that grand, wild, rugged land that although only some thirty miles North of Glasgow was a most attractive real Highland landscape. And, a major consideration for most of Glasgow's younger weekend climbers and hikers, the cheap return bus fare to Aberfoyle was usually just within our straitened means.

After hoisting their laden rucksacks on to their backs Gordon and Bob eagerly set out from the lively bustling Aberfoyle's crowd of kilted hikers, cheery hill-walkers and more serious real rock climbers.

They soon revel in the pleasant refreshing silence of the forest tracks that wander through the vast, freshly planted expanse of Achray Forest. They pass a newly-built Forestry Commission neat hamlet, its wooden houses all aglow with reddish resinous gleams in this fine June morning's smiling sunshine.

Effortlessly, climbing all the time, they follow a wide forest track that leads through what seems, endlessly ugly, untidy miles where all trees had been ruthlessly felled to help meet the Nation's insatiable greed for timber during the recent six long weary years of devastating war.

At last they reach the top of this devastated slope and are immediate cheered by brighter views. The closer views are of wee bright green fir trees all freshly set out in countless neatly ditched and ridged rows that seem to stretch from here to the South shore of that wee Loch that brightly and cheerily sparkles, as if amused by its own unique, (Glasgwegian inspired?) name: Loch Drunkie. And there, rising clear above Loch Achray is Ben A'an. Although small, the hill is most attractive with its steep rocky slopes thrusting defiantly skywards, more proud and imposing than many a higher, more rounded Munro. They smile as they eagerly anticipate climbing that grand wee hill quite soon.

But first they stand on the broad top of a fine new wooden stile that reaches across a high, tree-protecting new deer-fence and forms a grand vantage point to see and admire all the more distant views. They are awed by all they see!

Beyond wee Loch Drunkie there's Loch Venachar, Loch Katrine and, high in its hilly glen, Loch Finglas; and they get a mere glimpse of Aberfoyle's own long, narrow, attractive, Loch Ard. They see Scotland's only real lake: The Lake of Menteith, where our country's young Queen had been imprisoned. They are ashamed that they can only name a few of the countless hills that rise clear in the June sunshine. That one straight ahead of them has to be Ben Ledi, and there beyond The Duke's Pass surely that must be Ben Venue still valiantly guarding yon strange wee Goblin's Cave. And there, dominant in the West, is Glasgow's very own Munro, that much loved and frequently-climbed Ben Lomond.

They stare around and are wondrously enriched. Exchanging bemused grins they dizzily feel that perhaps cheeky wee Loch Drunkie has made them half drunk with all these intoxicating Trossachs pleasures that their eyes greedily feed on, their gulping senses almost drown on, and their future memories will forever treasure.

And surely they cannot entirely avoid being greatly influenced, being sub-consciously bewitched by the magic of Sir Walter Scott's words? His *Lady of the Lake* and *Rob Roy* had brought this fine Trossachs landscape to glorious glowing life as he clad it in his fantastic romantic tartans.

It was such best-selling epic poems and historic novels by Scotland's 'Wizard of the North' that brought this country's vital Tourist Industry into being. And he even got it started before there were any railways to make the long journey for all the awe-struck English tourists swift, comfortable and easy.

It was with Walter Scott's rose-tinted romantic vision and his history's misty fictions that these eager first tourists saw that land of *The Mountain and the Flood* with its ceaseless skirling bagpipes, its swirling kilt's intriguing mystery and the entire landscape coloured by attractive, or garish, tartans. And this was still the romantic vision of Scotland the re-born Scottish Tourist Board was starting to promote in these rather austere post-war years.

As wide-eyed they stare at his same tartan-hued Trossachs view as these hardy early tourists had, they wonder if future years will bring crowds of a new breed of tourists not just to stare, but, to climb these Bens and hike these Glens as they so delight in doing. 'Aye,' said Bob, 'I hope they do. But I doot they'll no' see this grand view we're admiring here today. In thirty years, or less, all these freshly planted wee trees will be well grown, so nothing will be seen from this site but dense woods of large dark fir trees,'

'Oh aye, of course that's true,' Gordon agreed. 'That grand track we've walked this morning will show nothing but monotonous miles of regimented firs, won't it?'

'Aye, I'm afraid it will. 'Bob sighed then grinned, 'Och, of course it's nothing new to have such conflicts between our country's economy and our people's aesthetic wealth and health.'

They scrambled from the stile and made their way down the slope with good easy happy speed towards what they hope will be the intoxicating delights of bright wee Loch Drunkie. They note the fine wide splendour of that high new road that eases traffic's passage over The Duke's Pass. They grin as they see all the twists and turns, all the blind corners, all the snake-like loops of the replaced auld road as it coils and sways its drunken way along by wee Loch Drunkie's shallow shores, its sheltered bays and its jutting promontory. They smile in anticipation of having a splendid refreshing drink of that wee loch's enticing water.

Before they quite reach that inviting shore they are stopped in their tracks by a sudden loud blast of bagpipe music. With mutual surprise they gaze around but fail to discover the source of this near, bright, cheery Highland sound. Bob laughs, 'Obviously Auld Walter Scott, that mighty 'Wizard of the North', is still up tae his tricks in this 20th century's still magic, Trossachs!'

'Aye,' Gordon agreed, perhaps it's the ghost of his larger than life auld Rob Roy boastfully showing off his braw piping skills.'

A path along by wee Drunkie's wandering shore lures them towards the unseen piper's echoing sounds.

As they turn into a narrow-entranced, birch-lined bay they seem to have suddenly entered an earlier century. There right before them are five wild, hairy, half-naked kilted Highland savages! Standing high and proud on top of a huge tumbled boulder the piper's gaze follows them as they rather hesitantly advance towards these wild Highlanders, while his skilled piping continued unabated. The four other figures were lying at leisure on a smooth stretch of fine dry turf with their bare chests and legs soaking up the enticing June sunshine. All had wild hair and bushy beards. Two of the largest beards, vividly glowed a defiant red. All were wearing ex-army kilts. Three kilts displayed the tartan of Glasgow's own regiment, the H.L.I.

(Highland Light Infantry) the other kilts were in the proud dark tartan of the Black Watch.

As we approached them they cheerily greeted us in loud, friendly, broad Glasgow voices. We grinned. These unmistakeable Glasgow accents assured us we were still in the 20th century and had not been enchanted back to some magic Brigadoon.

One fake savage asked, 'Well, lads, dae ye want a refreshing drink? Ye look a wee bit sweaty an' weary.'

We had noted, with real surprise, that they seemed to be only drinking mugs of tea. We'd expected these hairy kilted clansmen to be on something much stronger; perhaps some Uisge-Beatha, wild firewater from their own secret illicit whisky still.

Soon we were sitting with them enjoying their well stewed dark tea and their generously shared biscuits. When we told them we were intending to climb wee Ben A'an for the first time they assured us we'd really enjoy that grand wee hill just as they had done on the numerous times they'd climbed it.

Then, as was inevitable at any weekend campfire, bothy, or loch shore meet of Glasgow's keen climbers and hikers, the talk got round to politics. While most working class weekenders were well to the left of Attlee's praiseworthy, but over-cautious Labour Government, not all would agree with these modern wild Highlanders who proudly claimed to be founding members of a new, real, Scottish Nationalist Party which was going to bring Independence to Scotland very soon, and, if necessary, by means of armed revolution!

One big, sturdy, wildly red-bearded of these modern Rob Roys who was known as, 'Big Red Rab', heaved to his feet and said, 'Come wi' me, lads, an' I'll show ye a secret. A secret ye must promise tae keep tae yerselves.' We solemnly promised and he led us through a small dense wood of old birch trees and thick gorse bushes to a large cave well tucked away under an overhanging small steep cliff. He explained, 'This big cave is oor ain secret doss. We stay here maist weekends unless we're awa' climbing an' hiking somewhere else. Or when, wi' oor poor, long-suffering wives, we're awa' rallying like-minded folk in preparation fur The Great Day. But this secret place is where we plan oor Party's strategy an' tactics.' He proudly pointed, 'See whit's written up there? Dae ye ken whit it means?'

We read, 'H.Q. S.S.R.' printed high on a smooth rock wall surrounded by bright painted tartans and thistles.

'Ye ken whit it means?' Big Red Rab impatiently repeated.

We shook our bemused heads and his barrel chest expanded as he proudly explained, 'This secret cave is the Headquarters of the Scottish Socialist Republic!'

Lost for words, Gordon and Bob silently trailed after Big Red Rab as he showed them around this cave. As eager as an Estate Agent, he pointed out the many improvements and cosy comforts they had made. One flat dark corner was thick bedded with dry golden bracken; tree-trunk chairs were grouped together at a food-laden table; wooden shelves were loaded with more food or books, pamphlets and overflowing with papers.

Gordon and Bob exchange secret grins as they see what seems to be a secret hoard of bottles of whisky neatly tucked away in a dim corner. These wild modern Highland Clansmen went up in their estimation as they noted this proof that they were not, as they had almost unbelievingly feared, all been unaccountably tee-total.

Big Red Rab grinned, 'That's a' I'm going tae show ye, lads. We've got another cave somewhere aboot here, but we keep it real secret for, it's oor hidden armoury. That's where we keep oor guns a' ready fur The Great Day!' He raised his clenched right fist high and passionately exclaimed, 'It's coming yet for a' that; it's coming soon for a' that; the day when Braw Auld Scotia will be declared the Scottish Socialist Republic!'

We now rejoined the others. The piper had been playing all this time. He now stopped and said, 'Och my bare shoulders are damned burning in a' this hot sunshine. I'm going in for a swim tae cool doon. What about you lot? Do you fancy a swim tae?'

This suggestion met eager approval. The three who were still sitting threw aside their empty mugs and sprang to their feet. Big Red Rab asked us, 'Whit aboot you lads? Dae ye fancy going in tae?'

'Och no,' Bob said. 'That loch's very tempting, but we better push on if we're going to climb grand wee Ben A'an today.'

While Gordon and Bob heaved rucksacks on to their backs these five modern Rob Roys ran down the sloping turf in what seemed a fearsome Highland Charge complete with wildly shouted war-cries. They then threw off their kilts and, joyously primitively naked, plunged into the gasping, almost inebriating shock of sly wee Loch Drunkie's sun-bright water that, while invitingly gin-clear, was also perniciously icy-cold.

As we hurried away along the shore the agonised loud shouts and uproarious laughter of those intrepid swimmers echoed all around that amazing bay.

When we were out of sight of, although not quite out of sound of these Revolutionary Nationalists we paused and laughed as Bob asked, 'Well, Gordon, what did you make of, that lot?'

'I hardly know what to make of them. They certainly are interesting and amusing! I wonder are they mere wild but harmless eccentrics, or might their cause, prevail? Might our country really become the Scottish Socialist Republic? And might it become so quite soon?'

Bob grinned, 'Och I rather doot it! Perhaps if we live to ninety we might yet see their dream come about. But for now these extreme views are held by only a few Scots, and these passionate few are mostly rather eccentric dreamers like those five modern Rob Roys and like guid auld Wendy Wood who bravely endures imprisonment for her unshakeable beliefs and her symbolic burning of all those much-disliked Union Jack flags.'

'Aye, Wendy seems a really great character right enough. Perhaps there should be many more like her to stir things up and get things done. But what do you think of Big Red Rab's secret armoury? I wonder if he really has any hidden weapons.'

'Och, if they do have any they're more likely to be rusty auld muskets, claymores and dirks rather than modern guns.' Bob laughed, 'Although you never can be sure. Remember those stories we've heard about some of the characters associated with the Creagh Dhu, who are rumoured to have at least one rifle hidden away at a certain Highland bothy?'

'Oh aye, of course I remember that. But surely they use it not to bring about a Red Revolution, but to poach red deer, don't they?'

'Aye, they do. And I believe there are quite a few other active weekend climbers and poachers like them too.'

Gordon grinned, 'Perhaps this illicit poaching with secret rifles on wealthy landowner's Highland estates are the first steps that will lead to Big Red Rab's passionate dream of the Scottish Socialist Republic really coming into being.'

'Aye, maybe,' Bob rather doubtfully said, 'More likely to give the weekenders a bit of variety for their dinners, I would say.'

Some years later they learned through the Scottish Press that Big Red Rab *did* have real guns and explosives hidden in his secret armoury. Glasgow Police's anti-terrorist Special Branch had somehow discovered this, and poor Rab and others of that passionate, patriotic band of Scots spent some years in jail… no doubt still preaching their subversive message to their now, captive audience!

Apparently Rab had discovered, and had 'borrowed' from a secret war-time hoard of weapons hidden, then forgotten, in some Argyll hills. These weapons, like many other secret hoards, had been intended for the Home Guard and other brave volunteers to harass with guerrilla tactics, the vile Nazi Huns if they had successfully invaded and occupied besieged Britain in 1940 or 1941.

Their speeding feet now hurried them along the old disused road that twisted and turned through a thick forest of maturing firs. They then crossed the Brig o'Turk road and started climbing another forest track that led more or less directly towards Ben A'an.

As expected, they soon discovered an empty war-time Nissen hut that would be their comfortable bothy for the night. They dumped their loads, then, with some surprise, Bob saw Gordon pull out a neatly coiled white nylon climbing rope from his rucksack. 'Right then,' he laughed, 'what are you intending to do with that?'

'Och, I borrowed it from a rock climbing friend at work who couldn't get away this weekend. I thought I'd bring it along and perhaps we can use it on some not too difficult route on Ben A'an.'

'Aye, very well, come on then, let's hurry on to that wee hill and see what it's like, close up.'

This they did. In no time they were gazing with great pleasure at its stately, rocky shape. They were much impressed by the challenging steepness of its bare rock faces.

Gordon had sketched this hill's rock routes from a climbing guide book. From the sketch's easy lines to the hill's hard bemusing rock face they tried to trace the three new routes that Jock Nimlin had pioneered and named here before the war. Without direct human guidance they did not find this easy.

Bob then suggested, 'Let's go up that rock ridge to the left. It looks more or less an easy rock scramble rather than a tough rock climb.'

Gordon willingly agreed. Although the rope's reassurance was not really needed, they both tied on to increase their, as yet limited experience, of using a climbing rope.

Bob went first on the quite short, but steep, easy rock route. He soon gained the respite of a wide ledge. After tying the rope to a natural rock belay he shouted to Gordon to start up while he steadily hauled in the rope as his climbing partner, much faster than him, scrambled up.

'Well, where do we go from here?' Gordon laughed after he'd gained the ledge and had some time to look around.

Echoing his laughter, Bob asked, 'Wait a minute is this 'easy' route not challenging enough for you?'

'It's fine, but he pointed upwards and to the right, I wonder if I could take the lead on what looks a more interesting and harder route over there?' Seeing Bob's rather doubtful look, he eagerly continued, 'I should get a good secure belay up there at that ledge where that old birch tree is growing. What do you think, Bob, do you fancy trying it?'

'Aye, but the trouble with yon auld tree is that it seems to be precariously clinging on rather than happily growing, up there. Och, but just you go ahead with that climb and, willingly or otherwise, I'll follow you up once you secure a good belay, keeping a tight rope, you might need to haul me up the rest of it.'

Bob was most impressed with the smooth unhurried sureness of Gordon's ascent of that seemingly holdless, steep rock. He was delighted to see him reach the safety of the clinging lonely tree.

He was even more delighted to have the assurance of the tight rope to guide him up what seemed to be the sheerness of this all too smooth rock face with its all too tiny cracks and hand-holds. As Bob tip-toed his precarious way upwards, he hovered on the strange uncertain borderline between real deep, almost aesthetically sensual pleasure and outright stark fear. He wondered what grade of severity this unknown rock route might merit. He knew his rock-climbing limits and was well aware he would never dare attempt this standard of climb without the confidence-boosting security of a taut climbing rope.

After being reunited on the wide ledge where the auld birch tree tenaciously grew, they wasted no time in hurrying up the final easier slope to the heathery top at the summit of the small, but impressive, Ben A'an.

They sat for a time enjoying the surrounding glorious Trossachs views then Gordon drew out the sketch map he had made of the routes on the face. He studied it for a moment then, with a wide grin, said, 'Congratulations, Bob, you've just now climbed one of Jock Nimlin's severe rock routes.'

Bob stared amazed 'What? Are you sure? What's it called?'

Gordon re-checked his sketch then chuckled, 'Yes, that's it, aye, I'm sure it was, "Birch Wall".'

Bob thought for a moment then laughed, 'Jock's "Birch Wall" was it? Well, Gordon, it's now got a new name, after the time I had on it, I've re-named it Bob's "Bitch of a Wall"!

# Odd Things on the Cobbler

wo of those odd Cobbler things we definitely remember, the third, the most intriguing one, may only be an auld Cobbler legend, something laughingly passed down by word of mouth from generation to generation.

The first time we, Gordon and Bob, exultantly, climbed that fine rock route, Nimlin's Direct, that graces the South Peak of The Cobbler, we were amazed as we almost unbelievingly stared at a familiar Glasgow object in a very unfamiliar place: a bright red tin Glasgow Corporation Tramways Department sign that read, 'Trams stop here on request.'

Jammed into a long crack on this ledge's natural rock belay we thought at first it might be an extra, a most unnatural belay, but on feeling its shoogly insecurity we decided it was here for nothing more than some Glaswegian fun; something suggestive of the type of humour of the city's very own working-class climbers, the Creag Dhu.

We know a few hardy wee Glasgow cyclists who boast of having cycled, with much panting and pushing and, at times wearily carrying their heavy laden road-bikes right through the high, wild and rough Cairngorm mountain pass, The Lairig Ghru. But some, possibly again the aforementioned characters, have taken a bike to a stranger place than that remote mountain location.

Some months after we'd seen that strange request for trams to stop on The Cobbler, we were back again on that grand wee three-peaked Arrochar hill. At Gordon's keen urging we planned to climb a more testing rock route on the jutting and stern-looking, overhanging North Peak. After diligent study of his Cobbler guide, Gordon had chosen the 'Fold Direct' route. Graded 'severe', and needing delicate balance, he saw it as a worthy challenge to his increasing climbing skills.

Bob saw that severe route with something more than anticipation; he saw it with real apprehension.

'Do you fancy trying it? Are you game to have a go, Bob?' Gordon anxiously asked.

'Aye, all right, let's do it. As long as you take the most difficult part and lead the whole way, okay?'

'Aye, that's grand. According to the guide book there are some good belays. I'll keep a good tight rope on you and reassure you if you need it. Provided, I don't fall off, that is.'

Bob gave a rather forced grin, 'Aye, be sure you talk me up it, especially on the overhanging crux.'

So it was arranged, and so it was done.

As Bob thankfully left the severe moves at the crux behind him, Gordon shouted encouragement, 'Well done, Bob, you're over the worst. You'll soon be at the belay.' He laughed, 'This very special, unique belay.'

Bob, paused for a breath and called up to him, 'What's so unusual about it?'

'Och, just climb up and see for yourself.'

He did. He stood amazed. They both burst out laughing.

There, neatly parked at the back of this high ledge, half way up this severe rock climb, was a bicycle. Old, rusty, minus its seat, both wheels twisted and tyre-less, that pale blue 'Raleigh Roadster' had once been some keen cyclist's pride and joy.

Standing staring at the bike Bob and Gordon made wild guesses at why some daring climber had carried it up here. Could it be some strange memorial? Had it been merely a fantastic dare, or a light-hearted ploy?

Could this precariously placed airy bicycle claim to be the very first true mountain-bike?

The third odd Cobbler story takes us back to the South Peak, to that fine rock climb graded merely, 'Very Difficult', The Jughandle. As its name implies it has many large, sound, secure hand-holds. And, so the story goes, as one happy climber placed his groping hand into a large 'jug' he gasped in horror, snatched his hand back recoiled in shock, almost fell off.

Firmly gripping other holds, he pulled himself up and peered in to see what ugly vileness his reaching hand had touched. And there it was. That other thing he had shockingly gripped. Not, as he first thought, from a tailor's dummy, but a real human male's hairy hand, severed at the wrist, and oh so deadly cold and clammy. Oh so lifeless and toad-belly white.

Surely this bizarre mountain prank on this occasion couldn't be blamed on the Creagh Dhu. We were pretty sure there was none of the medical profession in the ranks of that club. Almost certainly it had been some medical student, perhaps a member of the august, Junior Scottish Mountaineering Club, who had placed that hand, 'borrowed' from some dissecting room, on the Jughandle, hand-hold.

We cannot swear to this macabre story's truth, but our climbing friend, auld Dave Martin, who told it, swore it *was* true. However, under our intensive questioning, he admitted he'd heard this tale from someone who'd heard it from someone else.

# An Abundance of Bothies

O nce more this party of five climbing companions were taking advantage of the newly-introduced British Railways cheap weekend fares to get out of Glasgow and into their beloved Scottish hills.

They were not going on the familiar Highland line to the wild West Highlands. This time they were steaming through the very centre of Scotland on the Perth to Inverness line.

Leaving the train at Blair Atholl, they delighted in the glowing brightness of yet another perfect day in this bliss of late May. Ignoring the Duke's imposing castle they strode along the path by His Grace's once salmon-rich but now Hydro-depleted River Tilt. Although, holding fewer salmon, this cheery wee, Atholl river had lost none of its modest beauty.

They passed tree-screened Marble Lodge, then were in the tree-less bareness, beyond the un-imposing, Forest Lodge.

Gordon, the youngest of this group of keen hikers and climbers, spoke up, 'It was on this Glen Tilt path that there was a confrontation between a hiking professor and the deer-stalking Duke of Atholl, wasn't it? Didn't the indignant Duke try to prevent the professor from completing his hike from the Linn o' Dee to Blair Atholl?'

Dave Martin, the oldest of these five, gave an instant passionate reply, 'Aye, that bastard 19th century Duke tried tae keep everyone off his vast estate except his posh cronies. But just wait, come the Revolution and we'll hang His Grace – or rather, his Bloody Disgrace – by his noble balls frae the top o' the highest tower o' his castle!'

More gentlemanly polite when expressing his hardly less deeply felt left-wing views, Lawrie Travers laughing, gasped, 'Oh, Dave! Oh, my dear fellow, you express yourself with such wonderful eloquence.'

Bob Scott, Podge Maurice and young Gordon joined in the loud laughter. Auld Dave now said, 'Och, it's a' very well tae laugh, but, when I think o' how that damned Duke so ruthlessly cleared oot so many o' his ain clans-folk tae make way for his more profitable sheep it fair makes my blood boil!'

Now Podge , remembering from his favourite author, Seton Gordon, said, 'Aye, but remember that brave man Professor Balfour stood up to that bloody Duke, he took legal action, to the highest Scottish court, to get this long Glen Tilt path declared to be (to the fury of the Duke) a right-of-way open to all.'

'Aye,' Bob agreed, 'and following on from that historic case came into being the Scottish Rights of Way Society that, to this present day, fights to keep all our Highland Glens and rugged Bens open to all stravaiging hikers and adventurous climbers.'

They now left the Glen Tilt path and started up the steepish climb to a heathery bealach. From the top of this pass they could see their weekend destination, 'The Tarf Hotel.'

This 'hotel' was actually a climbers' bothy. Over the years they had heard of it but had never been to it. Some fabled tales were told about it. On pre-war maps it was shown as, Tarf Lodge. The long, grim, six war years had brought about its demise as a comfortable lodge for the exclusive use of wealthy gentry.

One old timer, who'd used this bothy, had laughingly told them, 'We used to call it Tarf Mansion, but now it's more correctly known as the Tarf Hotel.'

'Oh and why is that, my dear fellow?' Lawrie had politely asked, 'Why the change of name?'

'Och, just you go and visit it and you'll see the reason for yourself.'

So here they were and down there they now saw The Tarf Hotel beside the brightly gleaming River Tarf.

When they reached the bothy, the reason for its change of name became obvious. At both sides of the front door were metal black and yellow Automobile Association signs that proclaimed it to be a three star establishment.

Amidst the laugher and jovial suggestions that they better remove their boots before entering this exalted place, Podge's ever ready camera recorded their arrival at this somewhat eccentric hotel. They were pleased to find the roof, windows and doors all more or less intact. The main room was, rather surprisingly, still completely wood-panelled, and had chairs grouped around its wide fireplace while a large table soon became laden with five primus stoves and heaps of food. There were even some old single beds, minus the mattresses, in a cosy bedroom.

After they'd finished their evening meal, Lawrie raised his dram in a toast to whoever had carried these A.A. signs over many wild Atholl miles to the Tarf Hotel. 'These unknown lads must have been real tough and determined characters, with a great sense of humour.'

Auld Dave agreed then got on to a familiar theme, 'Aye, and it's awful tae think of how much money was so recklessly spent building this sporting lodge in such a remote place. The almost slave-labour working conditions for the poor workers who built it in all kinds o' weather must have been terrible.'

'Oh yes, my dear fellow, that's very true,' Lawrie said. 'And in these hard Victorian days all building material and everything else must have been brought in over these many miles by horse and cart.'

'Aye,' Dave again agreed, 'and after all that desperate effort these wealthy selfish land-owning bastards would only use this place for two or three grouse-shooting and deer-stalking months each year.'

'Aye, that's true,'Podge said. 'I've also read that the 7th Duke of Atholl used to boast of how austerely he "roughed it", living the simple life in this remote Highland bothy. Somehow he never happened to mention the many ghillies and other servants who were also here dancing instant attention to His Grace's "simplest" of needs.'

Podge now took his camera to capture something of this endless lingering May evening's widespread sunset glory. Happy, enjoying his week-end, Gordon went with him.

An hour later they returned to the candle-lit comfort of The Tarf Hotel. Podge described what they had found about half a mile from the bothy. 'As expected, we came across the remains of large peat-banks where over the years much peat had been cut to supply the needs of this posh shooting lodge which, in those days, even seemed to boast the amazing luxury of laid-on hot water.'

Gordon now continued their tale, 'Aye, and we saw a long deep trench that looked terribly like those open mass graves of Nazi concentration camp victims we've all seen in Movietone's wartime cinema news.' He added, 'However I'm very glad to say that instead of seeing rows of stark dead bodies, we saw endless layers of dead bottles.'

'Yes,' Podge said, 'and these all too empty bottles had once held the best vintage Champagne, many grand malt whiskies, fine red and white wines and other exotic liqueurs.'

This information set Dave off on another of his frequent rants, 'Och, trust those wealthy gentry bastards not tae deny themselves onie luxuries even in this remotest o' places.'

Gordon laughed, 'I think you are just a wee bit jealous there, Dave, just because we have so little whisky ourselves?'

★ ★ ★

Sunday's hazy dawn promised another perfect day. After their hearty breakfast all five set out to climb Carn a Chlamain, a remote Atholl Munro.

On that pleasant summit there was a reluctant parting. Four set out for Glen Tilt then Blair Atholl and Sunday evening's return train to Glasgow. The fifth, Bob Scott, was going to return to The Tarf Hotel and from there continue on his fortnight's annual holiday by himself. Before they'd parted he'd again thanked them for the surplus food they'd left for him. He'd laughed, 'It looks like I'll have to stay a whole damned week here to eat that stack of food you've left me.'

However he did not stay a week, or even an extra day. That evening and the following morning he was somewhat bloated from all the heaviest of the leftover food he'd eaten. The lighter food he crammed into his bulging rucksack. Anxious to get into the heart of the Cairngorms and to use other bothies he soon set out to explore what was for him, an undiscovered wild land.

Pausing on the Bedford Memorial footbridge he thought of that poor man who had been swept to his death while trying to wade across the flooded River Tarf. He then had more pleasant thoughts of that well-known drawing of a royal party crossing the Tarf, before this life-saving bridge was built. He chuckled when he remembered how auld Dave had raved at the drawing of Queen Victoria and Prince Albert selfishly crossing dry-shod with uplifted feet on their sturdy ponies without a thought for their hardy kilted Ghillies who led the party, with the cold Tarf water coming up to their freezing arses. Then with acute observation, Dave had declared, 'Och, but that sturdy bearded highlander leading wee Victoria's pony is John Brown, her very special ghillie who, after Jerry Albert's death, at last got his well-deserved reward for his loyal service by becoming her secret lover!'

As he gazed down into the deep dark pool below the Falls of Tarf, Bob wondered if Dave's statement was historically true, or was it just republican, slander?

Bob now continued on his solitary, but not lonely, way along the ancient bridle path that rose to its gentle peak by modest wee Loch Tilt then sloped down to complete the link between the Tilt and the Dee and here he came across another bothy. His map declared this to be Bynack Lodge. Most of this large building was in a sad ruined state, but one almost intact room could be used as a reasonable bothy. But Bob's intended stop for tonight was another, the more remote, old shooting lodge – Geldie Lodge.

As he strode along the rising track by the Geldie Burn he noted a prominent rocky knoll that rose impressively steep above this pleasant glen. Again consulting his map he saw this steep knoll was called 'The Duke's Chair.' With an inward chuckle he thought, 'If auld Dave was here how he'd curse and swear at not being able to escape from His Grace, the Duke, even in this most remote of places.'

The track now forded shallow Geldie Burn then led directly to the front door of a large and, despite its abandoned state, still impressive, Geldie Lodge. And this old shooting lodge was not entirely neglected. One part of it, upstairs, was blessed with a weatherproof roof, and the windows and doors were still intact. These main rooms were by and large, quite comfortably furnished. Prominent on a clean scrubbed table was the bothy's visitors' book which showed it was looked after and often used by intrepid Rover Scouts from Aberdeen.

Having this fine place to himself Bob spread his sleeping-bag on the thickest layer of dried bracken that made a comfortable bed in a cosy corner of the upstairs bedroom. Then gazing through the clear, scout-cleaned window, across the Geldie Burn to steep, Munro high Beinn Bhrotain, he almost felt like a Duke, as if he was monarch of all he surveyed.

The following morning's continuing sunshine and his still ample supply of food made him decide to enjoy the bothy's comforts for another day and climb that impressive Ben that was impertinently staring down at him.

So he passed a perfect day of perfect weather in a perfect way.

After all the long day's fresh air, sunshine and pleasant activity he greatly enjoyed the candle-lit pleasure of drowsily nodding over his drooping book before he fell into deep untroubled dreamless sleep.

Next morning he once more dry-shod crossed the May-drained Geldie ford and eagerly set out for the larger River Feshie and that well known bothy that had often housed the Queen's favourite painter, the Victorian-knighted Sir Edwin Landseer.

As Bob made his quietly happy observant way amongst the widely-scattered, the rugged and ragged gale-battered auld Scots Pines that tenaciously clung to the steep eastern side of this part of Glen Feshie he was delighted to see a herd of red deer stags: those noble Highland animals that Landseer had so famously (and all too romantically?) painted here. Of course at this time of year these stags were not at their proud antlered Landseer prime.

As Bob neared Landseer's Bothy he was not sure if he was pleased or not to see a trickle of greyish smoke rise from its chimney. Surely in this warm sunny weather in the full glory of late May there was no need of a fire.

However he let no hint of this doubt escape him as he returned the hearty greetings he received from the only occupant, who, almost like a mind-reader, said, 'Nae matter how fine the weather is I think it's always real braw tae sit by a cosy bothy fire in the evenings, don't you?'

Caught off guard, Bob stammered, 'What? Aye, oh aye, yes I agree there's real pleasure in a fire.'

His new friend laughed, 'Aye, an' when there's sae much dry dead wood lying all aboot here it would be bloody daft tae leave it a' for some other bothy worthies tae burn up, wouldn't it?' Without waiting for a reply, he then said, 'I'm called Tam Weir, ye ken. Who are you?'

'Oh, my name's Bob Scott.'

Tam threw back his head and laughed, 'No, by God, you're not! I ken Bob Scott, he's the gamekeeper at Luibeg Bothy, I've stayed there often.'

'I assure you I am Bob Scott too.' He grinned, 'Or if you prefer, you can call me Robert.'

'Och naw, Robert's too damn formal.' He thrust out a hard strong hand, 'Glad to meet you, Bob.' His hand grasped with a crushing ex-miner's grip. 'By God it's quite a coincidence isn't it, you haeing the same name as guid auld Bob Scott an' me haeing the same name as grand wee Tommy Weir.'

As Bob laid out his food and gear he observed his new friend. Tam was not tall and his lack of height made his sturdy body seem all the wider. The dark green ex-army kilt he wore added extra width to his hips.

Tam now said, 'I'm going tae collect some mair firewood.'

Bob volunteered, 'I'll come and help you.'

'Dae ye want tae see a real Landseer drawing?' asked Tam as they headed for some sad-looking, fallen auld Scots Pines.

'What a real Landseer away out here? That doesn't seem possible.'

Tam led him to the gaunt remains of a house gable complete with a chimney. He grinned and pointed, 'There you are, Bob, a genuine Landseer drawing.'

Still fairly clear on the discoloured plaster above the fireplace was a Landseer fresco of an alert stag. Tam explained, 'This is a' that remains o' the original Landseer bothy, where he stayed an' painted a' his famous stags.'

Bob laughed, 'So the Landseer bothy we're staying in is an imposter?'

'Aye, it is.' Tam pointed, 'Dae ye see twa real bullet holes in yon painted stag?'

Peering closer Bob grinned, 'Aye, they do look like bullet holes, right enough. Are you responsible for them?'

'Och no, some sodgers training here during the war must ha' shot yon poor beast. I ken, we, usually when gae foo, sometimes took pot-shots at strange things when we were in Italy.'

'Oh, so you were in the Army during the war?'

'Oh aye, I was in the braw auld Argylls. I wis one o' the 8th Army's Desert Rats. Aye an' we fought a' the way up bloody Italy tae. That other Bob Scott ye've still tae meet at Luibeg Bothy, was a Desert Rat tae. We've shared many braw drams, twa ex-sodgers, reliving war-time memories.'

After their shared evening meal they sat by the well-stoked bothy fire and Tam lit a large, curved, Sherlock Homes pipe. Giving contented puffs he grinned, 'This auld pipe is my only real self-indulgence. '

'I see you've brought the luxury of a book with you too,' Bob remarked.

Tam said, 'Here, hae a look at it. Have you read it?'

'Oh aye, I've read it. Read it with great pleasure.'

This fairly recently published book was Tom Weir's *Highland Days*.

'Aye, I've read it wi' great pleasure tae,' Tam said. 'An' no only wi' great pleasure, but wi' life changing effect tae.' He gave a wide cheery grin, 'If it wisna' for wee Tommy Weir's book I widna' he here in this auld Argyll sodger's kilt. When I was demobbed after the war I was bloody sure I wisna' gaeing back doon thae damn coalmines an' never seeing onie real daylight for near half the year. I got odd labouring jobs here an' there, an' when I'd a good few bawbees in ma sporran, I took off an' tramped aboot.'

'Then I read wee Tommy's book and efter that I more or less followed in his footsteps, stravaiging a' ower the brawest, remotest, wildest parts o' the Highlands.' He gave a hearty carefree laugh, 'Aye, an' that's whit I'm still daeing.'

Bob's echoing laughter was not quite so carefree, 'Oh, Tam, I greatly admire your fine free life style. I feel very strongly I should do something like that too. But the book that influenced me even more that Tom Weir's grand wee book was W. H. Murray's, *Mountaineering in Scotland*. Along with all my climbing pals, I was vastly inspired by his wonderful example.'

'Oh aye,' Tam said, 'nae doot Murray was a great climber an' writer, but I found a' his deep philosophy an' religious mysticism much too airy-fairy. I wis far mair impressed by wee Tommy Weir's mair doon tae earth book wi' its much less flowery, but nane the less deeply felt love o' oor braw Scots Hills.'

'Aye, that's as may be,' Bob said, 'but would you recommend a life-style like yours for me?'

'Och aye, it's a really grand life as long as ye're young, fit an' free.' More solemnly he continued, 'Och, but it was sad tae when I visited a' thae remote hooses that, when wee Tommy stayed in them before the war, were a' occupied by gamekeepers or shepherds an' their large, well-contented families. Aye, but in these post-war years, thae poor hooses, a' lie desolate an' empty.' Tam brightened and grinned. 'But at least thae a' mak' braw climbing bothies, don't they?'

After an ample shared breakfast these new friends prepared to part; Tam to refill his empty sporran by working at one of the many Hydro-electric schemes that were about to bring electricity to every house in the Highlands; Bob to happily stravaig from bothy to bothy for the remainder of his holiday.

Following Tam's advice, Bob left the hard tarred Glen Feshie road and took a more picturesque forest track that, he'd been assured, would lead him to a little known and seldom used small wooden bothy.

And so, after many doubtful turnings in a maze of forest tracks, it did. For some unknown reason this dry and cosy wee shelter was known as 'Drake's Bothy' although the sign above its door proclaimed it to be 'Inshriach Bothy.'

Early the following morning Bob set out with even more eagerness than usual in his stride. Guided by his map and the enthusiasm in Seton Gordon's book he keenly anticipated getting into the large, natural Rothiemurchus Forest for the first time.

His great expectations for this largest remaining remnant of Scotland's Ancient Caledonian Forest were more than fully met. After yesterday's searching through a vast endless mass of neatly regimented dark fir trees, today's natural forest was a wondrous marvel.

Rising, well spread out, from a sea of tall thick old heathers, many ancient Scots Pines proudly displayed their rugged tenacious wild splendour. Slender silver birches and dense juniper bushes were scattered about to add additional pleasure to this marvellous scene.

This beauty was further enhanced as the winding path led Bob round by the glory of Loch an Eilein. Then the sight of the ruined Castle on this loch's only island brought less happy thoughts. For, according to Seton Gordon's book, that high castle was where the last breeding pair of Scotland's ospreys had been shot by a misguided blood-thirsty 19th century laird. As he sat and stared at that dark and gloomy ruin, he wondered if he might ever see returning Scottish ospreys again breeding and fishing here. It did not seem likely.

With a touch of urgency he hurried on. For, while this ancient forest tried to hold him with its ensnaring beauty, his complaining stomach reminded him that his supplies of food were almost finished. So he made straight for Aviemore.

He found this sleepy wee place to be little more than a neglected hamlet. The only activity was at the railway station as a main-line express came steaming in. Then, once it had gone and the branch line train to Speyside also steamed away, Aviemore again lapsed into drowsy peaceful ease.

The few shops and the one small garage seemed little more than rusty iron sheds. However he found one corrugated-iron roofed shop to be quite amazingly well stocked. After purchasing a few items, he hurried to the nearby Youth Hostel. There was no finesse in his urgent cooking. A small tin of beans was mixed in with a large tin of mince; eaten direct from the pot, the resultant mixture was delicious! A large tin of creamed rice completed the much needed meal.

Next morning, once Aviemore's wee shop's drowsy fat ginger cat was shooed off the freshly baked bread, Bob was served. He again stocked up, not with many heavy tins but with lighter food easier to carry the many rugged miles into the heart of the Cairngorm Mountains.

Shortly after he crossed the Spey he got a welcome lift on a timber lorry. The road they followed soon became little more than a rutted forestry track. After being bounced about on the hard metal back of this lorry he was pleased to be let off near that other beautiful loch in this wondrous Rothiemurchus Forest – Loch Morlich. Not only was he seeing this place for the first time, he was seeing it at its very best with the large loch's calm surface faithfully reflecting the high Cairngorms lingering late winter snows.

Striding along the ancient path that rose to Ryvoan Pass he was delighted to see that unique wee lochan he had read about. Neatly tucked away below a steep, Scots Pines dotted slope, Lochan Uaine did live up to its name. Its waters *were* an amazing green.

No need to re-read Seton Gordon's book – that book he had not shown to Tam Weir – to remember how this cute wee loch's waters had got their quaint green colour. They had been magically turned green by the Wee Folk washing their emerald coloured clothes in this hidden away lochan. With a grin he thought, 'Thank God Tam isn't here, he would dismiss this story of wee goblins and elves as all too airy-fairy!'

Bob soon reached Ryvoan Bothy. He was pleased with the cheery bright red colour of the metal roof that had replaced the original turf covering. He was impressed by the solid thickness of the old stone walls. He felt strongly that this building was impregnated with history. These other bothies he'd used had been built in the Victorian heyday of Highland sporting estates, but this building was centuries old. It had sheltered Speyside clansmen on their cattle thieving raids into the lush grasslands of Moray. Despondent defeated Culloden survivors had taken refuge here. In the terrible depression of the 1930's the first of Glasgow's working-class climbers had discovered and treasured this bothy's welcoming shelter. Some hardy Lovat Scouts and Commandos had used it on wartime winter mountain exercises. (Bob little knew how two Assynt ex-Lovat Scouts would influence his future Assynt years.)

After a quick snack he took an easy climb to the summit of Meall a' Bhuachaille. This shepherd's broad and smooth heather slope was in strong contrast to that other shepherd, the Buachaille Etive Mor, who so dramatically rose to dominate the eastern entrance to Glencoe.

Early the following morning he again strode on. Refusing to be backtracked by that tempting wooden bothy that during the deer-stalking season was still used as a stable, he eagerly headed into the ever more wild, remote and untamed Cairngorm Mountains.

Following the rough uncertain path that vaguely wound its way between Loch A'an's northerly shore and the steep stark enclosing slope that menaced with its tumbled boulders and its slowly advancing avalanches of unstable grey screes, his gaze was constantly drawn to that crazy maze of steep crags, age-shattered cliffs and deep-gashed gullies that savagely encircled the far end of this remote and lonely loch. And somewhere in there, below its rugged Shelter Stone Crag, would be his refuge for tonight.

A neat cairn on a huge fallen boulder confirmed that this was the famous Loch A'an Shelter Stone. The size of this one gigantic stone dwarfed all the countless boulders scattered around. While Ryvoan Bothy had been used for centuries, this Shelter Stone had been used for thousands of years, even from the time of the first post-ice-age Picts.

After the struggle through the small entrance the shelter's dim interior seemed quite spacious and was pleasantly dry. It even had an interesting visitors' book.

As he snuggled into his sleeping-bag that evening Bob refused to let his imagination dwell too much on thoughts of all those tons of solid rock poised just above his head.

The following day, keeping clear of Hell's Lum Crag, he had a steep but quite straightforward climb to the broad summit of Cairn Gorm. He wanted to see this mountain in its present pure state before any of these vague plans for ski-lifts on its Northern slopes might come about.

After another night of having this unique howff to himself and not having seen another human soul all the previous day, Bob left it and headed for a bothy where, if all reports were true, there should be good, if sometimes somewhat eccentric company.

After passing the mass of grey screes and steep tree-less slopes around Loch Etchachan it was pleasant to be amongst the scattered auld Scots Pines that increased in numbers as he strode along the fine wide path down through Glen Derry. Then, crowning the pleasure of this verdant glen, a golden eagle launched itself with heaving effort from a nearby old pine. Bob admiringly watched how that eagle's initial straining effort changed to effortless soaring ease as up-currents of warm air lifted it in wide lazy circles.

Just before reaching Derry Lodge he spied the first humans he'd seen all day; two men striding up towards him. One man seemed about the same age as Bob. Hatless, he had thick, reddish hair while a shiny beard enclosed his beaming weather-beaten face. A pair of binoculars hung around his neck.

The other man was much older, but his energetic pace and the jaunty swinging of his ancient kilt belied his advanced years.

As they approached, Bob thought, 'By God, that kilt really is old.' Most of its red tartan was very faded, but a large untidy patch glowed a vivid scarlet. A tweed jacket and matching deerstalker hat, both also rather faded, completed his outfit. A leather-cased telescope hung from one shoulder. His right hand grasped a sturdy cromach. He must be a rather eccentric Highland laird , Bob decided, one who's had his ancestral kilt handed down from generation to generation.

The 'laird's' cultured Scottish voice seemed to confirm this as he pleasantly greeted Bob. Returning that greeting, Bob suddenly remembered something. He had a clear memory of a picture in a certain book. 'Yes, surely that's him, that's the author of the book.' He smiled, 'Am I fortunate enough to be talking to Mr. Seton Gordon?'

The smile was returned, 'Yes, you are. And my young friend here is Mr. Adam Watson. How did you know me? Have we met before?'

'No, we haven't. I recognised you from the picture in your book.' Bob removed the book he had borrowed from Podge from his rucksack and handed it to its author.

'Ah yes, *The Cairngorm Hills of Scotland*. It's a good few years since I wrote it. Would you like me to sign it?'

'It belongs to a friend, but I know he would be really delighted to have your autograph.'

As the old author fumbled with his fountain-pen his young companion, Adam Watson, with a smile, said, 'It was reading that book of Seton's when I was a mere boy that set me on my true course in life. I decided to become a naturalist and devote my skills to really getting to know the Cairngorms and the varied wildlife which is to be found here.'

Adam was distracted by a soaring eagle. His binoculars followed its every move. And Seton Gordon's telescope quickly mirrored this action.

Bob eagerly told of his great delight in seeing the eagle further up Glen Derry. 'Aye,' Seton said, 'that's where we're going; to check up on the surviving chick in the eyrie. Well, we'd better get going.' They exchanged firm handshakes then parted.

Soon afterwards Bob stood on the wee wooden bridge that crossed Luibeg Burn. He gazed around. This was an idyllic place. The rounded high hills, the extensive heather moors, the ancient remnant forest of scattered auld Scots Pines all blended together to present a perfect picture.

Amongst and screened by a grove of tall pines, stood a modest but attractive wee cottage. That must be the home of the well-known gamekeeper, Bob Scott, thought the other Bob. Beside the house in amongst the trees, nestled a wooden, tin-roofed shed that could only be the fabled bothy that bore its owner's name.

As he neared this shed a sturdy stocky middle-aged man dressed in plus-fours and jacket of a fawnish shade that had a brighter thread almost red in colour glowing through the faded tweed, suddenly appeared. In a deep, broad, Aberdeenshire voice he asked, 'Well, lad, are ye here tae stay in ma bothy?'

'Aye, I am. Will that be all right?'

'Och aye, I dinna' ken why it shouldnae be. But it will cost ye a wee bawbee.'

Bob smiled, 'A wee bawbee? Exactly how much is that?'

'It's a shilling per nicht. To be paid in advance, tae.' He grinned, 'I don't want onie mair trouble wi' cheating bastards trying tae slip awa' without paying me. I've had tae chase some miserable buggers half way through the Lairig Ghru tae get ma bawbees frae them!'

Bob laughed, 'Och, I do intend to go through the Lairig Ghru, but I assure you I won't try to cheat you. I would like to stay for a least two nights.' He searched in his pocket, 'I've only got half-a-crown; here take it. That will pay for the two nights.'

The gamekeeper instantly accepted the large silver coin. He made no mention of the sixpence change. However he grinned cheerily as he opened the bothy door and warmly said, 'Come awa in then, lad, an' mak' yerself at home in ma braw bothy.'

And this wee bothy really was "braw". A large, well-used fireplace dominated the wooden gable end. There was no thick stone wall to make a real ingle-neuk, but the chairs set snugly on each side of the fireplace suggested real convivial comfort and contented warm ease. A strong wire ran from wall to wall above the fireplace for the drying of climbers' rain-soaked clothes. Some roughly hewn timber chairs were set by a large table. It even boasted the unusual luxury of some comfortable wooden bunks.

'Aye, it really is a fine bothy, right enough,' Bob enthused.

'Aye, an' dae ye see whit's up there?' The gamekeeper pointed to the bare electric bulb hanging from the ceiling.

Bob laughed, 'Surely that's just for show? You don't have electric lights in here, do you?'

'Och, but aye I dae, it comes frae the generator that lights ma hoose. An' that's whit ye pay bawbees for, tae help buy a' yon bloody expensive diesel oil. So you see, lad, I'm no' really mean charging ye for yer stay.'

'Oh I never thought you were,' Bob hurried to, not quite truthfully, assure him.

'A' weel, that's as may be. By the way, whit's yer name lad?'

Bob had been waiting for this, with a wide grin he replied, 'Actually my name's the same as yours. I'm a Bob Scott too. I've been looking forward to meeting you and staying in your famous bothy, of being, Bob Scott, at Bob Scott's.'

Rather suspiciously the other Bob Scott asked, 'Is that true? Is that yer real name, lad?'

'Aye, it is. Here look at this.' He handed over his Scottish Youth Hostels membership card. 'My name and other details are all in there.'

The gamekeeper grinned, 'Aye, richt enough, that a' seems in order.' He laughed outright, 'By God, Bob ye'll think I'm a damn customs officer checking yer passport before letting ye intae ma special domain!'

Bob echoed his laugh, 'Och, as long as you *do* let me into this truly special place you look after; not only this bothy, but all the glory of this surrounding Cairngorm land.'

'Och, ye're welcome tae mak' the maist o' both, lad. Dae ye ken the Cairngorms well?'

'Oh no, not very well, I've mostly climbed more Westerly hills. But I'm spending this holiday getting to know the Cairngorms better. I've been going from bothy to bothy. I've just come from the Loch A'an Shelter Stone.'

'Och I ken yon place weel, but I've nae slept in it. Yon's a gey wild, lonely an' eerie place tae bide on yer ain.'

Bob laughed, 'Aye, that would be true in dreich weather with smothering dull clouds and sleety rain, och, but it was fine at this great time of constant May sunshine with each brilliant cloudless day stretching out endlessly.'

'Aye that's true, lad, an' there's nane o' thae bloody midges at this time tae.' the gamekeeper laughed, 'Nor are there sae mony o' yon hikers an' climbers that at the height o' summer can become swarming pests tae, especially when we're stalking the deer.'

Bob laughed, Och I'll be well away from here by the time you're deer-stalking. Oh, another great advantage of this dry May weather here in the Cairngorms is how easy it is to cross all the wee rivers and the many large burns that are real low now. I've mostly crossed dry-shod, but when I've had to paddle I've never been deeper than half-way to my knees. These crossings must be an entirely different story in time of rain and flood.'

'Aye, they are. Aye, ower the years, mair than wan hiker has met his fate in wan o' thae big burns in spate.' The gamekeeper now grinned and his eyes twinkled, 'Aye, lad, I now ken ye've got a wise auld heid on your young shoulders. Aye, ye're a real genius tae tak yer holidays at this braw time of year. An' whit bonnie hill are ye planning tae climb the morrow?'

'Oh, I might not manage any hill. I'll need to walk to the Braemar grocers and get stocked up with food. I've not much left.'

'Och there's nae need tae gae intae Braemar. The grocer's weekly mobile shop ca's here the morrow at ten o' clock. Ye'll get a' ye need frae him.'

'Oh that's great. I'll wait for him, then still have plenty time to climb a hill.'

So the following morning, after stacking his re-stocked food in Bob Scott's braw bothy, the other Bob Scott was now sitting at relaxed ease at the large cairn on the stony summit of Derry Cairngorm. As he gazed around with delight he chewed voluptuously on a large Mars Bar and felt his pure aesthetic senses being challenged by the more basic sensual pleasures of appeasing his hunger. Vividly remembering the austere wartime years when all chocolate was extremely rare, his delight in the Mars Bar's luxurious splendour at last won outright.

But later, hunger appeased, deep aesthetic pleasure again took over as he drank in the impressive Cairngorm views that surrounded him, the mountains shading into a distinctive hue of misty blue.

After enjoying his fresh replenished evening meal, Bob wisely made the most of the lingering glory of this perfect May evening by contentedly strolling by the side of the drought shrunken but still attractive Luigbeg Burn. All nature was aglow with this late evening glory. Even the most ancient of the Scots Pines managed to pulse their dull grey auld trunks with something of their resinous reddish youthful vigour while their upper branches bravely glowed and green needles took on a strange purplish sheen.

Bob now saw the Luibeg gamekeeper coming towards him. His lively, friendly wee terrier accompanied him. So too, as far as the confining fence allowed, did his auld grey pony. Even the scatter of his wife's many hens seemed to be half-heartedly following him.

The two Bobs exchanged hearty greetings. 'Well, lad, did ye see mony o' my beasts oot on Derry Cairngorm the day?'

'Oh aye, I saw two herds of stags, one herd of about twenty, the other, almost fifteen.'

'Aye, yon's about whit I'd expect tae see on yon braw brae.' Like every experienced Highland gamekeeper he had a good idea of how many deer were on the various parts of the estate he looked after. 'An' whit condition did they seem in, eh?'

'Oh they certainly were not looking their best. Their coats were very ragged and untidy. I guess they were still moulting out of their thick grey winter coats. And of course their freshly growing new antlers were still quite small and covered in protective "velvet".'

The gamekeeper laughed, 'By God, Bob, I'll need tae look tae ma laurels ye seem tae ken an awfu' lot about yon beasts.'

Bob also laughed, then modestly said, 'Och, it's mostly what I've learned from reading Seton Gordon's books.'

'Aye, yon grand auld Seton Gordon an' fine young Adam Watson ye met yesterday, sure ken a lot aboot the deer. They ken as much as me.' He exploded into harmless mirth, 'Or they think they dae!'

Bob had also told this other Bob Scott about his friend, Tam Weir, he'd met at Landseers Bothy and how Tam's free and easy stravaiging life-style had so impressed him. He grinned, 'I'm also most taken with the great life you live here at Luibeg. Surely you must be quite content living and working in such a natural paradise as this. Oh I know the weather's not always as great as this. I know the winter conditions can be really terrible, but surely this is where you want to continue living, isn't it?'

'Aye it is.' He laughed, 'I saw mair than enough o' thae mucky Arabs an' a' the desert sands when I wis wan o' Monty's Desert Rats. Aye, an' I had enough o' the bloody Eyeties tae, even wi' a' their alluring vino.

'Aye, braw wee Luibeg is where I'm content tae bide jist as ma wise auld faither did afore me. I ken I could never live in Glesca' or onie other damned city.'

Bob sighed, 'Aye, that's what I increasingly feel, that I must get out of that constricting and depressing city. Aye, I must! Aye, I will!' (Even in his most fantastic dreams Bob never imagined that in not so many years time he too would wear tweed plus-fours and a matching jacket of a fawnish pattern that was kept for the exclusive use of Assynt Estate's gamekeepers, gillies, and the estate-owning Vestey gentry.)

The following morning Bob set out on the easy hike to another of the Cairngorms' legendary places: Corrour Bothy.

He again silently praised May's sun-glowing days of endless pleasure and its rainless weeks that had reduced the infant River Dee to no more than a subdued mountain burn, for the two hand-wires above the foot-wire that made the only bridge across to Corrour Bothy, were very loose and made the rucksack burdened journey rather precarious and as shoogily as a speeding Glasgow tram. However he got across without suffering the indignity of an unintended cold bath. (A few years later two members of a ladies hiking club were not so fortunate. They had fallen into this infant River Dee when it had been transformed to a roaring flooding fury. Dragged down by their heavy rucksacks both ladies drowned. The following year a fine new footbridge was erected and named in their memory.)

Despite its widespread fame, Corrour Bothy was modestly unpretentious. Its new iron roof and its one window and door kept its one wee room snug and dry. It boasted a unique concrete table and a grand auld visitors' book. Some entries were even pre-war. Bob glanced through that book and was delighted to discover some famous names: Tom Weir, Bill Murray and Jock Nimlin all there, making a roll-call of famous, and greatly inspiring Scottish climbers.

Bob now climbed up from the bothy by the obvious gully which rose directly by the steep smooth boiler-plate rock slabs of *The Devil's Point,* (as it was now coyly called, although its older rhyming name of *Auld Nick's Prick* was much more accurately descriptive.)

He then followed along above the line of curving cliffs that led direct to Cairn Toul. He made a brief call at the more pleasantly named Angel's Peak then continued on round by the wee waterfall, then in its drought-like state, not at the moment living up to its grander name of 'The Falls of Dee.'

Then, on the vast summit of Braeriach he sat for some immeasureable time, gazing all around. Awestruck, he tried to take in this endless Cairngorm panorama: all this vast, smooth spreading plateau and the slash of the Lairig Ghru pass, that great gash that lures hardy hikers from Speyside to Deeside.

Bob had Corrour Bothy to himself that evening, but he was not lonely. Through Seton Gordon's Cairngorm book he re-lived the time when Seton had shared this deer-watchers' bothy with its last auld occupant who not only watched over and fed the deer but entranced and bemused these beasts with his eccentric bagpipe playing. His fantastic Highland music had these stags dancing crazy Highland Flings with prancing hoofs and mad upflung antlers.

The following morning saw Bob pass the Pools of Dee and continue on through the impressive Lairig Ghru.

The Rothiemurchus Forest's mass of auld Scots Pines made a glorious contrast to the high Cairngorms much harsher mountainous environment, and there were supposed to be many wartime Nissen huts, ex-army or ex-forestry, scattered throughout this ancient forest. Rothiemurchus Lodge would also have made a fine bothy, but it was still used by the Army for training.

Bob remembered how his cousin had laughingly told of how when in the Army in winter 1944, he'd been trained here in skiing and mountain warfare, then, expecting to fight in the mountains of Norway or Austria, he'd instead seen battle at (or even below) sea-level in the dyke-breeched flooded flats of Holland.

Bob soon found an empty Nissen hut pleasantly positioned beside a dainty forest lochan. He quickly settled in and appropriated its wartime comforts for his peacetime uses.

He spent the next day in happy exploratory rambling. From Loch Morlich's pine-reflecting perfection he stravaiged this ancient forest's meandering tracks to the rising path that led him through that quaint, narrow, savage enclosing Chalmain Gap. From there it was a pleasant steady steepish climb to the fine wee peak of Lurcher's Crag.

Resisting the temptation to push on through the vast boulder field that, like an army of aggressive sentries, guarded the approach to Big Ben Macdui, he instead took the easier option of reaching and sitting on one of the cairns that claimed to be the true top of Cairn Lochan. This place boasted some impressive cliffs that tenaciously clung on to their gully smothering hard-packed snows.

Next day, hunger's rumbling reminded him of his body's urgent needs. If only he had had a shotgun, the many black grouse he'd seen in this forest would have made a regal meal. Then, suddenly he was startled by a much larger bird, one he'd never seen before. Although, as he discovered later, this bird was of the grouse family its huge size and obvious aggressive behaviour made it quite different from all other grouse he had seen.

As he stared amazed, slowly walking away from this large cock Capercaillie's angry grumbling rumbles Bob's own hunger pangs made him see that huge bird well stuffed and roasted. The Capercaillie was the size of a turkey and surely would be just as tasty. He again lamented his lack of a shotgun.

However that evening at Aviemore's Youth Hostel his tins of mince, baked beans and Ambrosia creamed rice, seemed even more delicious than usual.

As his senses revelled in this happy feed Bob tried to keep his thoughts from dwelling on tomorrow's train journey back to Glasgow, and then back to work. Instead he re-lived this great Cairngorm holiday and re-met these wonderful characters who had helped make these simple, not over-strenuous, not wildly adventurous past two weeks in that abundance of grand Highland bothies, so pleasantly memorable.

# At the Arrochar Caves

Pleased to be back in Arrochar and delighting in the thought of spending another weekend climbing that grand wee hill, The Cobbler, while being again snugly based in those almost legendary Arrochar Caves, Gordon and Bob hurried around by the head of Loch Long.

Anxious to claim themselves a comfortable dry place, not in one of the larger, well-known, well-used lower caves but in a higher, more secret cave, they continue clambering upwards through the confusion of huge boulders and impeding trees then climb up that half-hidden wee path that follows by the side of the Allt Sugach burn.

To those who know it and happily use it, this higher cave is fondly known as a real home from home, a place they do not want too many to learn about. They therefore keep secret its whereabouts and refer to it only as 'The Secret Doss.'

It can accommodate four in real comfort, any more than this is too much of a crush. The snug dryness of this secret place is greatly enhanced by the thick, years old, layers of tinder-dry bracken and dried out springy heather that completely covers the cave floor and lulls all dossers in this wondrous howff to splendidly-mattressed, comfortable sleep.

Bob and Gordon dump their laden rucksacks on the Secret Doss's magic bracken mattress then prepare to have a quick 'drum-up', a refreshing drink of tea before they head for the Cobbler's nearby slopes.

'I'll get my primus stove going while you fetch the water, Bob, all right?' Gordon suggested.

'Aye sure, I'll fill both our dixies.'

Gordon threw his sleeping-bag on the bracken mattress to get at his primus and the dixie, which was deeper in his rucksack. Bob fetched out his neatly packed dixies without needing to remove anything else.

Clashing the empty steel dixies together like discordant cymbals, Bob left the cave and started down to the nearby wee burn. Half way there sudden loud shouts halted him. He turned, stared and listened. What seemed to be loud agitated swearing was coming from their cave. Shouting, 'What the hell's wrong, Gordon?' he hurried back up the slope.

Gasping, he increased his speed as he saw greyish smoke pouring out of the low entrance.

All that mass of dry bracken and heather inside was rapidly becoming a fierce blazing inferno. Wasting no time or breath on words Bob frantically helped Gordon throw the last of all their weekend gear out of the cave to safety.

Gordon's fine, almost new sleeping-bag was the first thing he'd rescued. He'd managed to stamp out the lump of fiery bracken that was burning it and threatening to completely destroy it.

Their two rucksacks and most of their other gear seemed miraculously un-damaged by the fire.

Sitting well clear of the heat and dense grey smoke pouring out of the cave and rubbing their watering, smoke-reddened eyes, Gordon explained what had happened, 'It was just one moment's foolish carelessness. I had lit the meths that heats the primus stove then turned to get the tea out of my rucksack. My sudden movement overturned the primus. The flames spread like wildfire through the dry bracken. I managed to grab the primus and throw it outside. But by then the damage was done. That dry bracken and heather went up like a bloody furnace.'

Bob nodded, 'Aye, I saw that for myself. Och, Gordon, you did really well to save all our gear. The only real damage seems to be to your poor new sleeping-bag.'

'Aye, I know.' Gordon grinned ruefully as he inspected the hole in his eiderdown bag. He picked away some of the bracken that was fused to the bag's nylon cover.

Using up all of our joint stock of sticking plasters, Gordon patched up the large burn hole at the foot of his sleeping-bag. He again grinned, 'That should stop all the precious eiderdown feathers from flying all over the valley.'

After refreshing our smarting eyes and sweaty faces in the burn's pure cool water we made our way back down to the lower caves. We were lucky. No one was using these often quite crowded caves. Laying out our sleeping-bags we staked our claims to the best brightest and cheeriest places near the front of one of the largest and driest caves.

After some much-needed tea we rather belatedly climbed to the stark rock summit of The Cobbler's central peak and happily made the most of what remained of this fine bright June day.

About to re-enter the cave we were halted by the approach of two climbers. We recognised them as being a pair of the Creagh Dhu Club's finest climbers, Johnnie Cunningham and Mick Noon. They rather abruptly greeted us, 'Hello lads, have you caught sight of any bloody strangers hanging about here?'

'No, only ourselves, we haven't seen anybody else. Why what's wrong?'

Loudly and passionately they explained, 'Some bloody idiots have set fire to the dry bracken and heather in our secret doss up the hill from here. There's nothing left but a smoky mess. If we catch those bastards we'll give them a right good bloody tanking!'

Praying that no smell of smoke lingered on their clothes, Bob and Gordon gave the two angry climbers their deepest sympathy. They then exchanged a quick, furtive glance as the same terrible thought arose in both their minds.

'Eh, what have you got planned for today, anything special?' Gordon asked Johnny.

'Only to beat the living daylight out of those bastards that burned the doss,' was the angry reply.

Meanwhile, Bob slipped away, murmuring, 'I'll just go into the cave and make a space for you two. Only be a minute.' Both had remembered the damning evidence of Gordon's burned sleeping-bag.

Bob rolled up the tell-tale bag and threw it and his own intact sleeping-bag into the darkness at the back of the cave. He then heaved their rucksacks and all their other gear to the cave's rear. He got to the cave entrance as the two Creagh Dhu stalwarts were about to come in. 'There you are,' he said, 'there's the best place cleared for you two. It's only fair that you should get pride of place here.'

'What are you two up to?' Johnnie asked. 'There's something fishy going on here, but, nevertheless, it's nice to see folk with proper respect for their elders and betters.' He gave one of his trademark twisted grins.

Later Gordon said to Bob, 'Well done, Bob. I'm sure your quick-thinking saved us from a good hammering there.'

'If it had come close to that, I was going to say it was you that bloody well started the fire, not me, don't you worry,' was the cheery reply.

# Our Own Tyndrum Doss

How eagerly we looked forward to spending another weekend in our own Tyndrum Doss.

After being dropped off at Tyndrum's main hotel by good auld MacBrayne's always reliable Fort William bus, it was pleasant indeed to set out at a good steady pace and feel our bus-sluggish blood pulse in a way that was healthy and warmly thrilling. And more, much more, than merely 'pleasant' were our feelings as we steadily advance through this January day's sharp clear air under the cloudless blue sky while sunshine's brilliant glitter, transforms the snow covered Tyndrum landscape into something of splendid awesome wonder.

Accompanied by the magical musical crunch of effortless boots on frost encrusted snow, we tramp directly towards the West and ever nearer to that snow-glowing trio, Ben Lui, Ben Oss and more modest, tho' more grandly named Beinn Dubhchraig.

With its rugged track to guide us, we soon arrive at Cononish farm. After eager greeting, and being warmly welcomed by the auld sheep farmer, we push on beside the semi-iced tumbling burn that drains the Ben Lui Glen. Gliding past our own wee doss this burn provides us with our drinking water. Whenever he put a dash of this water in our hospitably offered dram, the auld farmer would grin, 'Och just a wee splash o' this water is fine. I ken there's nae deed braxy sheep further up this burn!'

This farmer was a real character. It was with his permission, and indeed his encouragement and active assistance, that we had this humble wee doss of our own.

This doss was nothing special; most certainly was nothing splendid. It could in no way compare with the solid rock-roofed vastness of the high Cairngorms' famous Shelter Stone. Nor could it come near the domestic cosiness of Ben Alder Cottage or of Geldie Lodge's fine dry, badger-like, bracken-mattressed bedroom and its other welcome comforts all kept in order by keen Aberdeen Boy Scouts.

No, our Tyndrum Doss was like none of those. It was made from a disused old sheep fank. As it was only the height of its dry stone dyke we could not stand up in it. We had to crawl in then sit to make our meals or lie in the welcome warmth of our sleeping-bags. It was roofed with sheets of corrugated iron and a layer of thick peat and further anchored with heavy stones. Inside it was dry under all reasonable weather conditions although in the coldest winter its bare stone walls would sometimes be rimed with ice. At least it had a wooden floor and the sleeping-quarters were snugly layered with dry bracken. It could sleep four in comfort; any more was an awkward crush.

There were four of us this weekend; Podge, his girlfriend, Margaret, Auld Dave and Bob. So, good old friends, we knew we would get on well together in the rather restricted confines of this fine wee doss we had all helped build. After a quick brew of tea and a light snack we, eager to make the most of what remained of this perfect winter day, set out towards Scotland's only gold mine. We had explored this disused mine before, but there was recent talk of it being brought back into use. The only sign we discovered of that possibility was that the heavy gate guarding the mine entrance, that had been wide open before, was now securely padlocked.

Later that windless cloudless night a keen frost set in and smothered the entire frozen snowy landscape in profound star-bright silence. A deep silence until the eerie banshee love-sick howls of a mate-searching vixen set a male fox into louder lusty howls of even more unearthly response.

These silence-shattering howls and the frost's ever keener, ever more shivery grip, made us once again admire the wisdom that had made us buy those post-war treasures, our Black's Icelandic sleeping-bags. The more the restless foxes howled and the more cruelly the frost gripped, the more we silently revelled in the snug luxury of our eider-down bags.

Early morning's searching sunshine peeped through chinks in our primitive wee doss's rough stone walls and, advancing with scalpel lances, deplored our snugly comfortable sluggish ways.

Crawling out into morning's reprimanding brightness we, with rueful smiles, apologise to Ben Lui's sun-snow glowing summit. We promise the neglected hill that we will not further delay our planned advance on its inviting snow slopes. But only more vivid imaginations than ours could truly feel that Ben Lui, with all its inspiring bright beauty, looks on us with anything but complete indifference.

Still, as we advance over neat drifts of snow towards these high steep slopes, the pleasure we get from this cold indifferent beauty is real, is fantastically real. Surely only the meanest most miserable human spirit would not be uplifted, would not rejoice either with loud articulated praise or with silent inaudible appreciation.

Rising straight before us is Ben Lui's smooth North West face. Showing clear in the searching light despite being in the North's sun-denying shade this face today is one huge smooth slope of pure rock-free snow. As it has nothing of the challenge of Ben Nevis's ice-coated rock ridges or its steep, snow-frozen narrow gullies, we advance with carefree high hopes and joyous spirits. This day's climb should be nothing really serious, but still we'll wisely not neglect to treat this mountain with all due respect.

We climb on two ropes. Podge and Margaret on one; Dave and Bob on the other. For some time Podge takes the lead with undemanding easy skill. He then lets eager, less skilled Margaret take over. This not too steep lower slope of Ben Lui is a perfect place for her to practise and improve her snow-climbing skill. Should she, or any of us, fall down from here and not be held by our partner's snow-belay we should come to no real harm. There were no rocks to hit, no ice-cliff to fall over; we should endure nothing but a long easy slide on smooth snow. In fact this was a place where in previous winters we'd all greatly enjoyed the thrill of long, well-controlled snow glissading and had practised the essential skill of effective braking with our long, wooden-shafted ex-army ice-axes.

For all British winter climbers at this free and easy post-war time these grand old ice-axes were indispensable (Some older climbers thought they would be for ever irreplaceable!) So, too, some thought our Commando-soled boots to be the ultimate perfection in climbing boots. Certainly they had almost completely replaced the heavy, tricouni-nailed pre-war boots that had scraped their silver tracks on the good old Cobbler's most popular rock routes.

Likewise Podge's recently bought new climbing rope had only lately become available through Black's Mountaineering Shop and the gleaming whiteness of this fairly thin, strong, light, water-resistant nylon rope showed up brightly against the dirty shade and sad grey of Dave's old hemp rope. This almost entirely obsolete ex-army or perhaps even ex-hangman's thick hemp rope seemed to delight in doubling its already heavy weight when used in heavy rain. Bob and forever optimistic Dave, sincerely hope this will safely take the sudden violent strain of a falling climber. However, we hope not to put it to that test today.

Despite being always conscious of the brevity of this mid-winter day, of the time needed to gain Ben Lui's summit and of that deadline for catching this evening's Glasgow–bound bus, still we cannot resist the thrilling pleasure of a few long, fast, whooping glissades on this perfect slope of perfect snow.

Then we again start eagerly climbing up this gradually steepening vast slope of purest snow. Podge and Margaret again lead the way while Dave and Bob leisurely follow in their wake. We wisely save our energies for the higher, steeper, more demanding slopes. And, much more obvious from here, we both take cautious note of how far that thick snow cornice near the summit bulges out into clear space. Overcoming that obstacle will be the main – almost the only – real challenge of this winter climb.

Dave now takes the lead, his weight-lifter arms effortlessly plying his ice-axe. With seeming ease he cuts step after snowy step while Bob, snow-belayed below him, plays out that thick old hemp rope that slowly but surely snakes up to where it pythons its coils around Dave's no longer youthful or slim waist.

At last Bob takes the lead. Eager to be warmly active after his belaying wait in this North slopes cool shade, he, too, swings his ice-axe with seeming effortless skilled ease then places each Commando-soled boot higher, ever more steeply higher in the next firm snow-step.

Soon – surprisingly and pleasantly soon – he's at the end of the rope and, thrusting his ice-axe vertically downwards into the snow, and tightly looping the rope around it and around himself, he gathers in the rope as Dave climbs up. Then Podge and Margaret follow in the comparative ease of his snow-cut steps.

Together, the four of them take a short rest. Then again Bob takes the lead on what is now the much steeper final climb. Soon, almost before he knows it, he's under the summit's snowy cornice that bulges far out into space directly above his head. After warning the other three to belay to the side well clear of his falling snow, he stands steady on the flat snow-platform, he's cut out of the steep slope and starts actively hacking away at this summit-defending overhanging bulge. With very little exertion, lumps of not too solid snow loosen and fall. They hiss away down the steep slope, each a miniature avalanche.

Securely standing and alertly watching at the belays, Dave, Podge and Margaret are pleased to see the confident ease of his progress through the snow cornice. As they see all these tiny avalanches rush past them at urgent hissing speed they again congratulate one another on having judged this steep slope's snow conditions correctly. The uniform firmness of the snow's smooth surface and its safe Northern shade make any danger from a full-scale avalanche most unlikely.

Soon Bob's channelling tunnel is cut right through and he clambers on, near to Ben Lui's sun-bright summit. After all those pleasant, but chilly hours in Northerly shade he silently rejoices at again feeling the sun's warming rays glow on his uplifted face.

Soon all four of them stand beside Ben Lui's snow-plastered cairn and once more drink in the vast, snow-bright panoramic views. Every way they look they greet old friends. That must be mighty Ben Nevis peering around the Big Shepherd of Etive. And that can only be fair Ben Lomond proudly and brightly standing, across from the almost hidden, Auld Cobbler.

After a summit halt that refreshes both hungry body and aesthetic soul they make their happy, easy, but always alert and cautious way down this friendly Ben's firm snow covered South-leading wide ridge. Again they rejoice at the pleasing sound of their reliable Commando boots' crunching crisp grip on firm bright snow.

Then, with loud celebratory voices raised in Pagan praise, they all joyously glissade down a large part of the snow-pure safe glen that guides its burn down to, and past, their own, their very own fine auld Tyndrum Doss

Then much later while companionably sitting and chatting of this and that in their Glasgow–bound bus they all agree that this has been a grand winter weekend at their own, the one they built, Tyndrum Doss. And today's snow ascent of Ben Lui's had been great. Yes, had been really great! Oh of course, they all know there had been no real technical difficulties in today's easy winter climb, but even so it had still been a wonderful experience.

Oh yes, they all fervently agree, this entire weekend with such grand friends has been perfect, absolutely gloriously Perfect!

# Hogmanay on Ben Nevis

The bus the Lomond Mountaineering Club had hired for this three-day Hogmanay Holiday was waiting at Glasgow's St. Enoch Square. The driver was a well-kent, well-liked character who gave friendly greetings to the club members as they arrived. He noted their rucksacks were especially bulky, partly no doubt due to extra provisions packed in amongst bottles of whisky.

He also approvingly noted that each ice-axe wore a web 'glove' that covered its sharp steel blade. And all the ice-axes long sharp points were firmly jammed into corks. The majority were corks from whisky bottles, but a few – those from snooty Kelvinside owners – were, of course, Champagne corks. An ice-axe minus its cork could have dire consequences; could result in a heated confrontation with an irate tramcar conductress who would loudly exclaim, 'Hey you, ye're no' coming on ma caur wi' that dangerous weapon!'

If the poor climber continued standing pleading on the tram's platform the stout wee Glesca conductress would angrily declare, 'If ye don't get aff ma caur the noo I'll fetch the driver tae sort ye oot!' Then came the oft-quoted final command, 'C'm on, get aff!'

But the pleased bus driver noted that all his climbing passengers had all their ice-axes cork-intacta.

When at last the hired bus halted at Glen Nevis Youth Hostel there was a friendly lively struggle to grab rucksacks, ice-axes and all other gear then secure a bunk in a waiting dormitory.

Over the leisurely evening meal there was much eager animated talk and bright anticipation of the climbs they planned to do the following day. Some were going to challenge The Ben's highest, toughest, snow and ice gullies. Some were going to take the easier tourist route to the summit. A group of three, Dave Martin, Bob Scott and George (Podge) Morrice planned to camp on The Ben's summit.

Podge was the author of this plan. He'd persuaded Dave and Bob to join him in this mid-winter adventure. They were now as keen as him.

It was Podge's avid reading of Seton Gordon's wonderful books about the Scottish Highlands that had decided him on this plan. Seton had spent some winter nights on the summit of Ben Nevis, not in a tent but in the wee hotel that had once crowned this Ben. Podge too would spend a winter night on Scotland's highest summit, and what more fitting night than that of Hogmanay?

Right on planned time the following morning these three left the hostel and set out with eager pace. Soon the tourist path's increasing steepness slowed their progress to a steadier rhythm. Deep snow and mountain-burn ice made this a different scenario from that experienced by summer tourists.

They soon reached the path's halfway point where there once was a path-keeper's wee stone shelter at which he would demand a one shilling toll from every passing tourist. As a token gesture, today, they merely 'spend a penny' before pushing on for the mountain top.

At last they reach and symbolically touch the snow-encrusted summit cairn. They clear away some deep snow then pitch their tent amid the snowy mounds that are the remains of the old observatory.

They spread paper over the tent's ground-sheet in the hope that this will help insulate them from the mountain snow's invasive coldness. Podge has a sheet of special paper, black tarred on one side and glossy brown on the other. Dave and Bob make do with layers of old newspapers. The large sheets of the Glasgow Herald were most favoured.

Although so familiar, they are once more amazed at how many handfuls of packed snow are required to melt down to make a meaningful dixie-full of tea.

After their patiently awaited tea and pleasant snack they set out to make the most of what remains of this calm, sun-bright, frost sparkling last day of December. They wave cheery greetings to climbers on the far side of The Ben's large summit plateau then set out to explore where the narrow snowy arête of the Carn Mor Dearg ridge joins up to the mountain top.

Back in the tent, sorting out food for dinner, they were made aware of a change in the light as the tent walls strangely warmly glowed. Podge grabbed his camera and hurried out. Dave and Bob keenly followed.

As Podge's camera captured the glowing scenes the two others stood in silent awe. This high Ben and every other snow covered mountain amazingly glowed with sunset's pulsing reds and blushing pinks.

This wondrous show of aesthetic pleasure quickly faded, dusk's dimness took over and directed their awed senses back to the more mundane, but no less real, pleasures of their snug tent, cosy sleeping-bags and waiting food and drink.

True to the wise old adage about 'too many cooks spoiling the broth,' Podge alone did the cooking while the two others tried to keep out of his way in the tent's limited space.

Once the ample, and tasty, dinner was all eaten, their mugs were filled with strong dark Jolly Roger Rum, generously laced with Crabbies strong green ginger. Each swallow of this potent mixture sent a glorious warming glow flooding through each body. With happy sensual pleasure each followed this delightful sensation as it spread out from food replete-belly to the furthest toe and to the deepest reaches of each exhilarated, if somewhat bemused brain.

This alcoholic feeling warmed Dave Martin's repertoire of comic songs into lusty life. Soon Podge and Bob happily joined in as Dave sent poor Eskimo Nell on her rude Alaskan adventures. They eagerly followed him in the Shooting of Dan McGee before taking a hectic rail journey on The Runaway Train. They also sang of their own lands; of lonely Mary in a Remote Highland Glen, and, with memories of auld clan feuds, of MacPherson's Rant with its promise to '*murder and to ravish in the lands of the Clan MacTavish.*'

The happily gregarious hours flew un-noticed by until, carried clear on the calm frosty air, the loud hooting clamour of Fort William's distillery and moored ships announced the birth of one more New Year.

Once the usual ritual of hearty handshakes and happy wishes was over, they wisely decided to drink no more but to get to sleep. Best keep reasonably sober in case this glorious weather should sudden turn to life-threatening blizzard.

Despite the giant allure of the Milky Way's fantastic glowing, million, million stars they spent no more time out in the bone-freezing coldness than was necessary to splash three separate tell-tale piss holes in poor Ben Nevis's pure snows.

Once deeply cocooned in eider sleeping-bags, the last candle blown out, each, almost instantly, fell into profound untroubled sleep.

This deep, noisy snoring sleep continued until the back of three, that dark time when the tide of human life is at its lowest, most vulnerable ebb. This time of body and mind's least resistance had been frequently used by Hitler's Gestapo and Stalin's K.G.B. as they ruthlessly rounded–up their real or suspected victims.

However these three, crammed into that high tent were awakened at this un-Godly hour not by the thuggish thud of jackboots or the bone-shattering smash of sadistic truncheons but by the silent deadly menace of freezing, creeping cold.

With ruthless stealthy purpose the snow's savage cold effortlessly crept through groundsheets and layered paper's puny insulation then insinuated itself through eiderdown's defeated barrier. Disdaining their many-layered clothes, that cold snaked its slithery stealth along tingling nerves, down shivery muscles, then buried itself deep in the marrow of thickest bones.

Auld Dave's plaintive voice was the first to break the solemn dark silence, 'Och, I'm bloody well frozen stiff! How about you lads, how are you doing?'

Podge and Bob assured him they were freezing as well. 'Well let's light some candles then make some hot, rum-laced coffee to keep the cold at bay.'

Later, once all mugs were drained and all candles blown out, they again settled down into the rum-increased snugness of sleeping-bags, gloves and ex-army balaclavas while their rum-laced blood volcanically flowed and urged them to deep, rum-induced sleep.

As dawn's bright light spread its pleasant message over the glowing summit of Scotland's highest mountain these rum-drowsy climbers welcomed its promise of another day of perfect frosty calm.

Two primus stoves were lit, two dixies packed with ample snow. Podge had intended to make scrambled eggs for breakfast but, finding the eggs frozen solid, he boiled them instead, allowing many extra minutes for them to unfreeze in the more or less boiling water.

Once the tent and all other gear were packed up they nobly resisted the temptation to do what was done when The Ben's summit observatory and small hotel were in use and throw the empty bottles and other rubbish down the handy Gardyloo Gully. Leaving no litter, they carried all rubbish down to the Youth Hostel's bins where Dave laughingly remarked, 'This good deed should earn us some extra Boy Scout points.'

That night, after the marrow-freezing stealth of The Ben's snowy summit, the Youth Hostel's simple ex-army bunks seemed havens of warm decadent luxury.

# Climbing the Aonach Eagach Ridge

Despite the utmost efforts of our sleeping-bags' eiderdown luxury we had spent an uneasy sleepless night in the freezing discomfort of Cameron's Barn at Altnafeadh at the East end of Glencoe. As we shivered through this frost-keen night of late January, we could well understand why farmer Cameron had refused to house his precious cattle in this ice-box of a byre. The byre was built pre-war, when the grand new road came bravely marching through Glencoe. All the latest materials were used in its construction: a solid concrete floor, walls of large concrete blocks, a strong roof of corrugated iron. While purpose built to withstand the fiercest Highland weather it was also unwittingly designed to gather in and tenaciously hold the worst of winter's freezing cold in its concrete and metal. Even the low walls that divide the cattle stalls, that are now climbers dossing quarters, are not made of warm wood, but of thin slabs of concrete.

Something else that added to the sleepless discomfort of that night for Gordon Nicol, Bob Scott and other members of their Lomond Mountaineering Club was the frequent need to get up and go out into the surrounding snow and pee. For another disadvantage of this Cameron's Barn was its all too tempting proximity to the fleshpot of Kingshouse Hotel and its endless flow of irresistible beer.

The glowing brightness of morning sunshine on fresh snow persuaded these two slightly hung-over sluggish young climbers to crawl out of their not fully effective sleeping-bags, grab some breakfast, then, belatedly follow the more abstemious climbers who had set out to climb the long, narrow, snow-plastered Aonach Eagach Ridge more than an hour before.

Bob and Gordon exchanged wry smiles as their uplifted hands shaded their rather bleary eyes from the sun's snow-reflecting glow. Like most climbers, and even skiers, in these post-war years they had no sun-goggles. Nor did they have any crampons. Again these things were only fairly rarely used, and then only on the severest ice-climbs on Scotland's most challenging gullies. Despite their slightly jaded state they were full of a confident youthful keenness that assured them that their faithful old ex-army ice-axes and their grand gripping Commando-soled boots would again see them through yet another wonderful day of snow-climbing.

Of course they were experienced enough to know that one advantage of leaving this bothy a bit later was the fact that these earlier climbers would have blazed the trail through this thick soft two day old snow. They would merely have to follow in these obvious tracks.

'Come on, better get cracking,' Gordon said. 'We don't want to keep auld Annie waiting any longer, do we?'

'No we don't,' Bob grinned. 'If good old gentlemanly polite Lawrie was here he'd reprimand us for keeping that old lady waiting.' For many young Glasgow climbers the Aonach Eagach ridge had been re-named, 'Annie's Eager ridge.'

They eagerly start out through the pre-ploughed snowy track that led directly from the bothy to the Eastern start of this five mile long 'Notched Ridge' that true to its name, was well notched with challenging pinnacles and sharp steep peaks, all now generously covered in bright glittering snow. Under these conditions this was considered one of Scotland's finest winter ridges.

Quickly getting into their easy, mile-devouring stride it does not take them long to reach their first easy peak, Am Bodach (The Old Man), is he perhaps the husband of eager Annie?

As they continue along in that clear snow-track it leads them by a detached small tower to the narrow exposed ridge of 'The Chancellor' and, also guided by the remains of a rusty fence, poking through the snow, they are soon on the broad peak of Meall Dearg.

As they reach the crux of this glorious bristling ridge, the ragged jagged steeps of the snow-plastered Pinnacles, they see, and soon catch up with a group of nine climbers. They are arranged in three roped parties of three. Each party is led by older more experienced men while the six being led seem little more than boys. All are well equipped with crampons, ice-axes, new nylon ropes and bulky rucksacks. The three leaders are members of an Edinburgh climbing club and are instructing these youths in the skills of safe, winter climbing. Even though they come from Edinburgh, they return Gordon's and Bob's cheery greetings with equal friendly warmth.

Rather surprised at these two young Glasgow climbers lack of, what he considers absolutely necessary safety gear, the oldest Edinburgh leader said, 'Just you two lads push on ahead of us. Obviously you're travelling much lighter and faster than us. Just be careful how you go.'

Carried away by the carefree exhilaration of this challenging long ridge's snowy bliss they laughingly reply, 'Aye, right, thanks, that's exactly that we'll do. Aye, and don't worry, we will be careful.'

Revelling in the narrow steepness of this sun-glowing ridge, Bob and Gordon make quick progress climbing up over the top of the largest pinnacles and scouting around the many smaller ones. In many places, instead of strictly following the already blazed snow-trail, they break away and eagerly pioneer their own daring new snowy routes.

Exultantly they continue on towards the West and are blessed by the cloudless sunshine glowing on their beaming faces. They gaze with wordless awe down the steep gash that is the formidable Clachaig Gully which so far has only been rarely climbed. Far below, neatly tucked away in the depth of Glencoe, they spot the Clachaig Inn, that magnet that has occasionally tempted foolish droothie climbers to try a short-cut down the rough, steep, vegetative gully and have their lives cut short, or be at least miserably be-nighted.

Although keen to get to the Clachaig Inn, Gordon and Bob wisely take the regular route that leads them down the easy Westerly ridge which points directly to the isolated Pap of Glencoe.

Pausing outside the front door of the Inn they smile as they again see the notice set boldly above the door: 'No Hawkers, Tinkers or Campbells served here!'

This was the way the MacDonald owner of this Inn kept his hatred of the murdering Campbells alive some 250 years after their treacherous massacre of the Glencoe MacDonalds.

Thinking of their climbing pal, George (Podge) Morrice who was not with them this weekend, but was busy eagerly courting his girlfriend, Margaret Campbell, Bob laughed, 'The sooner Podge marries Margaret and replaces her Campbell name by bestowing his own name on her the sooner she will be able to get served in this Campbell-hating Inn.'

Entering the Inn they meet up with their climbing club friends who had been ahead, blazing the trail before them. These earlier climbers mockingly laugh, 'Must have been an easy day for you two. We'd done all the hard work before you got there!'

'But,' Gordon smiled, 'in lots of places – and especially the most dangerous bits – we left your trail and forged our own much more interesting and testing route through the thick snow.'

All these happy climbers now agree that this has been a perfect day of wondrous snow-climbing on that perfect Aonach Eagach Ridge.

As arranged, their hired bus collected them at the Inn, took them back through Glencoe to their Cameron's Barn Bothy, waited as they grabbed some food, then returned them to Glasgow's dark dreich foggy misery.

# Companions of the Night

From the silence above, as I, Gordon, climbed up the stairs, I knew I'd be having no human company tonight. This was in Paterson's barn in Arrochar, a popular bothy haunt of week-enders from Glasgow, and usually it would be packed, but not this evening. Ah well, I could do without conversation for one night, I'd be back in town tomorrow for work the next day. Bob Scott, on the other hand would probably be at the doss in Coiregrogain, near Loch Sloy, on his way to Ben Alder cottage for a week's holiday. We'd had a good day's climbing on the Brack, a 2,400 ft hill on the western slopes of the Rest and be Thankful. It was a hill we hadn't been on before and gave wonderful views over Loch Long to Ben Lomond and beyond.

But for now, I needed a 'drum-up', making use of the one 'luxury' the barn possessed, a table. Admittedly, it was only a frame with some planks nailed across it, but, by the stains and melted candle-wax on its surface, it was obviously well-used by visiting week-enders. I took out my trusty old Primus stove, tightened up the valve, and pumped up the pressure. There was a roar as I put a match to the spray and my stove was ready for action. There was no doubting the efficacy of the Primus brand, Amundsen had used them on his way to the South Pole, so they were certainly adequate enough for the wilds of Arrochar. Mine, because I had enlarged the jet, was capable of boiling a pint of water in a minute flat. They had their disadvantages however, being quite heavy and sometimes leaked, leaving the contents of your rucksack smelling of and the food tasting of paraffin. They were also potentially dangerous, especially if one returned slightly befuddled from the pub, as a careless kicking over, converted your cooking device into a lethal flame-thrower. This happened to us once in the Arrochar caves (see an earlier chapter).

I drank my mug of tea and munched my supper-time biscuits in the silence created by turning off my stove. The sound, the heat, the light given off by the Primus were somehow comforting, even companionable, but now in the quietness, I might as well get some sleep. It took under five minutes after I had blown out the candle, before the scrabble of little feet could be heard running across the wooden floor. Nothing new here, they were the permanent residents, and besides, my food was in my rucksack hanging from a nail, out of reach, in the rafters. It was when I felt a tickling in my ear and heard a sniffing sound very close by that I shot up, switching on my torch. As I swung the beam round, half a dozen pairs of eyes glittered back at me. They scuttled off out of range as I shouted and made to throw my enamel mug at them, but I knew they'd be back.

If I wanted to sleep tonight something had to be done. If I could get up off the floor, where they couldn't go, that would be the answer. My torch-light fell on the table. Right, that would at least keep me from contact with them.

Transferring my sleeping-bag on to the table, I clambered up, lay down and blew out the candle once more. A short pause, then the scampering, rustling, gnawing and squealing resumed once again. I'd never get to sleep with this racket. The only thing the bloody rats seemed to be wary of was, light. I can't have my torch on all night but what about candles? With two lit candles at the top of the table and two more at the foot I lay down to see if this tactic might give me peace from my furry foes. For at least five minutes there was silence then, with a scuttle and a scamper, the din began again. I lay, flat on my back, staring up at the sky-light above my head, all four candles flickering in the gloom when, with a shudder, it struck me what I must look like – a laid out corpse surrounded by candles to keep the devil and evil spirits away, never mind bothy rats.

My boots were on, my rucksack packed and I was clattering down the stairs into the night in under a minute. Not a moment longer would I spend in that eerie place. There were always the caves in Glen Loin, just along the valley, but closer, I remembered, there was a doss about 100 yards or so up the hill facing me. It was only a large boulder which had tumbled down the hill and come to rest on two others, but anything was better than the bedlam in the barn.

My torch picked a way up through the tussocks of grass and clumps of heather and soon I neared my shelter. At first glance I thought someone was already sleeping there as a bulky grey shape occupied the space beneath the flat roof so I called out to alert them of my presence. I needn't have bothered. I now saw that the guest in residence was a large, very dead, sheep. I could be spending the rest of the night seeking somewhere more convivial to lie down unless I accepted the inconvenience of sharing my accommodation with this rather bulky, very uncommunicative, deceased, ram. Luckily my unfortunate companion wasn't long dead and I managed to drag him part of the way out of the entrance. The ground, on which he had breathed his last, was fine and dry, so I gratefully unrolled my sleeping-bag, lay down and, undisturbed by lively rats or very dead sheep, slept like a log.

# Hogmanay at Landseer's Bothy

e had all arrived at the correct time at the correct place, so there were no anxious waiting worries over annoying latecomers.

Five rucksacks, five ice-axes and much extra gear were carefully stacked in the back of our hired Ford van. Lawrie Travers, our driver and chief organiser of this Hogmanay outing to Landseer's Bothy, was satisfied by his final check. All was in neat ship-shape order. 'All right, my dear fellows, let's all get in the van and get on our happy way.' Then he was suddenly gentlemanly contrite. Turning to the one 'dear fellow' who was not a real 'fellow,' was in fact an attractive young female, Lawrie smiled, 'Oh, I'm sorry, my dear young Margaret, but it's so unusual, so pleasantly unusual, to have a lady in our rough and ready group of male climbing pals that for a moment I forgot about your most welcome female presence.'

'Oh, that's all right, Lawrie,' Margaret Campbell said. She smiled at her boyfriend, George (Podge) Morrice, 'Podge has warned me not to expect any special favours; I've to fit in to "be one of the boys"; just be one of your happy gang.'

'Aye, I'll set her on the right course,' Podge said. 'I'll keep Maggy happy under my protective wing.'

Not wanting to be left out of this smiling banter, Dave Martin, always susceptible to female charms, gallantly bowed and kissed a surprised Margaret's hand, 'You are most welcome, Margaret, it's great to have a charming lady join our happy band of hoary auld climbers.'

Podge laughed, 'Och, Dave, we're not all "auld and hoary", like you, you ken.'

Dave and Bob Scott clambered into the back of the van and, before Lawrie closed the rear doors on them, Bob asked, 'Have you got the key for the padlock on the Glen Feshie gate with you, Lawrie?'

Patting a zipped pocket on his anorak he beamed, 'Yes, my dear fellow, it's safe in here.' He now got settled in the driver's seat while Margaret and Podge squeezed themselves together in the happy intimacy of the passenger seat.

At this early Saturday hour on the last day of the year there was little traffic about so they soon got clear of the ugly, post-war expanding 'second city of the British Empire'.

Near Auchterarder the three in the front of the van noted, with approval, that signs now pointed not to a most posh hotel at Gleneagles, as they had done pre-war, but to that commandeered building's new use by the National Coal Board, as a centre for miners rest and medical rehabilitation, directly after its wartime use as a military hospital. Margaret was surprised to hear the vigour with which Lawrie approved of this change of use. Misled by his genteel manners, she had thought he might be a real Tory. She was pleased that he, like almost all of Glasgow's climbing and hiking fraternity, was a socialist, with many being well to the left of what they regarded as much too moderate Labour.

When they drove into the heart of the bustling 'fair city' of Perth there was much more traffic on the go. They suffered a slight delay at a minor traffic jam where an accident had blocked a city centre road. As they patiently waited for the traffic to flow, Lawrie said, 'I wonder if I'll live long enough to see this A9, this vital Highland artery, vastly improved with every town and village we now drive through being neatly by-passed?'

From the back of the van Dave's voice rang out with loud passion, 'Och, Lawrie, as I've told you often before, you've nae a chance o' seeing that coming tae pass until we've got oor own free, independent, Scottish nation again. No Westminster government is really interested in spending much on Scotland. You ken that, don't you?'

Before Lawrie could reply, Podge spoke up, 'Aye, that's true, Dave. The only thing Westminster's willing to spend unlimited amounts on is Dounreay Atomic Power Plant. And the only reason for that is to keep that dangerous, potentially disastrous, uncertain Atomic Devilry as far away as possible from London. As General Wolfe of Quebec fame would say if he was alive today and the North of Scotland was contaminated with deadly radio-active dust, *"It was no great matter!"* '

Bob smiled his agreement to Dave's and Podge's sincere sentiments. Podge and Bob had been influenced by older Dave's passionate espousal of

Scottish Nationalism. With him they'd even met that wonderful erratic Union Jack-burning Scottish Nationalist fanatic, Wendy Wood. They'd even been questioned by detectives from Glasgow's Special Branch when they'd raided that weekend hotbed of Scottish Nationalism, the Covenanter's Inn at Aberfoyle. This had been at that exciting time when Scotland's Stone of Destiny had been re-claimed from Westminster Abbey and some post-coronation pillar boxes had come under attack for displaying the false claim of her majesty being Queen Elizabeth the second of Scotland. As there never had been an Elizabeth the First in Scotland how could she be 'The Second'?

As the traffic jam now cleared Lawrie wisely concentrated on his steady reliable driving.

On a long straight stretch of the A9 road North of Perth where he could see the road clear before him Lawrie pulled out to overtake a slow tractor and trailer that had been snailing before him for the last few miles. Just as he was about to slide over in front of the tractor a speeding car rose up from an unseen dip in the road straight in front of him. As Lawrie's urgent brakes savagely gripped, Podge and Margaret braced themselves for a deadly impact. Cocooned in the back of the van Dave and Bob were unaware of any danger until they were violently thrown about.

Van and car halted with bumpers almost touching. The white-faced drivers exchanged weak smiles and pretended to wipe sweat from clammy brows. The tractor-driving old farmer continued on his unconcerned way.

Lawrie stopped at the first suitable place. He smiled, 'That was a bit too close for comfort!'

'Where the hell did that car come from?' asked Podge. 'The road was completely clear ahead of you, wasn't it?'

We learned later that this unseen dip in the long straight road was a notorious accident spot that had claimed a number of lives. Local councillors and M.P's. had long been urging it be rectified before there were any more deaths, as there had almost been just then.

A primus stove was lit and tea brewed up. Lawrie was given a strong, well sweetened mugful. We all praised his driving skills, the wonder of his instant correct reaction to that sudden danger. He modestly accepted our sincere praise then said, 'I suppose what could so easily, so quickly, have been our tragic deaths should make us all the more eager to snatch all we can from precarious Life's all too fleeting glory.'

We all passionately agreed. Dave quoted from our much read, much-loved, 'Hedonistic Bible,' *The Rubaiyat of Omar Khayyam:*
*'One moment in Annihilation's waste,*
*One moment of the well of Life to taste…'*

After half an hour we drove on. We passed through the pleasant wee towns of Dunkeld and Pitlochry then passed Blair Atholl's imposing castle. After the long, slow, engine-straining continuous climb up through Glen Garry, where its recently Hydro-electric vandalised river was a sorry sight, it was pleasant to get a reviving whiff of the Dalwhinnie Distillery's 'angel's breath.'

Then passing a field of sturdy Highland Garrons in Newtonmore we wished them success in their new Scottish sport of pony-trekking on wild Highland hills. At rather dour Kingussie we at last turned off this endless A9 highway and, passing under sad neglected Ruthven Barracks, took the minor road that led direct to Feshiebridge. Thankful that we were nearing the end of our journey, we unlocked the gate that kept the private road to Glenfeshie Lodge strictly closed to unauthorised vehicles.

As our van rumbled at cautious snail's pace across the seeming rather precarious old wooden bridge over the wide, fast flowing River Feshie, our noisy approach startled a grazing herd of red deer stags into a not too alarmed, not too long continued, flight.

'Oh, they're lovely aren't they?' gasped Margaret excitedly. 'That's the biggest herd of stags I've ever seen.'

'Aye, 'Podge eagerly agreed, 'they're real bonny. Especially now they're in amongst those grand auld Scots Pines. I'll make sure I get some braw photos o' them this weekend.'

Lawrie smiled and pointed ahead, 'Now we're truly at journey's end. That must be Landseer's Bothy.'

It was. Or rather it was the derelict house at Ruigh-Aiteachain also known as Landseer's Bothy.

With thankful relief Dave and Bob tumbled out of the crowded quarters in the back of the van and, after stretching cramped limbs and greedily drinking in all that could be seen through dusk's rapid gathering dimness, they helped get all the gear into this fabled bothy which they had heard of, and read about, but had never used. They hoped it would come up to their great expectations. A quick look around its homely comforts assured them that it would. Its roof, windows and doors were securely weatherproof. Its wooden floored main room was well provided with a table and two benches and rough hewn log seat was invitingly set at each side of the open fireplace from which there came the pleasant lingering scent of wood-smoke. In a corner near the fireplace was a generous heap of sawn up dry tree branches, some tinder dry kindling, and crumpled up dry old newspapers.

As he surveyed this welcome scene Lawrie said, 'Whoever last used this bothy certainly left it in great shape. We'll be sure to do the same when we leave here.'

We all wholeheartedly agreed. The table was soon loaded with heaps of food and, it being Hogmanay, many more than our normal ration of bottles of alcohol. Gazing at that groaning table Margaret laughed, 'Thank God we didn't have to carry that huge load all the way along those many miles up Glen Feshie's private road.'

Our five sleeping bags were soon set out in their chosen places in the adjoining snug bedroom. There was extra sleeping space in a loft should any more climbers arrive.

Podge and I left the others to prepare the evening meal while we went to use his latest acquisition, a unique chain-like saw that, rolled up, was only the size of a soup plate, but when uncoiled was transformed into a long, sharp, two-man saw. We did not have to go far to find many fallen old Scots Pines whose time-dried bleached branches would make excellent firewood. With the aid of the freshly risen, almost full moon's glittering glow on newly fallen snow and, when necessary our torches, there was enough light to safely guide us as we worked that savage-toothed saw between us. Then, trip after trip we carried those sawn branches to the bothy's door, until we were halted by news that the meal was ready.

The inside of Landseer's Bothy was now a glorious sight. The entrancing light from a gay array of candles and the flickering glow from the fire's high-leaping flames were brightly reflected and endlessly repeated in numerous bottles and many well filled glasses. With the five of us hungry revellers crowding around that laden table the food and wine soon disappeared and empty wine bottles gained their other noble use, as romantic candle holders.

Later, replete with food and aglow with wine, came perhaps the even greater pleasure of sitting, sprawling or lying around the freshly heaped fire's glowing gregarious warmth and hearing old tales being re-told or, coaxed by memory and coloured by wine and imagination, hear new stories being conjured up; fabulous tales, some of which might even be true, of those hardy characters who tramp Scotland's Bens and Glens and doss in those all too many semi-ruined auld 'Buts and Bens' that are falling into utter decay in this post-war land that now is home, to all too many sheep, and all too few people.

Wise from previous head-throbbing, stomach-churning sad experiences, we all agree not to take much more drink as we cosily wait for the New Year to coming ringing in. We all want to be fit to get up early tomorrow morning and, making the most of our short mid-winter day, get on to some high, sun-bright, snow-sparkling nearby hill.

And so our final pre-midnight nightcap is a modest measure of rum and green ginger, a heart-warming drink that was brought to our ken by Podge, when some of us had camped on the snow-deep summit of Ben Nevis on a previous Hogmanay.

As Podge's tiny, battery-operated wireless chimed the midnight bells five glasses were raised high, five toasts were given and five fine, if unusual, rummy drams were drunk. Margaret and Podge, as befitted a courting couple, tightly hugged and lovingly kissed. Dave, Lawrie and Bob confined their New Year greetings to happy wishes and hearty handshakes; none of us, thank God, went in for over-demonstrative hugging.

Pre-dawn candles were lit the following morning, primus stoves were set hissing, tea and coffee were drummed up, breakfast was made and leisurely eaten. Despite frost's keen sting, the grey-ashed, wood-smoke scented fireplace was ignored. If this room got too cosily snug and warm we might weaken and, enjoying its comforts, leave for the hills foolishly and potentially dangerously, much too late.

As dawn's winter dullness gave reluctant way to sunrise's glittering brightness we congratulated ourselves that we had, with stoic wisdom, refused to be delayed by a tempting fire. Tonight we would all the more keenly bask in our re-lit fire's welcome heat.

Before heading for the high, bright enticing Feshie hills, we had a proper look around our bothy's immediate surroundings in full daylight. We were all immensely impressed. Podge, frantic with his expert camera, and Margaret went stalking after the many seemingly semi-tame stags that alertly, but not alarmed, loitered among the large old Scots Pines, noble survivors of the Ancient Caledonian Forest.

Brightened by clear pure early morning light, that brightness enhanced by the covering of frost bright snow that so merrily sparkled, glittered and danced, each one of those noble old trees put on a brave display of its gnarled trunk's aged grey, its higher branches shining reds and its bottle-green needle's attractive purplish sheen. For some minutes, wonderful, almost silent, awe-struck minutes, we drank in the beauty of this scene.

We all now headed for the hills. Having studied our maps we were all agreed where we were going. In this perfect winter weather we expected to have a perfect day on the Glenfeshie Deer Forest hills that were all new to us and were companions to our more familiar Cairngorm hills

After passing Landseer Bothy we took the narrow path that sauntered past more fine old Scots Pines then, with steep zigzags, led us to Lochan nam Bo and then along the curving wide ridge to the rounded summit of Mullach Clach a' Bhlair. Despite the steepness of that path's ruthless zigzag climb, every step had been a pleasure on an inch or so of fresh snow. As always, it was pleasant to hear each squashing footfall give its quaint distinctive squeak. Then on the frost-gripped higher ridge not one footfall broke through the armour-plated surface. Each boot instead gave that sharp crisp crunch that we loved to hear. It was also reassuring and pleasant to have the reliable sturdy support of our good old ex-army ice-axes.

Then, even up here, not far from the summit cairn, we discovered the remains of another ruin. There were now little more than snowy mounds to show that this had once been a deer-watcher's frugal bothy.

As we all sat and ate and drank we also greedily took in the vast snow-glowing views that endlessly stretched in every direction. The impressive billowing vastness of the Cairngorm plateau was the dominant view. Although it had none of the jagged ruggedness of the Cuillins and other Westerly hills, it still profoundly impressed.

An unhurried descent brought as all pleasantly healthily glowing back to Landseer's Bothy. Podge and Bob again sawed firewood while the other three again got on with cooking.

Soon two more wine bottles became re-invented as candle holders, then again replete, we grouped around the delighted fire's high-leaping flames. Our ruddy, healthy glowing faces glowed even ruddier as the well-tended fire's generous heat forced some of us to sit further back. Again many tales were told and we talked of many things. We might even have talked *of cabbages and Kings; of sealing wax and string*. Our talk of books ranged widely. We all agreed that W.H. Murray's *Mountaineering in Scotland* was a classic; was more or less our inspiring climbing bible. Then somewhere we got from the pure aesthetics of noble mountaineering to much more earthy authors. Dave praised Emile Zola's novel *Germinal* for its vivid harrowing depiction of the miserable lives of French coal miners. Bob, in turn, claimed the novel *Earth* to be Zola's masterpiece. This book truly was crudely earthy as it revealed French peasants in all their filthy misery.

'Oh gosh,' Margaret smiled, 'neither of these books sound like a bundle of laughs, do they?'

'No, my dear, they most certainly do not,' Lawrie agreed. 'I thought Zola's novels were still banned in Britain.'

'Aye, some of them were until quite recently,' Bob said.

Podge smiled at Dave and Bob, 'You two can keep all your erotic novels. I'll go stravaiging all over my Highland Highways and Byways with my favourite author, good auld Seton Gordon. But I can tell you a story about a banned erotic novel too.' He did. He told of how, when serving in the R.A.F. police, he'd been ordered to search an airman's quarters. There were reports that this airman was, for a fee, hiring out a copy of a notorious erotic novel; a novel that was strictly banned in still rather prudish post-war Britain. This novel was D.H. Lawrence's *Lady Chatterley's Lover*. Podge had found this book hidden under a mattress. This airman was put on a charge and the novel confiscated and ordered to be destroyed.

'And was it destroyed?' Dave asked.

'Oh aye,' Podge laughed, 'it was destroyed all right, but only after it had been avidly read by me and all the other R.A.F. police at the airbase!'

'And was Lady Chatterley really a very shocking lady?' Margaret asked once the laughter died down. 'Does that book still deserve to be banned in Britain?'

'Oh aye, it really was quite shocking for a book that's supposed to be a great work of literature. I can well understand why the Archbishop of Westminster does not want it to be widely available to corrupt innocent maidens and put erotic thoughts into the minds of pimply youths.'

'Och that's all very well, Podge, but you enjoyed reading it yourself, didn't you?' Dave asked. 'I seem to remember you telling me that.'

Giving a rueful grin Podge admitted, 'Aye, I did enjoy it, or at least certain parts of it. Some pages were real eye-openers.'

The talk and laughter continued on until drowsy heads began to droop and we agreed it was time for our final nightcap of rum and green ginger and then to sleep. We planned to be up early in the morning for our long return journey to Glasgow.

As we all held aloft modest measures of our heart-warming drink, Lawrie proposed a toast, 'Here's to this perfect Hogmanay weekend in this perfect Landseer's Bothy with such perfect friends.'

With deep sincerity all echoed that toast then quaffed the last of the glorious rum and green ginger.

# Crossing Rannoch Moor

This was another thing we had often thought about, talked about, and even dreamt about: of hiking across part of that huge desolate peaty waste that was Rannoch Moor.

This tree-less wilderness of black peat hags, of dangerous deep bogs and gaunt moors of old, thick, wiry heather more or less stretched from Corrour Railway Station in the North almost to the Black Mount in the South, while the Fort William railway line enclosed it in the East, and the fine new road to Glencoe, confined it in the West.

We had first read of this challenging wilderness in Robert Louis Stevenson's grand adventure novel *Kidnapped*. After evading the red-coated Government soldiers in Glencoe this book's two heroes crossed the stark Rannoch moor on their way to the safer shelter of Prince Charlie's Cave on the lower slope of remote Ben Alder.

Gordon and Bob, we 20th century lesser heroes, would, after a fine climbing weekend in Glencoe with other Lomond Mountaineering Club friends, set out from Kingshouse Hotel to cross that daunting moor early on Monday morning. We would make the most of our two extra holiday days and on the Tuesday afternoon get a train at Rannoch Station to take us back to Glasgow. We would, if all went as planned, have spent a comfortable, although illegal, Monday night in one of the cosy, wee railway bothies we had, in strict confidence, been told about.

And, at first, all did go as planned. After seeing our friends off in their Glasgow-bound bus, we returned to Glencoe's Cameron's Barn to spend a further reasonably comfortable night in that chilly bothy. At least at this third weekend in March there did seem some hint of the warmth of Spring in the air and so this well-used bothy's concrete walls and corrugated iron roof were not coated with a sheen of fine ice as they had been in our last stay here in January.

Early the following morning, we nobly resisted the tempting aromas of sizzling breakfast bacon coming from Kingshouse Hotel's kitchen window, and pressed onward on the track that led to Black Corries Lodge. A lesser track led us on for a while beyond that old shooting-lodge and then we faced a pathless waste that stretched from dark, stark, Blackwater Loch to Stob Na Cruaiche's uninviting Black Corries that, with grim tenacity, held large patches of old ugly, yellowed snow in their sullen, North-facing corries.

After checking the map, our compasses and our watches we pressed on; we were well on time and well into our eagerly planned moor-crossing route

Although dull and overcast, this March morning had been quite mild at dawn when we had breakfasted, rolled-up our sleeping-bags, packed our rucksacks and left our Glencoe bothy, but now we both noticed a definite drop in the temperature as a rising wind set in from the East and thrust a decidedly icy chill into our faces. With some apprehension we also noted a solid dark mass of ugly black clouds that the increasing wind seemed to be surging in our direction.

We decided to press on with increased speed. But the more we tried to hurry the more this primitive landscape seemed, with devilish delight, to thrust dark obstacles in our way.

This entire Rannoch Moor was a vast graveyard of auld Scots Pines. Centuries ago these trees must have been an inspiring sight, part of the ancient Caledonian Forest that grandly clad all the Scottish Highlands. In a few notable places these ancient trees lived on, but not here. All that remained here were the countless stumps and tangled roots of long dead trees preserved in their dark mummified state by the moor's endless waste of boggy oozing peat.

The further we advanced towards the East the more of these ugly peat hags and stark, treacle-black bottomless bogs we came across and had to precariously time-wasting negotiate while these straggling roots of dead Scots Pines seem to malignantly reach and snatch and grasp our feet and legs like haggish auld witches or like slimy pre-historic monsters reaching out with ugly scaly claws.

Bob had often wandered by himself, had excitedly explored and rejoicingly discovered grand new parts of the Scottish Highlands and he never then felt in any way lessened, never felt any greater fear for being alone on top of wild Bens and the depths of rugged Glens, had indeed on some awed, almost mystic uplifting occasions been glad to be free to explore his deepest emotions by himself. But here today on this relentless endless waste of peat, bog, and mummified auld trees he was truly thankful he was not on his own. He delighted in having Gordon's cheery company, who agreed with Bob; this dark moor's endless deadness could become overpoweringly depressing if one faced it alone.

Suddenly we faced another, possibly a much more real threat of death than these half imagined dark dangers, as a savage blizzard slashed in from the East. With gasping urgency we continued on into the thick of this fierce storm.

As an ugly mixture of freezing snow and blinding sleet was driven into our numbed faces by a now almost gale force wind we forced ourselves to keep an alert look out for swallowing bogs and deep black peat hags while trying to shelter our storm-assaulted half-closed eyes by lowering chins to chests.

Wordlessly gasping, we struggled on, directly into this malevolent storm while ever thicker snow took over from the uncertain sleet and sent its keen searching fingers into even the slightest weakness of our tightly fastened clothes and, delighting in exploiting gaps at our anorak's neck and sleeves, making its triumphant entry and relentless torturing us with its soaking shivering misery.

But still Gordon and Bob silently continue on. Neither wants to be the first to articulate their secret strong doubts about the wisdom of continuing on into this seeming endless fierce blizzard.

At last Bob halts and with real relief turns his back to this relentless storm. Gordon does the same. Their eyes meet and they manage to grin. 'Well,' Bob says, 'surely this must be decision time. I reckon we've come slightly more than half way. Should we press on into this damn storm until we reach the railway track and the bliss of a railway bothy as planned? Or should we give up on that and return to Glencoe's Kingshouse Hotel? That way we'd have the blizzard's driving snow at our backs instead of slashing into our faces.'

'You think we've come more than half way? Gordon asked.

'Aye, I feel pretty sure we have.'

'Och well, in that case it would surely be a real shame to give up and turn back now. I think we should push on for the railway bothy, despite this bloody blizzard. Do you feel up to it, Bob? Do you think you'd manage to make it?'

Again Bob grinned, 'Och aye, I'm sure I'll manage it. I'll prove I'm as fit as you, even though you're a couple of years younger than me.'

And so we pushed on direct into that choking, soaking, blinding blizzard. Probably we were youthfully foolish. Almost certainly we should have turned back and returned to Kingshouse and have had this blizzard battering at our backs. Surely better to endure the ignominy of a defeated retreat rather than collapse exhausted and lose our lives.

Pausing only to often check these compass bearings we had wisely taken before this blinding storm set in, we struggled on for almost another two hours. By then we were both almost on our knees!

On the last part of this route we fortunately came across far fewer menacing peat bogs or black peat hags to confuse and delay us as we searched for safe ways around them while being viciously battered and near blinded by this relentless blizzard.

Then the auld Pagan Gods of this desolate ancient waste-land relented.

When we were almost at our last gasp they kindly let us, quite literally, stumble over our eagerly sought snow-covered railway track. Both smiled, both gasped, 'Thank God!'

Now one final vital question: which way to the nearest life-saving bothy? We knew there were quite a number of these cosy wee railway bothies positioned along by desolate Rannoch Moor's remote railway line. They were railway linesmen's much needed basic shelters that had saved more than one railwayman's life when they'd been benighted in one, miles from the nearest railway station, by the sudden fierceness of a January blizzard.

We soon decided we'd head South-wards along this reliable guiding railway line. While we were greatly cheered by the hope of quickly finding a wee bothy, we also greatly enjoyed the immense relief of no longer battling directly into this blizzard but having it battering at our left sides while we eased our numbed, anorak-cowled faces towards the right.

Once again we fervently thank our ancient Pagan Gods as a wee railway bothy sudden looms through the snow's blinding white and early dusk dimming light.

With freezing fingers we eagerly light cheerful candles. We rejoice to see what we remembered hearing being rapturously described – a neat wee iron stove. Our spirits further soar as we find the stove neatly set with papers, fine chopped kindling and well-placed small coals. It's easy to imagine that that fine wee stove, impatiently waiting, is just as eager as us for it to roar into joyous life at the touch of our match.

And it did, with the help of the blizzard's howling wind it well and truly roared to heart-warming life. The more that glorious stove roared the more our spirits soared. And there was no shortage of replenishing coals. A wooden corner bunker was high heaped with regular sized lumps of gleaming black gold, and we had also noted a large, partially snow covered mound of more coal outside the bothy door.

Exchanging beaming grins we expressed our delight that grand old Steam Trains still ply this romantic West Highland Line; that – at least not in the near future – there seems no fear of those historic old coal-guzzlers being superseded by perhaps more efficient, but the ugly unromantic Diesel Trains. Although this line, like all of Britain's extensive rail network, had been Nationalised and transmogrified into British Railways, to us, and to all those who worked on, or used this line it would always remain a grand route of steam, smoke and soot, a jewel in the crown of good old, ever-reliable L.M.S (London, Midland & Scottish) railway company.

The more we thrust ever more of our looted railway coals into this railway bothy's grand wee iron stove the more we heart-felt praise the L.M.S's great Steam Trains. Before too long this most efficient wee stove was glowing almost red-hot while the large L.M.S. kettle on it was exultantly rejoicing with its spout's hissing steam and its trembling lid's rattling din. We had been amazed at how many handfuls of snow had to be packed into that kettle to produce boiling water.

We too, were exultantly rejoicing. And we truly had many reasons to rejoice. First and foremost there was the life-saving warmth and shelter of this great wee bothy. There was the true luxury of now wearing dry warm clothes after quickly changing out of the snow-soaked clothes that were now hanging and dripping from rafters and ropes above the glorious hot stove. These steamy anoraks, trousers, shirts and thick woolly stockings were happily creating an atmosphere as cosy and cheery as a Glasgow Wash-House Steamie! And we heartily rejoice that our good old ex-army rucksacks had also kept our sleeping-bags quite dry.

Soon the bothy's wee table is happily crowded with our keenly anticipated simple, but delightful, evening meal. Then our very modest wee bottle of whisky is produced, is opened, is carefully poured, is eagerly gulped, and sincerely praised for its heart-warming glow. Shared memories again flow; happy old tales are re-told. We again toast these great Victorian engineers who undaunted, struggled to conquer this soggy boggy Rannoch Moor with their vast rafts of countless trees that at last kept their forever sinking railway line afloat. But most of all we heart-felt praise them for providing us with this life-saving railway bothy complete with its gregarious roaring wee stove and all that great abundance of free railway coals.

We agree that the least we can do in return is to leave the stove as we found it. Before we depart for Rannoch Railway Station tomorrow morning we will re-set it with papers, kindling and small coals, ready for its next user to set a match to.

As we drink off our last wee dram and hear the blizzard's unceasing howling we also whole-heartedly agree that, as Bob wrote in his poem about us 20th century adventurers:

> *We would not exchange our humble wee bothy's cosy bliss*
> *for any luxurious Savoy or Ritz…*
> *pampered luxury can not beat this!*

# Our Climbing Club's First Deaths

### (In memory of Johnny Harvey)

**W**ith justifiable pride, middle-aged Johnny Harvey thought back to that far-off pre-war year of 1932 when he formed one of the first, and one of the best, of Glasgow's new working-class climbing clubs. He was proud that his inspired creation, The Lomond Mountaineering Club, having survived the war that had brought about the demise of other climbing clubs, was still going strong in these more hopeful bright new post-war years; was indeed going from strength to strength. There had been a most welcome recent injection of fresh young blood. Six, keen 'Young Lomond Tigers,' were achieving things on the severest new rock routes that were being put up at the time, by hardy Creag Dhu pioneers. This latter club began inviting the young Lomonds to share Jacksonville and even to be climbing partners on the occasional route. This was seen to be part of the process of vetting new, potential members, an honour extended to the rare few. An invitation to join this elite band was considered to be perhaps the greatest accolade in Scottish climbing. To his immense pleasure his 'Young Tigers' remained faithful to Johnny Harvey's beloved Lomond Club and brought most welcome new prestige to the club that had been in danger of becoming rather dull, plodding and middle-aged, with most members being mere hill-walkers rather than real adventurers taking risks and proving skills on severe summer rock and savage winter ice.

Thinking back through the long, grim, weary war years to the hardly less grim pre-war years of the Great Depression, Johnny once again felt he could be truly proud of his fine achievement of forming this grand working-class climbing club under these unfavourable conditions. Glasgow – 'The British Empire's Second City' – was feeling the first full terrible effects of 1929's Wall Street Crash that was sending the entire Capitalist System into fear, despair, and that desperate world-wide Deep Depression that had closed down many famous Clydeside shipyards. It would keep them closed until a belated naval re-arming programme and then the outbreak of the Second World War only twenty years after the end of the 'War to end all Wars' brought them back into urgent production.

Yes, it had been grand in these terrible depressing pre-war years for him, through his great club, to help some of the brightest, most adventurous, most imaginative young men (and a few more notable women) to gain the healthy freedom of their fine Scottish hills with like-minded climbing friends.

Yes, there had been many really great, hugely rewarding climbing weekends in these well remembered years when on summer's challenging new rock routes or under winter's ever changing icy grip they had discovered something of what the hills and all-encompassing wider Nature could give.

So for these happy climbing weekends they almost forgot the dire effects of mass unemployment, the crushing means-tested poverty, the cruel hunger that often verged on real starvation.

It was little wonder that practically all the Lomond Club members were politically alert and active, were well to the left of the Labour Party that seemed to have lost much of the ardent fire of the Socialist beliefs of its Red Clydeside founding fathers. Some – taken in by clever Soviet propaganda – fervently wished they could live in Stalin's rose-tinted workers' paradise.

Yes, these climbing weekends had been grand escapes from the Great Depression's pressing problems, although there had been no complete escape, for how passionately the curse of poverty and the ever increasing menace of Hitler's and Mussolini's rise to power had been discussed around the frontal heat and the chilled back shivering of many a high flaming mid-winter camp fire, or when huddled with hopeful outstretched hands at some mountain bothy's pathetic suggestion of a warming fire in a wild, cold, tree-less Highland landscape.

Johnny took further justifiable pride in the fact that during his club's twenty five years of life he had been its President. At each annual general meeting he offered to resign his proud presidency to allow any who thought they could guide the Lomond Club better than him to do so, but no one wanted to remove him from his unique position. Indeed with each passing year there were even louder cheers and more thunderous applause as he was once again confirmed as this club's one and only President.

As he prepared his 25th presidential speech he promised in it he really would resign once he'd completed his 30th year as President. Looking back, he thought of the pre-war years when he with his Lomond Club was the first to pioneer the hiring of buses for weekend climbing. In those, car-less years these unique buses had been a godsend that provided quick, easy, cheap and warmly convivial transport to the wondrous Scottish hills.

Johnny found a gem in one bus owner who became their most constant weekend driver and a hardy, good-hearted friend. He, Charlie MacAteer, was known as 'Flee-on' in recognition of his bus's eager speed and the dauntless way he flew head on at the fiercest challenging conditions of drifting snow or slippery ice. After a few pleasant weekend trips with the Lomond Club he proudly named his bus 'The Mountaineer'.

'The Mountaineer' even managed some weekend trips during the early part of the Second World War, but when the German U-boats ever more deadly toll of Britain's vital oil tankers, made petrol a very scare, strictly rationed commodity, even Charlie could no longer 'Flee-on' and 'The Mountaineer' was laid up, to patiently wait for Peace to return.

Returning to preparing his 25th presidential speech Johnny remembered something he must mention, something that also made him proud. The uplifting fact was that in all these 25 years of his club's existence not one member had suffered a fatal accident on their beloved Scottish hills.

But did his proud (almost boastful?) mention of this happy fact, tempt Fate?

For, shortly afterwards, came sudden disaster! Not just one, but two, Lomond club members died on those hills they had loved.

What made those two deaths worse was that it had not been two 'Young Lomond Tigers' who had died testing their skill and nerve on difficult and dangerous rock climbs or ever dicier ice. Such deaths would be deeply sad, but would hardly be surprising.

Cruel Death's two victims were not rock or ice climbers; and, far from being 'Young Tigers,' were more-or-less middle-aged, almost sedate, lady hill-walkers. Although they'd been winter walking on the deep-snowed high Cairngorm Plateau, still they should have been quite safe. They had been experienced, had been well clad and equipped, complete with good old ex-army ice-axes.

That ever present, ever threatening danger of a sudden change in the winter weather, seemed to be the cause of these two tragic deaths.

A deadly combination of a strange unsure hazy light and of a sudden densely thick onslaught of blinding snow must have obscured their way and these two lady companions had veered away off their route and, struggling blindly through this white-out, had started down a thick snow slope that with deadly suddenness plunged from easy gradient to hidden precipice. They had helplessly slid over that deadly cliff.

That sudden blinding local blizzard only lasted a short time. Bright sunshine soon returned and guided two other Lomond Club climbers, who had wisely sat out that storm, along the still visible snowy track these two lady climbers had left. With dismayed alarm these experienced climbers saw these tracks veer away from the safe route and plunge straight down to where they were almost certain, was an unseen cliff.

Retracing their tracks they made a swift safe way down an easy slope that brought them round by the base of these cliffs. There, smashed against savage rocks, they found the two dead bodies.

Urgently returning to their Loch Morlich camp they broke the tragic news. The Aviermore police were informed. The necessary procedures were set in motion.

In these early post-war years proper mountain-rescue teams were not yet fully organised and there were very few rescue helicopters. In the most remote Highland areas local gamekeepers and shepherds were often called upon to find, and then carry back, injured climbers. Or they willingly took on the much grimmer task of carrying back dead climbers' frozen bodies.

But on this sad occasion not much local assistance was required. Instead of returning to Glasgow that Sunday evening on their hired bus all the Lomond Club members here for this Cairngorm weekend, stayed on, and the following day, they solemnly carried back their two dead club members.

These two tragic deaths overshadowed the Lomond Club's 25th annual general meeting. Poor Johnny Harvey could no longer be proud that his club had had no fatalities on the Scottish hills during all these years. But still, as these club members unanimously agreed, these truly tragic deaths in no way diminished the notable achievements of their club through all these many years.

Again they unanimously agreed that the last thing these two dead lady members would want would be for their sad deaths to curtail the fine activities of this club they had loved.

And so, after remembering them with two minutes of solemn silence and with bowed heads, their annual meeting continued on to other business and more happy hopeful things. As expected, Johnny was re-elected as President. He again promised he *really would* retire on the 30th anniversary of his presidency.

And so Johnny Harvey remained President until death claimed him. Suddenly, savagely, claimed him. He did not die on his beloved Scottish hills, but – surely more cruelly – in Glasgow the victim, of a massive heart-attack.

Johnny would be delighted to know that *His* Lomond Mountaineering Club lives on, though not with *His* wondrous weekend buses, but with today's members arranging their climbing car-meets through the wonders of modern technology.

It would also delight him to learn that while these present club members greatly enjoy their affluent life style – an affluence unimaginable to these pioneering pre-war climbing stalwarts – many of them still seem to love their Scottish hills no less truly passionately deeply, as Johnny's grand pre-war generation had.

# His First Glasgow Climb

Being an extremely keen rock-climber and a member of Glasgow's climbing club, The Lomond Mountaineering Club, Gordon had done many of the severest rock climbs on the Cobbler, the Buachaille and Ben Nevis, but, so far, he had not done any climbs in Glasgow. Should he rectify this omission he wondered as he sat pondering on the stone step of the stairs outside his four-storey high, Ibrox tenement home?

The reason for him sitting here was all too foolishly simple.

Returning this Sunday evening from another grand climbing weekend he'd climbed these all too familiar tenement stairs to discover he'd somewhere, somehow, lost his house-key. And his father who shared this flat with him wasn't in. He would, Gordon knew, be visiting his brother in Johnstone, a social call he made almost every Sunday evening. It would be the best part of two hours before he came home.

'So', Gordon pondered, 'should I get my sleeping-bag out of my rucksack, cocoon myself in it and wait here on this cold stone stair for Dad's return?' There seemed little real alternative. None of his unfriendly near neighbours would think of inviting him in.

Then he had a sudden bright thought, 'Hang on, we never snib the kitchen window. There's no need to. Who's going to try to get in that way?' He gave what he thought might be a crazy answer – 'Me!'

He went through the tenement close to the back court to have a speculative look. Yes, an iron drain-pipe ran all the way up the building, it passed his kitchen window and ended at the roof.

Like the true rock-climber he was, he thought through this possibly dangerous drain-pipe climb before he started. What did he have to watch out for?

(a) Not the verticality, he had been on rock-routes three times as high during many climbing weekends.

(b) A neighbour coming to their kitchen window as he climbed past? Would they believe him as he, desperately clinging on to the rhone-pipe, tried to convince them he really wasn't a cat-burglar? 'I live upstairs, just lost my key!'

(c) Much more important than this was his awareness of the likely fragility of that possibly corroded old drain-pipe and its iron attachments that were securing it to the wall.

If he pulled outwards too much that old pipe was liable to come away in his hands. To be safe he must keep the pressure downwards as he climbed and test how solidly each section was attached to the wall before he cautiously advanced any higher.

Put to this test the greatness of Gordon's climbing skills were again proved.

As he neatly eased himself through the raised kitchen window then clambered over the large, deep, wally sink he murmured, 'Och, that was a lot easier than sitting on the stairs.'

Finding that remark not quite adequate, he added that old, triumphant, war-time saying – 'A piece of cake!'

When his father returned, Gordon did not tell him about his lost key and, most diplomatically, he wisely refrained from mentioning his adventurous, and dangerous, clandestine entry.

Sitting up in bed he eagerly wrote up his climbing diary. What should he name this drain-pipe climb? He decided on *The Tenement Wall*. What to grade it? 'V-diff' made it seem a bit too easy. 'Very Severe' was perhaps going over the score. He finally decided that, considering the rather shoogly state of parts of that old drain-pipe, it, his first Glasgow climb, must surely qualify as a 'Severe'.

As far as Gordon knows, this *Tenement Wall* is not listed in any Scottish climbing guide book.

# Extreme Contrasts

O n this foggy Saturday morning in late November Bob Scott and
Gordon Nicol were sitting in a Drymen – bound bus.

When they reached the upmarket Bearsden, the worst of Glasgow's
thick foggy filth had been left behind. Then, confirming their confident
expectations, at pleasantly sleepy Strathblane the fields and woods frostily
gleamed under a windless, fogless, calm blue sky.

Leaving the bus at Drymen they eagerly head for Loch Lomond's famed
bonnie banks. As they hiked along by that rugged, pine-clad shore the low
winter sun blindingly glared and sprinkled diamonds over the isle-dotted
loch. Sun, loch and hills happily lured them ever further on and to their
bright cheerful young minds it seemed that Ben Lomond's snow-glowing
summit beckoned them – even seemed to welcome them.

At Rowardennan Youth Hostel they meet and warmly greet other
hostellers; some hardy wee Glesca long-distance cyclists; some jaunty kilted
keen striding hikers; some exultant hill-walkers and climbers. Through
their exchanged enthusiastic tales all learn more about this land they all
deeply love.

Once the heaped, hunger appeasing meals are eagerly consumed the
glowing-faced crowd near the huge, furnace–hot iron stove, leave the
kitchen's stifling heat, happy, and replete.

A little later these cheery faces were again set gloriously aglow as a skilled
accordionist guided their feet in lively jigs and wild reels.

Feeling the need for a refreshing breath of pure night air before retiring
to their crowded dormitory, the two friends strolled outside the hostel.
Glorying in the star-bright night's silent calmness Gordon grinned, 'This
profound silence is quite a contrast to all that lively music and frantic
dancing, isn't it?'

Bob returned his grin, 'Aye, it sure is,' after gazing at the billion glittering stars and the dim, frost-gripped landscape, he thoughtfully added, 'I suppose if we're wise we should make the most of these contrasting pleasures; should let the gregarious pleasure of one increase the more introspective (at times almost mystic?) pleasure of the other.'

Gordon smiled, 'Well done, Mr. Scott, spoken like a wise auld sage.'

'Aye, and this most not so auld sage, predicts that this perfect calm frosty weather will last all day tomorrow and we'll have a great day on the Auld Ben.'

As Sunday morning's chilly mists were reluctantly giving up their watery grip on the loch and were tenaciously clinging to phantasmagoric trees, the two pals were eagerly climbing not the main tourist path but an older, rougher, less-used track. They laughed as they again read that warning neatly painted on a small steep slab of smooth rock, *The Granny Stopper*. They could well imagine some cheery Glasgow families, looking like the *Sunday Post's Broons,* being dismayed by that steep rock and the gasping granny thankfully waiting here.

They quickly press on and soon they once again 'conquer' that grand auld Ben which, in turn, once more conquers them with its brilliant silent snow-pure perfection. They stand and exultantly gaze while awed senses are almost overwhelmed by all this widespread beauty. The calm November sky is an endless glow of pure eggshell blue. To the North and West, there appear limitless panoramic glories of snow-clad Highland Hills.

They continue to eagerly stare but decline to turn and look towards the South East. They are all too well aware of what ugliness lies in that direction.

They eventually force themselves to look round, and sure enough, there where Glasgow sprawls, is an appalling sight. The sky's countryside blue has sickened to the filthy misery of a fog-black funereal pall as countless domestic and industrial chimneys spew out their suicidal smoke.

They turn their shrugging backs on that grim city that, quite literally, is an ugly blot on the landscape.

They refuse to let the prospect of this Sunday evening's duty bound return to fog-shrouded Glasgow spoil the immense pleasure they get from Ben Lomond's sun-sparkling snowy purity.

When they do return in the evening's Glasgow bound dejected bus they see even Dumbarton's solid stoic castled Rock has almost disappeared in the ghastly mist ghosting in from the shivering, wide Clyde.

At Clydebank the gaunt walls of roofless, Luftwaffe blitzed tenements gloom through the shrouding fog, more gravestone grey and grimmer than ever.

As the much loved, much polluted, unseen River Clyde gets narrower the filthy fog gets even muckier, ever thicker, and their miserable bus crawls ever slower as Glasgow's ugly urban sprawl seems to spread out further and ever more pervasive. Finally the conductor has to walk and, with his searching torch, guide the snailing bus's fog–blinded driver.

At weary long last Bob and Gordon leave their very late bus and, almost Braille-like, grope their homeward way through traffic-less, even tram-less, fog obscured streets. With smarting eyes, gasping breaths and soot choked nostrils they endure the final awful miles through what is now no mere fog, but a killer, smog that condemns many Glaswegians to an ugly early death.

As they try to hurry their rucksacks' hunch-backed Hyde-like shapes through this blinding smog they stoically talk. Wheezing, they compare the extreme contrasts of this glorious day on snow-pure Ben Lomond with this befouled city's noxious smoggy misery.

They whole-heartedly agree that they really must escape from this man-made Hell; escape not just for more grand weekends, but for ever.

And eventually they did, in their own, very different ways.

# PART TWO

# At Vestey's Beach

'Well, do you feel a bit brighter now?' Bob asked as he watched Gordon eagerly gulp down the last of his second mug of tea.

'Aye, I do. I hate to admit it, but those Temperance fanatics with their praise of tea as "the cup that cheers but does not inebriate," really have got something. Those mugs of char have really revived me after my long weary journey. Of course the large plump trout you caught early this morning were great too. In fact they were the best fish I've ever eaten.'

Bob grinned, 'Och, I don't pretend to be a great cook, but my freshly-caught trout, well fried in my large auld frying pan's mature, oft re-used fat until the trout's tasty crisp skin peels from the succulent pink flesh really are, I honestly think, something very special.'

Gordon laughed, 'Aye, I agree. You are entitled to honestly, if not modestly, say that.'

Gordon's journey today *had* been long and weary. He'd taken a very early morning bus from Glasgow to Inverness; he'd changed buses there. Then at Lairg he'd changed buses again. He'd taken the slow mail bus that stopped at every isolated house on the long, single-lane road from Lairg to Lochinver.

It had been a real relief to be no longer wearily sitting, but to be tramping along the five twisting miles of narrow road that meandered through this truly unique Assynt landscape he was seeing for the first time. His destination was Achmelvich Youth Hostel where his climbing friend, Bob Scott, desperate to get out of Glasgow, had taken the summer job of hostel warden until, a few years later he got a better job as a trainee ghillie and gamekeeper on Assynt Estate.

Making the most of this fine warm June evening's bright lingering cloudless light, Bob and Gordon strolled along Achmelvich Bay. Their progress was slow as Gordon made many stops to gaze in wordless awe at this wondrous coastal scene: the spotless pure shell-sand white of this curving beach; the shimmery sheen of aquamarine where whispering sea and waving weeds meet; the lush green of the machair with its own milky-way of a million smiling daisies; then behind all this endless seemingly innocent bliss there's the sudden shock of the Lewisian Gneiss. Savagely thrusting upwards, these timeless rocks flaunt their contorted tortuous shapes at us and almost seem to growl with solidified thunder.

'Well, Gordon, what do you think of all this? Does it come up to your expectations?'

'Oh aye, of course it does. It's… it's fantastic, really marvellous.' It had been Bob's postcards extolling the unspoilt beauty of the wild landscape of Assynt that had made Gordon decide to visit and see this place with his own eyes.

They leisurely strolled on. 'Would you like a drink?' Bob asked. 'There's a fine wee well down there near Vestey's Beach.'

They lifted the neat wooden lid that protected this special Vestey's well. *We filled the jam-jar with bright nothing and drank down its freezing light* as Bob quoted, Gordon asked, 'Is that from one of your own poems?'

Bob laughed, 'Och no, it's from an even greater poet than me; Norman MacCaig.'

Making their way down to the isolated beauty of Vestey's Beach they passed a large, securely locked, beach chalet. 'I suppose that belongs to the Vesteys too?' Gordon asked.

'Aye, it does. They own almost all of the vast Assynt Estate and they think of this as their private beach.'

'That's a pity; that chalet would make a grand climbers' bothy wouldn't it?'

'Aye, it would, but we don't get many rock climbers coming about here.'

Bob's words were soon proved to be premature!

Being a truly natural rock climber, Gordon's searching gaze instinctively led him to an interesting red outcrop that rose intriguingly from the pure white sands of Vestey's Beach. He decided to climb it.

After a bit of a struggle up the steep lower part he saw a narrow crack offering a possible way to the top. Reaching up for a handhold, his groping fingers encountered something quite unexpected, surely not a piton here? But it was! And the absence of any rust proved it had been hammered in fairly recently. What a puzzle. He got to the top and sat on the grass to think. This mini-cliff was little more than thirty feet high; surely not challenging enough to merit someone equipped with technical climbing aids?

Bob again confirmed that he knew of no hosteller who had been interested in climbing these Achmelvich cliffs.

No matter. Someone's piton loss will be Gordon's piton gain.

So the following morning he borrowed the hostel's coal hammer, went back to Vestey's Beach and on this, the third ascent of the crack (as far as he knew), knocked out the piton and added it to his fairly meagre stock of climbing gear.

Some thirty years later when Gordon and his wife were teaching in Brunei, about as far away from Vestey's Beach as you could get, a possible explanation of who that piton's original owner might have been, emerged.

Gordon was reading *High Endeavours*, the life of Robin Smith, the brilliant Edinburgh climber who tragically fell to his death, aged a mere twenty three, while climbing in the Pamirs. There on page 23 he came across this, *After Skye, Robin headed off to rejoin his family who were now holidaying in Sutherland. It was here, on the rocks of Achmelvich Bay as little as a year ago, that his first scrambles, first hopes, had signalled the birth of his lifelong fascination with climbing.*

The year described was 1954, neatly tying in with Gordon's first visit to Achmelvich. Sometimes mysteries take a long time to be solved.

# Almost Disgraced

How pleasant it was to effortless row this wooden boat over the calm, trout-rich loch then let it guided drift and allow the two youngest grandsons of this estate's owner to cast their favourite trout-flies under their ghillie's watchful and expert guidance.

Especially pleasant for the ghillie was this morning's gentle breeze, warm glittery sunshine and a few high white clouds after his four successive days of long and strenuous deer-stalking under dark louring clouds and gale-driven soaking rains.

At lunch time the two boys with joyous boastfulness display their many plump trout to their white-haired grandmother. After she and the lady with her had given due enthusiastic praise, she addressed the ghillie, 'Oh, Robert, the boys have done excellently well, thank you.' She smiled, 'You've made good use of the landing-net, now how would you like to try using one of Lady Emily's butterfly-nets?'

So it was arranged and after lunch Lady Emily drove Robert in her gleaming dark blue Rolls-Royce to locations along the coast from Lochinver village. This titled aristocratic English lady was an expert entomologist. She was hoping to find a rare butterfly that was usually only found where sea and heather meet.

After unsuccessful searching some distance from the village, Lady Emily and her ghillie were diligently combing the shoreline heather near Lochinver's almost tide-girthed kirk. As he carried the large butterfly net at the ready, Robert furtively glanced around and fervently prayed that none of his hardy climbing pals from Glasgow, now camping at lovely Achmelvich Bay, would appear and see him employed in this sissy way.

All too vividly he imagined how they would react. He could almost hear their cutting remarks, their rude jokes and jeers. With these hardy lads in past years he'd tackled The Cobbler's rock routes, had braved Ben Nevis's exhilarating winter gullies, had on one memorable (and real scary!)

occasion, even done a severe rock climb with one of the less mad of the crazily courageous and often outrageous members of the famous Creagh Dhu climbing club.

Now, after such exciting adventures, was he reduced to this – to fluttering about with a butterfly net? How would he ever look them in the eye? How would he ever live down the disgrace if any of these hardy climbing pals should see him now?

As he continued his diligent search he could not stop thinking that this is quite some come-down from risking life and limb on summer's bare mountain rock and on winter's often decidedly dicey ice.

Then he spied, eagerly chased after, and finally captured not just one, but two of those rare butterflies.

Delighted, Lady Emily loudly exclaimed in a clear, distinctive, la-di-da voice, 'Oh, jolly good show! Oh how clever of you, Robert!'

Again he cast a quick furtive glance; again he was pleased that none of his hardy Glasgow pals were in earshot.

Happy with the success of our hardy intrepid hunting we drive away in Lady Emily's posh Rolls-Royce and turn up the narrow private road to Glen Canisp Shooting Lodge. Rounding a last blind bend her ladyship jams on the brakes and stops as we suddenly meet three of Robert's climbing pals.

Sweaty and dishevelled, they are returning from climbing that fantastic mountain, Suilven. Impressed to see Robert so stately and coolly ensconced in that Rolls-Royce these Glasgow pals obstreperously laugh and cheer, then with mock obsequiousness bow low while, with a wide grin, Robert asks, 'Well, my dear fellows, have you had a good day?'

The nearest one, Gordon, speaks for all, 'Oh yes, Bob, we've had a great, but real sweaty day climbing Suilven, how about you?'

Robert glanced at gentle smiling Lady Emily before he grinned his reply, 'Oh yes, we've had quite a strenuous day too'.

'Have you bagged any beasts today?' Gordon asks.

Again Robert glanced at her quietly amused Ladyship then said, 'Oh yes, Gordon, we got two.'

Lady Emily then drove on while Robert dismissed his old pals with a stately almost Queen Motherly gracious wave and hopefully left them thinking that they'd bagged two stags; had had a strenuous day of strenuously stalking Assynt's wary red deer instead of feebly searching for silly butterflies.

# Doubled Week-end Dangers

These pages tell something of a little known part of Scottish mountaineering history; of these exciting post-war years when Creagh Dhu's finest climbers and the Lomond Club's 'six young tigers' often met together, bothied together, drank together and, although great rivals, sometimes climbed together.

The climbing dangers these two groups shared were suddenly drastically doubled when some of the Creagh Dhu, quickly followed by those Lomond's few, bought motor-bikes. The ensuing reckless weekend races on the old A82 from Glasgow to Glencoe were really quite hairy. The return Sunday journeys, tired after their week-end exertions, were even more exhilarating, thrilling and scary! These mad bikers even invented their own word for those notorious races – their 'habble' where they defied death even more than on the severest rock routes.

The Lomond Club's daring six were joined together in great camaraderie and trusting climbing compatibility. As they became more experienced they formed into regular climbing pairs. At times they climbed with others, but most often Gordon climbed with John Anderson; Alex Shanks with David Johnson (known as 'Big Mur'); Tony Garman with John Eccles.

As each climber's partner had the same level of rock-climbing ability this allowed them to 'lead each other through,' at every climb's belay, with the second on the rope continuing on and taking over as climb leader, rather than having the delay of changing places, at each belay. This made for greater shared enjoyment and much greater speed, even on the severest climbs.

These three teams of young 'Lomond Tigers' were now 'knocking off,' and succeeding in not falling off, many of the Severe and Very Severe rock routes on The Cobbler and Buachaille Etive Mor. In quite a short time they had ticked off, routes like, Whether Wall, Cupid's Groove, Whither

Whether, S-Crack and Punster's, on The Cobbler's North and South peaks. On the Buachaille's fabulous Rannoch Wall, that spectacular airy steep wall of red Rhyolite that occupied many of these keen young climbers day-time thoughts – and some of their night-time dreams too, dreams that could wander into vivid nightmares – they again were successful on routes like, Red Slab, January Jigsaw, Satan's Slit, Whortleberry Wall and Fracture Route. And they continued to add other 'conquered,' climbs to this impressive list.

A lot of this success was due to the frequency of their visits to these supreme climbing locations brought about by their purchase and use of powerful motor-bikes.

Tony Garman's second-hand Rudge Ulster was the first bike bought. Alex Shanks soon followed suit by buying a second-hand Royal Enfield. These purchases were capped by Big Mur's acquisition of a brand new Triumph Tiger 110.

Now the six of them could leave Glasgow and be 80 miles away in Glencoe, in well under two hours. Bill Smith of the Creagh Dhu was thought to hold the record for doing this journey in the fantastic time of one hour and ten minutes.

This travel by motor-bike was much more than just a fast and more convenient form of transport; it was also amazingly exciting. Roaring up the old Loch Lomond-side road with its countless wild bends in a vain attempt to keep up with the speed of the likes of Bill Smith, and Mick Noon, was an incredible adrenalin rush. Speed added another layer of danger to their already high-risk, rock-climbing past-time.

Quite frequently a wet patch or a misjudged angle on a bend would have them sliding and skidding along the road relying on their primitive protective gear of Harris tweed bunnets which, firmly pulled on with skip to the back, usually stayed on even at the highest speeds, and their below-the-knee raincoats to keep them from injury.

Once when Gordon was on the pillion of a different bike, one belonging to Sandy Crawford, another Creagh Dhu lad, on the way to Arrochar, they leant over to take the bend just beyond Tarbet Hotel in true Isle of Man T.T. style, only to crash down as the bike shot from under them. The impatient bike continued on its rider-less way up the road leaving these dazed two sprawling on the tarmac behind it. Sandy picked himself up and ran after his precious bike leaving Gordon in a still spinning daze by the side of the road.

'I had to make sure my bike was O.K. first,' Sandy said when he returned. 'There are always plenty of blokes to climb with, but that bike cost me an awful lot of money.'

On another occasion Gordon was on Big Mur's bike at a set of traffic lights on Glasgow's Great Western Road and what should have been a patient wait turned into abject embarrassment. A bus full of Rangers football supporters pulled up alongside them and all in that blue and white bus gazed down at them. Gordon and Mur imagined they must make an impressive sight; the big, powerful, shiny motor-bike purring away, the rucksacks with climbing ropes stuck through the flaps; two daring climbers off on a dangerous adventure.

But this pride came before a fall.

As he waited for the lights to change, Big Mur leaned over to look at something low down on his bike. Gordon, curious, did the same. The next moment they toppled over and lay under the bike. Amazed, foolish, dejected, they stared up at the row of highly amused mocking and jeering faces on the bus.

They exchanged rueful glances then Gordon grinned, 'My God, Mur, if we can't keep our balance on a motionless bike how the hell will we keep our balance on the sheer Rannoch Wall?'

It seemed quite a pertinent question.

It was some small consolation to roar past that mocking bus a few minutes later with Gordon's arm raised and two fingers extended in one of Churchill's famous 'V for Victory' salutes.

These 'Lomond Tigers' and the Creagh Dhu characters fell off their motor-bikes more often than they fell from rock climbs. It was amazing there were no motor-bike deaths and really quite few serious injuries.

In some seven years of climbing Gordon recalled only three serious accidents involving his friends.

Once John Eccles and Tony Garman were attempting a new route on the line, which was later to be called Centurion, on Carn Mor Dearg Buttress of Ben Nevis when Eccles pulled up on a large rock flake. Fortunately he was only about sixty feet from the ground when the rock, with Eccles attached, came away from the sheer face. Rock and man instantly parted.

Soft human flesh and all too solid earth violently met. Falling rock met other rock and exploded in a saltpetre gasp of fire and brimstone.

Eccles suffered no worse than a fractured pelvis. He later told his anxious companions he really enjoyed being carried down the hill by the Mountain Rescue Team in a state of euphoria brought on by the pain-killing shot of morphine he'd been given.

Willie Gartshore, also of the Lomond's Club, suffered an identical injury to his pelvis, in a fall on The Cobbler. In an example of press inaccuracy, his story the following day in the *Glasgow Daily Record* was headlined, '*President of the Langside Mountaineering Club injured in fall on Ben Lomond.*' Perhaps the reporter should have checked the veracity of the account given to him by a mischievous young Lomond's climber keen to keep his club's name out of this report.

Another incident showed the importance of the drinking sessions that helped climbers wind down after a hard day on the hill. These events followed on from Charlie Vigano's fall in the Lost Glen area of Glen Coe. This member of the Creagh Dhu had sustained a badly broken ankle and was in considerable pain. Some of the club's lads brought Charlie back to the car-park above Jacksonville in one of the few motor-bike and side-car outfits owned by weekenders at that time.

This was around seven p.m. and coincided with the time when everybody was getting ready to go along to Kingshouse Hotel for the Saturday 'thrash'. Charlie's ankle and lower leg were black and swollen to twice their normal size, but, despite his obvious pain, he insisted on going to the pub rather than being taken to hospital. 'I'm O.K., I'll get my anaesthetic along at the pub,' he declared to those who advised medical treatment. They thought this showed immense fortitude and self-sacrifice in the social interests of his fellow climbers.

The usual boisterous evening ensued but was somewhat marred by the abandonment of the darts match when a loose dart fell from the board and landed point down into the back of an Old English Sheepdog lying sleeping on the floor. The poor beast, whose master owned the hotel, ran howling out into the night, the dart impaled in his back, leaving the players stranded with only two darts.

The dog never again slept under the dart board and it, and Charlie, recovered in due course from their injuries.

The three injured climbers, being young and hardy, soon returned to climb again in these compellingly seductive Highland hills.(These hills that never quite relinquish their grip, even when age and infirmity dictate that decrepit old climbers must view them from well below their summits.)

On one sunny summer's day the six young 'Lomond's Tigers' were camped across the River Coupall from Jacksonville, where the boys of the Creagh Dhu were gathered to re-furbish their bothy. These friendly rivals suggested to the Lomond's six that if they gave a hand to help in this work they might be offered membership of the exclusive Creagh Dhu Club.

After some discussion the temptation of a glorious rock-climbing day on The Buachaille's fabulous Rannoch Wall, compared to hefting lumps of wood and struggling with awkward tarpaulins was too much. The Buachaille won, and besides, could they have trusted the Creagh Dhu about that *almost* promised membership once the work was finished? They'll never know.

Just as this great club only very rarely offered membership to other climbers, so too were they extremely sparing in their praise of rival mountaineers' exploits. So Gordon was surprised and a bit chuffed when Hugh Currie, one of the Creagh Dhu's slightly older, highly respected members approached him near Jacksonville and said, 'I hear you've climbed The Nook, a nice wee route. Well done, Gordon.'

These few words were high praise indeed!

John Cunningham and Mick Noon had only recently first climbed this very severe route up The Cobbler's huge overhanging rock nose on its North Peak. All previous attempts had failed and these outstanding climbers only succeeded through the discreet use of artificial aids.

Gordon and his climbing partner, John Anderson, also completed this climb with the help of pitons and an etrier. Their reasoning was that, 'anything the Creagh Dhu can do we can at least try!'

They went up by the familiar Punster's Crack then on the very exposed and airy *Nook* itself, Gordon hammered in some pitons in the overhanging crack before precariously clinging and reaching up high above his head to hammer in one more piton.

Clipping in a karabiner to this, he used the etrier (a short, four-runged rope-ladder) to move up the crack and round the corner below the dark, grimly-overhanging Ramshead Peak. Another fifteen feet of strenuous climbing and he was safe on the flat, summit rocks.

Once Gordon was safely tied to a secure belay, John came clanging up behind cluttered with removed pitons and etrier, leaving the route clean and clear for the next hopeful candidates.

To complete the day, and to get some practice, they abseiled back down the overhang, admitting that they'd found the launching of themselves out into open space more scary than the testing upward climb.

While pleased at proving they could, if necessary, confidently use artificial climbing aids they agreed that they much preferred their usual free style climbing.

In later years, on more mature reflection, Gordon thought their participation as teenagers in what was, by any standards, a really dangerous past-time gave them an outlook on life which otherwise they might not have had. It trivialised the usual problems teenagers have, and led them to develop greater self-confidence.

They knew the risks they were taking, that the stakes were high, but seldom did they feel they were not up to the task. They were certain that what they were climbing, with a certain amount of care, was well within their capabilities.

Surely the great success of their glorious climbing years proved their youthful confidence was fully justified.

# High Jinks at Jacksonville

On this beautiful warm summer morning a mixed party of the young Creagh Dhu and the Lomond Club's six young 'tigers' were lazing about outside what was a legendary name in post-war Scottish climbing history: Glencoe's Jacksonville Bothy.

The disorganised leisurely playfulness of these apparently slothful youngsters painted a most misleading picture of these young climbers. Soon, as one of them laughingly declared, they would be, with their nerves of pure steel coiled like fine tight springs, risking life and limb on the severest steepest rock climbs on The Buachaille's fabulous Rannoch Wall.

But for now all were at relaxed ease, were enjoying simple, innocent, almost boyish pleasure until one impish wee devil suddenly started his mischief-making game.

Tony Garman, one of the Lomond's six, was crouched at the River Coupall filling his dixie for another brew of tea when Alex Shanks, also of the Lomonds, playfully threw, what he said was 'a small stone', but Tony angrily described as 'a bloody great boulder,' into the water beside him.

The soaked Tony, was instantly transformed from an inoffensive young man into a raging fury, screaming, 'Ya bloody evil wee bastard!'

Poor Alex was appalled by the fury he had fairly innocently unleashed. Before he could abjectly apologise a dixie-full of water was thrown over him.

Alex's volatile mind instantly flashed thoughts of diabolical retaliation. Mumbling dark incantations he hurried into the Jacksonville bothy. He quickly re-appeared with Tony's anorak grasped in one hand.

'Don't you fuckin'dare!' screamed a dripping and frothing Tony.

Undeterred, the bold Alex casually dropped Tony's old, tattered, but highly prized anorak into the bubbling river.

Tony erupted from the water clutching the rescued wet garment in his hand. His eyes glared savage rage as he passed Alex and threw himself through Jacksonville's open doorway.

The other young 'Lomond Tigers' know that, under some stress, Tony can 'lose the place', and they think this silly incident has triggered his flashpoint.

This is soon confirmed as Tony emerges almost hidden by the mountain of Alex's gear he's hugging to his heaving chest. He's got the lot – sleeping-bag, clothes, boots, even rucksack!

Alex realizes that no humble pleading, nor more active intervention, would have any real effect on this transformed demon as he rushes to the river, all the time gurgling almost hysterical giggles.

Alex decides that if that chortling devil finds this so funny, well, two can play at that game. He too dives into Jacksonville. He emerges half-hidden by all of Tony's plundered gear that swiftly joins his own in the river.

The picture in this beautiful Glencoe setting now became rather confused; became a maelstrom of surging foam, high splashing spray, joint hysterical screaming and loud cursing as these, by now half naked, half drowned frantic young climbers urgently run from pool to pool searching for their drowning heavier gear and their gaily floating lighter clothes.

Over the years ancient Glencoe has witnessed much history, but never before had it seen, and heard, the strange spectacle of, now again more or less best friends, Alex and Tony once more making themselves ridiculous objects as they repeatedly thunder up and down the Glencoe road on their powerful motor-bikes in the hope that the sunshine and the speed-made breeze might dry out themselves and their fluttering, tied-on clothes.

★ ★ ★

Some months after this crazy day, the Glencoe road witnessed another weird motor-cycling spectacle.

That weekend Jacksonville was crowded, had room for Creagh Dhu members only, so five of the young Lomonds were dossing in nearby Cameron's Barn.

After a great long day of climbing many demanding routes on the Buachaille's rocky walls, the boys in Cameron's and the characters in Jacksonville were about to set out for their customary Saturday evening session at the Kingshouse Hotel.

The Creagh Dhu decided to walk. Four of the young Lomonds were also thinking of walking when the fifth, Big Mur, announced that he was going on his motor-bike, 'So I can give one of you a lift.'

'Only one? That means you're letting three of your mates walk. You're a selfish big bastard, Mur,' Gordon observed. Then, playing on Big Mur's pride in his powerful motor-cycle, said, 'Surely that bike could easily take more than two of us?'

This strategy worked and so a few minutes later the walking Creag Dhu scattered to each side of the Glencoe road as the strange spectacle of a triumphant Triumph Tiger motor-cycle with all five young Lomonds desperately clinging on to it, came along at a speed of about sixty miles an hour.

The crowded motor-bike flashed passed these, for once upstaged, Creagh Dhu walkers, who suffered a blast of the horn, a roar of jeering voices and a forest of raised 'V' signs. Raucous, but grudging approval was reciprocated from the roadside.

Years later, in 'The Swinging Sixties', when television sets were appearing in most British homes, when the great British Public 'had never had it so good', these still fairly young Lomond veterans were not impressed by a certain highly praised performance at the televised Edinburgh Military Tattoo.

What was certainly the greatest motorcycle display team in the British Army certainly had more than five on one bike in their grand finale, but that lot only travelled at walking-pace and had all the large clear space of Edinburgh Castle's esplanade to manoeuvre in, whereas the Lomond's five on Big Mur's bike had travelled at over sixty on Glencoe's narrow and curving public road.

And another thing, the team's heads were well protected by crash helmets, while our daft young heroes were shielded by nothing more than their de rigueur, back-to-front, tweed 'Glesca bunnets.'

# Various Climbing Types on
# The Buachaille

The Lomond Mountaineering Club was having another weekend meet at that grand auld favourite place: Glencoe.

Their crowded hired bus deposited many gregarious club members and some Creagh Dhu guests at Altnafeadh's Cameron's Barn. That stark concrete bothy quickly became happily and noisily crowded.

That tough breed, the Creagh Dhu climbers, did as they had to do in summer's pleasant heat or in winter's icy grip, wade barefoot through the wee River Coupall to get to their own, their very own, squat, black, tarpaulined cosy bothy, Jacksonville.

The Lomond Club's own group of hardy young climbers, its six 'Young Lomond Tigers', camped across the river from Jacksonville. These 'Young Tigers,' and the Creagh Dhu's 'climbing marvels' were drinking pals and friendly rivals.

The glory of Sunday's beaming dawn, its promise of a bright, warm, dry June day enticed all out of cosily seductive sleeping-bags, hurried them out of bothies and tents and sent each in their own eager way to go and have a wonderful long day on those marvellous Glencoe Hills.

And so on this perfect day the glorious monarch of this glen, the fabulously shaped Buachaille Etive Mor was, by the standards of those un-crowded post-war years, really very busy with various climbing types all extremely keen to do their own thing.

That easy, but greatly rewarding rocky scramble, The Curved Ridge, was the favoured route for the greatest number of today's eager climbers. Most of the older more cautious Lomond Club members, including almost all of the club's ladies were taking this most enjoyable route to the top of The Buachaille.

Thinking themselves exhilaratingly daring they waste no breath on needless talk as they concentrate their grasping hands and thumping boots on this ridge of rough bare rock. Their entire world is compressed into this airy space around the glory of their haloed heads. They rest on a convenient flattish ledge. They gaze amazed. Their startled senses almost disbelieve what they see.

Over there is that vast, almost vertical rock-face that rises so amazingly sheer and is the fearsome Rannoch Wall. And on some of that intimidating face's most difficult rock climbs are *real* climbers. They quite literally hang on for dear life on that place of *real* airy space. These young 'rock tigers' with their dangling ropes and soaring hopes put the puny fears of those on the safe Curved Ridge to shameful rout.

The exhilaration those happy cautious climbers feel on the thrilling bliss of the Curved Ridge is more than matched – is a thousand times magnified – by what those young lads of the Lomonds and Creagh Dhu, feel. The adrenalin, singing through their pulsing blood-stream and thrilling their taut violin-string nerves, soars to a glorious life-enhancing crescendo as the dangerous crux of their latest, severest, Rannoch Wall route is skilfully climbed and 'conquered'.

Little wonder that after their latest, most awesomely dangerous very severe rock climb has been completed, those 'Young Rock Tigers' should let out roars of savage joy; should let off pent up emotion by giving loud ironic cheers and rudely merry insults at some of their Creag Dhu rivals.

Some of those, who watch and disapprove from the easy safety of the Curved Ridge, think that all that noisy banter coming from the Rannoch Wall is 'not quite the thing'. Other almost Luddite climbing traditionalist, austere followers of their God-like guiding light, W.H. Murray, think those noisy young climbers should – like Victorian children be seen and not heard. And how they hate to hear that woodpeckerish hammering in of those terrible things, artificial climbing aids, those, un-godly abominations – metal pitons.

One traditionalist who's not too bigoted and is one of the Lomond Club's most popular old stalwarts is Lawrie Travers. Today he's gaily leading his party of six, including four keen and hardy lady hill walkers, up this wondrous Curved Ridge, this rocky highway that leads directly to The Buachaille's alluring summit.

They meet two of the Creagh Dhu's expert rock climbers who, having claimed a severe route on the Rannoch Wall, are making their way down this easy ridge to get to the foot of that formidable sheer cliff to climb again. They greet Lawrie with cheery warmth, 'Oh, Lawrie, you old rascal, trust you to be taking it easy with these dear ladies while we're sweating our guts out on that devilish Rannoch Wall.'

Lawrie's reply is equally cheery, 'Oh, my dear fellows, how delightful to meet you again.' After giving them a keen scrutiny he gives a disarming grin, 'Oh but, my dear fellows, I'm not so delighted to see those things slung around you; those hammers, pitons, karabiners and slings. Surely these artificial climbing aids are more suited to solving Civil Engineering problems rather than spoiling the wholesome peace and deep aesthetic thrills of our noble Scottish Hills.'

With a laugh, one of those fearless climbers shouted over his shoulder as he hurried away, ironmongery clanging at every step, 'Oh, don't worry, Lawrie, I promise we won't go over the score with our hammers and pitons.'

As he waved them on their way, Lawrie shouted, 'Be careful how you go there, on the easy rocks. Remember the tragic fate of poor Jackson.'

Answering the ladies' questions, Lawrie explained, 'Jackson was one of the Creagh Dhu's earliest, keenest, post-war members. He was also one of the most enthusiastic builders of their first rough simple bothy near the foot of The Buachaille. After climbing a severe route on the fearsome Rannoch Wall he, just like those other two, was recklessly hurrying down this easy Curved Ridge, when he suddenly slipped and plunged to his death on the rocks below. The Creagh Dhu's new bothy by the River Coupall is named *Jacksonville* in memory of him.'

As Lawrie's happy party sat on the summit of the Buachaille Etive Mor and greedily eagerly drank in the glorious views that stretched in every direction two of the Lomond's young 'Rock Tigers' joined them.

After warmly greeting them, Lawrie said, 'Oh, my dear fellows, it's great that you should come up here to this grand summit, should not live as if the intimate close view of your loved rock faces was all that our mountains can give.'

One of those two 'Rock Tigers', Gordon, smilingly replied, 'Lawrie, I can assure you we don't wear rock-bound blinkers; while we love the thrill that rock climbing gives us we also appreciate all the much wider, much more varied pleasure that the hills can give. In fact I think one enhances the other.'

'Oh, my dear fellow, that's very well said. Yes, our great Scottish mountains are glorious places for many different climbing types; for Murrayish introverts and Creagh Dhuish extroverts; for those who climb with cautious care and those who climb with dangers dare.'

*Bob on An Teallach (late May snowfall)*

*Gordon in Martin's Doss, Cobbler*

*Dave Martin & Bob 'take a look at' ice-wall, Ben Nevis*

*Masterchef Bob in Cairngorms*

*Dave, Lawrie Travers & Bob on Ben Nevis, (ideal conditions)*

*Three 'Lomonds' & a bike at Cameron's barn, Glencoe*

*Bob on skis at Glenshee, Round house YH*

*White Ghyll, Lake District, six Lomond Tigers on wall*

*Glesca' bunnets. Garman, Eccles and Anderson in fifties 'helmets'*

*Achmelvich Bay after winter storms*

*Gordon, The Nook, Cobbler*

*Bob at peat-bothy, Achmelvich*

*Poacher turned Gamekeeper*

*Canisp*

*Eiger & Jungfrau, Grindelwald*

*Gralloch, Bob, Charlie Ross & Dr. Ferguson's son*

*Setters waiting for the Glorious Twelfth*

*Bob & Eileen and dogs, heat-wave in Assynt*

*Dhampus camp-site, Himalayas*

*Hinko cave, tea-break*

*Avalanche debris*

*Annapurna Base camp*

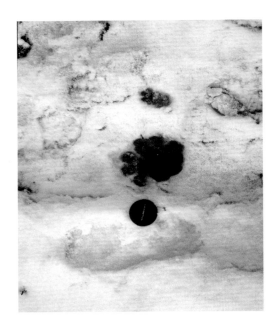

*Snow leopard paw-print*

*End of trek*

*Mount Kinabalu*

*Bob & Lass on Suliven*

*Bob, kilt and Quinag*

*Gordon & John Anderson in Jacksonville, 1983*

*Bob on his hill, Craigower, Pitlochry*

*Gordon & Mary, Mount Kinabalu*

*Bob & Gordon, Pitlochry, main street, 2013*

# The New Pony-Boy

This dreich September day Charlie Ross and I, Bob Scott, were to take Assynt Estate's recently taken on pony-boy on his first day deer-stalking on this vast, wild and rugged West Sutherland sporting estate.

This trainee pony-boy and ghillie, Jamie Ogston, was a tall sturdy seventeen year-old youth. With cheerful outgoing self-confidence he described himself as being an Aberdeenshire farmer's braw loon, strong, hardy and hard-working. He had experience with horses as well as the usual farm animals. He claimed to be expert at shooting rats, rabbits and wood-pigeons and was keen to learn about deer stalking and grouse shooting and to become a Highland gamekeeper.

Finding Jamie to be a real cheery, eager worker and learner, Charlie, the head-gamekeeper, and the estate's other keepers willingly taught him, although for the older West Highlanders this braw loon's broad Aberdeenshire accent was rather difficult to understand. For the wealthy English owners of this estate and their gentry friends Jamie seemed to be talking in a strange foreign language.

Jamie's invariable cheery comment about anyone who could not understand him was, 'Och, man, they must be glaikit if they dinna ken whit I'm saying!'

Jamie now led Auld Nell, the steady, sturdy, grey Highland garron, from her stable behind Glen Canisp Lodge over to where Charlie and I were waiting.

With his usual expertise Charlie quickly and thoroughly checked over the large deer-saddle and its many neatly tied up leather restraining straps. He then slid his strong fingers between the saddle's wide securing girth and the warm bulge of the patient pony's well fed belly.

'That girth's no' tae slack, is it Charlie?' asked the eager-to-learn, new pony-boy.

'Och no, lad, it's just fine. We'll tighten it up later before we load the dead stag onto Nell.' With smiling kindness Charlie gave the pleased youth some further praise, 'Aye, Jamie lad, you've learned well, you've got the deer-saddle and a' else correctly fitted on Auld Nell.' After casting his expert eye over the new pony-boy Charlie grinned and said, 'But that's mair than I can say aboot how you're fitted oot yourself, lad.'

'Whit dae ye mean? Whit's wrang wi me?'

'I'm no' sae keen on those skin-tight new jeans you're wearing. Jamie.'

'Och Charlie, man, whit's wrang wi' them? I bought twa pair o' thae special braw new jeans just tae wear as a pony-boy.'

'Aye, nae doot you think them real "braw", but the trouble is that they're far too tight, lad.'

Jamie frowned then grinned, 'Och, man, at least thae braw new breeks o' mine are much neater than yon awful baggy tweed plus-fours the twa o' you are wearing.'

'Aye, Jamie, perhaps so, but just wait until you get soaked in a day o' torrential, gale-driven Assynt rain. Then you'll ken why we prefer tae wear oor tweed plus-fours.'

Laughing, I confirmed Charlie's remarks, 'Aye, loon, once these new, skin-tight jeans get sodden and start shrinking and chaffing your legs, you too will wish you were wearing a pair of these tweed plus-fours.'

Jamie laughed and mocked them, 'Och, man, I wouldna' be seen deid in a pair o' thae awfa' tweed bloomers! I ken I'll be fine an' dandy in thae braw new jeans o' mine.'

Charlie and I grinned at one another, glanced at the low, rain-threatening clouds, then almost as one, said, 'Aye, all right, Jamie, we'll soon see about that.'

We set out. Charlie led the way, I followed with the rifle, secure in its cover, slung over my back; leading the willing pony, Jamie kept close behind me.

At Charlie's usual steady unhurried, but mile-devouring pace, we strode mile after wild Assynt mile along the stalkers' path that stabbed ever further Eastwards, ever deeper into the heart of Glen Canisp Deer Forest, ever nearer to the glen's guardian mountains, Canisp and Suilven.

Canisp's bare sandstone lower slopes loomed dimly beneath the dismal shrouding clouds. Even when clearly visible, this mountain, despite its slightly higher height, was completely overshadowed by its flamboyant near neighbour, Suilven. Thrusting its brutal steepness above Assynt's wildness of rugged heather moors, its quagmires of black, bottomless peat, its rushing, salmon-filled rivers, its trout-teeming countless lochs and weed-choked lochans, Suilven dominated this fantastic landscape like a louring pagan god.

Even with our many years of familiarity with that mountain Charlie and I again felt something like mysterious awe as we stood and stared at it. I smiled, 'Oh, Charlie, surely Auld Suilven, even if not a "Munro", is one of Scotland's greatest, most unique, mountains.'

Seeing Suilven from close up for the first time, Jamie Ogston stood staring in wide-eyed, wide-mouthed silence. Charlie laughed, 'Well, lad, you seem tae be struck dumb!'

Being an "Aberdeenshire farmer's braw loon," Jamie was accustomed to a tamed countryside of neatly enclosed fields; he felt almost overwhelmed by the primitive power of this untamed Assynt landscape, but was unable to express anything of his strange, powerful feelings of wonder and awe.

My laughter joined Charlie's, 'Aye, loon, yon Suilven's a bit more impressive than Aberdeenshire's braw wee Bennachie, isn't it?'

The stalking party now continued along Glen Canisp's seemingly endless stalkers' path until they reached and climbed the steep rocky track that rose up towards Canisp's Westerly slopes. At the end of this track the rain, driven by a strong West wind, began to pour. As the men fastened their jackets more securely and pulled hats down more tightly, the pony turned its broad backside to the wind and rain, tucked its long, thick, grey tail snugly between its legs and settled with stoic patience to wait here as long as necessary.

Charlie patted Auld Nell and said, 'We'll dae oor utmost no' to keep you waiting too long in this damp miserable weather, lass.' He grinned at the new pony-boy, 'That goes for you too, Jamie. Just you coorie doon behind that boulder and patiently wait here wi' Auld Nell. Don't leave this place even after you hear a rifle shot. One o' us will come back then guide the pony an' you to the dead stag. Have you got that?'

'Aye, okay, Charlie, I hope you shoot a stag soon. It'll be bloody miserable hunkering doon here in a' this teeming rain.'

Charlie and I set out to find and shoot a suitable stag. In this dreich weather of shrouding low clouds and obscuring heavy rain this would be no easy task, but I had absolute confidence in Charlie's great stalking skills.

After almost an hour of steady walking, cautiously clambering around steep heathery knolls and expertly searching with keen telescopes we discovered a group of nine stags. Some were lying down. The others stood with drooping heads and dripping bodies in a huddle of sodden misery.

After lying, studying them through his telescope, Charlie wiped away the rainwater dripping from his bushy eyebrows then grinned at me, 'Thae poor beasts look about as miserable as you an' me! Come on let's go an' see if we can put one o' them oot o' its misery.'

After a few thousand yards of cautious crouching, then some miserable crawling through soaking heather we were in position to take a shot. As I eased the rifle out of its cover and slid it to Charlie he whispered, 'I'll take yon eight pointer standing tae the left there. He's a poorish looking beast.'

Charlie took his usual perfect heart-shot. The selected stag instantly dropped dead. The other stags leaped up and ran through thick heather in a glittering mist of high splashing spray.

I hurried back to fetch the impatiently waiting new pony-boy and the stoic old pony.

Having heard the shot, Jamie was on his feet eagerly searching through the dismal rain. He saw me waving him forward. Auld Nell also saw me, and giving a vigorous shake, without needing my urging, she started plodding towards me. Obviously she, like the soaking humans, was eager to get this work done as quickly as possible. No doubt she had bright visions of her waiting dry stable and its generous helping of tasty hay.

The new pony-boy seemed s wee bit queasy as the dead stag was expertly gralloched and he saw a huge mass of grey guts come obscenely slithering out. Charlie grinned at him, 'Are you all right, lad? You look a wee bit green aboot the gills.'

Jamie smiled bravely, 'Och no, Charlie, I'm fine now. A' they spilled guts were just a wee bit startling, ye ken. I've shot an' skinned an' gutted rabbits, ye ken, so I'm used tae seeing blood an' guts. But maybe no' as many as these.'

After tightening the pony's girths they heaved the stag onto her large deer-saddle then firmly secured the dangling carcass with its head twisted sharply upwards to keep the antlers eight sharp points well clear of the pony's body.

As the stalking party started out for the longed-for shelter of the distant shooting-lodge their speed was dictated by the steady plodding pace of the laden pony as it clattered down the stony track that led into Glen Canisp.

For eight long, rough, Assynt miles, they trudged along the stalking path that now led them direct into the West, led them face-on into the battering storm sweeping in from the Atlantic. As the heavy rain relentlessly poured down, the two gamekeepers and the new pony-boy's soaking clothes became so saturated that it seemed that even the keepers' thick tweeds could not absorb any more water. Although he nobly refrained from complaining, Jamie's sodden too-tight jeans were giving him painful chafing misery.

At last they reached the blessed shelter of the shooting-lodge. They hung the stag in the deer-larder then Charlie said, 'Right, Jamie, now take Nell to her stable, unsaddle her an' give her a good rub-doon while we skin the stag here.'

The stag was quickly skinned. The rifle was soon dried, cleaned and thoroughly oiled then locked away in the gun-room's secure cupboard. We now turned our attention to the two generous drams left by the lodge's housekeeper. Charlie beamed, 'Now that the rifle's been taken care of we can see aboot getting ourselves well-oiled tae!'

As the excellent whisky's wondrous reviving warm glow spread through his soaked body, Charlie grinned, 'Ah, that's better! Aye, that uisge-beatha truly is the water of life!'

I heartily agreed, 'Aye, it is, it certainly is. Now let's complete our transformation from drookit misery to warm comfort by going over to my place and getting changed into dry clothes.' We hurried through the pouring rain to the three bed-roomed flat above the lodge's garages which was, for the present, my home.

My wife and our two dogs warmly greeted us. After having conscientiously dried Auld Nell and seen her comfortably settled munching her hay in the cosy stable, Jamie joined us. 'Right,' I said, 'now let's get quickly changed into dry clothes then we'll see what hospitable food and drink the wife's got waiting for us.'

The three of them hurried into the three bedrooms where, in wise anticipation, they had left dry clothes.

Revelling in the luxurious comfort of our dry clothes, Charlie and I went into the sitting-room, 'Where's Jamie, 'I asked my wife, 'hasn't he got changed yet?'

'No, the poor drookit loon must still be in his bedroom.'

Charlie and I went to Jamie's bedroom. I knocked on the door and asked, 'What's keeping you, lad? Have you not changed yet?' Unable to make out his muffled reply, I opened the door and entered the room. Charlie followed me. We stood and stared at the dejected figure. Sitting on his bed, Jamie was a picture of absolute misery. He seemed to be resolutely holding back unmanly tears. 'What's the matter with you, lad?' I asked, why are you still wearing these soaking jeans?'

'They've shrunk sae much in a' yon bloody rain that I can't get the bloody things aff me! I've struggled an' struggled wi' them, but they won't budge!'

Charlie grinned, 'Ah weel, Jamie, now ye ken why you should have been wearing a pair o' oor baggy tweed plus-fours, don't you?'

'Oh aye, I ken that noo, Charlie. Oh but how the hell am I gaun tae get thae shrunken jeans off my soaking an' freezing legs?'

Taking a leg each, Charlie and I tried to pull Jamie's sodden jeans down over his knees, but our best, strongest struggling efforts were to no avail. We soon gave up.

As Charlie drew his large, razor-sharp gralloching knife from his jacket pocket he again grinned, I doot there's only one thing for it noo, lad, we'll have tae slit up the seams o' your jeans to above your knees. Is that all right?'

'Aye, I suppose that's a' ye can dae tae help me.' He gave a nervous shudder, 'Oh but please be damn careful how far up ye slit thae jeans.'

'Och, don't worry, lad,' I laughed, 'we'll try not to inflict "the unkindest cut of all" on your vigorous youthful manhood!'

As soon as Charlie and I had, with cautious care, slit up his jeans, Jamie struggled out of them with profound thankful relief.

Charlie and I laughed and pointed. I mocked, 'Just look at you, lad, I've heard of turning blue with cold, but your legs are now brawly woaded a gaudy denim blue!'

Years pass, then that new pony-boy, Jamie Ogston, that "Aberdeenshire farmer's braw loon," visits my wife and me in our new home that looks out across Inverkirkaig Bay.

Time has transformed him; he is no longer a callow immature loon, he is a big, sturdy, black-bearded gamekeeper with a wife and a two year old loon of his own.

There is sincere sadness when I tell Jamie of Charlie's recent sudden tragic death. We stand, clink well-filled glasses, then, drink a solemn toast in memory of Charlie Ross, that greatest gamekeeper, greatest friend; that man of rare good nature, that soaring fount of glorious uproarious laughter.

I heave another sigh then force myself to brighten, 'Och, Jamie, we know the last thing Charlie would want would be for his friends to remember him with too much solemn misery. That man of endless friendly goodness would want to be remembered with hearty gregarious laughter.'

And so, laughing over convivial drams, we recall in vivid detail Jamie's first day as pony-boy with Charlie and me. With beaming face and glittering eyes he said, 'Och, man, I fair learned a richt lesson yon day when Charlie an' you had tae cut yon sodden, shrunk, too tight jeans frae my chafed, frozen, demin-dyed legs. Noo, I always wear a pair o' yon gamekeepers tweed plus-fours that I sae foolishly youthfully mocked as we set oot yon day. Or, as you see, I wear this braw Gordon Highlanders kilt an' enjoy the comfort an' freedom o' its jaunty swinging pleats.'

'Aye, Jamie,' I grinned, 'you look real braw in that kilt. Aye, you certainly learned your lesson well that day,'

# GLAIKIT!

'**B**e sure Robert and you only fish one at a time and have only one of our rods in use. Don't exert your great fishing expertise to catch too many salmon, Charlie. Leave some for us when we come down to the river later this morning.' Mr. Vestey, the millionaire owner of this large West Sutherland sporting estate, smiled pleasantly as he gave his head-gamekeeper these instructions.

Charlie Ross grinned as he replied, 'Och, sir, I don't think that even with my best skills I'll catch many, if any, fish under these conditions.' For all of May and June there had been a sun-bright drought. The River Inver had become a sorry, shrunken, dried-up ghost of its usual tempestuous self. Then, the previous afternoon and through all of the night there had been a deluge of torrential rain. The river was now in roaring spate. 'Nae doot loads o' salmon will be surging in frae the sea, but they'll keep rushing non-stop for miles up the flooded river.'

And these were exactly the conditions the two gamekeepers found when they arrived at the river

Although his vast experience confirmed that conditions for salmon fishing were pretty hopeless, Charlie again felt that old familiar glorious thrill of eternal optimism that every true fisherman feels as he made his first cast and sent his glittering 'Green Highlander' artificial fly gracefully sweeping over the salmon-filled river.

And this July morning the River Inver truly was fantastically filled with salmon. Hugely excited by this roaring spate after their weeks of weary waiting in the salty estuary, many hundreds, perhaps thousands, of silver bright, firm-muscled, peak-conditioned, wild Atlantic salmon were frantically rushing up this lovely West Highland, river.

As Charlie expertly fished the Star Pool, the largest and best pool in the river, salmon after salmon arrowed itself high from the rushing water, gracefully curved, then joyfully dived back into its true element, and splashed a bright glittering fountain skywards. It almost seemed as if, with its tumultuous rushing and these joyous glittering spoutings, this river was rejoicing in its re-invigorated flooded state as much as these exultant salmon so obviously were.

Expertly fishing as he went, Charlie made his careful way along the concrete walkway that curved out towards the middle of this pool. The full turbulent force of the river flowed along one side of this concrete and it was in this flood that countless excited salmon were ceaselessly leaping then eagerly swimming ever further up the river towards where they had been spawned and where in November they in turn would spawn.

As with persistent skill Charlie cast his fly ever further down through the pool he would often see four or five, or even more, high leaping salmon in the air at one time. And not one salmon, seen or unseen, took any interest in his alluringly-presented, shining fly.

After some fifteen minutes of this quiet torment, Charlie turned and said, 'Och, this fishing is useless. Thae buggers are just mocking me.' Then as a large salmon leapt only inches from him and sent spray cascading over his legs he ruefully grinned, 'Och, damn it tae hell, noo the buggers are trying to bloody well droon me! Here, Robert, you take the boss's rod an' see if you can dae any better.'

'Och, Charlie, if even you with all your years of experience can't catch one o' those buggers how do you expect me to do any better?' However he readily took the long, double-handed, split-cane Hardy rod (the Rolls Royce of rods) and with eagerness, but with little hope, started fishing.

While concentrating on his unproductive fishing, Robert noted that two wee boys had come running up the riverside path and were now standing open-mouthed staring at the flooded river's high leaping salmon.

Urgently beckoning their parents who had now almost caught up with them, the excited boys shrilly screamed, 'Hurry, hurry, mum, dad. Come and see the salmon! Look, look, there's hundreds o' thae big salmon! They're lowping a' ower.'

'Aye, thae fish are a braw sight right enough, boys, but don't jump aboot like that, you'll fa' in the river.'

'Aye dae whit yer mum tells you, Tam, and you tae, Wee Eddie. Sit doon here wi' us an' watch the man catch one o' thae big braw salmon.' Even as he gave these sage instructions, their father felt almost as excited as his sons. He, and they, had done a little very amateurish fishing for trout in some of the many lochs in this Assynt district, but none of them had ever seen anything like this awesome sight of so many salmon so wildly leaping.

Listening to that excited, broad-spoken Glasgow family as he continued fishing down through the Star pool, Robert smiled to himself and thought, 'I only wish I could catch one "o' thae big braw salmon." But this seemed unlikely. The rushing and leaping salmon took as little interest in his best 'Jock Scott' fly as they had of Charlie's various flies. Exasperated and frustrated, he began to hate the sight of all those exultantly leaping fish which showed such mocking disdain for his best fishing efforts.

And now it was not only the salmon that were mocking his useless endeavours. He distinctly heard the shrill voice of the oldest boy contemptuously ask, 'Och, dad, why isn't yon stupid man catching onie o' thae braw salmon?'

Before the father could answer, his youngest son loudly joined in his brother's heartfelt disdain, 'Aye, Tam, yon man must be real glaikit!'

While trying to restrain her laughter, their mother gasped, 'Och, be quiet, boys. That "glaikit" fisherman will hear you.'

With a rueful smiled Robert thought, 'Aye, I will be real glaikit right enough if I waste much more time on those damn frustrating fish.'

Then he saw what he had been hoping and praying for.

In the sheltered calm water between him and that critical family on the river bank one large salmon had quietly risen, gently disturbed the flat surface and then sunk down.

From where he was sitting contentedly smoking his favourite auld briar pipe Charlie had also seen that gentle rise. He shouted friendly encouragement, 'There you are, Robert, yon resting salmon's waiting for your "Jock Scott" tae come tae him.'

Robert laughed, 'It's a long cast, Charlie, but I'll do my best tae introduce Jock tae him.'

And he did. As his accurate long cast swept the "Jock Scott" over the resting salmon, it quietly rose, gently sucked the deceptive fly into its mouth then turned and sank down.

And that was the end of its quiet resting. Sudden desperate panic took over. Its terrible fear of this strange unknown danger sent the firmly hooked salmon racing across the Star Pool like a glittering silvery torpedo. It sliced through the pool's central flood and sent many salmon desperately leaping in shared blind panic.

The long, upright, fishing rod bent in a graceful arc, as it bowed to its strong and noble foe. The rod's reel was a blur of fantastic motion. Its whirring song became a screech of wild triumphant joy. The fishing line hissed through the water in urgent pursuit of that desperately-rushing, distant salmon.

Rejoicing in adrenalin's familiar tingling rush, Robert knew that his nerves no longer ended at his fingertips but, racing down that quivering fishing line, were in direct contact with the desperate fish; were in direct touch with his ancient hunting and fishing ancestors.

And his wondrous singing reel was accompanied by the chorus of those two wee boys' loud excited jubilant shouts of, 'He's caught one! He's caught one!'

'Aye, I hope I have caught one,' Robert grinned, 'I hope these boys' jubilation is not premature.' He knew all too well that a salmon was not truly 'caught' until it was safely in the landing net.

Far down at the distant tail of the large pool the hooked salmon leapt high and for a few exciting seconds displayed the beauty of its impressive size for the first time.

Then in another fast hectic charge it sliced back through the pool's fierce central flood and again sent many other salmon into soaring nervous leaps.

Frantically reeling in the fishing line, Robert tried to keep in touch with his salmon as it sped unseen back up towards him. Then from the calm water between him and his excited audience that salmon again leapt high and brightly displayed its impressive size.

This much nearer graceful curving splashing leap triggered ever louder, ever more excited shouts from the two wide-eyed Glasgow boys, while, lost for adequate words, their parents joined in the excitement with loud gasps of admiring wonder.

After other less strong rushes and less wild leaps the salmon was tiring. With calm experienced assurance, Charlie held the landing net ready in the water. Applying steady pressure Robert guided the fish over the net. With a smooth accurate movement Charlie lifted the net and the captured salmon.

This success was applauded by cheering boyish voices and loud clapping adult hands.

As the gamekeepers finished weighing the dead salmon the boys' father approached and asked, 'Will it be all right if my twa bairns come over to see the fish?'

'Aye sure,' Charlie replied, 'bring them over.'

Their father's encouraging wave brought his excited sons racing to him. They flopped to their knees beside the eighteen pound salmon. Stroking the wonder of its silvery streamlined shape they gasped in admiring awe, 'Oh, dad, mum, it's a real braw huge salmon, isn't it?'

Robert winked at the parents then smiled at the salmon-worshipping boys, 'Well, lads, do you still think I'm glaikit?'

Tam and his wee brother Eddie, blushed, in embarrassed confusion. Between them they managed to stammer an awkward apology. Then with re-gained self-assurance and sincere admiration, Tam stoutly declared, 'Och no, mister, you're no' glaikit. The way you caught this braw salmon was real magic.' Grinning up at Robert he made a desperate effort to find greater words to more exactly express his praise, 'Och no, mister, you're no' glaikit at a'. You're a ... a real braw Wizard Fisherman!'

# My Brief Visit to the Alps

Thishis must be the most inattentive pitching of a tent in history I thought. The three of us had arrived by train from Paris only half an hour previously, and we were now attempting to lay out the tent, hammer in pegs and assemble tent poles, whilst simultaneously staring up at the array of mountains facing us. Legendary names to the climber, the Grande Jorasses, Aiguille du Midi, the Dru, with its famed West Face, all overshadowed by the snowy bulk of the highest of them all, Mont Blanc. No wonder we were distracted. We were in the Chamonix municipal camp-site, on the banks of the river Arve, at the beginning of our first Alpine climbing holiday. Eventually our tent was up, our gear stowed inside and we stood, in a row, silently taking in the mountains, thinking to ourselves, where do we start? Obviously not today, so a meal and a glass of wine might stimulate some positive ideas. The problem was we didn't have enough information yet to make any real plans, so over dinner, we agreed that things would be better in the morning when we knew more, and therefore we ordered another bottle of wine to celebrate this emphatic decision.

Next day over coffee and croissants in the camp-site café, we bemoaned our lack of planning and concluded that a visit to the tourist office might be more productive, supplying us with information on mountain huts, distances and grades of routes which would all help us in our ignorance of the terrain. (A visit to the camp-site toilet, a wooden hut with a hole in the floor, perched on a plank above the icy waters of the glacial river would also provide us with a very uncomfortable new experience).

On the way into town I remembered that a fellow engineer on the *Port Dunedin*, my last ship, had written to me in Glasgow before we left suggesting there might be a position for me on a coastal vessel, *The Glenshiel*, now being fitted out in Peterhead. I had replied and told him that I would be on holiday but could be contacted at the poste restante in Chamonix, if necessary. As we were entering Place Balmat, named after the first man to scale Mont Blanc, I saw the Post Office and thought, well, I'm here anyway, might as well check. Blow me, if there wasn't a telegram waiting for me. The job was mine if I high-tailed it directly from my Alpine sojourn back across the miles to North-East Scotland. After a few moments, as thoughts went swirling round my brain, I decided that this time, my head would rule my heart and my Alpine venture would be over almost before it had started. 'Sorry lads,' I said, I'm going to have to go back to Scotland for this job. The Alps will always be here for the future, the job won't be. Sorry about this.'

I sensed, very slightly, some relief in the reply when it came. 'That's OK, Gordon, you're probably right to take the job. We'll manage fine without you. Hard luck, you never even got up the hill.'

As I went back to the camp-site to pack up – I couldn't even bear to go with them to the tourist office – I thought to myself, of course it makes more sense to climb in pairs. Three on a rope is a bit clumsy and takes longer. Good luck to them. So off I went, dreaming of rocky spires and razor-edged ridges, to my job of making sure the *Glenshiel's* engine kept going, crossing and re-crossing the stormy waters of the Minch. This wise decision saddened me, but I resolved I would return to the Alps some other day.

# My Return to the Alps

I
t was to be some twenty-three years before this resolution was fulfilled. We had been back on holiday in Scotland from Saudi Arabia, where I was teaching at Riyadh University and our air-ticket allowed a stop-over anywhere in Europe on our return to the Middle East. I had suggested Grindelwald, in the Bernese Oberland and Mary, my wife, agreed. After a flight to Paris and a train journey to Zurich, we found ourselves standing waiting for the 18.58 p.m. train to Grindelwald. The Swiss are well-known for clock and watch-making (and of course Army knives) but allied to these crafts, it was their time-keeping that really impressed us. As the second hand on the platform clock ticked round past 18.57, I looked at Mary and said, 'Looks like its going to be late, I don't hear anything.' Precisely as the second hand reached the vertical and 18.58, the train swished to a stop beside us. Accuracy to a 'T', or was the clock rigged?

Arrival again on the dot, at the scheduled time in Grindelwald, further impressed us – I take back what I said about the rigged clock – and we made the short walk across the street to our hotel.

In the morning, I was wakened by Mary, who was standing at the window. 'Come and see this,' she said. I gasped as I looked out of the window. The towering North Wall of the Eiger loomed above us dark and menacing, (Eiger is German for 'Ogre') but, despite its almost overpowering presence, it is nevertheless, a hypnotisingly, attractive mountain. This is the arena of so many dramatic episodes, (at least sixty-four climbers have died on it) and a visit to the local cemetery is a sobering experience, seeing the many tombstones with coiled rope and ice-axe engravings.

That day with the aid of a local map I made plans to get closer to the Wall and I saw that a path was marked, running east to west across the foot of the face. I was certainly not going to try any climbing, but this would suffice as a near-enough experience.

Early the next morning found me, perhaps being taken for a railway employee by passengers on the train, walking up the maintenance track of the Kleine Scheidegg railway. This seemed to be the most direct and obvious way to the foot of the West Flank and indeed as the railway veered off to the meadows around Kleine Scheidegg station, I left the track and headed in an easterly direction. Soon after, I found a narrow path which undulated through the scree slopes at the foot of the wall. In twenty minutes, casting watchful glances up to my right, as the North face during the day has frequent stone-falls and occasional avalanches, I was directly under the centre of the face and tracing with my eyes a possible line of attack. The scale is the first aspect to hit you at this distance, (the face is in total, 1500 feet higher than the height of Ben Nevis, from sea-level to summit) and the second noticeable feature, is the gloom, being seldom in sunshine.

Soon I came upon a small flock of about twenty sheep on the path ahead, which trotted happily along before me, seemingly unconcerned about the possible bombardment from above. They kept to the path, pausing when I paused, then, trotting on as I moved. Perhaps I was being accepted as an honorary shepherd. They stopped and waited while I tried to pick out the 'White Spider,' the famous snowfield featuring in Maurice Hertzog's book of the same name, then they obediently walked on as I did. This continued for about a mile until I began to think I'd eventually be marching into the centre of Grindelwald in the company of my woolly friends. Luckily, they seemed to tire of me when I reached a steep gully, crossed by a simple wooden bridge spanning a raging torrent of white water coming from above, and trotted off merrily downhill. Over the bridge I stopped to take in the magnificence of the surrounding scenery. Behind rose the immense bulk of the Western Flank, the descent route normally used by successful climbers of the North Face, whose almost vertical wall was on my immediate right. The North Face, or 'Nordwand' in German, had earned the nickname, Mordwand or 'Murder Wall, and was releasing a constant shower of water falling hundreds of feet from its lowering brows. Ahead of me at the eastern end of the wall was the striking silhouette of the Wetterhorn, which in the sun, looked benignly down on the colourful buildings of Grindelwald below. The path, on which I hadn't seen another person all morning, had one last surprise for me. On a stone, basking in the sunshine, sprawled a shiny, black, Alpine salamander, the first I had seen. It seemed unafraid as I took its photograph, and, as I carried no matches, was unable to test the theory (almost certainly a myth), that salamanders were fire-resistant, could even extinguish fires. Soon my route took me downhill to Alpiglen with its forests and meadows of beautiful Alpine flowers. So, I had managed to get close and get a strong impression of the Wall, the scene of heroic deeds and dramas, without doing anything more dramatic myself than stroll along a good path preceded by a flock of friendly sheep, but it gave me memories that I carry to this day.

# Yet Another Alpine Visit

I managed another visit to Grindelwald, this time twelve years later. The area had held a fascination for me for some time and I felt I had unfinished business there. Under similar circumstances as the previous visit, on leave, this time from Brunei, where I was now working, I had formed a more ambitious project, this time I would attempt to reach an Alpine summit. To this end I had utilised the services of the internet to hire a local guide from the town to guide me up the mighty Jungfrau. The guiding company had a wee shop in the main street and supplied all the gear, boots, clothing, ice-axe and crampons, and in July 1994, there I was, being kitted out, ready at last for an Alpine ascent.

A feature of much of climbing in the Alps, perhaps frowned upon by the purist, is the use of mountain railways to get you effortlessly and quickly up to five or six thousand feet, and on, in our case, to eleven thousand, where the real climb to the summit begins. Thomas, my guide and I took the last train to Kleine Scheidegg and there transferred to the cog railway which journeyed upward through the centre of the Eiger to Europe's highest station, Jungfraujoch at 11,000 feet. This was a style of mountaineering I was really beginning to appreciate. The station, at this hour, was empty apart from us and, leaving the lights and warmth of the spotlessly clean building, with its gleaming glass and chrome, its cafes and shops, and stepping out into the darkness and the ice and snow of the Aletsch glacier, was quite a shock. Switching on our head-torches, Thomas said, 'OK, off we go, follow me but stay about twenty metres behind my tracks in case there are any crevasses.' The mind boggled, just off a train and next minute, perhaps down a crevasse. Amidst flurries of snow, I followed Thomas across the glacier. It was relatively easy walking yet nevertheless somehow unreal having been transported from the bustle of evening in the town and now, thousands of feet up in the clouds, tramping across a dark and silent landscape. After no more than an hour, our torches picked out the dark shape of rocks towering out of the snow. The guide stopped and called, 'We are here. We are at the hut.' Above us rose a steel ladder and at the top I could see a large metal cabin perched precariously on a rocky spur. I followed Thomas up the ladder and suddenly, as he opened the door, a blast of light, heat and noise rushed past us out into the silence of the mountainside. As I stood blinking in the light, slightly deafened by the noise of voices raised in singing and shouting, I saw rows of tables and people on benches, eating drinking and making merry. So much for the solitude of mountains, Bacchus must have been a mountaineer. 'Come,' said Thomas, 'we must register and then eat, as they close the restaurant in half an hour.' As I tucked into an excellent dinner of veal escalope and rosti, with a stein of Louwenbrau, I thought back to our climbing days in Scotland, sleeping in caves and barns and scrabbling about with tins of beans and sausages. What I would give now to have my old mates here to enjoy this.

At ten o'clock precisely the singing stopped, the hubbub of noise ceased, and people started going upstairs to the dormitories. It was almost as if everybody had said, 'Right, fun is over, sleep now and climb tomorrow.' Thomas confirmed this by saying, 'OK, we get you a sleeping-bag and then bed. We have an early start. I will wake you at 4.00 a.m.'

Our dormitory consisted of a raised wooden platform on which people simply found a space to unroll their sleeping-bags and lie down. I likened it to a giant tin of sardines as I glanced over the rows of supine bodies stretched out in the half-light around me. Then all was silent as the effects of heavy meals and alcohol took over.

Where was I? What were those 'beeping' noises? Thomas was shaking my shoulder and saying, 'Morgen, it is four o'clock, time for breakfast.' All around me people were sitting up and switching off wrist-watch alarms. It seemed that as well as going to bed at the same time, everybody was also getting up together.

Over muesli and coffee, Thomas informed me that there had been a heavy snowfall during the night and that there might be problems on the mountain. 'I'll go to the manager's office to find out what the forecast is.' Some time later he returned looking a bit gloomy. 'It looks impossible. I'm afraid with so much new snow the avalanche risk is very high. Climbers have been advised not to climb today.' Overhearing this, some climbers quizzed him in German, sighed, nodded, and trooped off back to bed. He turned to me and said, 'I'm very sorry Gordon, I think we go back down to town, we can catch the 8 a.m. train, and you will get a refund for one day, from the office. Damn the refund I thought, I want to go up the mountain. What is it with me and the Alps? Yet another disappointment, but then again, I suppose being buried under tons of snow, would also count as a rather drastic mountain experience, one I'd be quite prepared to forego, so fair enough, let's go down.

We ploughed through the knee-deep snow, back across the glacier, following the steps of some who had left before us, back to the lights and luxury of the Jungfraujoch, 'The Top of Europe' as it is called. There was to be one final 'experience' on the journey down. The train stopped briefly at one of the two viewing platforms in the tunnel, and it is a short distance to the Stollenloch, a window that opens out on to the North Face. As well as providing a magnificent view, the window has been used to make many rescue attempts, and also as an escape route for climbers in trouble. My first thought was how unpleasant and how unwelcoming it all was. The whole wall was soaking wet and a constant shower of water fell from above. The rock looked very unstable, fissured and cracked, ready at a moment to break away and plummet to the screes below. (In 2008, a piece, the size of two New York skyscrapers detached and fell into the valley, luckily in an uninhabited area). The 'Ogre' seemed to want to shed any surface intruder, be it water, snow, loose rock or climber. How unlike the warm, sunlit cliffs of sound rock of say, the Dolomites. Nevertheless it had been, and continues to be, a magnet for hundreds of climbers, drawn by its scale, reputation and the challenge it presents.

And, as I looked down I sensed I could see, on a faint undulating path some 2,000 feet below, a small flock of sheep standing as if waiting for some visitor to come along and accompany them on their morning stroll. I think it's about time I left here!

Surely being twice jinxed from reaching an Alpine summit is enough. A third time might *not* be lucky. Best not tempt fate.

# On and Around Suilven

Having resolved to make the most of this perfect bright dry June weather we, Bob Scott, my wife Eileen, and our two dogs, Lass and Chico, set out fine and early from our estate flat behind Glen Canisp Lodge.

We had a long day before us, long and, we happily felt sure, full of these simple pleasures our familiar Assynt hills and lochs can give. Simple natural pleasures which are bright with grand deep meanings.

As we steadily strode Eastwards on that stalkers' path that stabs into the heart of Glen Canisp Deer Forest, this long glen's twin sentinels, Canisp and Suilven, loomed through their clinging white mists and seemed to hazily urge us to hurry ever further on.

We cast our sympathetic glance at that old, sadly ruined shepherd's cottage, Suileag, which seems near to its final decay. (We, in later years, rejoice to hear that auld Suileag has been re-born as a fine climbers' bothy.)

As we cross the rickety wooden bridge that leads the path towards Suilven we again smile to see these robust wee rowans that so eagerly thrust up from a large boulder's thick heather wig. Bob is pleased to know that these autumn rowan berries he threw up there, have so strongly taken root. Given enough time, these groping rowan roots, as they tenaciously search through dark cracks might force that boulder apart. It was Assynt's head gamekeeper, Charlie Ross, who, after the Second World War, had started dispersing rowan berries in rocky cracks and gaping fissures in miniature ravines and other wild places inaccessible to hungry deer and sheep. Bob copied Charlie's wise example, and now hundreds of these hardy rowans were tenaciously growing.

Bob gives a nod to that familiar pony track as it clambers up towards Canisp's lower slopes. He's pleased that today he's not going up there with rifle and ponies, that great stalker, Charlie Ross, and the eager, stag-stalking, posh-talking estate-owning gentry.

Nor today is he wearing these Assynt Estate tweed plus-fours with their pattern that's kept for this estate's exclusive use, no, today he's enjoying the even greater comfort and freedom of his Scott tartan kilt.

After avoiding the treacly peat that pretends to be a path, they reach Eileen's fishing destination, Loch Na Barrack. There she'll happily stay and fish for that loch's grand trout while Bob again climbs Suilven.

Fairly young and very fit he takes Suilven's steep slopes with ease. He soon passes through the gap in that strong, high, wide stone dyke that was built in that desperate time of potato blight to keep sheep from Suilven's surprisingly lush but dangerously steep Westerly summit.

Standing at the grey stane cairn he gazes all around at this amazingly ancient Assynt land, this landscape that has almost as many peaty lochs as it has exposed bare rock, thrusting hills, rocky knolls and sheep-devouring bogs.

Beauty is in the eye of the beholder, and what, to many, would seem a solemn miserable wilderness of rock and peat, is to Bob, a place of sublime deep and elemental beauty.

Having drunk his fill, he climbs back down, is warmly greeted by rejoicing dogs, is less demonstratively welcomed by Eileen who proud displays her freshly caught large trout.

Spurred by Eileen's success Bob hurried to where his rucksack and fishing rod await his return. His assembling fingers seem to feel the fine light split-cane fly-rod eagerly quiver, be as keen as him to get going.

June's glaring sun the loch's bright glitter and the lazy breeze's gentle whisper hardly seem conducive to successful fishing. However he is not disheartened. Much better this than, as all too often happens, having a half-gale fling almost horizontal rain and your own awkwardly cast fly in your cowering face. Under today's bright conditions your gentle dry-fly can prove its worth.

And it did!

After patiently waiting for a large trout to quietly rise, his accurately cast dry-fly parachuted down and as it settled on the loch's glittering surface, that neatly deceived trout rose and urgently grabbed it.

For fish and fisher and even the wild screaming reel, there is a mad adrenalin rush. Then the madly racing, now distant trout suddenly leaps high, splashes back and fountains a glitter of rainbow spray.

Well content with their catch of some large plump golden trout, Eileen and Bob sit at relaxed ease. They smilingly imagine that Auld Suilven, mellowed by the glorious sunshine, smiles down on them.

They again note that faint outline, almost hidden by thickening heather, of the wee bothy where Assynt's tough and hardy 19th century Highlanders had lived while they built that robust dry-stane dyke high on Suilven's narrow ridge.

'These dyke builders would have to climb up from this wee bothy every day to that ridge then come back down at dusk, wouldn't they?' Eileen asked.

'Aye, they would. It's quite a strenuous way to get to your work. But of course they would not work every day. In the Highlands there was no work done on the Sabbath then. They would probably 'rest' on the Sabbath by walking those many miles to the kirk in Lochinver.'

'And the landowner paid them for building that high dyke?'

'Aye, he did. At that grim time of the Potato Famine the best landowners paid the Highlanders a mere subsistence wage, just enough to keep them and their families from actual starvation. That was when many deer-stalking paths, long estate boundary dykes and even some public roads, like Wester Ross's, Destitution Road, were built.'

Bob grinned, 'Aye, and I bet these hardy Highlanders largely lived on these big trout from this loch. They would not catch them in our fancy sporty dry-fly way but would set fixed lines baited with worms each morning before setting out to climb to work. Aye and I expect they, like us, despite our very different ways of catching them, felt something of that grand feeling of being in touch with their ancient hunting/fishing ancestors every time they caught these trout.'

Eileen smiled, 'Oh it makes all these remote wild places so much more alive when we know something of their history. And even if the story is sad, like that poor lady who slipped on wet grass and fell to her death down Suilven's steep heathers and screes, still it's good to know that story.'

'Aye,' Bob agreed, 'there's not many who know that sad story. There's very many fewer who, like us, have seen that small aluminium lonely cross set in her memory on Suilven's low North West screes.'

As that happy couple and their two tireless dogs hike the long return Glen Canisp miles the Western sun ceaselessly beams its gregarious smiles on them.

# A Quiet Weekend in the Lake District

Although climbing was the central purpose of my weekends, other activities occasionally featured. A case in point happened once when the Lomond climbing club's hired bus took us for a visit to the Lake District. Amongst the members on board were a few guests, namely, John McLean, Pat Walsh and Bob Hope, three of the famous Creagh Dhu Club's finest climbers who fancied a wee change from Glencoe.

We camped at Langdale, near the Old Dungeon Ghyll pub, the legendary haunt of rock climbers. Feeling thirsty after our journey down the A6 we thought a few pints were called for and set off across the camp-site. Some of the local lads had the same idea and started emerging from their tents. To our amusement, some of them began looping slings and karabiners over their shoulders. They were getting geared up, not for a climb but for appearance's sake to impress others in the pub! Now, one of our group, Duncan who was known for his low tolerance of fools, began ridiculing them and a fair bit of fairly good-natured banter flew back and forth before the lure of the beer took us away.

After a fairly quiet evening, despite the earlier friction, we had our sing-song, our pints and eventually went back to the comfort of our sleeping bags. Duncan, who'd done the ridiculing earlier, obviously had some difficulty in getting off to sleep, (as had the rest of the camp-site) as he sang song after song at the top of his voice. He had reached verse ten of the *Ball of Kirriemuir*, when an equally loud voice with a Northern English accent was heard to 'request' him to, 'Shut the fuck up and let everybody get some sleep.'

Trouble ahead as the jolly balladeer shouted back, 'You gonnae make me ya English bastard?' The response was inevitable.

'I will that, you Scottish twat, out you come or I'll come in and get you.'

Out charged Duncan, our singing hero, straight at the English upstart. Now he's for it. Yes, he was, as the English climber effortlessly grabbed him by an arm and a leg, raised him above his head and threw down on the ground in a crumpled heap. To emphasise this superiority he bent down, picked him up, and did it all again.

'Are you going to shut up now or do you want me to do this to you all night?'

There was a chorus of shouts from the Lomond tents, 'For God's sake Duncan, do as the man says. There's none of us going to get any sleep tonight if you keep on thumping down on the ground like that.'

The next day we found that our minstrel had made a serious miscalculation. He had chosen to serenade the reigning All England Cumberland wrestling champion.

That morning I paired up with Bob Hope and we had a very pleasant day climbing on White Ghyll Crag doing some of the Knots/Nots, routes called, Haste Not, Slip Knot and Gordian Knot, at the time graded Very Severe. One big advantage for the rock climber here was the easy access to the crags from the roadside, with no long slog up the lower slopes as was the case on most Scottish hills. On the way back to the camp-site we stopped at Raven Crag, above the Dungeon Ghyll, to have a 'wee look'. The classic climb here was Kneewrecker, which went up a crack in the central face of the crag. It was so named for a move on the crux which necessitates the use of your right knee-cap on a tiny wrinkle in the rock, to gain, somewhat painfully, enough height to reach the next handhold. The broken branches on a tree below were testament to the number of climbers with sore knees who had come off at this point. Fortunately, we both got over that painful crux without falling and breaking any more branches of that long-suffering tree. All in all, a grand day's climbing.

That evening the consensus was for a change of venue, not by any means because the Old Dungeon Ghyll might have the possible presence of a certain Cumberland wrestling champion, but just for a drink in different surroundings, so the club bus took us to a pub in the town of Grasmere. Our evening was going well there as one of the older Lomond's on guitar, was leading a rousing sing-song of favourites like, *McPherson's Rant* and *Step We Gaily*, until a group of lads in the corner started a counter rendition of

*Ilkley Moor Bah Tat.* Fair enough, we had no monopoly on the singing, so we respectfully quietened down and let this melody ring out. The trouble came when in response to our next song, *Ilkley Moor* was bellowed out once again. Now, this seemed to be an instance, less of a limited repertoire than an outright act of aggression. Obviously, so thought Pat Walsh as he put down his pint and walked over to our rivals' table. John McLean said quietly to me with a wee smile, 'Oh Oh, Gordon, here we go. Pat's taken off his specs and put them down the back of a radiator. That means only one thing.' Pat stood before our rival choristers. We didn't hear what exactly was said but one assumes it wasn't complimentary, as in a flash, he had dived over the table, scattering glasses of beer as he slid towards the far end. The 'Ilkley' ringleader sitting there suddenly stopped singing as a series of punches rained down on his head. In the general melee which followed not a lot of damage was done, perhaps not what the lad with the well-punched face might have said, but it all calmed down and was over when the landlord of the pub, ironically chucked out the English climbers, calling them troublemakers. Obviously he was a very perceptive and discerning man.

As I said at the beginning of this, occasionally we had distractions other than climbing at the weekends.

# Introduction to *A Dream Cargo*

L ike many of the Glasgow weekenders in the early 1950's I served my apprenticeship in engineering and as National Service was still in operation, when my time had been served, I had my medical and was asked which regiment I wanted to join. My reply of, 'Merchant Navy,' didn't go down very well. It seemed the lesser of two evils but trips to Africa and New Zealand left me concluding that in joining the Navy you saw very much of the sea and very little of the world. On return from N. Z., I was offered the position of first engineer on a small cargo boat which was being fitted out in Peterhead. The *Glenshiel* which would ply the coastal trade, mainly on the waters of the West coast of Scotland, so I thought, more in port than at sea, that sounds better than the other way round, and I accepted.

The following story was one of many 'Para Handy' like experiences I had in my one year on the boat. Sadly, the *Glenshiel* foundered in the Firth of Clyde in June 1973 with the loss of all but one of the crew.

★ ★ ★

# A Dream Cargo

The last bucket of seaweed went swinging up over our heads, and rose out of the hold to be tipped into the waiting truck. Throwing down his shovel, Sammy, the first mate, gave a shout, 'Right lads, that's it, we're finished. Let's get cleaned up, snatch a bite to eat and get down to the bloody pub. I think we've bloody well earned it.'

I looked at the blisters on the palms of my hands, and chipped in, 'You can say that again, look at the state of my hands.'

'Och away ya big lassie, ye're no' used to hard graft, that's your problem,' laughed Chunky the deckhand, 'Now let's get up that ladder and out of this stinking place, my mouth's like dust-pan fu' o' ashes.'

We were tied up in the harbour at Girvan after bringing 200 tons of semi-rotten, malodorous seaweed, 'tangle', as it was commonly known, from the Outer Hebridean island of South Uist across to the mainland, to be unloaded and delivered to the alginate factory in Ayrshire, where it was processed. This had been the latest of a number of unpopular cargoes we'd had in recent weeks, coal, cement, salt, shell-grit, each unpleasant and back-breaking to work with, and now, the smelly, 'tangle'. Despite the praise the Scots song, *The Tangle o' the Isles*, heaps on this island seaweed, we never wanted to see it ever again.

Next morning, we were seated round the table in the galley, nursing a few 'sair heids,' and somewhat reluctantly, trying to force down mugs of tea, when Charlie West, our skipper, and uncle of Charlie West the deckhand, 'Chunky' to us, to distinguish between them, squeezed his bulky frame through the narrow doorway. 'Right, lads, I've just been on the phone to head office in Glasgow and you might be interested to know that, on the next tide, that's around two o'clock, we're on our way to Skye.' A groan went up, quickly choked off, as he went on, 'Aye, I know, I know, but wait, I've no' finished. We've to pick up 250 tons, in barrels, of malt whisky and bring it to the bonded warehouse in Campbeltown. They'll be no complaints aboot that, now will there?'

Despite the hangovers – in fact almost curing them – a roar of approval greeted this, led most enthusiastically by Jimmy from Stornoway, our alcoholic cook and deckhand –we once found him hiding with an empty bottle of whisky, inside a wardrobe, dead to the world – who was doing a wee jig round the table, as he celebrated.

A chorus of remarks rang around the now much-animated galley; 'About bloody time we got a proper cargo like, after the shite we've had…'

'My God, the fumes alone will keep us going to at least, New Year…'

'Aye, let's hope it washes away that bloody coal and cement dust we've been breathing in for the past couple o' weeks.'

Two days later, our vessel, the *Glenshiel*, lay alongside the distillery pier at the head of Glen Carbost in Skye. I was standing outside the wheelhouse gazing up the loch at the magnificent Cuillin mountains, lightly dusted with snow, and thinking, 'What a magical setting, beautiful mountains, glens and rivers, all right on the doorstep of one of the best malt whiskies in the world. That's some combination!' My reverie was broken as Charlie popped his head round the door and said, 'I can see you're miles away, up there in the hills, but I wondered if you fancied a wee walk up to the manager's office? I've to sign the cargo manifesto, and, while we're there, ye can never ken, there might just be a wee dram to force down as well.'

'Best words I've heard today,' I replied, 'With this scenery and the chance to have a glass of Talisker while we're in amongst it, there'll be no stopping me.'

A secretary led us into the manager's office and he rose from behind his desk greeting us warmly, 'How are you doing Charlie? How have you been keeping? Still battling the Force Nines across the Minch?'

'Aye, we are that. The new boat's doing quite well I must say being the first of the diesel-engined Puffers. The only thing is I miss the steam 'puff' rather than the diesel 'thump,' if you get what I mean?' Then he said, 'Oh, and by the way, I'd like you to meet my new engineer, Gordon Nicol.'

'How do you do Gordon?' said the manager. 'How're you finding working with Charlie? They say he's that crabbit with everybody, he's been offered a harbour-master's job in Rockall, miles away from every other living soul, bar the seagulls. Isn't that right Charlie?' Amid the laughter he turned to a glass cabinet behind his desk and, over his shoulder, said, 'Och, I'm sorry, I'm forgetting my manners. You'll both be having a wee dram, will you not?'

'I thocht you'd never ask,' replied our skipper. 'Yes, please, just a wee one,' with a wink to me. 'That'll be grand.' Almost as if he was surprised by the question.

Our host took a bottle and three glasses from the cabinet and handed us one each. I watched in silent alarm as first Charlie's, then mine, was filled to overflowing – the whisky was running down the sides of the glass and pouring onto the carpet – producing not a flicker of reaction from either the manager or the skipper. Half-filling his own glass, the former, raised it and toasted our health, 'Slainthe,' he said, and we responded appropriately. After exchanging a few more pleasantries, and finishing our business (and whiskies) we said our farewells and made our slightly unsteady way down the road back to the pier.

'A fine man,' said Charlie. 'Even for a manager.'

'Tell me something,' I asked, as we walked along the narrow road, 'Why on earth did he overfill our glasses, it was running down the side. Is there a problem with his eyesight?'

'Na, na, he was just showing his generosity, to show there was no space left in the glass. He always does that. Did you no' see the state of the carpet? I'm telling you if he ever throws it out, I'm grabbing the bugger and putting it through the wringer.'

I was asked to re-tell this story several times, especially how good the whisky tasted, as we made our steady way back down the Inner Hebrides to our destination in Kintyre, and to where it was anticipated, some 'accidental spillage' might occur.

★ ★ ★

'What's keeping the buggers, it's nearly 8-30?' said Sammy, as we looked anxiously about for any sign that discharging the cargo would begin. Then, a long, half-an-hour later, a large truck trundled down the pier and out climbed two dockers, accompanied by Stevie, the aptly-named, stevedore. Watched closely by several pairs of eyes from the wheelhouse, they worked away, unloading barrels, for the rest of the morning, the layers growing lower and lower, as our unease increased apace. Eventually, Sammy, with the boldness of the desperate, sidled up to Stevie and whispered, 'Any chance of any of it coming our way?'

'Sure there is, I'm just waiting for the lads to knock off for lunch. Just have a big hammer and some empty lemonade bottles ready, and then we'll get started.'

After about ten long minutes, the two dockers climbed up the ladder and into the truck and headed off for lunch.

'Right Jimmy, get a hammer from the tool store and three of you run up to the shop and buy some lemonade,' said Sammy, now being decisive as our prize became more tangible.

We ran back down the pier carrying a dozen bottles, the three of us guzzling and pouring away as we went, sacrificing the fizzy, sugary drink to make space for its incomparable replacement, liquid gold! We stood fascinated, looking down into the hold where Stevie, standing on top of a barrel, raised a 14 pound hammer above his head.

'Christ, that's a bit drastic isn't it?' said Sammy, 'That'll make a hellova mess.'

Then we saw skill, art, precision and experience of someone who had obviously done this many times before, come into play. With a gentle tap on each side of the bung, which was sawn flush with the waist of the barrel, Stevie coaxed the plug, bit by bit, upwards until it popped out. He then pulled out a length of rubber tubing from his jacket pocket and proceeded to siphon off a bottle-full of clear liquid. Tapping the bung back in again, he looked up at us from the hold and said,

'Only one from each barrel, that'll be put down to evaporation, or *Angel's Share,* as they call it. They'll never miss it. More bottles lads,' he called out. As they were being passed down we realized that there were about twenty barrels left in the hold and we only had a dozen empty bottles.

'Quick. Back up to the shop!'

'You lads have some thirst, I'll say that for you,' said the woman from behind the counter, 'but I'm sorry to say I've only got six left. We'll be getting more delivered tomorrow if that's any use to you?'

'Thanks,' replied Chunky, 'I'm afraid it's more urgent than that, we canny wait that long.'

We wonder what she would have thought if she had looked out of the window of the shop and seen us running, unscrewing and emptying out, 'urgent' lemonade, all the way down the pier.

With our booty secure and divided amongst us, Stevie, strangely, declined to have any. 'Don't like the stuff,' he said, 'but I know you do and I don't mind helping you out. D'you know that I've worked for this company for ten years and never had a pay rise. They're a tight shower right enough. This is my last week with them, I've got a job with a distillery up Oban way so I don't feel I owe them anything other than a slight loss in profit. So enjoy your drink. I'll be away for a spot of lunch myself.' He gave us a wave and disappeared up the pier.

Clutching our 'gift' we made a beeline for the galley to have a spot of 'lunch' for ourselves. With a coffee mug holding a treble measure of whisky in front of each of us, we exchanged grins of mutual satisfaction. Mugs were raised and with a chorus of, 'Slainthe' the five of us took a big gulp. Almost immediately, spluttering and coughing, faces screwed up, there was an explosion of curses,

'Christ, that's terrible, it's like anti-freeze or paraffin'.

'Unbloodydrinkable, what's wrong with it? It tastes nothing like whisky.'

'Gordon you bastard, you said this whisky was the best you'd ever tasted.'

'Aye, your taste buds must be in your arse.'

Sammy, as usual, had the explanation. 'Do you ken what's wrong wi' it? It's only a week old, it'll be 100 proof. That's why it's clear and why it's put in the warehouse in sherry casks for years to mature before it's bottled.'

'Very good Sammy,' said Jimmy, 'but we've got eighteen bottles of it, we can't let that go to waste, so how the hell are we going to drink it?'

'There's only one way,' replied Sammy. 'We'll need to dilute it wi' lemonade. Quick up to the shop and ...Oh no! ... Oh fuckin' hell!'

# The Colonel's Special Barley Wine

Once again Colonel Wise and his fishing friend, Major Horne, had rented one week's salmon fishing on the attractive River Inver.

The retired colonel cautiously drove his old Bentley down the steep hill to where this narrow Assynt road narrowed even more to meet the horse and cart width of the hump-back stone bridge that crossed the Inver and let the road enter the lovely, sleepy, one-street village of Lochinver.

Colonel Wise stopped his car beside this auld bridge then he and the equally keen Major Horne draped themselves over the bridge's wide parapet and eagerly peered into the river's dark waters in the hope of seeing some resting salmon.

Ignoring the satanic black disapproving glares of some strict Sabbatharians making their solemn way to their cheerless, 'fire and brimstone' kirk, these keen fishers excitedly pointed at the indistinct wavy shapes that were salmon waiting at restless ease in that mixed peaty and seaweedy tidal water.

These experienced fishers did not need these grim kirk-goers to tell them that salmon fishing was not allowed on the Scottish Sabbath. These old army veterans were following Napoleon's wise adage that: 'Time spent on reconnaissance is never time wasted.' The information they gained today they hoped to put to good use tomorrow.

And they did!

Between them, by lunchtime that Monday, they had five, fine Inver salmon in the bag. Fresh in from the Minch, these five streamlined silver beauties were at their powerful wondrous prime.

After a pleasantly protracted lunch, Colonel Wise and Major Horne got on with their wonderful fishing. Of course, to their ghillies, this jolly pair were secretly known as 'Morecambe and Wise'. And, although they were authentic English 'Officers and Gentlemen', there was nothing snobbish about them. In fact, they were often almost as funny as that famous comic duo.

Again with the expert help of their Assynt Estate ghillies, Charlie Ross and Robert Scott, they hooked, and after a quite titanic battle, got three more splendid, wild, strong and active Inver salmon in their landing-nets.

Rightly well satisfied with their grand day's fishing, the Colonel and the Major invited Charlie and Robert into the auld manse they had again hired from the needy (or greedy?) Lochinver Minister. After getting their salmon put into the manse's large freezer the beaming Colonel genially invited, 'Come through to the kitchen with us and we'll all share a celebratory drink'.

As Charlie followed the old army officers through to the large kitchen he grinned and secretly winked at Robert. Knowing Charlie well, Robert knew exactly what these signals meant. They were obvious signs of his eager anticipation of receiving at least one large dram to celebrate and toast this grand day's fishing.

But, inexplicably ignoring the bottles of whisky so invitingly set on the auld kitchen's large sideboard, Colonel Wise opened a cardboard box and lifted out two small bottles. He smilingly explained, 'As you know, Charlie, I own an old family brewery. This is a new line we've developed. It's a special beer we call "Barley Wine." It's very strong and very bitter.' He handed one small bottle to Charlie and one to Robert.

Charlie carefully inspected his bottle. It was very small, about the size of a 'Babycham.' It looked tiny and even seemed to shrink as it nestled in the palm of Charlie's large powerful hand.

'That one bottle of Barley Wine is equal in strength to a double whisky,' the Colonel enthusiastically extolled. 'Now what would you like, Charlie, that bottle of Barley Wine or a dram?'

Charlie took his time about replying. He turned the small bottle around and continued to inspect it. Then he slowly raised his eyes and silently gazed at Colonel Wise. His mouth broke into a broad grin. His eyes twinkled.

The Colonel, Major Horne and Robert patiently waited for Charlie's well considered reply. They expected him to come out with some appropriate humorous remark.

They were not disappointed.

'Och weel now, Colonel,' Charlie said in a slow, deliberate, judicious voice, 'I'm sure a *wee* bottle o' your Barley Wine wid be very nice...*after* a double whisky!'

# Not an Admirable Admiral

O beying orders received from Assynt Estate's factor, who had received his orders from Mr Vestey, the owner of this estate, Charlie Ross and I were waiting for the retired Admiral to arrive at Glen Canisp Shooting Lodge. For some reason that had not been revealed to us lower ranks whose mission was 'not to reason why, but to do or die', this old retired Admiral who had never been here before, had been given a day's free fishing on Loch Druim Suaradlain, the attractive, isle-dotted, trout-rich loch that nestled at the Lodge's doorstep.

Our awaited Admiral's arrival was announced by his Silver Bentley's rather fast and erratic parking at the back of the Lodge.

With a welcoming smile and outstretched hand, Charlie introduced himself to the Admiral. He was rewarded with a brief handshake and the glint of a return smile. Charlie then introduced me, and the handshake and smile I received were even more cursory. It was obvious that this crusty old sea dog did not want to waste precious fishing time on prolonged social niceties.

As Charlie assembled the Admiral's long, double-handed, 'Hardy's' split-cane salmon rod he asked, 'Have you a smaller trout rod to assemble, sir?'

That innocent question was like a red rag to a bull. 'Trout rod? …Trout rod? … What the hell would I want with a trout rod? I fish for salmon and nothing else, is that perfectly clear, Ross?'

'Och aye, sir,' you've made that abundantly clear.'

Listening to this exchange and seeing the Admiral's ruddy cheeks glow even ruddier, I thought, what a bad tempered old bugger! The result no doubt of a lifetime giving loudly barked, instantly obeyed, naval orders. With an inward smile I wondered if, instead of replying 'Och aye, sir,' Charlie should have replied, 'Aye, aye, sir,' in the correct naval manner.

The Admiral seemed to relent slightly as he said, 'I don't mind catching a good sized sea-trout that fights almost as well as a salmon, but I don't have any interest in these piffling brown trout. Mr Vestey informed me that there's quite a good run of salmon going through, or resting in this Lodge's loch. Is that true?'

'Oh aye, sir, that's perfectly true. The two gentlemen Robert and I had out on the loch yesterday caught four salmon between them.' Knowing Charlie as well as I did I was not surprised to see a mischievous gleam in his eye as he glanced at me then returned his gaze to the Admiral, 'Aye, and they also caught a good bag o' a dozen braw brown trout tae!'

The Admiral greeted this mention of brown trout with a snort of disdain. 'Come on, Ross, let's go and see if I too can bag two brace of salmon.'

As soon as we came out from the tall trees and mature rhododendrons that sheltered the lodge we were buffeted by a strong Westerly wind and splattered by fiercely driven rain. Once the Admiral was well settled in the broad stern seat, Charlie and I sat side by side in the middle seat and with an oar each, got our sturdy boat going. We were pleased, and rather surprised, to find that the old Admiral did not bark orders at us to direct which way we should go. Obviously he was an experienced enough fisherman to know the wisdom of leaving the boat's guidance in the hands of his ghillies, and to rely on their expert knowledge of this loch. The Admiral's fishing expertise was clearly confirmed when he started casting with his long rod in these all too breezy and difficult conditions.

As Charlie and I heaved with each oar we forced our unwilling boat to make progress against the prevailing wind and head for the West end of the loch. Once there we'd turn then drift back, with us guiding it between small islands and allowing the Admiral to fish where, from experience, we knew were the most likely places to catch salmon.

After we had turned, it was pleasant to rest at our oars while our boat drifted and the Admiral repeatedly cast and enticingly drew his salmon flies through the restless waves. But all to no avail. Although we saw a few salmon leap high then splash back into the waves in a wild commotion of spray, not one of the fish showed the least interest in the Admiral's skilfully presented flies. 'God damn these uncooperative buggers,' he growled. 'Take the boat back up to the end of the loch, Ross, and then take me on another, a more productive, drift.'

'Aye, very well, Admiral. There are quite a few drifts we can try, but if the salmon stay in their present sulky uninterested mood, I certainly can't promise that any other drift will do any better than this one.'

'God damn it, man, you're not very optimistic are you? Isn't it every ghillie's job to do everything he can to encourage his fishing gentleman?'

'Aye, it is, and I'll do everything I can to help you catch salmon. I was just making it clear that I cannot guarantee that any other drift will be more productive than this one.'

The Admiral scowled but said no more. And now, Charlie needed all his breath for rowing, not talking. We had turned the boat and with straining oars were urging it against the waves and buffeting wind. While Charlie and I strained and sweated the old Admiral sat huddled under his oilskins and trolled his salmon flies behind the boat. Even this 'not quite cricket,' method of fishing, caught no fish.

At the more exposed Westerly end of the loch the wind and waves rose higher and wilder. Black clouds raced low over land and water and released their heavy load of rain. While Charlie and I strained and silently cursed, the Admiral consoled himself with a generous dram of excellent old malt whisky from a large silver flask. With almost unbelieving dismay Charlie saw that enticing flask being returned directly to an oilskin pocket. Then he thought, surely we'll be offered a dram later when we're restfully drifting.

But this hopeful wishing proved to be a rosy pipedream. On the next drift that flask remained concealed in its secure pocket, while the Admiral continued his skilled tenacious, but again unproductive, fishing. As the wind gusted to gale force and the waves surged to higher crests, the salmon seemed excited into a stormy madness of frantic leaping. For a time everywhere you looked you saw at least one salmon high in the wild air then heard its spray-splashing return. But still not one salmon showed any interested in the Admiral's well presented flies. He did catch a few small brown trout, but they were returned to the loch with disdainful curses.

Hour after hour, drift after unsuccessful drift, the old Admiral stubbornly fished. Time after time, with ever increasing effort, the two ghillies manfully overcame the grim competing gale. With dram after delightful dram the Admiral consoled himself for this terrible frustrating fishing. Not once was the flask offered to the ghillies.

As the wind howled and the rain poured and no salmon were caught even the Admiral, that crusty old veteran of many a stormy ocean, eventually had had enough. With rainwater dropping from his bushy eyebrows and his ruddy cheeks whiskily aglow, he curtly barked, 'Turn the boat around, head for the jetty. This fishing is hopeless! I'm wasting my time!'

With eager willingness Charlie and I started turning the boat. There were anxious moments when we were broadside to the turbulent waves. The boat rolled wildly and shipped a load of cold water. Then the bow came round and we were safe. The boat now responded like a greyhound released from its trap. It raced before the storm with joyful speed as if it knew it was heading homeward to the security of the sheltering jetty. No strenuous rowing was now required from the ghillies. They had ample leisure to observe the Admiral as he again produced his silver flask, raised it to his lips, and with his head tilted well back, poured the last of the whisky down his throat.

Charlie had given many un-subtle hints such as staring longingly at that flask and licking his lips, but now he silently cursed the Admiral and wished the miserable old bugger would choke on those last few drops of whisky. Instead he returned his flask to his pocket and brought out an already filled pipe and a box of matches. He huddled for shelter and struck match after match. All failed to light on the damp matchbox. Purple with annoyance he swore, 'Oh God damn it, is there nowhere dry on this damned boat where I can light a match?'

I glanced at Charlie and noted the roguish gleam in his eye. I waited expectantly for his reply. I was not disappointed.

Charlie gently drawled out his answer, 'Och, well now, Admiral, you could try striking a match on the back o' my throat… it's certainly dry enough!'

'What? What?' the Admiral gasped, 'What was that you said, Ross? I'll let Mr. Vestey know of your damned impertinence!'

The Admiral wasted no time in getting ashore, getting his rod and fishing gear into his Bentley and leaving without any handshakes, and most certainly without giving any tips! 'Och Charlie,' I laughed, 'I bet that auld Admiral is wishing for his good old navy days when he would have had you put in chains, or even be flogged, for your damned insubordination.'

'Aye, nae doot he is. Och, but he was a real miserable bastard with his braw whisky, wasn't he? Thank God there are no' many o' the real gentry as bad as him.'

I nodded my agreement then grinned, 'Before you leave in your van, Charlie, you better come up to my wee flat. My wife should be there now and I'm sure she'll give you a cup o' tea,'

'Aye, thanks, I sure could do wi' a drink o' tea. And dae you think there might be a wee dram there tae?'

'No, 'I grinned, 'there won't be a *wee* dram there. I'm damned sure I'll find a *good big* dram for you there, and we'll drink a toast to that miserable not very Admirable Admiral, won't we?'

# Wee Hamish's First Salmon

Gordon decided to take his four year old son, Hamish, on that return trip to Achmelvich he'd been promised and was constantly clamouring for.

Gordon himself had been wishing for some time to get out of Glasgow and return to that familiar wild Assynt landscape he loved so well.

Gordon and Hamish soon got themselves settled in the simple (some might say 'primitive') comforts of this wee hut that for some happy years had been Bob Scott's Achmelvich home, and was now rented out as a very modest, holiday 'cottage'.

As, promised, Gordon once again took his wildly eager son trout-fishing on some of Assynt's countless lochs. Normally at this sunny time of early May, many aquatic flies would be hatching and many hungry trout would be greedily feeding on them. But, despite the clear skies and bright sunshine, the weather was not normal. A strong, biting cold wind was driving in from the North West; directly from the freezing Arctic.

Gordon respected an old adage he'd heard from Bob in past years, "When the wind is in the North the wise fisherman does not go forth." That traditional wisdom was proving itself true today. Almost no flies were hatching and no trout were rising.

Soon even wee Hamish's boyish keenness waned as his fingers froze and water constantly dripped from his nose.

They returned to their Achmelvich cabin, warmed themselves with tinned soup and tea then, had a Mars Bar each.

Soon after they had eaten, wee Hamish, looking out of the window at the glowing sunshine, hopefully said, 'Dad, can we go out fishing now, it's nice and warm?'

'We've just had a plate of soup, that's why it's warm. But O.K. let's have a look.'

Together they ventured outside. Gordon smiled at his son, 'Sure the sun is shining all right, but the wind is still very cold. The fishing will still be hopeless.' Sensing, and sharing, some of his son's terrible disappointment, Gordon cheerily decided, 'I tell you what, Hamish, we'll go over to Inverkirkaig. You can try to catch salmon in the River Kirkaig Estuary. And we can also visit Bob Scott and his wife in their new home there, how about that?'

Gordon parked their car and Hamish with eager excitement led the way to the River Kirkaig Estuary.

Hamish's enticing silver spinner was soon brightly swimming through the brackish tidal water.

Gordon knew that the wild and lovely River Kirkaig's salmon fishing was strictly controlled, could only be legally obtained, at a stiff price, through Lochinver's posh Culag Hotel. So even here at its tidal estuary they were illegally poaching. He also knew that as early in the season as this there would be very few, if any, salmon coming fresh in from the sea to this late-fishing river. Still, blissfully unaware of this discouraging knowledge, wee Hamish fished on with undiminished optimism.

Shivering in the cold North wind sweeping in from the glittering sea, Gordon was about to suggest they pack up this unproductive venture and head home to their cosy wee holiday hut, when Hamish suddenly wildly shouted, 'Oh Dad, Dad, I've caught a fish!'

And so he had. Or at least he'd hooked a salmon. It was not yet caught. Although his own excitement was almost as great as his son's, Gordon tried to calm Hamish while instructing him how to keep in control of the fish as it sped off in a wild rush and sent the thin nylon line slicing and hissing through the salty brine.

Then in a commotion of silvery spray the salmon leapt clear of the water. Father and son's pounding hearts leapt as high as that soaring salmon.

'Reel in! Reel in!' Gordon shouted as Hamish's fish, came racing in towards them.

After much "toil, sweat and (almost) tears" the 8 lb. salmon weakened and Gordon managed to grab it and heave it on to the land while wee Hamish shouted triumphantly and did a wee dance, hopping from one foot to the other, on the stony shore.

When some of the excitement and the proud inspection of Hamish's great salmon had subsided Gordon anxiously looked around then said, 'Right Hamish, we better get your poached salmon hidden in the car before the river-watcher or any gamekeepers see it and take it from us.'

Appalled by that awful possibility, Hamish raced back towards the car and urgently called on his dad to hurry up, as Gordon, with one hand behind his back holding the salmon, tried to make an innocent-looking exit from the scene of the crime.

Back in the car, the salmon hidden in the boot, Gordon now had another problem. How would he ever manage to cook a fish that size? The hut's wee calor gas cooker and the small frying-pan and cooking pots would never cope with it. He grinned at his son, 'Well, Hamish, there's only one thing for it. We'll throw ourselves on Bob Scott's mercy. Although he's now an Assynt Estate gamekeeper surely he's bound to turn a blind eye to our poaching exploits.'

And he did. Bob and his wife, Eileen, loudly and sincerely lavished their laughing praise on wee Hamish's cleverness in catching such a fine fish.

With eager skilled speed the streamlined silver beauty was transformed into thick salmon steaks. Then Eileen's expert cooking wizardry turned these fresh fillets into a wondrous succulent mouth-watering feast.

Wee Hamish eagerly tucked in to the meal he had supplied, and ate with something of the relish of his primeval hunting/fishing ancestors.

Bob poured Gordon's celebratory post-dinner dram with wise moderation; he had to drive back to Achmelvich over those narrow and endlessly twisting Assynt roads.

The following morning the bright sun still shone and that North West wind still bit with Arctic chill. As if resting on his laurels, wee Hamish for now had had enough of fishing. Remembering past summer holidays, he insisted on going on to Achmelvich's beautiful white beach to make sandcastles.

So, sometime later, Hamish and Gordon were sitting admiring their handiwork. Then the sun went in behind high grey clouds and to their utter amazement large snowflakes came fluttering down. Soon the freezing wind swept in a smothering blizzard.

Striding through this May-time mini-blizzard, came an Achmelvich crofter, Donald Pollochan, with his two collies. He had been conscientiously once more checking up on his vulnerable young lambs. He waved, smiled and then shouted, 'Fine day Gordon, aye it is that, now wouldn't you and wee Hamish there be much better off making a snowman rather than daft sandcastles?' He laughed as he looked down at the two figures, 'Och, but I wouldn't worry about it, just sit there a wee while longer an' somebody passing, will see a couple of daft tourists doing a damn fine impersonation.'

# A Long Point on Quinag

F eeling that we're almost cheating, we leave our car parked almost
800 ft high by the Skiag Bridge to Kylesku Ferry road.

Starting from this elevated position on this bright June day might
seem to make our climb of Quinag's long, many-peaked ridge all too easy.
Bob Scott justifies his decision to climb those 800 ft. in the lazy ease of the
car by the thought that, for him, this climb is not being done entirely for
fun. It is partly work, pleasant work admittedly, but a type of work none-
the-less.

As if reading Bob's thoughts his old climbing pal, Gordon Nicol, on
holiday from Glasgow, grins and says, 'Oh it must be great to be paid for
doing what you like doing; what you would more or less do in any case.'

Bob placidly smiles his contented agreement.

His petite wife, Eileen, joins in with, 'Aye, that's what I think too; he
should be truly grateful for having his great game-keeping job.' Her loving
eyes sparkle with an impish glitter as she laughs, 'Aye, and not only does he
have his great work, he has great wee me too!'

Bob laughingly orders, 'Oh come on, let's get going before we have any
more, any even more soppy, romantic talk.'

So that happy party of six eagerly set out. There were three humans and
three dogs. Two of the dogs are Eileen's and Bob's own: Lass, Bob's working
fox-terrier; Chico, Eileen's medium-sized white poodle. The third dog, a
young, English Setter bitch, named Shadow, belongs to Assynt Estate. As
part of his game-keeping duties, Bob is in charge of Shadow, is training her
ready for her grouse-pointing duty on the next 'Glorious Twelfth,' the
annual August start of the grouse-shooting season.

All three dogs are actively eager as they start to effortlessly climb Quinag
Ridge's easy Easterly approach.

Under Bob's encouraging guidance Shadow makes controlled sweeps over slopes of uninteresting grouse-free grasses, then with ever more alert and eager nostrils, searches through every patch of heather where, she frantically hopes, some coveys of red grouse might be hiding.

Undeterred by every disappointment, Shadow, with tireless energy, continues sweeping through all fresh heather clumps with her sensitive quivering nostrils forever testing every scent the Westerly wind brings her.

But all her eagerly keen grouse-finding expectations are sorely disappointed.

When the entire party reach the long ridge's first summit, Spidean Coinich, not one grouse has been heard, seen, or scented. Only a few old yellow droppings are evidence that grouse have been here.

They drop down to Quinag's narrow Bealach then they, or at least the three humans, strenuously make their way up the steepest part of this long ridge to get to 2,653 ft. high Sail Gharbh, the many-peaked hill's highest summit.

After a short rest they push on to the most distant final summit, Sail Ghorm. There's more heather, a few more yellow old grouse droppings, but still no grouse for the sorely disappointed Shadow to scent and point.

As the three humans leisurely start walking down the final easy slope that leads to their waiting car they continue happily talking while two dogs, Lass and Chico, contentedly walk with them.

Engrossed in his talk with Gordon of some of their grand old climbing days, Bob does not notice that Shadow is missing. It is Eileen who suddenly notices and, alarmed, asks, 'Wait a minute, Bob, where is Shadow?'

With searching eyes all three scan the surrounding slopes, but nowhere is there any sign of Shadow.

'She must be back there much higher up the hill,' Bob says. 'I'll go back and find her.'

'I'll come with you,' Gordon says.

'Just you wait here with Chico and Lass, Eileen,' Bob instructs. 'If Shadow should return to you just keep her with you until we come back, O.K.?'

'Oh, yes, yes. Oh, Bob, hurry and find her. Oh, what if she's gone over those Westerly cliffs!'

With eager anxious speed Bob and Gordon climb back up the slope they've just descended.

They scan the higher rougher ground that rises to the first summit, Spidean Coinich, but still there's no sign of Shadow.

They climb on a bit further then Bob gives a delighted shout, 'Oh, there she is!'

'Where? Where? I can't see her,' Gordon exclaims. Bob points and laughs, 'Over there, look. She's doing what I'm doing, accurately pointing.'

'I'm damned if I can see her yet, 'Gordon complains.

'See what looks almost like a large white stone amongst those smaller grey stones? That 'white stone' is actually Shadow. She's scented hidden grouse and is standing motionless, pointing at them.'

'Oh yes, I see her now,' Gordon said. 'Surely she's not been standing there 'pointing' all this time?'

'Aye, almost certainly she has. That's what she's been trained to do. Usually she'd only have to hold her point by herself for some minutes until I had joined her. Then we'd silently wait until the gentry 'guns' joined us and took up their shooting positions on each side of the patiently waiting man and dog.'

'And exactly what happens then?' Gordon asked as the two of them hurry towards the motionless, waiting Shadow.

'Well, gently urged on by me and guided by her unerring nostrils, Shadow in slow-motion, stalks forward towards these as yet unseen grouse. The two 'guns' advance slowly, on each side of us. Then, although expected, there's that always startling sudden explosion of a covey of grouse bursting into scattered flight. Then, sportingly giving the erratic grouse some distance, the usually accurate guns blast out.'

By now Bob and Gordon had almost reached Shadow. Seeing a 'pointing' setter for the first time, Gordon was most impressed.

Standing motionless, as statuesquely still as if carved from marble, her silky white, slightly black and tanned body one arrow-straight 'point' from end of quivering nostrils to tip of outstretched 'feathered' tail, her right foreleg held up poised ready to instantly step forward as soon as ordered, she truly was a most attractive sight.

Reaching Shadow, Bob quietly, sincerely, praised her, 'Well done, lass. You've excelled yourself holding this point for so very long.'

'Now we move forward to see the grouse, do we?' Gordon asked.

'Aye,' Bob grinned, 'we move ahead to where Shadow's pointing, but I rather doot if we'll see any grouse.'

'Oh why shouldn't we? I thought that seeing and, in season, shooting grouse, was the *whole point* of Shadow's amazing long point.'

Without answering, Bob slowly moved forward with Shadow stealthily stalking with questing nostrils by his side. A mystified Gordon walked beside them.

Almost under Shadow's pointing nose a lump of greyish 'stone' rose up and scurried away. Two other 'stones' anxiously hurried after it.

'There you are, Gordon, that's what Shadow's been steadily and accurately pointing all this time, not red grouse but ptarmigan. Those hardy birds of the mountain's higher slopes are of the grouse family and, I suppose, must have the same scent as red grouse. So Shadow did amazingly well to stand and point these ptarmigan, these mountain grouse, for such a long time.'

Watching these birds running, halting, then again hurrying like clockwork toys, Gordon said, 'They seem most loath to fly, don't they?'

'Aye, they certainly do. Even when disturbed by men and dogs they usually run for quite a distance before at last taking reluctant flight.'

'Oh, I see, and do the gentry shoot ptarmigan too?'

'No they don't. At least on this estate they don't. There are so few ptarmigan here that our sporting gentry leave them to breed in peace.'

As he patted and praised Shadow, Gordon said, 'It's surely quite amazing that she held that motionless point for all that time. Would most trained setters wait so long?'

'No, many would have got impatient of waiting. They would run forward and put up the birds after pointing for some ten minutes or so.' Bob grinned, 'So perhaps I deserve a pat on the back too for training Shadow so well.'

'Aye,' Gordon laughed, 'I suppose you've done quite well for a lad who, not so many years ago, worked in a Glasgow office and the only grouse you ever had was about what a hellish job you were doing.'

# A Perfect Heart-Shot

With eager skill, Scots Guards officer Lieutenant James Bradshaw, drove his bright red two-seater M.G. sports car up the narrow private road that twisted and turned towards Glen Canisp Lodge. He was a friend of the son of the owner of this shooting lodge and its surrounding vast West Sutherland sporting estate. He was looking forward with great anticipation to his first Highland deer-stalking expedition and to bagging his first red deer stag.

After parking his car behind the shooting lodge, the young officer hurried to meet the three men and one pony who were waiting for him. Charlie Ross, the estate's head gamekeeper, advanced with outstretched hand. With firm handshakes and warm greetings, introductions were made all round.

'Well, sir,' Charlie said, 'I was told that you'd be bringing your own rifle and that you were an expert shot on army shooting ranges. Is your rifle in your car?'

'Yes, it is. I'll get it now. Then I'll be ready to set out and with your help and guidance bag my first stag. I've heard high praise of your great stalking skills, Charlie.'

'Och weel, I've had many many years o' practice.' He grinned, 'Sometimes my aching an' creaking auld knees strongly hint that I've been stalking for just too many years! But before we set out we better have proof of your expert shooting skills. I want to see how well you dae on the lodge's target. Anyone that's nae good on oor target is not allowed to shoot at, an' possibly only wound oor stags, all right, sir?'

'Oh yes, of course. I've been told about, and entirely agree with this wise rule.'

Lt. Bradshaw's first shot accurately smashed into the chest of the life-size stag painted on a large steel plate.

Watching through his telescope, Charlie said, 'Good shooting, sir. A perfect shot.'

The young officer fired two more shots. They were equally accurate. The three bright bullet marks on the painted stag were grouped almost touching one another.

As Charlie slid his telescope into its leather case he smiled, 'Three perfect heart-shots, sir. I've nae doot you'll dae as well when I lead you to your first stag.'

The stalking party set out. Charlie led the way, Lt. Bradshaw eagerly followed, I came next and the pony-boy, leading the sturdy white pony, brought up the rear.

Whenever the width of the path allowed it, the keen young officer strode by Charlie's side and bombarded him with questions about the life of red deer, the art and skill of stalking them and the history of this expensive, elitist sport. He also asked many questions about this wild Assynt landscape and its wildlife. He was thrilled when Charlie grinned and pointed, 'There you are, sir, there's your first sight o' one o' Assynt's golden eagles that you were asking about.'

Seen in vivid detail through the officer's powerful binoculars and the gamekeepers' telescopes the eagle as it effortlessly circled and soared on lazy wings high above them, truly was an impressive sight.

As the stalking party advanced ever deeper into the tree-less wilds of Glen Canisp Deer Forest the white early morning mists that had cosily cloaked the surrounding mountains gradually melted away and left these distinctive peaks bright and clear under a sky of luminous cloudless eggshell blue. Slanting sunshine flooded the receptive glen with welcome glowing warmth. A steady gentle breeze set in from the East.

Lieutenant Bradshaw said, 'It's a glorious day now. All this fantastic wild landscape is wonderful, is truly awesomely wonderful, isn't it? But will this clear brightness make the stalking more difficult, Charlie? Would it be easier on a dull day of cloud and some rain?'

'Aye, it would be, right enough. Och, but it's a real braw change tae be flooded with bright sunlight instead o' being flooded with almost constant drenching rain. But this East wind that's brought this welcome sunshine has forced me tae change oor plans. We'll need tae take a different route an' advance into this steady breeze an' make sure oor strong human scents are carried away from any stags ahead o' us.'

And so the stalking party left the main Glen Canisp path well before they would normally do when the prevailing South Westerly wind was blowing. Charlie guided them along the less used path that went close by the deserted, semi-ruined former shepherds' cottage at Suileag* then by the East of Loch Suileag and up a steep narrow wee glen that led to another loch. From there they made their way along the rough, heathery, lochan-scattered ridge that led to the Western slopes of that fine, isolated mountain, Canisp.

Leaving the pony and her attendant pony-boy waiting behind us, Charlie, the keen young officer, and I, made our cautious way through this wilderness of steep rocky knolls, narrow heathery ridges, well hidden boggy wee glens and secret weedy lochans.

From his years of experience Charlie knew that many stags were likely to be making the most of this welcome warming sunshine by lying in drowsy ease enjoying this infrequent dry weather on the South-facing bright slopes of some of these rugged wee knolls But while many stags would be lying in relaxed contentment, there would always be one or two older, more cautious, stags standing by on ceaseless alert.

And this was exactly what they found one hour later when, lying well concealed, they scanned one more knoll through expert telescope and less expert binoculars. 'There you are, sir,' Charlie whispered, 'see yon nine-pointer stag standing in front o' that large slab o' vertical rock there; he's a fine beast for your first stag.'

With eager enthusiasm Lt. Bradshaw whispered, 'Oh yes, I see him Charlie. Gosh yes, he would be perfect stag to bag. But do you think I'll manage to get within range of him unseen? He seems very alert and there doesn't seem much cover between him and us.'

'Och aye, sir, you'll manage it fine. It'll mean us crawling many yards through yon thick heather in front o' us, but that won't be a problem for you, will it?'

'Oh no, of course not, I'd crawl miles to get that stag!'

Charlie grinned, 'Och, I hope we don't need tae go as far as that. Anyway it will be quite a pleasure to crawl through dry heather; we're much more used to getting soaked by squirming through awful sodden heather.'

---

*This cottage is now a comfortable climbers' bothy.

'Well, Charlie, I only hope I keep up my high standard and get another accurate heart-shot when we get within range of him.'

'Och I'm sure you will, sir.'

With a grin I added my whispered encouragement, 'Aye, there's no doubt you will bag him, sir. That pair of ravens circling high above us are confirming this.'

Charlie smiled his agreement, 'Aye, those wise auld ravens are patiently waiting for us to get on wi' the stalk and supply them wi' a fine feast o' gralloch.'

One behind the other, the three of us silent crawled our wary reptilian way through the gentle rising slope of thick dry heather.

In due course, unseen and unsuspected, the stalkers were within range of the standing, nine-pointer stag.

Lt. Bradshaw's rifle was slid out of its cover, the safety catch was flicked off and one bullet was slid into the breech. The young officer eagerly, almost lovingly, hugged his rifle's smooth wooden butt to his right shoulder. The alert but unaware stag loomed large in his telescopic sight. The rifle's muzzle was aimed straight for the stag's heart. His trigger-finger steadily tightened. The loud shot blasted out.

Lying in the heather beside the young officer, Charlie and I had our telescopes firmly focused on the stag. We both clearly saw the officer's bullet smash into the vertical rock just behind the animal and a mere inch or two above its shoulder.

Expecting to see the stag run off in wild panic, we were amazed to see it stagger a few yards then drop dead.

Charlie threw me a quick meaningful glance and gave a warning shake of his head, so with instant understanding I smothered the remark I had been about to make.

Lt. Bradshaw happily grinned at us, 'Well, Charlie, another perfect heart-shot as I promised!'

Obviously he had not seen his bullet hit the rock and not the stag. Again obviously, as Charlie and I had instantly surmised, a sharp splinter must have flashed from the rock and fatally sliced into the stag's heart. Wisely adapting to the occasion Charlie readily agreed, 'Aye, sir, another fine heart-shot it seems for your first stag, my hearty congratulations.'

I joined in with my equally false, sincere congratulations to Charlie's, then when the lieutenant was bent over almost gloatingly inspecting his dead stag, Charlie gave me a secret impish grin, a cheery wink and a quick thumbs-up sign. I knew exactly what he was meaning and why he had said nothing about that bullet missing the stag. As Lt. Bradshaw was a 'pukka English officer and gentleman,' he would be well aware of the strongly established sporting tradition that, in celebration of a British gentleman bagging his first Highland stag, he had to donate a bottle of malt whisky to the gamekeepers whose stalking skills had enabled him to shoot his prize. Had that young officer known that his bullet had missed he almost certainly would have regarded his stag as having not really been sportingly accurately shot but having been killed by a mere fluke; a killing which was 'not quite cricket!' And therefore there would be no justification for giving bottles of malt whisky to the disappointed gamekeepers.

Keeping up another good old Highland sporting tradition Charlie dipped his fingers into the small pool of blood at the neat, fatal 'bullet wound' on the dead stag's chest then smeared that blood on the expectant, wholly delighted young officer's glowing cheeks. This ancient Pagan ritual confirmed that Lt. Bradshaw had truly sportingly bagged his first Highland stag and had been correctly 'bloodied.' As far as Charlie and I were concerned he would never learn that it was not his accurate bullet, but the amazing once-in-a-lifetime chance happening of that sharp splinter of deadly rock slicing into the unfortunate beast's heart that had bagged him his longed for first kill.

While the stag was being gralloched, the pair of ragged hovering, ugly cawing ravens impatiently waited to gorge on their eagerly anticipated offal feast.

The 'heart-shot' stag was loaded on the sturdy pony and the long, sun-bright, return journey started.

After steadily striding many sweaty but happy rugged Assynt miles, the stalking party reached Glen Canisp Lodge and the stag was hung and weighed in the lodge's deer larder.

As Charlie and I started skinning the hanging stag, Lt. Bradshaw said, 'I'll take my rifle to my car. I'll clean it later. There's also something I want to get. I won't be long.'

As soon as the young officer was well clear Charlie grinned and said, 'Come on, hurry up wi' skinning this beast. There's an operation I want tae carry oot on this "heart-shot" stag.' Once the hairy skin was peeled off, Charlie examined the small neat wound in the beast's chest where the deadly splinter of stone had so amazingly entered. With his large, razor-sharp gralloching knife, he slightly enlarged the fatal wound. Then, stabbing his knife into the opposite side of the stag's chest, made a much larger wound between its ribs and exclaimed, 'Aye, that looks a correct exit wound where the "officer and gentleman's" high velocity bullet smashed oot after slicing through the stag's heart. Aye, there's now nae doot that this was a perfect heart-shot!'

When Lt. Bradshaw returned, Charlie and I, perhaps rather unconvincingly, pretended not to notice the bottle of malt whisky he held in each hand; but when these bottles were forcefully thrust at us there was no doubting the sincerity of our grateful delight at receiving these traditional gifts that set the confirming seal of authenticity on the young officer having bagged his first Highland stag.

'What about the pony-boy,' asked the lieutenant, 'where is he? Should I reward him with a bottle of whisky too?

'The young lad's in the stable unsaddling and rubbing down the sturdy sweaty auld pony. Och no, he won't expect a bottle o' whisky.' Charlie grinned, 'We don't want to encourage him to become too fond o' the demon drink too soon, do we?'

Lt. Bradshaw laughed, 'Oh no, we don't want that. I'll give him a generous tip instead.'

The young officer now stooped to examine the hanging stag's chest. With something that suggested complacent, almost boastful self-praise he happily enthused, 'Gosh, that really was a jolly good heart-shot that bagged me my first stag, wasn't it?'

Unseen by the stooping young officer, Charlie glanced at the two alluring bottles of mature malt whisky, slyly winked at me, then with seeming sincere agreement, brightly enthused, 'Oh aye, sir, it truly was one of the best I've ever seen!'

# Shooting the River Inver Rapids

E ven for the notoriously wet West Highland weather, these last three weeks of almost non-stop rain had been exceptional.

The oldest, most experienced Assynt gamekeepers had never seen the River Inver so high. And now its flooding fury had washed the footbridge on the Star Pool dam clean away.

So instead of the usual walk from the Northern river bank, where their cars were parked, across the footbridge to the lunch hut on the Southern bank, from which they did their salmon fishing, these keen fishermen and their equally keen fishing ladies had now to be ferried across in rowing boats by their ghillies and gamekeepers.

Fortunately the Star Pool was large enough to count almost as a lochan, through which the River Inver rushed in impetuous flood, and so could easily accommodate two sturdy wooden boats.

As if conscious of the high value of their cargoes of Vesteys: grandparents; son and daughters; in-laws and many grandchildren, plus their dogs, the most reliable and experienced gamekeepers and ghillies were extra careful as they made each cautious Star Pool crossing.

They rowed each boat high up the pool and were vigilant never to allow their boat to be caught broadside on in the surging flow of the river's strong current. With expert rowing skills they kept each boat's laden bow pointing up the rushing flood then crabbed across and neatly gained the river's other bank.

For two days this ferrying went on with no mishaps. The river's level was steadily falling, but a rush of tempestuous flood still poured through the smashed dam's wide gap.

The most experienced gamekeepers and ghillies were now needed at the deer stalking, so some less expert ghillies were left to do the ferrying. For another few days all went well. Then came what could have been tragic disaster.

Colin, one of the younger, youthfully over-confident ghillies, perhaps rather bored by all this cautious toing and froing and weary rowing, thought he could hurry through his latest river crossing. He did not row far up the Star Pool and foolishly, failed to keep his boat's bow pointing up into the river's lower, but still powerful, current.

Too late he desperately tried to correct that slewing bow as the rushing river grabbed it and turned the boat broadside on to the flood.

Colin's urgent splashing oars were useless. The boat was being rapidly swept towards the dam's rushing gap. Colin urgently shouted, 'Hold on, Mrs Vestey, we're going over.'

White-haired Mrs Vestey was the only human passenger in this boat. She, perhaps even before the young ghillie, had been aware of the fate that might await them. Like the true British (Scottish actually!) lady she was, her first concern was not for herself but for her two spaniels sharing this endangered boat with her. Instead of grabbing the boat and holding on for dear life she grabbed hold of each dog and lovingly protectively hugged them to her.

Watching in horror as they saw their grandmother's boat about to go broadside over these rushing rapids, her young grandchildren screamed and wept.

Also standing on the river-bank above the dam another young ghillie shouted, 'Oh God, they're going over!' He turned and urgently ran down the steep path to the pool below the dam.

There he saw the boat half full of water but, amazingly, still afloat. Both its soaked humans seemed otherwise unharmed.

After broadside shooting these rapids and shipping a load of water the boat had, by some miracle, remained afloat and had surged out of the river's rushing flood into the calmer waters of a small bay. Having lost both oars, Colin leapt into the waist-deep water and started pulling the water-logged boat towards the gravel shore. The other young ghillie waded in and helped Colin pull.

One spaniel leapt ashore, vigorously shook itself and then stood expectant ready for any more of this watery fun.

Unconcerned about her own shivering freezing soaking state, Mrs Vestey's only fear was for her missing dog. 'Oh, Robert,' she gasped, 'have you seen Jasper?'

Jasper was her missing spaniel. 'No, I've not.'

'Oh God, he must be swept down river!'

Turning and starting running, Robert shouted, 'I'll try to find him.'

He rushed down the narrow rough path that went from pool to pool down this wild, rocky, in places ravine-like, lower part of the River Inver.

As he quickly checked each pool, with no sign of the dog, he increasingly feared the worst.

Then, again quite miraculously, he heard Jasper's plaintive whining, as he stood dejectedly on a narrow shelf of slippery rock, just above the river's rushing flood.

Putting his old rock-climbing skills to good use, Robert without too much trouble clambered down the steep rock slope. He grabbed Jasper by his strong collar and urged, pushed and shoved the shivering spaniel up the worst of the rocky cliff.

As the ghillie tenderly inspected the soaked dog, the spaniel, despite some bleeding gashes and ugly bruises, seemed quite un-worried by his half-drowned, river-battered state. After giving a vigorous shake, he eagerly started back up the rough riverside path that would lead him to where he had been so dramatically parted from his loving owner.

When the delighted spaniel and the even more delighted lady met there was wild rejoicing... an explosion of love and adoration.

# Some Dandy Glen Affric Days

(In memory of Nollie and Stewart Robertson)

'Why don't you come with us and share our week or so in lovely Glen Affric?' Nollie asked.

'Oh yes, I'd love to,' Eileen enthused. 'I've never been there, but from your last year's photos of that glen and its trout-rich lochs it's a place I'd love to see.'

'What about you, Bob, would you like to see it too?' Stewart asked.

'Och aye, I'd like to see Glen Affric…' I paused, smiled, then added '… once again.'

'Oh, so you've been there before?'

'Yes I have, many years ago, on one of my youthful summer stravaigings through the Highlands. A building contractor's lorry gave me a lift from near Beauly to the Hydro-electric dam being built in Glen Affric.'

'Oh yes,' Stewart said, 'we know that dam well. It's at the East end of Loch Benavean in the heart of Glen Affric.'

'Yes,' Nollie agreed, 'it's quite near where we park the Dandy, on a bonnie flat wee grassy site overlooking that lovely loch.'

'Did you camp at that loch, Bob?' my wife, Eileen, asked me.

'Och no, I didn't. I had no tent with me. I hiked on towards Loch Affric and slept out on its bonnie shore. The following morning I continued stravaiging Westwards past Affric Shooting Lodge and along the path that pleasantly meandered to one of Scotland's smallest, and certainly most remote, Youth Hostel. Named Alltbeithe on some maps, when it's shown at all, it's tucked away by itself in that wild road-less land between Loch Affric and Kintail's five high steep Sisters. It used to be a gamekeeper's stalking bothy. That remote hostel had no warden, and for the three nights I stayed there, it had no other visitors, so I had the place and all the surrounding glorious land to myself.'

'And how did you pay for your hostel stay when there was no warden to take your money?' Nollie asked.

'Oh there was an honesty box where hostellers were trusted to put the correct money.'

Stewart laughed, 'Aye, we were all much more trusting in those far off post-war years. Nowadays an honesty box would be likely to have all its money quickly stolen.'

'Yes,' Eileen added, 'and even the box itself would soon disappear!'

'And where did you go from there, Bob?' Nollie asked. 'Did you return by Glen Affric?'

'Och no, after climbing Kintail's five charming sisters, I wandered further Westward. I passed the impressive Falls of Glomach with their sheer drop of some 350 ft.'

'Oh yes,' Stewart said, 'these falls were thought to have the longest single drop of any Scottish waterfall, weren't they?'

'Oh aye, that was once, incorrectly thought,' Eileen said. She now spoke up in passionate praise of her beloved Assynt, that fantastic wild place where she now delighted to live. 'But Assynt's Eas-Coul-Aulin waterfall near Kylesku, is now well known to have a single steep drop of about 660ft. So it far surpasses Glomach's false upstart falls!'

I smiled affectionately at my Assynt-praising wife and then continued my happy reminiscing story. 'I dropped down the steep path from Glomach Falls to Shiel Bridge then took the more gradual climb up Mam Rattachan Pass, to the fine Youth Hostel that stared over Loch Duich and smiled out to greet Kintail's Five Sisters.'

'Oh, we've stayed in that Youth Hostel too,' Nollie said. 'Again, like you, many years ago.' She turned to her husband, 'Remember, Stewart?'

'Aye, I remember fine, even 'though it was all those years ago. The hostel warden was quite a "character," wasn't he?'

'Yes,' I eagerly agreed, 'he certainly was. If I remember correctly his name was Dom Capaldi, a Glasgow Italian, he was much more Scottish than Italian. He always wore a kilt, played the bagpipes, organised local Highland ceilidhs and Scottish Country Dancing.'

'Aye, he certainly liked being a "character," Nollie said. 'I also thought him a wee bit peculiar.'

Eileen grinned at me as she said, 'Oh what else do you expect, Nollie?

Aren't most hostel wardens peculiar in some way or another?'

Nollie laughed, 'Well you should know, Eileen. You married one of them, didn't you?'

This was true. For a few years I had been warden at Achmelvich Youth Hostel in Assynt. Although I did not play the bagpipes, I, too, had worn a kilt, not at wild ceilidhs, but for its jaunty swinging comfort as I strode long wild Assynt miles to fish that unique district's countless trout-rich lochs.

'This pleasant reminiscing is all very fine,' Stewart said with a grin, 'but you still haven't answered my original question, Bob. Would you like to come with Nollie and me and stay in our Dandy in Bonny Glen Affric?'

I smiled at my wife as she spoke for both of us, 'Aye, we would love to share your Dandy in that lovely glen.'

So everything was now perfectly arranged.

Two days later our small convoy left our Assynt Estate home near Lochinver, where I now worked as a ghillie/game-keeper. Our middle-aged good friends, Nollie and Stewart Robertson, led the way in their pale blue Austin mini with their Dandy camper trailer in tow. Eileen and I, plus our two dogs, followed in our green Skoda.

Our journey went smoothly and quite quickly despite Stewart's speed being rather restricted by the modest constraining weight of the Dandy he was towing. Then after a brief stop at Beauly, came Strath Glass's narrow road, with its many twists and turns and its Hydro mutilated river rushing deep below us. Then at last came, Glen Affric which also required driving care, with its even wilder twists and more sharp turns. With Affric's demanding caution came sudden wondrous glimpses of its famed rewards; a long narrow loch brightly sparkling in June sunshine; distant Westerly hills rising steeply; glimpses of auld Scots Pines clad in their high dark greens.

When well along Loch Benavean, Stewart cheerily tooted to let us know we'd arrived at last. After some careful reversing and much painstaking manoeuvring he got the Dandy positioned exactly as he wanted it on this small, flat, neat green sward that overlooked that sparkling loch some fifty feet below us. Eileen and I were amazed at how easy that Dandy trailer, under Stewart's experienced guidance, transmuted itself into a fine, commodious, comfortable wee caravan. Its sides folded out to reveal two double beds, a tiny fitted sink and a twin-ringed Calor cooker. Its thick plastic walls and roof enclosed and protected everything. A clear plastic window looked out over Loch Benavean.

'Nollie smiled, 'Well, Eileen, do you think you'll be comfortable here?'

'Oh yes, of course I will. It's really wonderful how snug yet quite roomy this wee caravan is.'

'Aye,' I agreed, grinning, 'it really is all fine and Dandy!'

'Yes,' Stewart said, 'that's why its manufacturer gave it that name: "The Dandy Trailer Caravan."'

As this June evening's lovely twilight lingered endlessly on, it sent 'our' loch's trout into that feeding frenzy known as 'the evening rise'. It also sent us, after our hurried meal, into a pleasant urgent frenzy of fitting our fishing rods together and selecting and tying on the artificial flies most likely to be of irresistible interest to those hungry rising trout.

Fortunately we did not have far to go. The large burn that provided our drinking and washing water flowed by the side of our flat green site then rushed 50 ft down a steep slope to enter the loch. This burn's food-rich estuary flowed into a small bay and, despite the many trees crowding this place that delighted in snagging our eagerly cast flies, all four of us keen experienced anglers, managed to find enough clear space to cast out trout-deceiving flies. We all got great pleasure from catching some trout. These strong fighting wild brown trout were not huge, most weighed half a pound, but their firm pink flesh made a perfect breakfast treat next morning.

Then, guided by previous visits, Nollie and Stewart decided to fish a better place on this bonnie loch, a place that held bigger trout. So, while they took Eileen in their car to try their luck at this more promising place, I took our two dogs to walk the modest miles to where later, I would join them in their fishing.

After being cooped up in the car for most of the previous day, these dogs, like me, revelled in our walking liberty. As we headed happily westwards, the dogs were more intent on eagerly sniffing at the musky scents of nocturnal foxes rather than, like me, admiring the wondrous distant views. At times Lass, my tough, wire-haired, fox-hating working terrier, was annoyed at not being allowed to follow the strongest, most recent, of these intriguing fox odours that might lead to another fierce conflict and another dead fox. Chico, Eileen's medium-sized bouncy lively white poodle, also seemed keen to follow these fox scents, but if he ever met up with a cub-defending snarling vixen he would probably turn-tail and run back to his loving 'mummy'!

I saw Stewart's parked car then saw my three fishers at that long, tree-clear estuary where a small river sped from Loch Affric and urgently flew into 'our' Loch Benavean. I, and the eager greeting dogs, quickly joined them. Soon my impatient fly-rod was in expert use and my five fine trout were added to their glorious catch. It was wonderful to be once again in direct touch with strong fighting trout and our ancient hunting fishing ancestors. So, too, on successive Dandy Glen Affric days they ceaselessly fished, while I hiked, climbed and also fished. One day, I explored the rushing burn that flowed by our camp site and climbed the nearby steep slope that led to Beinn a' Mheadhoin's attractive, although modest, 2,000 ft. summit. But the best of all those enchanting days was when Stewart dropped me off at Loch Benavean's hydro-electric dam and I took the long walk along the little-used forestry track that hugged the loch's southerly shore.

This truly was an enchanting place. Although this was forestry land there were few over-regimented massed ranks of light-denying dark firs. There were many noble auld Scots Pines, the struggling remains of the once mighty Ancient Caledonian Forest that had covered most of the Scottish Highlands. Between these spaced out pines there grew a natural forest of graceful silver birches, healthy lusty rowans, thrusting bushes of juniper, thick layers of high heathers and in damper places the grace of bog-myrtle's sharp tang. Crushing some myrtle leaves in my hand and sniffing its pungent scent, I wondered, did it really keep the savage Highland midges at bay? At least it had, in years past, given strong-stomached Highlanders their home-brewed powerful beer.

As my meandering fancies of past years mingled with the magic of these tenacious auld Scots Pines, I was sudden aware of my terrier, Lass, demanding my immediate attention. Why was she standing staring with raised hackles and deep throated growls?

Then with startling suddenness, a capercaillie appeared from between thick juniper bushes. This was only the second time I had seen one of these rare Highland birds. Turkey sized, it was the largest of the grouse family. This bird's aggressive display made clear it was a mature cock guarding its hidden mate and chicks.

As I held her back, Lass, annoyed, gave further growls and challenging barks.

Obviously also annoyed, that huge bird answered back with strange low-pitched ticks and, appropriate for a true Highland bird, a noise as of popping corks. As it pompously strutted nearer with wide fanned tail held vertically upright, and bulging chest proudly displayed, it thrust its regal head ever higher and stabbed its intimidating beak in our direction.

To my fearless terrier's great annoyance, I decided discretion was the better part of valour, and, leading her hurriedly away, left that macho Capercaillie popping more corks, sounding very much like a celebratory Champagne party!

Continuing through this enchanted natural forest we soon encountered more of its inhabitants – a pair of glossy glowing red squirrels. Then again, a little further on, we had another brief encounter with even more beautiful forest creatures – a pair of roe deer fawns. These tiny fawns were only, (as described in my later poem) *a few moments seen, then vanish into summer's dappled green,* but those few moments were glorious.

While the red squirrels had given a fine show of beauty, this was perhaps lessened and confused by their ceaseless active scampering and mischievous animated chattering, but that swift flow of those roe deer fawns graced this place with a perfection of pure Beauty.

Nearing the end of this delightful track, I had, framed by rugged auld Scots Pines, perfect views of those distant Five Sisters of Kintail, I had climbed many years ago.

A final fine bonus before I re-joined the others in the Dandy, was the pleasure of watching entranced as a large flock of sand martins performed their swooping, soaring, insect-snatching ceaseless dance around and above the nesting burrows they'd honeycombed in the steep walls of an old sand quarry.

Later, after enjoying a filling evening meal, I rounded off this perfect day in a perfect way by catching a fine plump trout that put up an amazing, almost salmon-like, strong fight, before being netted and found to weigh just over two pure firm pounds.

On the final evening of our stay we celebrated the perfection of this Glen Affric holiday with generous, but not excessive drams. Nollie confessed she'd had some doubts about having two, perhaps unsettled, dogs in the wee trailer caravan, 'Oh but they've been no trouble at all. From the first they've settled in fine and dandy.'

'Aye,' I grinned, 'Lass and Chico have enjoyed this holiday almost as much as Eileen and me.'

'That's grand,' Stewart said. 'We've enjoyed this holiday too. We've had great weather and great fishing, haven't we?'

'Aye and great company too,' I sincerely added.

After two more drams Stewart mentioned things he rarely spoke about. 'I often used to dream of returning to holidays like this in this:

*Land of brown heath and shaggy wood,*

*Land of the mountain and the flood.*

This was when I was stuck not just months, but weary long years in the arid sands of North Africa.' He smiled at Nollie and she returned his smile with understanding sympathy.

I knew that Stewart had been a 'Desert Rat,' a soldier in the British 8th Army fighting in North Africa. After his years there he also fought in Sicily and then in the long, slow, bloody campaign up the length of Italy. For four long years he had never been home on leave. And during these grim years Nollie too had been caught up in the cruel maws of war. Not only did she bring up their two young boys by herself while their father was away fighting, but they had lived in Clydebank, and their home had been flattened by the Luftwaffe's devastating blitz.

'Yes,' I said as Eileen and I raised our glasses in a toast to Nollie and Stewart, 'your age group, only a few years older than ours, rose to noble brave heights in that long grim struggle to defeat Hitler, Mussolini, and the despicable Japs.'

'Oh I know,' Nollie said, 'and although it happened years ago, it still remains vividly clear in our remembering minds.' She smiled brightly, 'Now how about a mug of char before we turn in for the night?'

The following morning just before we parted, Eileen and I heading back to Assynt, Nollie and Stewart, with their Dandy in tow, back home to Glasgow , I said, 'Thank you both for this holiday. These past Glen Affric days have been Dandy...Really Dandy.'

# Gordon's Trek to
# Annapurna Sanctuary

4/1/83. A long day, left Diryah at 4 a.m. and then a flight to Dubai (one and a half hours). Then on to Delhi with wine and beer on offer and a good mutton curry. The Indian sitting next to me mixed his milk powder sachet with his water then looked aghast at the result. From then on he copied my every move with my lunch. Flew over Karachi, the land looks very dry, some sand dunes (could it be the Thar Desert?).

Arrived at Delhi, very busy with a huge queue at immigration. I was standing at the end of this when a policeman came up and said, 'British? Come with me'. We marched up to the head of the queue and he pushed in saying, 'Priority', and handed my passport to the officer. After the way you are treated in Saudi this is more like it.

Took something called the ex-servicemen's bus to Connaught Place and checked into the Alka Hotel, which, despite its name turns out to be dry (and also vegetarian). At 200 rupees a night I got a double room for the price of a single, though I don't really need more space – I suppose I could sub-let the other bed. Had a shower and went down for a meal in the hotel restaurant. I sat beside an American photographer who works for Time/Life, named, John Hiller from Detroit, who is here on a mission – wouldn't elucidate.

I opted for Thali which is a lot of small dishes on a round platter with poppadums and a chapatti. No beer, despite almost pleading, so I settled for a fresh lime juice. The wee dishes were pretty grim and hot, dal, keema, tapioca, yoghurt, potato and rice with chillies dotted in amongst it. Not great but tolerable then up to bed for a sound sleep.

25/1/83. Started my first Indian day with an unspectacular omelette for breakfast. Decided to move to the Hotel Hans as this one is a bit tatty (and dry). I walked to the Nepalese Embassy to apply for a visa. Round the shops, bought a couple of books and got my passport back. Took a taxi to the Red Fort passing a sign on the way which said, 'To the Red Fart', told you the curries were hot. Got there half an hour before closing and hired an informative old Himalayan guide. Amazing lattice-work carved in solid marble. As the market area was near I walked down the Chandi Chowk, (choc-a-bloc more like it). The India of the imagination, jammed with humanity, noisy, colourful, chaotic but relatively trouble-free. I was approached by several locals, change money, sell, buy etc., but no real hassles. I couldn't get a taxi back to the hotel, so took a cycle rickshaw. The young guy was obviously out to impress, pedalling furiously through the chaos, through red lights, dodging traffic, continuously ringing his bell. On to a new ring road with a steep flyover which caused him some effort, standing on the pedals to keep moving. It was a strange vulnerable feeling sitting in this flimsy contraption, amidst motorway traffic. I gave him 20r. ( just over a pound, which delighted him) then I saw he had been doing all this with one arm being withered, nevertheless, some pair of legs for motorway pedalling.

In the evening went to Kwality's Restaurant which was supposed to be shit-hot. Reverse this and you'd have a fairer description. Tarted up for the tourist market but helping sizes were designed for skinny Indians (I guess to keep them that way).

I got a half sparrow tandoori with rice which I needed to follow with a keema egg curry and nan bread. Even then I was still hungry. Back out in the street lots of hippies around, mainly Americans. Time seems to have passed them by. Caught up by the mood, I sampled pan on the way back to the hotel. Supposed to be mildly intoxicating but I didn't find it so. Like a true local spitting out red betel juice all the way back. In the room cracked open the duty free Black Label, now that's what I call intoxicating, a dram at the elbow, reading the Observer, the perfect way to end an evening.

26/1/83. I moved hotels but not really much for the better. I decided to go and see the National Day Parade. Big crowds had gathered and I couldn't see any decent vantage points so I asked a police sergeant where I could find one. He was standing on the flat roof of a public toilet and he put down a hand and helped me up beside him. Immediately the surrounding crowd began to clamber up the walls. My new friend soon put a stop to this by whacking people on their up-stretched hands and uplifted heads until they gave up on attaining my privileged position. I don't know what the fuss was about as the parade was quite short, and unimpressive, they had camels but no elephants. As the last group passed, the crowds burst out onto the street to be charged at by a group of stick-wielding policemen who chased them back up the road leaving behind hundreds of flip-flops which had come off as the mob ran away in panic. I took a photo of the Sergeant and got his address and promised to send him a copy. For some reason Indian people all try to look as stern as possible when their photos are being taken, no smiles or waves at the camera, just stand up straight and look grim.

As it was National Day all the shops were shut but I managed to find a restaurant which brought me keema curry in a dirty dish. In a park near Connaught place I took a seat and gazed around at the chai-sellers, peanut vendors, hamburger salesmen, pan-purveyors, monkey trainers, illusionists, hippies, squirrels and green parrots in the trees and all the holiday parents and weans. Sikh Dads were playing badminton and there was even street cricket. I talked to Shari an Indian leather salesman who had worked for Clark's in London. He told me that Delhi is the most varied place in India, every where else is all the same, which somehow I doubt.

I walked to the Hotel Janpath and bought a ticket for tomorrow's trip to Agra. It's an early start, 6.45 at the hotel so no drinking tonight. An unnecessary observation as it turns out as it is a 'dry day' in Delhi. There doesn't seem to be any pubs anyway, only the hotel bars although I was told back at my hotel that if you wanted a drink on a 'Dry day' you could get an M.C. from a doctor, saying on it that you had to be sold a bottle as you were a registered alcoholic. I somehow doubt this also.

Headed back to the Gaylord restaurant but it doesn't open until 7-30. A rest and switch on the fan to get some colonial atmosphere but it is the same tatty room, where's the punkah-wallah?

Rain in the evening with lightning flashes as I entered the Gaylord (slightly apprehensive about the type of place it might be, given its name, but it seems to have the original meaning). It's a big, chandeliered, old-fashioned place with candles on the table and, incongruously, a four-piece band (2 electric guitars, drums and sax) playing reggae music.

Had murg al jaswani, kurma, yoghurt and nan bread, filling enough.

A very fat Indian, (fairly rare) was shouting his head off about the quality (kwality) of the food, the slowness of the service (hard to keep up with the speed at which he gobbled down the food) and everything else in sight. He finished off by picking his teeth and spitting the debris on to the table, blowing his nose furiously on the cloth serviette and stomped his way out, a good customer obviously.

As you waddled and belched your way out of the restaurant hordes of starving beggars descended on you, hands, (if they had any) outstretched, pleading for money, somewhat detracting the enjoyment of the meal you had just consumed. As you try to come to terms with it, muttering, 'It's not my problem, what can I do? Maybe if I give them my holiday money it will at least help some.' Right, I'd better get out of here or I'll be joining Sister Theresa.

27th Jan. Early call at 5.30, breakfast then had to wait for the bus as it gathered up passengers from other hotels. An odd assortment when it arrived with some very strange coincidences. In the back seats 5 out of 6 people were working in Saudi Arabia. In the two seats in front, one bloke, a German, was due to travel on the same plane as me to Nepal. He had also had just come from Riyadh where he was something to do with the new embassy, and after Nepal was going to Shanghai. His neighbour was Chinese from Shanghai who was going to Detroit where a black American, up the back of the bus, was from. Across from them were two Russians who were in Delhi lecturing to Indian students on the Chinese economy. This also happened to be the job of the Chinese man and all three jabbered away in Mandarin. One of the Russians had German grandparents who were from the same town as the German in front. The, 'I don't believe it', 'What a coincidence', 'That's real amazing', echoed for some time round the bus.

One of the other people working in Saudi was a middle-aged nurse at King Faisal hospital who had just been on a trekking holiday in Nepal and was going back to Riyadh the next day. This was her first job overseas (her husband had died leaving her a pile of money and a curiosity about the rest of the world). It seemed a strange choice of holiday for a woman of her age and background. (Late fifties and had lived most of her life on a farm in Texas) but she claimed she had always wanted to see Nepal. In the summer she was intending to travel on the Beijing-Moscow railway.

It was a long run on the bus through country similar in appearance to rural Thailand though less lush. We stopped for food at the Kosi restaurant

– pure white, wet, scrambled eggs and a potato rissole. The plates had a large letter 'T' embossed on them and I joked, 'Must be a 'Trust' house'. Back came the German with typical Teutonic humour, 'I think it is eggs', and gave a roar of laughter. We had a few more stops at 'crafty' shops and, on pulling away from one, had an alarming experience. A young lad, about 7 or 8 years old, had been running alongside the bus below the open window of the American nurse, one open palm inside, asking for money. As the bus picked up speed he jumped up and clung to the window. Fearing the worst a couple of passengers stuffed some notes into his still open hand.

Only then did he release his grip and fall onto the dusty road. All the passengers were on their feet looking back through the window of the bus and, on cue, the lad got to his feet, gave us a cheery wave and started counting his money. A trifle more enterprising than sitting begging at the side of the road!

The first sighting of the Taj through the entrance gateway was breathtaking. O.K. we've seen the pictures of one of the most recognisable buildings in the world, but, really it's nothing like the first glimpse. It is so white and delicate looking and sort of floats at the far end of the garden. Far and away the most impressive building I've seen. The foundations are 130 ft. down so that the river can't wash it away. The 4 minarets lean outwards by one and a half inches so that, in the event of an earthquake they'll fall outwards and not damage the main building. The brass crescent is 33 ft. high and the Farsi writing round the door has larger letters at the top so that the whole appears the same size. It is all inlaid with semi-precious stones, lapis lazuli, malachite, jasper, carnelian etc., forming flowers and decorations. All the lattice work is carved from the solid marble of which the whole thing is made. Inside is rather unspectacular being empty however an echo lasts ten seconds if you care to speak. I suppose the wonder is that it looks so good after 350 years although they are worried about pollution from the factories and traffic from Agra.

I had a curry lunch with a big screw-top and on to Agra Fort. It also is quite impressive and was built with the left-over marble from the Taj. Then the long haul back to Delhi, arriving at 9 p.m. and yet another early start tomorrow, 5 a.m.

Friday 28th Very heavy rain during the night and still bucketing down as my taxi arrived. I find an old eccentric English woman already seated in it babbling away about how things were much better under the Raj. Set off through the heavy rain with the driver, one hand on the wheel and the other out the window clearing the windscreen as there were no wipers. About halfway to the airport my fellow passenger pipes up from the back, 'I do hope the train isn't late'. Turns out she's going to the railway station, not the airport, so, about turn.

At the airport I'm first in the queue but find I have to pay extra on my ticket. Change another traveller's cheque to find I now have to pay airport tax. Once through into departure I find I can't use rupees to buy duty free, they'll only accept US$. Forget traveller's cheques, nobody wants them, US$ however!

The rain is really belting down now as I take my carefully selected window seat near the front, on the side which will face the Himalayas. Served a breakfast of omelette, bean-stuffed tomato and a vegetable rissole, O.K. until the inevitable turbulence caused me to slop my coffee over my lap. No sign of the mountains through the thick cloud, I hope we're higher than them. One thing that's in its favour, it's only a 1 hour 10 minute flight. A bumpy, and pretty hairy descent into Kathmandu through dense cloud.

Trouble-free immigration and customs. I took a taxi straight to the Yak and Yeti Hotel in heavy rain. Nice hotel, very good room. Dumped my rucksack and walked down to the Sherpa Co-operative to see about my trek. Mike Cheney seems a bit doddery for an organiser of expeditions. Because of the weather there is a bit of doubt if we'll get to Annapurna Sanctuary but it's going ahead at the moment. It appears I'm getting five or six porters to accompany me. This is because we'll be away from habitation and need enough supplies for 13 days. I went and bought second-hand climbing breeches and socks. Rained all day (this will be snow in the mountains).

29th Saturday I decided on a do-it-yourself sightseeing tour of Kathmandu today. It really is a step back in time. Narrow winding streets, full of rubbish which is thrown from the upstairs balconies. There are hens, ducks, goats, dogs and cows all grubbing about in the muck. Tiny open booths as shops, selling everything imaginable, (saw a man making Primus stoves, hammering away at a sheet of brass and bending it round into a fuel tank, the pavement his work-bench). Streets packed with vendors of flutes, drums, peanuts, sweets drinks, bikes, rickshaws and the odd car threading its way through the chaos. In the midst of this are ornate temples every 100 yards or so. Specialist sections for coin-sellers, barbers, restaurants and the tourist additions – pie shops, guest houses, souvenirs. There can be few places left in the world like this. Constant pestering by people selling things, beads, kukri knives, prayer wheels, Buddhist scrolls, carpets, marijuana, cocaine, heroin, morphine etc. I found the best technique was to smile, look directly at the person and say, 'No thank you', firmly. Tourists (women in particular) walk about with a cluster permanently around them, some clutching the harassed and bemused woman's arms. It's a riot of sights and smells, enough to fill the senses and memory for a long time. As an anti-climax, went round the Royal palace which was dull and untypical of the extravagance usually found in such places.

I had lunch in an Austrian-owned restaurant in the old bit near Durbar Square, very good, goulash, chips, veg. and a beer for less than 2 pounds. Looked to be a hippie haunt but there weren't any around, in fact there doesn't seem to be many in town at all, perhaps over-dosed or gone south for the winter.

Took a walk down Pig Alley with its pie shops, and Freak Street with its cheap lodging houses; rooms for 5 rupees (20 p) per night. The number and variety of restaurants is amazing. You can buy any kind of food you can mention and most of it is very good, (generally the best is found in places whose outward appearance belies the quality of the food that can be sampled). Hotel Crystal looks handily placed for this area and a lot cheaper than the Yak and Yeti.

Got back in the late afternoon, knackered and had a nap.

In the evening I went to the nearby Sun Khosi Nepalese restaurant. It looked a nice place, with an open wood fire, which was given better service by the waiters than was obtained by the hungry clientele. The wood resolutely refused to catch alight, despite frantic blowing, paraffin, old candles, paper and the efforts of all but the kitchen staff. I recognised two blokes who had been in the Kwality Restaurant in Delhi at the same time as me. World travel seems to be a case of re-meeting people in different locations.

Back to the hotel and as I have a very early start, packed and paid my bill. I went down to the bar in my trekking gear and met Evelyn and George, from Riyadh University. He seems O.K. but has a bit of the, 'I bloody told him where to get off. They'll not bloody mess me about. There's no way I'm paying that,' sort of thing about him.

Sunday 30th Kathmandu – Pokhara – Hyendra.
Up at 4-45 a.m.

Left my luggage in the store in the hotel and got a waiting land-rover to the bus station. Families were sleeping on the pavements along with the dogs and cows. A shitty old bus with some Americans screaming about the best seats and don't tip anybody. Set off at 7-15. After leaving the outskirts the bus climbed a road similar to the Glencoe – Kinlochleven stretch, but 20x times steeper and twistier. Constant stream of people walking along the road carrying bundles of firewood, green leaves, vegetables. There was much more to see than on a bus journey in India. Families were working away in the fields and on the slopes of the mountains and ravines. Stopped for a pee and a cup of tea – not much difference! Hair-raising journey as the bus swerved to avoid cows, weans, pigs, hens, and other buses. We stopped for lunch at a really simple shack of a restaurant. My team – 2 Sherpas and 3 porters led the way through the back to the living quarters where we got a surprisingly good curry, potatoes, a sort of leek, radishes, mutton and various spices. The team ate about 3 tons of rice in about 5 minutes. Now I see why I have so many of them, it is to carry their own food! We arrived in Pokhara at 2 p.m., about a 7 hour journey. I got many jealous looks from the other trekkers as I set off with my six porters, (we hired another in Pokhara), ice-axes, down jackets, the lot. Pokhara very spread out and not much to see. We walked past a dam being built entirely by hand. The men were standing in the river breaking up stones and passing them up to others on the bank, who were piling them into the dam wall. So many people walking about, true trekking country now. We stopped at 4 p.m. I was given a wee stool to sit on while the others lit fires, pitched tents and prepared food. If only my old climbing mates could see me now. A touch of nostalgia when I saw the tents were Blacks of Greenock.

I've had my dinner, rice, mutton, potato, an apple and endless cups of tea, and am ensconced in my double sleeping bag and the rain is belting down, which means snow higher up, mmm. Some traders from the Chinese border have camped next to me so I have a couple of horses tethered, adjoining the tent. Ang Nuri was telling me earlier on that he was from the Solo region of Everest. He says there are 23 different ethnic groups and languages in Nepal. He is a Buddhist, married with one son. His

English is quite good and he has been on several big expeditions (French Everest last year.) Before being a guide he was 5 years in the Army and told me that a private gets 110 rupees a month (5 pounds) where are my $550 dollars going?

We are in an area of known thieves who steal lots of trekkers' gear. It seems they slit open the side of the tent and steal cameras, boots etc. I hope the rain and the horses keep them away tonight.

### Monday 31st. Hyendra – Dhampus

I wakened to another great view, Machapuchare and Annapurna in the sunlight. Tea and a bowl of hot water to wash in, was delivered to my tent at 6 a.m. Porridge, tea and biscuits, then off. We passed through some very picturesque villages, Hyendra and the Tibetan refugee camp. Solid stone built houses with wooden windows, red plaster and thatched roofs. Banana trees, poinsettia and flowering cherries. Kids were heading for school, barefoot, and having to walk miles. The valley opened out to a flat flood plain which fills during the monsoon. Padi rice, harvested in June, with barley planted on the terraces up the hillsides. At the end of the valley we stopped for lunch. During the fire-lighting the cook suddenly jumped up and started throwing stones into the trees. He kept staring upwards and occasionally throwing another stone. I asked him what was up and he said there was a bad bird in the trees. He pointed out a kind of magpie and explained it brought rain. I joined him in throwing stones at it.

Out came lunch, hot orange on a silver tray to start, then chips, egg, tomato, pancakes and jam. We are on an important trade route from Pokhara to Jomsom and Mustang, and on to Tibet. Flour, salt, wool, grain and even firewood are still brought through here.

On the way again and we left the valley and had a steep and constant uphill climb to the ridge which runs to Dhampus. It rained on and off all afternoon so there was something in the jinx bird after all. As we walked through the strung out village of Dhampus we passed a group of people dividing up a pig which had just been killed. Three large eagles soared above looking for a chance. We set up camp beside a pond and a manure heap at 5,900 feet so the last climb was 2,100 feet.

While waiting for dinner a strange sight hove into view. A man, obviously English, with long wide khaki shorts, khaki shirt, black boots, wearing glasses, accompanied by two porters, came striding past. One of the latter was pleading with him, 'Sahib, I can't go any further.' The reply came in a loud pukka English accent, 'Oh yes you bloody well can, and you bloody well, will'. About half an hour later he came back again, looked around and came over to me. He was an officer in the Gurkhas (God help them) and he was doing a recce to find out the best place to take his General who was going on a trek the following week. He caused a wee stir in our camp anyway.

Had another good curry with garlic and ginger soup and a gallon of tea. I took the team's photos with the Polaroid and then one of a wee girl who was standing watching. Everybody was chuffed and the girl went for her mother who had to have one taken. Soon the whole village was out clamouring for photos, but I drew the line there. After dark, I saw a moving (not shooting) star going right across the sky. Then I saw another going at right angles to it. Ang Nuri said they were satellites but for a moment I thought I was becoming one of the U.F.O. mob. Went to bed at 7-30, nothing else to do after the fire has burnt out and firewood is too precious to simply burn for heat or sing-songs. The team are very cheery, although only one speaks any English, but I keep forgetting this is work for them. Sitting at the fire with a mug of tea and feeling very contented, I said, 'Ah, this is the life,' realising that when there was no response, what their opinion of it all might be. There may be no great drive to get to Annapurna Sanctuary, I'm the only one who really wants to go there. Maybe the prospect of gratuities and my spare long-johns at the end of it will keep them going.

### Tuesday 1st February Dhampus – Lanndrung

A very cold night, I woke up this morning to a very spectacular view of Annapurna and Machapuchare. Ice on the flysheet and the puddles are frozen. Some weans have been put outside to have their morning crap, in bare feet and virtually no clothes in temperatures below freezing. An older brother or sister stays with them and won't allow them back into the house until they have performed. Now that's toilet training with a vengeance. I took some photos in the clear blue skies and then we headed off. Just before we descended into the next valley, we met an Australian couple who have been trekking for 18 days. The wife was fed up, no bath, cold at night, food rotten, tired of climbing up and down. The bloke on the other hand was rapturous in his praise of the venture but obviously marital problems ahead. Later we passed 8 Sherpani who were portering for a large party. Lots of banter flew between the two groups. The young lad from Pokhara we hired on a porter only basis gets no meals or accommodation. He is clad in baseball boots, jeans, and a thin shiny jerkin and looks pretty miserable at times, not unsurprisingly. Ang Nuri was telling me that a headmaster of a high school here earns about 33 pounds per month or my earnings for three hours. He has been discussing climbing trips with me for August and reckons it is not a bad month in Manang where there are a few good peaks over 20,000. He is going to give me his address and we'll cut out the big companies, if I can ever afford it.

We are going along around the shoulder of the hill in nice warm sunshine, which has brightened up the mood, especially from the lad in thin clothing. At Landruk the trail splits – to Ghandrung high up on the opposite hillside – and a trail staying on this side to Chemro, further up the Modi Khola. The latter is crossed by a bridge at the Modi Khola Hotel, where we will stop for the night. The valley is narrow, steep-sided with lush vegetation. Down there the rain started again and all the way it was dark and gloomy. A cold wind blew down the river through the shelter where we had dinner and the tents are already soaked. One advantage is that the shelter had a thatched roof and we have a fire going. We are now at 6,500 feet and tomorrow we'll be at 8,500, probably amongst the snow. Each day begins with clear skies and good weather until about 2-30 when it clouds over and begins to rain.

We had vegetable curry and soup with garlic and ginger for dinner, supposedly suppresses altitude sickness, and an apple. I had about three platefuls of it so it seems my appetite isn't suffering. Entertaining evening talking to Ang Nuri about the Sherpas, his climbing experiences and the animals he claims to have seen. He told me he went out of his tent one night for a pee, about 11p.m. and, facing him was a tiger who growled loudly at him. He said, 'I so scared I forget why I go outside,' and he dived back into his tent. He says we may see wild boar tomorrow in the forest. I asked him what his opinion was of trekkers, and he said Americans and diplomats were the worst. The former he claimed, were stingy, bossy and fussy about everything, and the latter for constantly complaining about cold, tiredness, and discomfort. The idol of the Sherpas is of course, Hillary, who has collected lots of money for schools, hospitals and the airstrip at Lukla. At the opening of the latter, the plane from Kathmandu, which was carrying Hillary's wife and daughter, crashed, killing all on board. I asked the obvious question about the existence or otherwise of the yeti, and Ang Nuri claimed to have seen its footprints. He said it was also in Buddhist records. Sherpa Lawry also said it existed and told the story of how, four years ago, villagers had heard a dreadful commotion amongst their animals during the night but had been too scared to investigate. When the noise had died down the bravest went out and found four yaks dead, with their backs broken. A much better evening with some conversation, I think they are getting used to me.

### Wednesday 2nd Feb. Landrung – Khuldi Gar

Again, wakened to a stupendous view, there was South peak, Annapurna with a plume of snow streaming from its summit. Alongside it, towered its shapely neighbour, Hiunchuli. We started the day with a long diagonal climb up to the ridge. The sun was warm and the views spectacular. On the descent down to Chumro, we passed a school with a superb situation (and small classes). We met a French man who had been to the sanctuary with two friends, so it looks possible. We have saved a day by cutting out Ghandrung. It was also reported that a Korean group is up there attempting to climb Tent Peak, which frustrates me once again as Mike Cheney had said it couldn't be done at this time of year. Now we get here it might have been on. Ah well there's always the Cobbler. I think I'll need to be less cautious in future, state what I want to do and go all out for it.

At least Chumro, where we stopped for lunch, was a delightful place, well, it seemed to be while the sun was shining. Just at the side of the path on the way out of the village, we found a cow breathing its last. It had fallen down a steep slope and looked nearly dead. Around the village there is evidence of land slipping and I said to Ang Nuri it looked a dangerous place. He agreed but said it was the local people that posed the most danger. Several trekkers had been robbed and killed here and some they had never found. Not mentioned by the tourist companies, but he may have been exaggerating.

We headed on up the valley climbing steeply in the warm sun. The common problem on a trek is that every morning is very cold (and also at night) but warm through the day as you are walking, causing you to sweat, but then chill rapidly when you stop for a rest. On this trek to complicate things so far, it has rained every afternoon. Today we were high enough for this to fall as snow. I saw a rhododendron beginning to flower, a beautiful dark red. Spring must be nice here. It was quite a climb up to Khuldi Gar where we were spending the night, ploughing our way through heavy snow to get there. Some French blokes, passing us on the way down said that the snow was a metre deep. We'll have a look anyway.

Tonight's highlight was some rum I had bought in Chumrong. We put it in the coffee and it was excellent. It raised the spirits no end, so to speak. Ang Nuri told me that as a Buddhist he was allowed two wives and had a son by each. Apparently they have to have two marriages to each wife, which can be costly. I'm not sure if this is what he meant but if true, presumably, it involves having two mothers–in–law. He then told me a gloomy tale about how, on one trek, they had found an 18 year old girl drowned in a river, apparently suicide. This reminded me of when we came into Pokhara, as we crossed a bridge spanning a deep chasm, I asked why there was a big crowd standing around. Ang Nuri had said at the time, it would probably be a suicide. Turned in at 7-30 with a slight headache, hoping it wasn't altitude as we are only just over 8,000 feet and going higher tomorrow.

Thursday 3rd. Feb. Khuldi Gar – Deurali

My headache persists although not incapacitating. We paid off the boy from Pokhara, probably as well before he expired from the cold. Through uncertainty I didn't tip him, but he didn't hang about looking for it, just grinned, said cheerio and off he went. We heard that the porters had deserted the Korean team because of underpayment. There seems to be a fixed, non-negotiable rate. We set off at 7-30 into some very unpleasant going. The trail went through tunnels of overhanging bamboo laden with snow. One touch and a mini-avalanche fell on you. The next two hours involved going up and down, sometimes through a stream which was flowing down the path. The vegetation has closed in on us so no views at all. At 10 a.m. we stopped for lunch and soon after the sun reached the valley and it became pleasant.

I'm really beginning to enjoy lemon tea, had 4 mugs of it before lunch and ate a hearty meal – headache disappeared. The path now got more desperate, even steeper. With the snow and ice some parts were quite dodgy. After a couple of hours a frightening sight. A big avalanche had come down from Hiunchuli shortly before we arrived. The debris was composed of large round boulders of ice which would have given you no chance. This spot was well known for this danger, and three years ago, seven Japanese trekkers had been killed by an avalanche as they crossed the track.

Our method of crossing was to go individually after listening for any tell-tale sounds of a descending mass of snow. The worst part was the area in the middle as you probably couldn't have made it back or across in time.

The usual afternoon snow was falling quite heavily by the time we reached Deurali. The decision was to stay in the bothy, rather than pitch the tents. The plan now is to leave all the gear here and make a run for the base camp tomorrow and return here. It makes sense as there is about two feet of snow outside and it continues to fall. It all depends on how much more snow there will be, whether we make it or not. The Korean team attempting Tent Peak is going to have a lot of trouble on the glacier with the amount of new snow.

The bothy is solidly constructed with walls of drystone, woven bamboo matting on the roof and, separating the inside into compartments, kitchen, sleeping areas etc. We have plenty of wood and it is a bit like the old week-ending days in Scotland, except for the lack of banter and of course, yours truly getting the VIP treatment instead of just being one of the crowd. My dinner of noodles and veg. is somewhat unfortunate, as it gives me severe flatulence in a rather confined space. During the meal a cat was heard mewing somewhere in the bothy. The cook put a big dod of rice and dhal in a tin and left it in the other room (my bedroom) for the cat's dinner. It is still in here somewhere so I expect with my completely unwanted attraction to the beasts (I don't really like them) it will come and try to sleep on my face at some time during the night. Before bed we had a final nightcap of rum coffee, which is very popular with all.

Friday 4th. February. A day I'll never forget.

We had a latish start, didn't leave the hut till 8 a.m. Once away, Ang Nuri set a cracking pace. We were traversing steep, snow-covered slopes, kind of dangerous as we were hurrying along. Added to that, we crossed another avalanche track with snow and rocks obliterating the path. Then we reached the Machapuchare Base Camp where the Koreans are camped. They immediately began asking us the names of the peaks around. It turned out they didn't even know which one was Tent Peak, their objective. Glad I'm not with them. We followed a narrow spine of rock towards Annapurna South. The Modhi Khola divides here. One branch goes towards Annapurna 3 and the other towards Annapurna itself. On reaching a high point on the ridge above the Annapurna Base Camp we found ourselves, at what must be one of the most astounding viewpoints anywhere in the world. A vast amphitheatre of mountains surrounds you. A place you could spend hours silently gazing at 180 degrees of sheer beauty. Clockwise, these mountains are Hiuchuli, South Peak, Fang, Annapurna 1, Tent Peak, Roc Noir, Annapurna 3, and Machapuchare. We watched an immense avalanche come thundering down Annapurna and I had a moment of worry, would it reach the spot where we were now standing? Every now and then there would be a tremendous rumbling and crashing, coming mainly from the Annapurna 3 area. We met an English photographer from the Sun newspaper who kindly took photos of us for posterity. What a spot to eat your packed lunch! It had taken us two hours from our bothy to Machapuchare Base Camp and another 45 minutes to the Annapurna Base Camp. The peaks were gradually clouding over, so reluctantly we decided to descend. Again this was at a cracking pace and we reached the hut at 3-45. So for about 8,000 feet of ascent and descent we had taken 4 hours. This I was going to pay for later. A party of trekkers popped into the bothy on their way down and we gave them some coffee. They reciprocated with some rum to add to it, much appreciated. After they had gone I got a blinding headache which also made me feel sick. It was like the worst hangover, but for some reason, I felt slightly better if I was standing up. Eventually I had to lie down and Ang Nuri suggested some garlic and ginger soup. I tried a little but couldn't finish it. I refused dinner and had a long miserable night, my headache troubling me all night. As I say, 'A day to remember.'

## Saturday 5th Deurali – Khuldi Ghar

When I awoke, the blue sky looked as if it had been polarised. It had also been very cold as my boots were frozen solid, likewise my toothpaste, and the cooking oil. I took some porridge and felt better. We packed up and set off in deep snow. It was proving to be quite tricky going with each of us falling over at various times. As we were crossing the avalanche track, Ang Nuri looked up and shouted out, 'Quick, run for it'. Over the top of the ridge a small snow avalanche was cascading towards us. Perhaps, the advance party of a larger one? We scampered across, stumbling over the snow boulders one after the other, unscathed, but it was a scary moment. Soon after, walking down the track, I stood on a snow-covered boulder, skidded, and slid over the edge. Luckily my bamboo pole jammed between two boulders and I was able to hold on, avoiding a nasty drop to the river. I clambered up covered in snow, shaken, but otherwise unhurt.

We arrived back at Khuldi Ghar with sleet falling and everything soaking wet. We all spent some time drying out over the fire. The dinner hierarchy makes me feel a bit guilty. I get mine first, then Ang Nuri, then Sherpa Lawry, then the porters and when everybody is satisfied, sitting back belching, the kitchen boy gets anything that's left over. Ang Nuri told me that in my selection of trekking agencies I had made a wise choice. Sherpa Co-operative takes 15% of the fees and pays the rest to the guides and porters. They also have a monthly salary scheme, health insurance and bonuses. The other agencies take about 60% and have no benefits.

I've been thinking about the extremes of experience one has, when trekking, at least during this time of year. Night-time is way below freezing and mid-morning is swelteringly hot with the sun plus your physical exertion. Afternoon is wet, either snow or rain. Evening is drying-out time, choking on wood-smoke. The others all seem to have colds which, luckily, I seem to have avoided (immunity gained from Scottish winters?) The porters wear baseball boots which have only one merit, they dry easily but are immediately wet again as soon as the walking begins. I'm missing conversation now in the evenings. We stop for the day about 3-4 p.m. leaving quite a long time before you turn in. The weather, being bad in the afternoon, means you either sit in front of the fire or in your tent for hours. I'm thinking that now that our goal has been reached and we are heading back to Pokhara, albeit by a different route, I'd just as soon go faster. A bath would be nice.

I mused over this and dropped a bombshell this evening by suggesting we walk faster and further each day to get back earlier. We have already saved one day and I feel we could cut another off the total. The dismay that this news caused was considerable. I then realised why. The team were thinking that if the trek was shortened by two days that would mean two days less pay for them. I assured them that, as it was my decision, I wouldn't be trying to get a refund and they would get full pay. They were happy enough about this but a bit dubious about going faster. I think it can be resolved by cutting down on the long lunch, when the weather hasn't yet deteriorated, and walking for longer in the afternoon.

### Sunday 6th Khuldi Gar – Ghandrung

An early start on the first day under the new regime and after ten minutes walking, we came across freshly-made paw prints in the snow on the path, obviously made by quite a large animal. I said to Ang Nuri, 'Big dog, eh?'

'No,' he replied, 'this is a snow leopard.' The tracks went along our path for some yards then Ang Nuri stopped abruptly, and raised his hand. Cautiously we moved round a bend and in front of us, the path, the snow and vegetation were all torn up. Just above us, on the hillside, there was a crashing of something moving quickly away through the bushes so ending my first and only brief encounter with this exotic and rare animal. As consolation, I took a photo of one of the paw-prints with the lens cap beside it for scale.

We arrived back at Chemro, which still looked picturesque in the sunshine and reached the place where the cow had been dying on our way up. That it had expired was indicated by the presence of a dozen large vultures, now sitting on the spot. I was going to take a photo of them when some kids came up and scared them off by throwing stones at them.

Up from Chemro, there is a biggish school and the kids attending, have steep slopes to climb and descend every day. I counted 1,500 stone steps from Chemro to the top of the ridge. A long trek down the hill again and lunch at 11 a.m. The sun came out briefly as we dropped down to Kymno with its riverside location and attractive stone-built houses. On the opposite bank were numerous water-driven rice-mills, similar to the Norse mills found in the north of Scotland. A steady slog to the pass at the top of the ridge then down again to Ghandrung. This is a much bigger village, where it is said that every second house has someone serving in the Ghurka regiment. There are about 700-1000 inhabitants. The first campsite we went to had a trekking party already there. There they were, all ponsy, sitting on their stools with posh anoraks on. Not like us hardened lot, been to 14,000 feet in the snows and sub-zero temperatures. We moved on to another wee site round the corner. This was ideal, with just enough room for our party. We are directly above a stone platform where they cremate the dead before throwing the remains down into the ravine and river (another popular spot with the vultures).

Camaraderie good tonight, must be the longer walk extended people a bit and now the relief is setting in. I suppose I pushed a bit hard today as we compressed two days walking and camping into one. To ease the guilt, I sent Dilkumar up to the teahouse for rum and beer. A new spirit has entered the group! Just before sunset a great howling and wailing broke out from one of the houses above. It is reckoned that somebody must have died.

Ang Nuri told a story about how he was guarding the family's yaks one night when he was about 9 or 10 and a great beer (sic) attacked a yak and killed it. The bad beer, (sic) over the next few months killed many yaks, goats and dogs until the locals managed to shoot it. When they examined the body they found it was wearing a wrist watch (strictly speaking, a paw watch). A bit of a mystic, Ang, he seems to believe all these things. However, as a Buddhist, he must never kill anything or tell lies, so I'm not sure how true this story was. The other peculiarity in his tale was that Nepalese bears are black with a white front, and this killer, with a penchant for time-keeping, was all black. He also told the story of an American Peace Corps teacher who taught in the local school. She had been here three years and had a house in the village. One day she came home from school and found thieves had stripped her house of all its possessions. Disgusted, she left a week later, never to return.

A much more social evening tonight, a late night, stayed up to 8 p. m! Maybe the drinks helped.

## Monday 7th. Ghandrung – Naudanda

We were away by 7 a.m. Good, gradual descent to the Modi valley on well-laid flagstones. The irritation today is that Ang Nuri is a walking snotter-box. Every six feet there is a yellow splat on the stones. As we crossed the river, we encountered a profusion of bird-life, some brilliantly coloured. Many have scarlet rumps and tail-feathers. Apart from vultures, and the 'rain' birds this is the only avian life we've seen. From there it was a slow climb up the other side of the valley to Chandrakot. I imagine it must get the locals down to see the route ahead so clearly. Up one hill, look down into the next valley and see the path winding its way down, then up to the top of the next ridge. At Chandrakot we meet the main track from Pokhara to Jomson. Immediately it is a lot busier. This is the route for many trekkers and traders, provided for by a profusion of lodges and hotels along the way. We are now on the opposite side of the valley from Dhampus. It's been a long day: ten hours walking so far, but we keep on going past Khare to Naudanda, where we will camp in the play-ground of the local primary school. Before we reached there, a Hindu priest came up and tried to put a spot of red paint on my forehead. Of course I declined, thinking it might involve some kind of monetary donation. I am Scottish after all. Ang Nuri approved of my refusal, not because of my stinginess, but because the holy man was a Hindu. A woman with a small baby, sitting chatting to some friends broke off from what she was saying to ask me cheerily in perfect English, 'Hello, would you like some marijuana? I've got some good stuff.' Again, I declined.

The kids in the mountainous regions have pretty responsible jobs to do. Tiny girls are carrying babies on their backs and clambering over walls and down steep slopes herding gigantic buffaloes. Other small children are carrying huge loads of herbage for feeding the animals, bundles of firewood for cooking and heating, even flagstones to repair the paths. One tiny boy with an Australian type bushman's hat jammed on his head had been sent (I presume) out on to a sloping roof, tiled with large flagstones to bring in the washing which was hanging on a line. The roof was overhanging a near vertical slope down into the valley, but there he was, wandering about, unconcerned, folding up the clothes. I made a note at the time, 'Every boy and girl has a living doll – a little brother or sister on his or her back'. It is bit of an eye-opener to see how much responsibility these kids are given, and how well they react.

So now we have saved two whole days and we'll be back in Pokhara tomorrow.

## Tuesday 8<sup>th</sup> Feb. Naudando – Pokhara

Ang Nuri left early to take a short cut back to book seats on the bus. It's easy walking now, along the ridge to Sarangkot. We're meeting dozens of trekkers now. I think this must be a popular route, evidenced by lots of kids saying, 'Namaste, how are you? Give me school pen or one rupee'. At Sarangkot, on the top of the hill, is the old fort of King Sarang. From here you get a good view of the valley and the mountains. We reached the place where we are having lunch but two of the porters haven't arrived. Leisurely walk down through the town to the airport. Cows are actually grazing on the runway and have to be shooed off when a plane is due to arrive. We are camping next to the runway. Strange location for the tents considering we are leaving by bus tomorrow. Still, it is flat. An Australian couple have just arrived back from a trek and appear to be shattered. I joined in a game of football with some local kids but I noticed my porters were a bit disapproving afterwards, undignified behaviour for a sahib?

At dinner, Ang Nuri produced some rakshi, which tasted very like sake. Under the pretext of getting some more, Lawry and Ang and I went up to the porters' pub. They left me there saying they'd be back in a minute or two, so I had a beer while waiting. I was joined by the Aussies and we had a few beers. By ten o'clock the two Nepalese hadn't come back and when I got back to the tent, the others, apart from Lawry, had gone to bed. Staggering about, falling over and laughing uproariously, he obviously had found a livelier pub than me, but quietly crawled into his tent after I shook hands with him and said goodnight.

## Wednesday 9<sup>th</sup> February

We were up very early, at 4-30 a.m. for some reason, packed up and went for the bus. Ang Nuri delivered some disturbing news that, the previous day, a Pokhara-Kathmandu bus had gone over a cliff and 31 people had been killed. In Nepal, if an avalanche doesn't get you, a bus journey will! Our bus wasn't due until 7-15, and I couldn't see the reason for the 4-30 start. However, it was a chance to see Pokhara waking up. All the little shops along the bus stop street contained families, sleeping on the floor. When the wooden shutters opened, a woman would lean out, hawk and spit and come out to sweep the ground in front of the shop. Looking inside you would see that the bundles of clothes lying on benches and on the floor would gradually reveal themselves to be wakening kids and adults.

The bus was packed when it came and I saw the prudence of pre-booking. It remained that way for the next seven hours. It was also very cold for the first 3 or 4 hours as some window glass was missing or didn't fit, so that a constant blast came whistling round your head. The last two hours were the opposite with the hot sun streaming in the window. Not a comfy journey and smelly too. One old woman in front of me, wrapped in sacks, really stank.

Back in Kathmandu I met Mike Cheney and he was very pleasant. I also got my ticket changed so that I fly to Delhi and Bombay tomorrow, then on to Dhahran and Riyadh on Friday. Decide not to stay at the expensive Yak and Yeti and got a decent room with heating, and a hot shower for $16. Ah, the luxury of a shower, washing my hair and walking in light shoes again; I fairly bounced up the street. I went for a Chinese meal which was a bit disappointing, so I cheered myself up with a few beers. Got back to the hotel and the barman, obviously skimming, gave me huge measures of the local whisky. Woozily, I made my way to my room to be wakened at 2-30 with a violent headache. Vowed, for yet another time, never to overdo the consumption of strong drink in future, and with this resolution, eventually fell asleep.

Thursday 10th

Up at 8 a.m. feeling fine, maybe I will drink again, but only in moderation. Had omelette and coffee and went for a wee walk (as one does after a 12 day trek) it was still cold this early in the morning, and the shops remained firmly closed. Found the tourist office open and was told that I would get Nepalese posters at the Airline office. After a long trudge there and many sorties through offices I was told that they were all finished and I'd be better off trying the tourist office. Eventually had some mixed success in some of the shops in Freak Street and Basantpur. Ran out of time however so had to hurry back, check out and get off to the airport.

Smooth operation, got a Himalayan-side seat with a good view but unfortunately couldn't identify anything. We were all given cans of Heineken and I decided to test my moderate drinking rule. When I popped the can it almost exploded and poured all over the table and onto my lap, soaking my trousers. Luckily there was an empty seat between me and the aisle and I was able to slide over. The Indian gentleman in the aisle seat then went to open his can (which was upside down) and I told him to be careful. He said, 'Don't you worry, I know all about these,' and set the can on the floor of the plane in the aisle. When he opened it, it sprayed everybody within 10 feet. All around people were muttering and wiping themselves down. To cap it all he asked for another can saying to the stewardess, 'Make it really cold this time'. This one got him and me a direct hit in the face. By now the plane was reeking of lager and a few of us looking as if we had peed ourselves. Lunch was two chicken legs each, which tasted of fish (maybe they were fish legs), a packet of peanuts and a lump of cherry cake. On arrival at Delhi, I bought some assorted packets of tea for gifts, when I was struck by the thought of their imminent destruction by the ultra fussy customs at Dhahran.

Flight to Bombay went O.K. with yet another chicken curry. I had a long wait for my rucksack when we got there but got a pleasant surprise at the Air India desk about my onward flight next morning to Saudi. The sleepy girl at the desk (10-30 p.m.) nodded as I explained my next flight and wrote me out a voucher for Searock Hotel plus taxi fares both ways. Trouble is I'll have to check-out from the hotel about 4 a.m., so 4 hours luxury then off again. I shared a taxi with an Indian statistician working for U.N. in Lusaka. Problems arose at the very plush hotel as there were too many passengers for the number of rooms. I got mine at 11-45.

### Friday 11th February

Had a call arranged for 4 a.m. but awoke anyway at 3-50. I grabbed some breakfast and headed back to the airport. This would be a very busy flight with hundreds of Indians all scrabbling and pushing at each interminable desk, money-change, and check-in, Immigration, Customs, Security and finally Departure Gate. My flight was scheduled to leave at 7-15 and at 8 a wee man came into the lounge and shouted that it wouldn't leave until 9 a.m., due to technical problems, leaving a mass of perspiring people all stuck in the Departure lounge. No services of course and about half the required number of seats. The Departure screen was filled with various airline flight numbers and one-by-one they disappeared leaving the two remaining Air India flights, well, remaining. That's two with technical problems. Some satisfaction as the Saudis present were at last getting a taste of their own medicine as obstructive officials sent them to the back of the queue, pretending not to understand and asking for various documents necessary for clearance. The weans present, were by now screaming the place down. Altogether it was an experience to be missed. Ah, the glamour of air-travel! It must be the most unappealing and unpleasant form of travel nowadays, like being at the dentist, even to the seats. Eventually told we have to change planes and was very glad they found that out before we took off. Every seat was taken with no sign of any service (such as drinks), only a film, Al Pacino in 'Author', which was mildly distracting. At Dhahran the Indians in the forward part of the plane refused to get off and blocked the aisles. The reason: they were showing a Tamil movie in this section and it hadn't finished. Christ, some of them go on for eight hours!

The on-going fight was due to leave in seven minutes so we were rushed through formalities only to find that in the domestic departure all hell was let loose. Thousands have no confirmation, causing absolute pandemonium at the wait-list desk. Joined a queue and, after about three hours, no movement. A Saudi marched past me and headed for the front of the queue. Something snapped and I ran forward and grabbed his arm. 'There is a queue I shouted,'

'Where's your place?' he asked. I walked back and stood in line and he said, 'O.K. I go behind you,' pushing aside a poor Indian who had been standing behind me. Five minutes later the man at the desk called out, 'Mohammed', and he marched forward to get his boarding pass. As he strode off, and with an upward flick of his gutra, he turned and gave me a cheery wave, the bastard.

Been in the airport 13 hours now and met a running friend, Bob Walton who is also trying to get to Riyadh so we collar a couple of Dutch guys and agree to share a taxi. Very hairy journey through the night through the desert with the four of us, eyes glued to the road, roaring out every time the driver drifted off to sleep. A four hour road journey but we got there.

At the airport car-park, my Cadillac started O.K. and I drove to the compound. I took the short detour to the Panda mini-mart for milk and bread, and then straight to bed. Just as my eyes closed, and much like the opening sequence of a movie, the majestic snow-clad peak of Annapurna soared above me, before, oblivion.

# A Long Gone Wee Bothy

I, Bob Scott, almost certainly am the last person still alive who had used that grand wee wooden bothy, that's now long gone.

Assynt Estate shepherds used to stay there at lambing time, each year until into the 1960's. These shepherds also kept a watchful eye on the estate's herd of black cattle that spent their winters in their Black Isle farm then were turned loose to graze all summer on this vast estate's many thousand acres, most of which was rough heather moor, rocky knolls, steep hills and countless lochs and boggy lochans. Each year, perhaps led by ancestral memory, many of these hardy beasts made their way to the verdant lushness of that grassy paradise that was the glorious heart of Drumrunie Deer Forest. There, in that gentle glen snugly tucked away between the threat of Cul Mor's Westerly cliffs and its more modest neighbour Cul Beag's grassy slopes, these cattle contentedly grazed on this precious, and all too rare, oasis of lushness. In days of August's welcome heat, replete cattle would motionlessly stand for drowsy hours almost knee-deep in the refreshing waters of the bothy's sandy lochan, as if waiting, and statuesquely posing, for some latter-day Landseer.

When all Assynt Estate's sheep and cattle were sold off, these shepherds were made redundant or were re-employed as estate workers and summer ghillies.

No longer needed for its original shepherding use, that grand wee wooden bothy in its wondrous loch-side, location, was left unused and securely locked and shuttered. The fact of that disused bothy being there was known to only a few. Even fewer knew the secret of where the flat stone was that hid the bothy key securely coffined in its old tobacco tin.

Now that I was working on this estate as a trainee gamekeeper, I was entrusted with the knowledge of where the bothy key could be found. I was told glowing reports of the trout-rich lochs all around the building. I was amazed by descriptions of the beauty of its location right by a loch-side shore of firm sand that glowed with the brightness of finely powdered ancient sandstone. In this largely tree-less land, that haven was further graced by having a welcome stand of stunted auld tenacious trees, birches, rowans and alders, around it.

It was a few years before I, now married, managed to get to that special wee bothy. I had secret fears it might not live up to all these great glowing stories I had heard about it. But even before my wife, Eileen, and I got near the place, these fears were swept away. Even if there had been no bothy to look forward to, the views from the top of this fine ridge were alone well worth the effort of our steep climb. In the pure clear June sunshine these near hills, Cul Mor, Cul Beag and Stac Pollaidh showed and proudly glowed at their prime best. More distant in the North, Suilven modestly shrouded its flamboyant shape in indistinct haze. To the South, eagerly reaching above Loch Lurgainn, the long Ben More Coigach ridge tried to show it could outdo any of its Assynt rivals.

And down there where we were eagerly heading, sparkled four lochs, all of which were supposed to hold an abundance of attractive trout. Sitting and holding the map spread out between us, we struggled to correctly pronounce these Gaelic names: Loch Lon Na Huamha and Loch An Doire Dhuibh.

Lovely, large Loch Sionascaig's name we already knew. That Lochan Gainmheich where the bothy rested, at one of its fine bright sand beaches was, to the annoyance of local Gaelic speakers, being anglicized to 'The Sandy Loch'.

With our two dogs keenly leading the way, we hurry down that little known and rarely used path to the first loch. We cast not very productive exploratory flies into its rather solemn waters, then carry on to much more attractive, huge Loch Sionascaig's, narrow Easterly bay, where a large burn rushed and chuckled in from the 'Sandy Loch'. After catching some fine trout we dragged ourselves away, hurried up that burn, crossed a narrow footbridge, and arrived at that sand-bayed wee loch with its overlooking wee wooden bothy.

Now of course, there were no drowsy cattle standing motionless here, but for us keen fishers, there was a much better sight: an active hatch of may-fly, which delighted the greedy trout almost as much as it delighted us.

In the almost flat calm and bright June sunshine our best dry-flies only rarely convinced the wary trout that they were irresistible food. Still between us, Eileen and I caught a few of this glorious wee loch's plump golden trout.

Well content with our morning's fishing, we now went to have a proper look at that wee bothy we had ignored while these trout were rising. We soon found the hidden key. There was no need to remove the large shutter, the glorious brightness of this June day peered in glowing eagerness through the wide open door and revealed all we had come to see. Compared to the rather spartan standards of the many mountain bothies he had used in the past, Bob found this unused shepherds' bothy, to be truly luxurious. There were two built-in wooden beds complete with mattresses and neatly folded blankets. There was a fine wee iron stove and a calor gas cooker; there was a large table and a couple of wooden chairs. There were two roomy cupboards and an abundance of storage shelves.

Eileen and Bob smiled at one another and happily agreed that they would soon spend a night in this great wee bothy in this grand location. And they wonderfully did.

At least once each May or June in the next few years they stayed overnight in this bothy. Much more often they went just for a day of pleasant walking and wondrous fishing. Despite the strong lure of all their grand local Assynt walks, this hike to this, their own, 'Sandy Loch' then the return up through that lush glen and around by the East end of Loch an Doire Dhuibh and along its steep, birch-clinging slopes, to the bealach between grand wee Stac Pollaidh and Cul Beag was now their favourite walk.

During these few happy years, the only others who sometimes used the bothy overnight, while fishing these lochs, were a group of great Assynt characters: Charlie Ross, Angus MacLeod , George Mackay, and their great poet friend Norman MacCaig, who while not Assynt born, was of Assynt by choice.

The one time Eileen and Bob met this gloriously gregarious gang of great fishermen at the Sandy Loch, they berated them for taking the easy way in, by boat down the length of Loch Sionascaig, to a mere hundred yards from the bothy, while that hardy two, had walked and climbed many wild miles to get here.

In beaming reply, Charlie Ross laughed and pointed to the bothy table with its load of unopened whisky bottles, 'Och, but you see we had such a precious burden tae bring in wi' us that we really had tae use the boat!'

Yes, these were grand happy years. Then, after yet another long, gale-howling winter, Eileen and I returned in the glory of May to our 'Sandy Loch' where we were shocked to see a blank gap where that grand wee wooden bothy had been. Even the narrow footbridge that had led to it was gone.

We later learned that Assynt Estate had made an arrangement for some government body, perhaps the Countryside Commission, to look after this no longer used part of their vast lands. And it seemed that, in these misguided years, these bureaucratic government officials were as guilty as the worst private landowner, in trying to discourage hikers and climbers from coming on their land. They had therefore removed the bothy and its footbridge.

Oh of course all this happened a good number of years ago and, hopefully, now in the 21st century, all the many organizations looking after Scotland's wild land have a much more enlightened, a much more welcoming attitude to today's vast invasion of hikers and climbers.

Looking back and warmly remembering, yes I am sure I must be the last to have used that long gone grand wee bothy. Eileen, these Assynt shepherds and all in that gregarious fishing and bothying group, are now all dead.

Should this story ever guide you to our 'Sandy Loch,' you might just see, (almost hidden by the rank invasive bracken, that's no longer kept under control by the former bothying shepherds), the former building's concrete foundations, at least you will know something of this place's not all too ancient history.

# Before the West Highland Way

A s I, Bob Scott, minutely study a friend's detailed modern map of The West Highland Way, I smile as I listen to the passionate eagerness of his description of this now justly famous long distant walk's many truly beautiful views, its many varied joys, the many testing challenges to be boldly overcome, and all the relaxing evening pleasures enjoyed at the fine hospitable accommodation to be found along the route.

It seems that all, from the poshest hotel, the more modest guest-house, the humblest bed and breakfast, the more basic Scottish Youth Hostels and those more recent arrivals – and keenest rivals – the back-packers spartan bunk-houses, are well geared up to meet the demanding needs of the many Summer thousands who now so eagerly journey this now so well marked, so extensively improved, long distant walk.

As, with the essential assistance of strong reading glasses, my auld eyes follow that well displayed West Highland Way's well used path as it eagerly trips along by famous Loch Lomond's bonnie Eastern shore, my memory, seeing much brighter and clearer than my tired eyes, sped me back to that time some sixty years ago when I, either alone or with equally keen youthful friends, at different times, tirelessly walked different parts of what is now this braw West Highland Way.

Journeying under memory's guidance, I remember some cash-strapped weekends when for only five pennies a fine speedy Glasgow tram, shoogily took us all the way to Milngavie's water works, from where we hiked the route that is now the start of the West Highland Way. But our more usual way, was to get off an Aberfoyle bus at Drymen, and then, hiking past Buchanan's imposing castle, hastily pass by Balmaha Bay with its re-awakening bustle of boating and fishing activity after its deep sleep of six long, lean, wartime years. Then all that noisesome hustle of drumming up post-war business is instantly forgotten as our track squeezed through the

Pass of Balmaha's redeeming narrow gap between a steep ridge's Scots-pined slope, and the isle-crowded waters of Loch Lomond.

The track from here runs free and clear as it swings along by the loch's greatly praised, 'bonnie banks' to what, not so many pre-war years ago, was a large imposing shooting-lodge set in its jealously guarded private land. But now these so bright and hopeful post-war years have brought about a strange change; Rowardennan Shooting-lodge is wondrously transformed into Rowardennan Scottish Youth Hostel. It is no longer a place for the exclusive use of wealthy pampered gentry, but now opens its welcoming doors to all: to excited youths, to eager young men and women, to those who have not allowed mature years to dull their bright outlook. But there are some few to whom these doors are firmly closed, for, most wisely, motor cars and motor-cycles are strictly banned.

Most weekends this hostel is gregariously crowded with some of the wiser, brighter, country loving Glasgow proletariat who come kilted hiking, tireless climbing, sweaty cycling. And every one, no matter how old or how young, must at least once climb Glasgow's most loved hill, Ben Lomond, that so inspiringly rises close by this great youth hostel's door.

Spending another happy weekend here I decided this time, not to again climb 'The Ben' but to explore that unknown shore between Rowardennan and Inversnaid. What starts as a well marked track all too soon gets hopelessly lost in a dense jungle of overgrowing shrubbery and a confusing maze of fallen trees. Smiling, thinking myself an intrepid adventurer, I push on along this challenging route that seems determined to deny my right of way.

Squeezed between Loch Lomond's rocky Eastern shore and the towering Ben's dominating bulk this place is a real confusion of massed woodlands of varied lichened auld oaks and stands of stunted birches. Underfoot, despite this late May's bright dry weather, there is much soggy boggy ground and a wilderness of rough damp turf. Giving up long before Inversnaid, I return to my youth hostel, to an enjoyable, if belchingly hasty, meal, before the evening hike to Drymen, to catch a Glasgow-bound bus.

Exactly one week later I return, my confidence boosted by a friend's cheery company, and we are determined to struggle all the way up that long, lonely, unknown shore then spend the Saturday night in a remote wee bothy we had heard about.

How this challenging route's hardships lessen, how its long miles shrink when our sweating endeavours, our frequent stumbling curses, and our many uplifting jokes, are shared in true youthful friendship.

Then, long before expected, we reach Inversnaid's attractive waterfalls and cross the rushing Snaid Burn by a rather dodgy footbridge and some decidedly dicey stepping stones. Keeping well clear of this picturesque place's posh hotel which we had been warned shuts its inhospitable doors on all grubby, thirsty Glasgow hikers, we push on then sit and admire the view, back the way we have come, to Inversnaid. We think it little wonder that Snaid Burn, as it eagerly tumbles down through these tree-cloaked steep slopes to plunge into the loch's deep cold depths, has inspired many great poets. That hotel had welcomed Walter Scott as he searched this place for vividly remembered tales of his next novel's brave hero, Rob Roy MacGregor. Had imaginative Scott invented, rather than discovered, Rob Roy's sheltering loch-side cave and his constantly guarded rocky prison?

And some 150 years ago this remote hotel had not closed its posh doors on three sweaty grubby great long distance walkers: Wordsworth, his sister Dorothy, and that other great poet, Coleridge. Little wonder that Wordsworth, knowing something of this place's Rob Roy history, hearing a Highland Lass singing in Gaelic, should wonder if she sang of:

> *Old, unhappy, far-off things,*
> *And battles long*

And deeply moved by the beauty of her dream-like song and her picture of visionary innocence, he thinks:

> *Thou wear'st upon thy forehead clear*
> *The freedom of a mountaineer.*

Then I remember a gentlemanly cleric who had also been made welcome at this Inversnaid hotel and had also been deeply moved by this remote place's overwhelming beauty and unspoiled wilderness. And so I quote the greatest lines of G. M. Hopkins' greatest poem, 'Inversnaid':

> *What would the world be once bereft*
> *Of wet and wildness? Let them be left,*

*O let them be left, wildness and wet*
*Long live the weeds and wilderness yet.*

While my friend and I wholeheartedly agree with Hopkins' fervent plea for Wildness to remain, we have oor grinning doots about his plea for the wet; for, suffering beneath our auld country's louring grey skies, we have often fervently pleaded for much less of their wet!

'Aye,' my friend laughed, 'and I doot if many gardeners would agree with his praise of weeds!'

Then, bright with the light of our remembered verses, we eagerly continue our happy youthful literary journey.

As we labour through ever more closely packed auld oak woodlands that grimly cling to ever steeper slopes plunging down to the loch's hidden shore, we cheerily praise our mature-like wisdom in undertaking this sweaty struggling wearying journey at this fresh bright May-time. For we are spared later summer's terrible additional burden of forcing a way through dense high bracken while being cruelly assaulted by ugly bloodthirsty clegs and clouds of buzzing flies or what can be the overwhelming torture of unbelievably sadistic tiny midges.

As with effortless ease, we cross another large burn which could be difficult when in full flood, we at last leave the dense oaks dappled green shade, and rejoice in the appealing openness of a sun bright grassy glade where we have a clearer view of the more distant land across the loch. This place is shown on our good old one inch to one mile map as Doune, and there, exactly as we had been told, was the rather tumble-down bothy that was to be our home for tonight. To us, in our rather weary state, that humble bothy seemed a perfect palace! Soon, despite the floor's knotted hardness, we slept with the undisturbed deep peace of youthful ease.

Returning from memory's journey to my present day study of that 'West Highland Way' map, I think that the Loch Lomond section must surely be the best part of this long distance walk.

Then a certain name leaps up from that engrossing map and grabs my stravaiging eye – Inverarnan! What a jumble of further happy memories that name conjures up.

Inverarnan Hotel, also known by its older historic name of The Drover's Inn, dates back to the start of the 18th century, and for us few still alive who knew it after the end of the Second World War, it seemed that the warmth of the welcome we always received there was a glorious continuation of the hospitality this old Inn has given through two and a half centuries, and so too, the simple homely comforts of its basic amenities have remained little changed through these 250 years. The convenience of electricity was the only really important change. Oh, and some of the largest, most expensive guest bedrooms now boast the luxury of their own wash-hand-basin, with, usually, an ample supply of hot – or tepid water laid on.

The infrequency of the weekends we could afford to spend in this inexpensive auld Inn made these few visits all the more enjoyable and memorable. The small bedroom I shared with a friend cowered under the high roof's steep slope and we too had to constantly stoop if our heads were not to painfully meet the low sloping ceiling. Of course this modest bedroom did not have a wash-hand-basin. On the fairly rare occasions when we really needed a good wash, we used the large, bright flowered Victorian china bowl and huge jug that stood on the table beside our bed. The only warmish water we received was brought by an unseen chamber-maid who early each morning, left what she thought was our prissy hottish water in what seemed like an old watering-can, outside our bedroom door. For all the small bedrooms hidden up here in the maze of dim passageways, there was not one bathroom and only one lavatory. We were thankful that at least it was a real water closet that usually condescended to thunderously flush after the third impatient tug of its dangling chain.

In these far-off early post-war years central heating was unheard of and there was little heating in this Spartan auld hotel, apart from cheery log fires in the largest lounge and the spacious dining room on the coldest winter evenings. Our frugal small bedroom had absolutely no heating even in the severest weather and as the hotel's precious hot-water bottles were strictly kept for the auld and decrepit, we got none of these bed-warming pleasures. Although we were young, tough and fit, even we longed for a hot-water-bottle as we went through the nightly ordeal of getting into our large double bed's smooth starched white linen sheets which stretched as uninvitingly as sheets of smooth snow and felt as freezing as real ice.

As we two young males lay shivering, individually, firmly apart in that large double bed, how we envied the hotel's married guests whose blood-warming passion would quickly heat their starched white sheets.

I must point out here that although my friend and I shared a double bed in this hotel, as did many of the mostly male climbers who were this hostelry's main customers we did so in all innocence. This sharing of weekend and holiday beds was quite common then and as far as I know, (although this must be very difficult for modern readers to believe) there was never any hint of any illicit, and at that time, illegal homosexual activity. And the innocent owners of this old-fashioned hotel saw no need for many, if any, single beds.

As I study a photo of this auld Drover's Inn, all so unchanged on the outside, I wonder has the interior changed much. Are all its stuffed game birds, all those chipped plaster-cast haughty salmon and bleary-eyed trout still sad prisoners in their dusty, spider-webbed glass prisons? Is the sedate small library and writing room now a bustling busy bar that eagerly meets the urgent needs of thirsty long-distance-walkers? Is that stuffed auld black bear still lurking somewhere in the gloom to startle unwary guests? That bear was moth-eaten then, more than fifty years ago, if still there, what must it look like now? It must be a real sorry sight, a more or less fur-free bare bear.

The long-time owners of Inverarnan Hotel were two sisters, the Miss Girvans, who, seen through our young unflattering eyes, seemed really auld old maids. The unfailing warmth of the welcome we received from these sisters was equalled by the generosity of the high-heaped plates of home-cooked local food we received, and with eager youthful appetites quickly consumed.

But amidst all this great Highland hospitality there was something amazingly missing. This hotel was 'Dry'! Due to the strict restrictions of the landowner's feu conditions, absolutely no alcohol could be sold at this arid, teetotal hotel.

Although the Miss Girvans turned a blind eye to some of their most regular guests bringing table-wine with them, they did not encourage it, and so at this hotel's fine dinners most of us were none the worse for pure water being the order of the day.

This quaint old-fashioned legal restriction, which then applied to quite a number of Highland hotels, did not detract from the great pleasure we got from our occasional weekends there. By far the most thrilling of these pleasures was to meet some fellow guests who were almost legendary heroes from pre-war years when they pioneered a wider, more working class bright new era of Scottish climbing.

First and foremost there was great wee, forever cheery, Tom Weir, who was always willing to share his extensive knowledge of Scotland's hills and wildlife with us mere novice young climbers.

We were struck with awe when a fellow guest discreetly pointed and whispered, 'That's Bill Murray. You know the great W. H. Murray. You've read his wonderful book, of course?' And of course we had. His first book *Mountaineering in Scotland* had become our, and many other young Scottish climbers, inspiring climbing bible. Although at first this climbing God seemed rather reserved, we later found him quietly, genuinely friendly.

Here we were also delighted to meet Alastair Borthwick, the modest author of that other Scottish classic, *Always a Little Further*. It was great to hear direct from him further vivid descriptions of these pre-war years all so crowded with colourful erratic characters who hitch-hiked out of Glasgow, then so light-heartedly, climbed, then dossed in their own secret caves, or in more well known bothies.

If I remember correctly, it was at this hotel we also first saw Ben Humble, his total deafness no hindrance to the keenness of his climbing. So too we met Jock Nimlin escaping from the high heights of his shipyard crane to the more inspiring heights of his beloved Scottish hills. These two were also great pre-war climbing heroes who, with quiet pride, brought something of that fabulous era with them as they no less keenly continued their grand climbing on the summer rocks and winter snows of those now post-war hills.

For me it was a special pleasure to meet Jock Nimlin who had pioneered so many new rock-routes on The Cobbler, that great wee hill that for so many young Glasgow climbers was where they honed their rock-climbing skills. My first real rock-climb had been on Jock's own 'Nimlin Direct' on The Cobbler's South Peak. I think I started climbing it with some apprehension, but I do remember I completed that first rock-climb with a great surge of excited exhilaration!

As I see Inverarnan Hotel conspicuously marked as a fine resting place on this West Highland Way map, I imagine it must now be brightly alive with the hearty bustle of catering for hordes of thirsty long-distance-walkers. Surely the ambience of that historic auld Inn must be quite different from when it was a gently friendly 'Dry' hotel sedately run by those two dear old-maids and was brilliantly alight with all those great auld Scots climbers – all, alas, now dead.

My eyes continue on through the map's Glen Falloch as quickly as our speeding MacBrayne's bus did as it often hurried us to Crianlarich, then a most modest hamlet boasting a small railway station, one dowdy wee hotel that sometimes closed in winter, and a useful youth hostel. But for us our weekend home was not here, but was in our own cosy bothy at nearby Ben More Farm.

Although Tyndrum proudly boasted of having two railway stations, this wee town usually seemed no busier than any of its sleepy, one station, neighbours. It was near here, by the banks of the remote wee River Cononish, that we had our own secret wee doss. From this well placed rudely primitive base we enjoyed many bright summer days traversing the imposing Ben Lui and nearby Ben Oss. On memorable sweltering sun-blazing days, we made the brave effort to strip and plunge into the heart-shocking waters of high Loch Oss. I also remember some fine winter climbs above towering Ben Lui's North-facing, snow-holding high corrie. When the weather was very bad we would, Midas hopeful, further explore the deep reaches of the nearby old gold mine.

Moving on, I remember a fine wee camp site, well sheltered from stormy weather and from disapproving landowners by a grand canopy of majestic auld Scots Pines that nobly graced this hidden place by bonnie Loch Tulla.

Now this enticing map leads me to great places that are still wondrously aglow with many bright old happy memories. I, like all Scottish climbers, will never forget my first clear sight of the Buachaille Etive Mor's towering solid rock pyramid of pure perfection. Then, as I stared in awe from the much less challenging safety of the Curved Ridge, I wondered if I might ever dare to follow the lead of those intrepid young Creagh Dhu Devils or the Lomond Club's Young Tigers as they tip-toe and finger-tip cling, to the almost vertical slabs of the Buachaille's nerve-testing Rannoch Wall.

Then I see Glen Coe's three impressive steep sisters who hide away the secret of their Lost Glen. Again I remember the exciting thrills of perfecting our winter skills on the jagged steeps of the long Aonach Eagach Ridge in its dangerously demanding snow-plastered, ice-coated state.

But these memories have led me astray from the West Highland Way's present route, and so I return to a hotel that never was, is not now, and never will be, 'Dry'. This wise place is the King's House Hotel where red-coated soldiers used to guard Glencoe's Eastern entrance; then, centuries later, it tried to meet the almost insatiable alcoholic needs of always drouthy, young Scottish climbers. I imagine the alcoholic needs of today's long-distance-walkers will be much easier to meet; many will be only concerned to foolishly replace their un-needed, large, expensive, bottles of pure water! How stupid to be so blind to our free-flowing Highland Burns.

The next name I note is Altnafeadh, but for us who remember the good old climbing days, that place was, and always will be, Cameron's Barn. This climbers' frugal bothy was perfectly situated for reaching 'The Buachaille' and all the Eastern Glencoe hills. With concrete floor and walls and a corrugated iron roof, this bothy was freezing in winter. While being much too cold for farmer Cameron's precious cattle, it was truly good enough for the youngest, toughest, and keenest of Glasgow's most active climbing fraternity.

As this walking way now climbs up the steep zig-zags of the 'Devil's Staircase,' it is easy to imagine, and perhaps earnestly repeat, the curses of General Wade's sweating soldiers as they back-breaking labour to complete his impressive and, so that English officer hoped, repressive Great Military Road.

Memory again led me away from the West Highland Way, and I re-trace a route I took on my own many years ago. I had made for a place where not hundreds of Wade's soldiers, but thousands of mostly Irish navvies had sweated, cursed, and endlessly laboured to build, high, remote, Blackwater Dam.

At the top of The Devil's Staircase I had left that track that is now eagerly followed by many happy thousands, but was then a little used, almost forgotten, auld military way where one could walk day after day and never meet another living soul. But then, as I happily strode through that expanse of trackless heather that stretched to meet the isolated dam, I kept an observant eye searching, not for other living souls, but for long dead unburied human remains. For quite a few of these Irish navvies had died out here on that auld military track or on these remote heather slopes because of the 'Temperance' of another Highland hotel.

While Kinlochleven Hotel was the nearest to these navvies hutted encampment at the Blackwater Dam they were building, this too was a hotel that was strictly 'Dry' with all alcohol completely banned. So the navvies most desperate with Saturday's urgent drouth, determinedly walked the long miles to the alcohol available at that strictly non-dry King's House Hotel at the mouth of Glencoe.

While, even in some of the wildest winter weather, these tough and hardy navvies usually safely made it to those desperately-needed drams, it was a different story entirely when, all too well alcohol fortified, they struggled on their return journey up that dreadful steep, that all too well named, 'Devil's Staircase'. And so there, and there about, in the years when the Blackwater Dam was being built, quite a few navvies died, overcome by alcohol, exhaustion, or smothering snow. Each spring, once all Glencoe snow had thawed, the local police searched that deadly route to recover the remains of these poor misguided souls who had, quite literally, fallen by the wayside.

As I had heard that the last navvy skeleton had been found as late as the war-time 1940's, I thought it not impossible that I might stumble across yet another long lost skeleton in what was then, in the early 1950's, a rarely disturbed expanse of heathery wilderness. But the only old bones I found were the remains of an old stag, its high pointing antlers and exposed ribs eagerly gnawed by other calcium-deficient deer.

I walked over the solemn grey length of Blackwater Dam then made my way along the Northern shore of that rather dull, dreary, featureless, aptly-named Blackwater Loch, to the almost equally grey and dreary long abandoned remains of Blackwater Lodge. As the lowering grey cloud's thick drizzle mingled with the dark loch's rising mist, to hurry in an early dusk, this entirely tree-less landscape became nothing but varying shades of dull grey. Here on my own it was all too easy to see this crumbling old shooting-lodge's misty misery as a perfect setting for a wandering Frankenstein, a blood-seeking Dracula, or, nearer to his former Highland home, a re-incarnated Aleister Crowley.

I was pleased to leave early the following morning.

I was even more delighted to discover another much more attractive and welcoming bothy that afternoon.

This great wee bothy, that had pre-war been a gamekeeper's cosy cottage, was pleasantly sheltered by trees, mostly stunted auld birches and some ever welcome protective rowans. I rejoiced to hear cheery blackbirds and the cheeky robin above the rushing sounds of a modest wee river as it passed in front of the house on its way to Loch Treig. After two pleasant days here I headed west, and happily followed the Water of Nevis down through the savagely wild upper reaches of Glen Nevis, which I remember good auld Tom Weir describing as the only place in Scotland that could almost compare with a wild Himalayan mountain pass.

At Glen Nevis Youth Hostel I replenished my food and energy. Then I fittingly rounded off my own West Highland route by climbing Ben Nevis once again.

I then walk what is now the final part of the official West Highland Way where I can again trace the amazing influence of tenacious old General Wade as I enter what was his Fort William. I hurry to the railway station and to those good old steam trains which, with their smoke, steam, and fussy speed, have taken over from the old military ways with their iron permanent ways which had been constructed with even wearier labour, even more sweat and much worse Irish cursing.

As, returning to this all too frantic 21st century, I make a final study of that West Highland Way map, I suddenly remember Fort William being famous, not only for the welcome end of this long-distant-walk, but for the quality, and quantity, of its fish and chips. Or were these great fish and chips really so wondrous only because of the insatiable urgency of us young Glasgow climbers' youthful hunger?

I fold up that map and also fold away many happy old memories. My younger friend as he takes back his map hopes that in future years it will recount great happy memories for him too.

Later, by myself, I think back on that inspiring map and wonder what these pre-war Scots climbing pioneers would make of these, not mere thousands, but tens of thousands who walk all, or part, of this West Highland Way each year. Would they approve? Oh, I think they would!

Perhaps they would 'hae some doots' about the path being so vastly improved; all the removing, so greatly taming of every, even the most minor, possible dangers; all the over-sanitizing, over-signposting of even the most straight-forward parts of the route. They might fear that too much of the wild challenge had been removed from this natural wilderness.

But oh surely they would truly approve of that route, no matter how over-crowded, that points the way for those, all too many, in danger of living – and all too-soon dying – of their sofa-bound city ways. And many, after completing that West Highland Way, will surely be inspired to move on to other things, to higher Scottish hills, to perhaps re-capture something of the great convivial camaraderie of these pre-war pioneers and those, like me, of the immediate post-war years; us who truly were, *We few, we happy few, we band of brothers.*

With a smile, I think that in this 21st century I should perhaps add, 'and sisters' to that quotation.

# Kinabalu: The Haunted Mountain

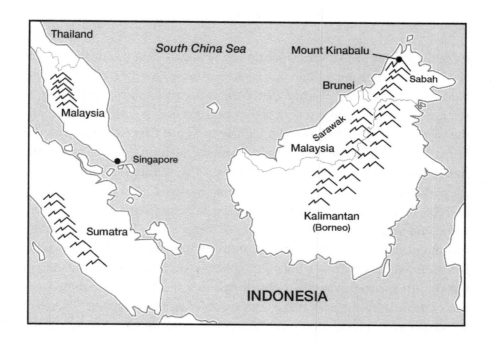

*S.E. Asia showing Brunei & Mt. Kinabalu*

I, spent three years in Saudi Arabia, but, unlike Wilfred Thessiger, for whom 'The Empty Quarter' held a lifelong fascination, I found that the landscape of the country and its lack of variety, led me to think of, and seek, pastures new. I applied for and got a teaching post in Brunei on the island of Borneo and, instead of finding new pastures, settled very happily for tropical rain forests. One day at the coffee break in my new college, a colleague, knowing of my interest in mountains, mentioned Mount Kinabalu, (see map). 'Why don't you go there during the April break?' he said. 'It's only a short flight and the mountain isn't far out of town. You should go, I think you'd like it, but one thing, be careful, it's called the haunted mountain for good reason. I'm sure your students would miss you if you didn't come back. We wouldn't, but they might,' he said, with a laugh.

The more I read and heard about the peak the more interested I became. So I made up my mind, haunted or not, I would be heading for Sabah on my next holiday.

★ ★ ★

In geological terms, Mount Kinabalu is a relatively new mountain, having been formed some ten million years ago. A massive, granite rock cooled and hardened and began to rise and pierce the softer rocks above. Still rising, at the rate of two inches per year, it is the youngest non-volcanic mountain in the world, and at 13,455 feet, the highest in South East Asia, between the Himalayas and New Guinea. The peak and the surrounding area, some 288 square miles, were made a national park in 1964. Within the boundaries of the park is one of the world's most unique ecosystems. In an altitudinal range of 7000 feet one goes from lush, tropical rain forest through temperate woodland and the stunted trees of moss forest to the bare granite of the summit plateau. Not surprisingly, the number and variety of flora and fauna, the mountain supports – a botanical survey estimated between 5,000 and 6,000 plant species, more than North America and Europe combined – is one of the reasons the park attracts thousands of visitors each year. There are 1,500 species of orchid alone and 25 types of rhododendron, however, the plant which probably arouses most interest, is most definitely the smelliest. This is a parasitic plant called *Rafflesia arnoldii* (named after Sir Stamford Raffles the founder of Singapore) and is one of the world's largest flowers. Its three foot diameter bloom has the fragrance of rotten meat which attracts pollinating flies. As well as attracting flies, the smell, likened to that of a decomposing buffalo, is a sure way park guides can locate it, and steer gagging tourists towards it, anxious to take their vacation photographs alongside this relatively rare plant. Another spectacular plant found in the park, is the giant pitcher, *Nepenthes rajah,* which gets its nutrition by trapping insects, frogs, mice and even rats in its half-full jug of rainwater, then digesting them, being in the broadest sense, a carnivorous vegetable! It is sometimes called locally, the 'monkey cup' as monkeys have been seen drinking from it, the largest specimens of the plant being able to hold a litre of water.

The climatic gradient from tropical heat to frost at the summit, and the huge variety of plant life also means a corresponding wealth of insects, birds and mammals. There are 326 species of birds; some of them only found on this mountain, ranging from the iconic hornbill, to the serpent eagle, which is sometimes spotted, living up to its name, as it flies over the trees, clutching a wriggling snake in its talons, the evening takeaway meal for the family. Animals are usually hard to see, being wary of people and camera shy. The wild boars, sun-bears, civet cats, monkeys and the 'men of the forest,' the orang-utan, are all here, hidden away somewhere among the trees. Pangolins (ant-eaters) porcupines and leopard cats and many species of bats can sometimes be caught in the beam of a torch if you are having difficulty sleeping, and fancy a nocturnal stroll.

The knowledge that this profusion of wild life is all around one, albeit generally well concealed, makes a trip here a truly unique mountain experience. Many visitors restrict themselves to the tourist trails on the lower slopes, content to explore the diversity of the forest, around the Park head-quarters, whereas climbers usually take the path leading upward, their minds on higher things. Both tourists and climbers, especially from temperate countries, are unlikely to have previously encountered any of the numerous exotic hazards associated with this environment. Side by side with the cute squirrels, the colourful butterflies and the engaging monkeys, lurk the 'nasties'. The forest that you are walking through harbours terrifying, relentless, stinging giant hornets, blood-sucking leeches, always ravenous, poisonous snakes, unlikely to attack unless threatened, but just keep your eyes open and try not to step on one. Likewise, check before you sit on a log to rest the weary legs, it is the favourite home of scorpions and ferocious biting fire-ants. If all this doesn't temper the enthusiasm of the nature-lover, there's always the mosquito, as tormenting and as numerous as the midges of Scotland, but with the added threat of the victim possibly ending up with malaria or dengue fever.

Why then has Nature bestowed such natural wealth and diversity on this particular mountain? Unlike other parts of Borneo there has been little depletion or degradation of natural resources. The steep slopes and rocky gullies are not conducive to clearing for farming or timber extraction and the mountain is therefore relatively unspoilt. The protected status established on the park's creation has led to a strict enforcement of rules for visitors and locals alike, but maybe there's something else!

The mountain has the reputation of being haunted. Its name is 'Aki Nabalu', meaning 'the revered place of the dead,' the name used by the local Kadazan people, since time immemorial. The Kadazan believe the mountain top to be the home of the guardian spirits of their ancestors. This reverence for the mountain is, of course, echoed in all parts of the world with some of the most famous being sacred, like Mount Everest, Mount Olympus, (home of the gods) Mount Fujii, Uhuru (Ayers Rock) and countless others. But as well as reverence, in Mount Kinabalu's case, it is important that the guardians are appeased, kept in 'good spirits' as it were, to avoid mishaps and misadventures amongst those who hope to reach the top. This takes the form of a ceremony, now held annually near the Timpohon Gates, the starting point for climbers scaling the peak. Called the 'monolob,' the ceremony involves a 'bobolian' or shaman and three assistants chanting before a bundle of roots and wood with seven white sacrificial roosters, tobacco, betel, areca leaves, lime paste, eggs, rice and salt, as offerings to the guardians of the mountain. It is fairly obvious why this ritual, once carried out for each party climbing the mountain, is now limited to an annual event as around 30,000 people climb the peak each year. A kind of 'blanket coverage' as it were, as a large chicken farm would need to be employed to keep up with demand. To this day visitors and climbers are informed about local taboos and regulations by the park management team before they walk any trail, be it up to the summit or in the surrounding forest. Although stricter in the past, those regulations still demand the principle of not harming, removing or disturbing the creatures and plant life of the mountain and its forests. It's not just physical acts that should be moderated. The way people talk or act should be in a respectful way, mindful of the reverence local guides and porters feel. I'm sure W.H.Murray, the Scottish mountaineer known to have held an almost spiritual approach to mountains, would have approved. And beware, violation of these rules, it is claimed, has resulted in some high profile misadventures, some fatal, over the years.

Given its popularity, terrain and range in temperature, Mount Kinabalu has had relatively few serious accidents, far fewer, than Ben Nevis for example. There have been some deaths from falls and hypothermia, but the most publicised drama and perhaps the most interesting unfolded in 1994.

On the 21st. February a British Army team of ten men, (two officers, three NCO's, two Territorial soldiers and three Hong Kong reservists) set out from the park HQ with the intention of descending Low's Gully, the very understated name given to the immense chasm that drops from near the summit, down the North Face to the jungle 3,000 feet below. The team became separated during the descent, due to disputes, misunderstandings, errors and poor organisation, and split into three groups, one group of three men emerging at a village, Melangkap Tamis, some nine miles from the gully, nearly three weeks after leaving the HQ. Gaunt and haggard, their clothes in tatters and visible skin in shreds, they were fed by villagers and in the morning taken by truck to the city, Kota Kinabalu for hospital treatment. On the same day another two soldiers staggered into another village a few miles from Melangkap Tamis. Near naked, one was gulping water from a pipe-stand, the other on his hands and knees crawling, calling out deliriously, 'Mummy, I want something to eat.' (Their food had run out seven days previously). The villagers were at first frightened by these apparitions in rags, suddenly having arrived amongst them through the jungle from the direction of 'Aki Nabalu'. One of the men had a badly infected cut on his hand, swollen and putrid, and as he had some medical experience, feared it was gangrenous. Seeing they posed no threat, the headman and his wife, kindly gave them food and washed and treated their wounds. Luckily for the soldier the local people had their own effective treatment for this kind of infection. Unfazed by the sight of the heavily infected wound, the headman's wife produced a jar of unpleasant-looking, murky, oily liquid and encouraged him to submerge his hand in it for twenty minutes. Whatever it was (extracts from bear bile? centipedes? amino acids from snake fat?) the infection subsequently cleared completely, although the soldier later required surgery to repair tendon damage. Over the centuries, the people who live in and around the forest have become well-versed in traditional remedies based on plants and substances available to them. They know for example that cuts and scratches in the heat and humidity of the rain-forest will almost inevitably become infected, if untreated.

Meanwhile the five who had reached safety realised that half the team was still missing. In torrential rain the two officers and the three Chinese soldiers had been unable to proceed and were trapped in the gully. Short of food and carrying injuries, having fallen several times on the perilous rocks, their survival depended on the rescue efforts now being organised from all over the world. A Royal Air Force Mountain Rescue team was flown out from United Kingdom. Helicopters from Malaysia and British military personnel from Hong Kong arrived in Kota Kinabalu and were ferried up to the mountain. The first attempt was made by the Mountain Rescue team. For two days they abseiled down the gully, but were eventually turned back by a full-flowing, massive 400 foot waterfall. The nature of the terrain, altitude, torrential rain and the biggest free abseil drop in the world, combined to defeat their attempt to find the missing men. Doubts were being expressed whether they were still alive or even if they would ever be found as the five had been in the gully for nearly a month (with ten day's rations). Efforts now were concentrated on helicopter searches over the jungle and lower reaches of the gully. This was extremely difficult and dangerous as the downdraught created in the gorge's natural wind tunnel, required 100% power from the engines to prevent the craft from being blown back out of the gully's five mile long course. Two days later a helicopter crew caught sight of the stranded party stretched out on boulders in the gully. The pilot managed to get low enough to lower food, medical supplies and a radio. Two subsequent attempts managed to evacuate all the men successfully, bringing to an end a saga that looked for some time as if the 'guardians' were going to invoke terrible vengeance on those responsible for this intrusion and had then decided, ' Right, we'll let you off with a warning this time!'

★ ★ ★

My own particular experience of climbing the mountain was, as for most of those following the tourist path, relatively uneventful. First of all I had to overcome the problem of not being allowed to climb unescorted or unattached to a party. I was able to circumvent this difficulty when, luckily, I met Martin, a teacher from Brunei who had just arrived at the park office with a group of eager students. My name was attached to his party as an extra teacher, and this seemed to satisfy the park authorities. Once outside the office, we agreed to meet up at the rest-house, Laban Rata, at 11,000 feet, as Martin intended doing some field work on plants by the path on the way up, kindly allowing me to go at my own pace, instead of hanging around sketching flowers and taking notes. The path was a bit of a slog being steep and muddy, and, although not raining, the exertion and the mist soon had me soaked through. Higher up, the vegetation began to thin out and become more stunted and after three hours with a couple of stops to admire the colourful pitcher plants, I reached the rest-house.

Above the building on the skyline, the rocky pinnacles of Donkey Ears and Low's peak appeared and disappeared in the swirling mist. It was up there that the Army team had camped before their descent of Low's Gully. One of the team, a soldier from the 3rd Commando Brigade had endured a difficult night. He later claimed that he arrived there with a sense of spookiness, which had come on him on his way up the mountain. That night he was very restless and heard a noise outside the tent in the early hours. He looked out to see a large shambling creature lumbering away from the camp-site. Terrified, he spent the rest of the night desperate for the reassuring daylight. A Sabah yeti? The Grey Man of Ben Kinabalu? A Malaysian Sasquatch? Who knows? It later emerged that one of the officers in a nearby tent confirmed that he had heard a noise and seen a shadow outlined against the fabric of the tent. He said he felt disinclined to investigate further.

An hour or so later the group, to which I had attached myself, arrived and sank down on the rest-house veranda. Soon, everybody was putting on sweaters and jackets as the temperature variation between the Park HQ and the rest-house is around 20 degrees C.

The usual weather pattern is for the peak to be clear of mist until mid-morning and then be shrouded in cloud for the rest of the day. For this reason it is standard practice for climbers to reach the summit in time for sun-rise around 6 a.m. This of course means an early rise and an 'early to bed, early to rise' philosophy is the rule.

Over the evening meal of chicken, rice and pako, (ferns), I mentioned to Martin that earlier, I had caught a glimpse of Donkey Ears, where the yeti had been seen. Immediately he became quite agitated and, glancing around, leaned towards me and said, 'For God's sake don't say 'yeti' or 'haunted' or 'spirits' or 'ghosts' in front of the students. They're terribly superstitious. They'll abandon this trip in terror if they get a hint of anything like that.' This was very true. We recalled the time some students at the Girl's School, in the capital, Bandar Seri Begawan, claimed to have seen a ghost ('hantu' in Malay) in a clump of bamboo in the school

275

grounds. An outbreak of hysteria followed and had girls collapsing all over the place, sobbing and screaming. After a few girls were hospitalised, they closed the school for a week and called in a 'bomoh' (shaman) to try to exorcise the evil presence. This method of dealing with the problem was surprising in a country that had strong Islamic beliefs. Yet it was widely held amongst the locals that in the jungle and, particularly after dark, being amongst the trees, were places where evil spirits reigned supreme and should be avoided.

We left the Laban Rata around 2 a.m., two teachers and 15 students, the lights from our head-torches bobbing up and down as we climbed the steep wooden steps leading upwards from the rest-house. Leaving the last of the moss forest behind, we came to a vast area of smooth granite slabs and ahead, as far as the eye could see, was a procession of lights, like an army of fire-flies, winding its way slowly up the rock, earlier risers than ourselves. This section is the most dangerous, especially during heavy rain and/or foggy conditions. In the monsoon season, the whole surface of the rock can be knee-deep in fast-flowing water and can sweep the unwary off their feet and over the cliff. The park authority has been aware of this hazard and, fixed ropes, attached to metal posts embedded in the rock, are strung out across the entire face. It is important that climbers follow the line that the ropes take, both for route-finding and also for maintaining one's footing. Once the roped section is passed the slope eases off and the summit plateau is traversed until the outcrop of the peak is reached. Around this, in the dark, sit and stand dozens of people waiting patiently for the main event, sunrise. My particular jinx around summits was about to manifest itself once again as our torches picked out the shivering crowds. It got lighter as dawn approached but, instead of the rays of the sun, creeping over the horizon, a thick mist descended from nowhere, shrouding the whole of the top of the mountain and reducing visibility to about 50 feet. Groans went up all around and cameras were lowered as Nature went about its merry way. A local guide was heard to say that sometimes the mist could lift as quickly as it came down, and that it was only a matter of waiting. People were taking photographs of each other, waiting in turn to drape themselves over the sign which said, "Taman Kinabalu, Low's Peak, 4,095 metres", and bars of chocolate were consumed, but the mist showed no signs of lifting. When eventually Martin announced to the disappointed students that it was time to go down, as conditions didn't look like changing, there was a chorus of, 'Please sir, can't we stay a bit longer, we haven't seen the sunrise?

'Sorry everybody, the sun has risen already, we just can't see it. We'll freeze if we stay here any longer, I'm afraid we're going to have to go down.' Turning to me he whispered, 'I'll tell them the ghosts are unhappy with us being up here. You won't see them for dust.' Thankfully, he didn't though, and we slowly made our way back down the rope trail, passing people on the way up who sometimes asked if it was misty on top. Our stock answer to this was, 'Yes, but it might clear, it's only a matter of waiting.'

Back in the hotel, I picked up the guide-book and once again read about summiteers rapturously describing the experience of how they had stood on the top of Mount Kinabalu and seen the sun rising in a cloudless sky, with the magnificent panorama of Borneo laid out before them. Oh well, I have been up there, but I'm afraid I'll need to use my imagination to see that wonderful scene in my mind's 'inner eye.'

# The Last 'Scholar'

*...a stag*
*paused in the thickening light to see that strange thing, a twelve-legged boat*
*in a bog...*

From *'Among Scholars'* by Norman MacCaig

Sitting alone at contented ease in my warm, comfortable, Pitlochry retirement flat this dreich October day of thick dull mist and constant drizzly misery, I once again pick up my well-read copy of *The Collected Poems of Norman MacCaig*.

What wonderful nostalgic memories many of that great poet's Assynt poems conjure up for me. Oh but as I grow older, how increasingly difficult it is to believe that so many years have passed since MacCaig died in 1996. And how much more difficult it is to realise that so many more years have passed since the 1970's when so many special Assynt men had died. Many of those larger than life characters had been MacCaig's friends. Some had also been my friends.

Dipping at random leisure into this book's many treasures, I halt at one special page. I re-read a poem that re-wakes old, but still vivid memories of another October day.

★ ★ ★

'Well, Robert, how are you this bright October morning? Are you feeling strong?'

I smiled at Bob MacDonald as he asked these questions then replied, 'Oh, aye, I'm feeling fine. But is there some special reason why I should also feel strong today?'

'Aye there is. Charlie Ross was on the phone last night and between us

278

we've organised a team of six strong men to carry out a special task today. You and me will be part of that team.'

'Oh, and what exactly is this special task?'

Instead of answering me, Bob asked another question, 'Are you nearly finished cleaning out all the kennels?'

'Aye, I am. I've just to finish this last one.'

'Well hurry up with it then come up to the kitchen for a cup o' tea and I'll explain all about the strong-man task six o' us are going to carry out today.'

Stimulated by the promise of this welcome tea in that hospitable kitchen and eager to learn what strenuous work was in prospect, I applied the long, stiff-bristled kennel brush with extra vigour. Soon this last of the four adjoining kennels was thoroughly brushed and hosed out and clean fresh straw was thickly spread on the wooden beds in the cosy inner kennels.

With effortless healthy ease I climbed the steep slope that thrust up from behind the kennels and led directly to Torbreck House. This house had been a Church of Scotland minister's spacious manse and was now the comfortable home of Assynt Estate gamekeeper, Bob MacDonald, and of his two sisters. As I climbed I was joyously accompanied by all the dogs on the other side of the high chain-link fence that securely enclosed their large, grassy, birch-dotted dog-run. The novelty of having those estate owned dogs as friendly companions was still fresh enough to fill me, a Glasgow born, but Assynt adopted, young trainee gamekeeper, with thankful delight. These well trained gun-dogs were Cruft registered thoroughbred silky haired English Setters, plus a brace of smooth-coated Pointers. The English Setters combined elegant beauty with tireless keenness when, with obedient methodical sureness, they quartered the undulating Assynt grouse moors then stood statuesquely still as they 'pointed' an unseen, but unerringly scented, covey of grouse.

I found it a truly rewarding fulfilling experience to, under the expert guidance of the gamekeeper, help train and exercise these graceful dogs. However, as Bob MacDonald explained while I drank my steaming tea and scoffed the tasty home-made scones that I had once again been given in this hospitable Torbreck kitchen, we would not be taking the dogs out today.

The more strenuous task that lay before us was to help carry a badly damaged wooden boat some two rough roadless miles from its trout loch to Inveruplan, the isolated home of Charlie Ross, Assynt Estate's head gamekeeper. This boat would later be collected by a lorry and be taken to Lochinver village where the estate joiner would repair it. The boat had been hauled well clear of the water and the last two weeks of dry, bright, bracing October weather would have dried it out and, hopefully, made it considerably lighter to handle.

'I've arranged to collect Alastair Mathieson, while Charlie is going to collect Angus MacLeod and his great fishing and drinking companion, Norman MacCaig, so that, with you and me, the six of us should manage to move the boat without too much trouble.' Bob grinned, 'I don't quite know how Charlie persuaded Angus and Norman to help with this estate work; perhaps he enticed them with glowing promises of many generous drams awaiting them at Inveruplan once they completed this task.'

I laughed, 'I only hope Alastair, that very conscientious river-watcher and gamekeeper will get on all right with that, I believe, very skilled poacher, Angus Macleod, and his great fishing and probably sometimes poaching friend, Norman MacCaig.'

Bob's laughter joined mine, 'Aye, I wondered about that myself at first. Och but Charlie assured me that, with his great natural diplomatic skills, he would keep those two poaching rascals under control; would keep the entire six of us, those employed by the estate and those usually very critical of the estate, working harmoniously together.'

With Bob driving his estate van we went and collected Alastair from his small cottage that overlooked attractive weedy Loch Culag. Returning, through the autumnal sleepy and now tourist-free village of Lochinver, we drove the narrow, almost traffic-less road past Brackloch then cautiously crossed the rumbling and shuddering old wooden bridge over the River Inver. From there a rough track led to Inveruplan.

The column of grey peat smoke rising lazily from one chimney scented the surrounding air with that wonderful unique peaty smell that, once experienced, is never forgotten.

The only activity about the place came from Charlie's two working fox terriers as they barked their questioning greetings from their kennels and from the annoyed muttering of a large black rooster as it went after its disturbed hens.

Standing by his parked van Bob glanced at his watch and said, 'We're already ten minutes past the appointed time for all of us to meet here. I hope

Angus and Norman have not changed their minds about helping us with this estate work.'

Alastair grinned, 'Aye, or maybe they've been led astray by some tempting sinner waving a bottle o' whisky at them!'

I smiled and perhaps rather naively asked, 'Oh surely they would not start drinking whisky at this time in the morning, would they?'

Bob and Alastair exchanged a quick glance then exploded into laughter. 'Och, Robert,' gasped Bob, 'it's obvious that you're not a true born Highlander and have not lived in the North West Highlands all that long.'

We then saw Charlie's fast approaching van and heard its cheery tooting. Soon the six of us were standing together exchanging animated cheerful greetings. Then Charlie led us all through the field behind his house and along the narrow rough path that followed along beside the wide, fast rushing burn that flowed quite steeply down from Loch an Leathad where the damaged boat was stranded. The narrowness of the path meant we went in single file behind Charlie who set his usual steady, unhurried, but mile-devouring pace that ensured we all had ample time to look around at the rugged heather slopes that surrounded us.

Once again I was impressed by how well the Assynt Estate tweed jackets and plus-fours that Charlie, Bob, Alastair and I were wearing blended in with the Autumnal heathers.

Having also noted this, Angus grinned and said, 'Oh, Charlie, if Norman and I come with you on many more estate tasks we will expect to get outfitted in these posh estate tweeds too!'

Charlie laughed, 'Och Angus, I've more than once heard ye declare that you would never wear the degrading garb o' us servile estate gamekeepers.'

Norman's laughter readily joined in, 'Och aye, Angus, I too have often heard you make that declaration!'

'Och I see I'm outnumbered and outvoted,' Angus grinned. 'Let's move on again, Charlie, and change the subject.'

We started moving, still in single file, but in changed order. I now had Norman MacCaig in front of me with all the others ahead of us. It seemed fitting that we, the only townies here, Norman from Edinburgh, I from Glasgow (although now settled in Assynt) should bring up the rear and let these other, much more country-wise men lead the way. Like me, Norman was keen to learn all he could from Charlie, Bob and Alastair, these experienced Highland gamekeepers whose fathers and grandfathers had also been gamekeepers. And we had no doubt we could also learn from Angus, that expert crofter, part-time ghillie, and – if local rumours were true – very experienced poacher whose Pagan Assynt blood flowed with ancestral Highland knowledge.

And we did learn. These excellent observers saw, and pointed out, many things that Norman and I might not have noticed; a fox's fresh paw marks in soft mud; a compressed pellet cast up by a large buzzard; a dying wee rowan tree, its bark rubbed off by a stag's itchy 'velvet' antlers.

However when we reached the loch even the two of us, not yet very experienced in country lore, did not need these experts to point out the quite obvious conical verdant heap that, crowned with glaringly-white fish bones, was the tidy latrine of otters. But we might not have noticed the disturbed soil at the entrance to an old fox den halfway up a nearby heather slope. Nor was it likely that we would be aware of the reason for that small neat splash of green that showed so vividly against the surrounding dark heather moor. We were intrigued to hear Charlie explain that that verdant green splash clearly marked the spot where an old hind had died and over many years the remains of her predatory plundered body had sunk into the heather moor while its calcium-rich bones altered that poor peaty soil to a lush grassy grave.

Norman said, 'Oh, Charlie, you make me feel like an eager scholar humbly sitting at your feet and drinking up all your profound nature-wise knowledge.' He turned and grinned at the other gamekeepers, 'And that applies equally to all of you.'

With a rueful grin, Angus, that skilled poacher, asked, 'What about me, Norman, have you learned nothing from me?'

Norman again grinned, 'Oh yes, Angus, I've learned some things from you, but as we're in the company of so many gamekeepers perhaps the less I say about exactly what special skills you've taught me the better for all of us!'

The six of us now sat in companionable ease while two pipes and four cigarettes were leisurely enjoyed. A low flying heron which had also followed up that burn from Inveruplan suddenly saw us and with ugly alarmed croaks violently turned away in ragged laborious flapping panic.

Angus smiled, 'There goes your 'Umbrella Heron', Norman, away to find a less crowded loch to land at and turn itself into a predatory walking-stick.'

Recognising that reference to one of Norman's Assynt poems I thought, 'Yes that startled heron does look *like a large umbrella ungainly flapping in a gale.*

Heaving himself to his feet Charlie said, 'Och, I suppose we better get moving too. The sooner we start hauling that boat the sooner we'll get to any whisky that might be awaiting us at Inveruplan.'

This bright incentive spurred us to our places at the damaged wooden boat. Although now going slightly downhill, the hauling, heaving, carrying and mildly cursing return journey was much slower. It demanded many more halts and rests. Our longest, most welcome rest came when we saw a rutting stag and heard its fierce challenging roars from the steep heather slope above us. Rising to that challenge Angus said, 'Let's see if we can get that sex-mad stag to charge us instead o' yon rival stag.' With a defiantly raised head and megaphoned hands he roared what seemed accurate, rutting roars.

For silent moments the uncertain stag stood and stared, then loudly bellowed his response. As Angus returned challenging calls for each of the stag's angry roars the madly annoyed beast, his normal fear of men much weakened by his obsessive rutting lust, started charging down the slope towards the source of that mysterious challenge.

Then with a violent slamming on of braking hooves, the stag halted. For confused silent moments it intensely stared at *that strange thing, a twelve-legged boat in a bog.* Then it turned and rushed back up the heather slope; back to his harem of sexy hinds and to jealously challenge and fiercely drive away any more normal upstart rivals.

Eventually we reached the field behind Inveruplan and with profound relief left that truly strange thing – a boat that got heavier the longer we man-handled it.

With her face brightly glowing, and with eager urgings, Charlie's wife, Jess, shepherded us all into their wee, cosy, hugely hospitable home.

While Jess handed around tea and home-made scones Charlie attended to the whisky, and six generous drams were quickly, expertly, unspillingly poured.

When the twice refilled large teapot was again almost empty and most of the excellent scones scoffed, more drams were hospitably offered; were gratefully accepted by Angus and Norman, but were decisively refused by Bob MacDonald who, in an authoritative voice, also spoke for Alastair and me. He smiled and explained, 'The three of us will have to leave now. I've to drive Alistair back home then return to Torbreck where Robert's to put the dogs into their kennels and feed them before it gets too dark.'

With deep regrets at having to leave this warmly welcoming house and its fine gregarious company, I scrambled into the back of Bob's van. I knew that even then, in these easy-going years before strict driving and drinking laws came into force and there were no car seat belts, Bob did not approve of taking too many drams before driving. He was fairly unique in having such views at that time, especially here in the remote "Wild West" of the Northern Highlands.

Returning to the present pleasure of re-reading Norman MacCaig's familiar poem *Among Scholars*, I, inwardly smiled, again regretting I had not been able to stay on at Inveruplan as Angus and Norman had done, and enjoyed many more hours in that glorious gregarious company; that place, that company so glorified in some of MacCaig's great Assynt poems.

In midst of glowing thoughts of these fine men who, "lurching and slithering", had laboriously hauled that boat with me all these years ago, I shudder with sudden sadness at the thought that these wonderful characters are now all dead.

Although he was the second youngest of these men, Bob MacDonald was the first to suddenly die when heather burning on an Assynt grouse moor. Then, in one really tragic year, both Angus MacLeod and Charlie Ross suffered sudden deaths at Inverkirkaig. Alastair Mathieson was the oldest of this group and he had a peaceful death after a fine peaceful life. Then when Norman MacCaig died in January, 1996 he did so with all the cheers, laughter and applause of his 85th birthday party still echoingly lingering not only in his, but in many other privileged and vividly remembering minds.

Now looking back from my own 85th year I'm truly thankful that I, the last of Norman's "scholars", had known such grand men; had, with them, been part of *that strange thing, a twelve-legged boat in a bog.*

# Just One Great Painting

S itting in my bed propped against a heap of pillows, I hold a mug of hot toddy with both hands and hope this favourite auld remedy's generously poured whisky will stop my cold's misery from progressing into vile flu. Dull with familiar male self-pity my heavy eyes go on a weary journey around this warm bedroom in my cosy small retirement flat in Pitlochry.

With a sudden surprising surge of remembered past joys my eye's heavy burden lightens, these searching eyes even seem to joyously brighten as they focus on one painting on the facing wall. This large watercolour landscape of what, to me, is a very special part of Assynt was by an old friend, John Fielder. John was from Yorkshire, but for much of his life he had somewhat frugally, but truly creatively, lived in a caravan at beautiful Achmelvich Bay, some four long, winding miles North of Lochinver village. Profoundly moved and inspired by the stark wild beauty of the surrounding Assynt landscape and its often fierce, always changing, weather, John created many wonderful, or even great, paintings. Of all of his paintings that enhanced the walls of my flat, this one facing me in my bedroom was my favourite.

In this painting John had perfectly captured the bright beauty of one of these seemingly endless Northern June days with its vast cloudless sky a pale eggshell blue, the rugged heather ridges and massed layers of ancient rock all vividly clear and subtly reflected in Loch Roe's ripple-free salty narrows. I stared at that great painting and sighed with nostalgic pleasure, remembering when such perfect West Highland weather, day after day, week after week, used to be the expected norm all through May and June.

As I sipped my warming toddy and wiped my dripping nose, I was once more amazed at just how many vivid memories that painting held for me… so much in just one great painting.

The strong dark green foreground depicted the steep grassy slope that

285

slid down to Loch Roe's bare North shore. Every stunted birch tree that tenaciously clung to this slope leaned wearily away from the West, all too clearly remembering the abundance of prevailing Westerly gales. Then with brilliant skill John's painting revealed the drowsy June beauty of Loch Roe's breathless calm perfection. And with further masterly skill, Ardroe's rugged rocky landscape was wavily reflected in that sea-loch's smiling brightness.

Then over there, accurately revealed in their bare paleness by June's bleaching sunlight, were two low rocky isles where Arctic Terns nested. With unclouded memory's clear brightness, I remembered how, many years ago, I saw that vulnerable colony of graceful 'Sea-Swallows' come under deadly attack from a pair of huge Black-Backed Gulls. On reporting this to my Achmelvich crofter friend, Donald MacLeod (known locally as 'Pollochan'), he at once agreed that we must try to save Loch Roe's precious, precarious colony of Arctic Terns. And this was long before Ecology and Conservation became today's hugely popular 'in thing'!

Under the guidance of Pollochan's years of experience and his vast treasure of Nature Lore, we, after considerable trouble, managed to get within our gun's buckshot range and killed both these ruthless Black-Backed Gulls that had threatened to gulp down every helpless Tern chick.

I had also enjoyed the great privilege and deep pleasure of accompanying Pollochan on night-time salmon poaching expeditions on Loch Roe when that Loch's thrilling dark mystery was fantastically enhanced by the glowing beauty of our stealthy boat's glittering phosphorescent oars. On one of these poaching occasions I enjoyed the most interesting company of one of Scotland's greatest 20th century poets.

Of course my salmon poaching ceased when I became a trainee ghillie and gamekeeper with the estate that 'owned' Loch Roe's wild Atlantic salmon, and I developed a diplomatic 'Nelson Eye' towards certain poachers.

Beyond these Terns' isles, well shown in the great painting, was where I had seen my first otters, proud parents and playful young, near their holt on the boulder-strewn South shore of Loch Roe.

Beyond that, just seen in the painting, was Loch Dubh; its fresh water held large brown trout, but the stunted birches that crowded its shores left very few places where I could cast my keen rod's artificial flies. However near the middle of the Eastern shore there was a small ledge of bare rock, free of trees with a wee burn flowing vertically down. Occasionally, when the trout were not rising and the weather was hot, I used this wee waterfall as a cold shower. This natural shower was especially useful when I was warden at Achmelvich Youth Hostel in the years when that hostel had no running water and such cissy things as hot or cold showers were unheard of!

Further along Loch Dubh's Eastern shore was where, later, as a trainee 'keeper under the guidance of experienced gamekeeper, Bob MacDonald, I had for the first time helped to shoot foxes, driven out by our hardy terriers, as they bolted from their underground den. That den's surroundings were littered with the pathetic remains of fox-slaughtered crofters' lambs.

Much higher, and steeply up from the shore we had discovered, and dealt with, another fox den. Then even higher and further up that rugged slope we came across not yet another fox lair, but the tell-tale remains of another type of den – an old, abandoned illicit whisky still. The size and darkness of the smoke stains on the huge overhanging grey cliff that rose above and sheltered this illicit still suggested that its peat smoke had been rising for many years, perhaps centuries.

We took some of the old still's curving copper coils home with us. They were in surprisingly good shape. Some local Assynt people, who best remain nameless, were keen to put these copper coils again to illicit distillery use. For some time there were strong rumours and even solemnly stated 'facts' that they really were again in use, 'somewhere in Assynt.'

Even although all this happened many years ago, perhaps the less that's said about it the better, but I do seem to remember at least one time when I desperately gulped and choked, my throat burned, and my stinging eyes wept a flood of scalding tears after having foolishly downed a special – a very special – dram of 'Uisge-Beatha' that most certainly had never been seen by any Customs and Excise Officers.

The long, rugged, undulating heathery ridges of Ardroe spread out high above Lochs Roe and Dubh and gently touched the painting's pale blue June sky. Then, thrusting up as if in competitive eagerness, there rose the stark, remote, isolated peaks of Canisp and Suilven. Both mountains wore the same vague purplish hue, but poor Canisp was completed overshadowed by the sheer dominance of Suilven's fantastic shape. Surely that mountain's sheer thrusting steepness and its unforgettable flamboyant shape make it Scotland's most unique mountain.

After having downed the last of my toddy and completed my clearly remembered reminiscent journey over that great painting I felt somewhat better; no longer shivery, no sign of flu's advance. Inwardly grinning I cosily wonder what had worked this quick cure: the glow of the toddy's miracle heat, or the warmth of that great painting.

# PART THREE

# Our Great Reunion

As mentioned in the introduction, Gordon and Bob completely lost touch with one another for almost forty years. Neither knew if the other was alive or dead. Then out of the blue in July, 2012, Bob, in his Pitlochry retirement flat, received a phone call from Gordon who was home on holiday in Scotland from Brunei where he and his wife, Mary, taught English. These old climbing pals spoke to each other as if they had only been a short time apart.

They both arranged to meet up at a Pitlochry restaurant. 'Has your appearance changed much in those past forty years?' Gordon asked. 'I fear I've aged quite a bit.'

'Och, I doot I've aged too. How then will we recognise each other?'

Gordon laughed, 'Och, we better both wear a sprig o' lucky white heather in our lapels.'

'Aye,' Bob replied, 'white heather seems a most fitting flower to wear; we both are real lucky to be alive and more or less thriving after the passage o' all these forty years.'

Even without the aid of floral signals they did recognise one another. With almost instant recall, they saw the bright ghosts of their eager climbing young selves linger on in these two bald auld men.

They ate and drank and talked about the past. With rueful grins they solemnly agree that those grand auld friends, those familiar auld hills, The Cobbler, Buachaille Etive Mor, and Assynt's noble Suilven, are now outwith their climbing reach.

In the comfort of Drummond's, they also agree that they might still *just* manage to climb Pitlochry's grand wee hill, Craigower.

And the following morning they do. They climb to the top of Craigower, despite the physical restrictions of Gordon's artificial hip; despite the threat of both Bob's knees seizing-up under the aching weight of their 85 active years.

Sitting on this familiar 1,300 ft. peak Bob once again drinks in this modest Perthshire hill's grand unpretentious views. Gordon on his first visit to Pitlochry's very own, very special wee peak is most impressed by the grandeur of its Westerly views.

Bob grins, 'Well, Gordon, is this an ample reward for all our slow, wearying, climbing effort?'

'Oh aye, it is. The view's grand and the stopping to admire it, is even better.'

Below where Schiehallion proudly displays its majestic pyramidal shape, Loch Tummel glitters in the mid-day sunshine while Loch Rannoch reveals no more than a tantalising glimpse of its hidden treasures before the desolate peat wastes of Rannoch Moor lead Gordon's searching eyes to distant Glencoe.

'That other pyramid shaped hill I can just make out must surely be The Buachaille,' mustn't it?' he asks.

'Aye it is. The grand auld Buachaille Etive Mor, that Glencoe hill we ken so well.'

What memories that hill held for those gazing auld men. While Bob remembers the uplifting bliss of climbing its glorious Curved Ridge, Gordon re-traces with memory rather than with his searching eye, some of the severe rock routes on that forever challenging Rannoch Wall, that he so youthfully climbed as one of the Lomond's 'Young Tigers.'

Bob now voiced their joint thoughts, 'Oh, Gordon, it's almost impossible to believe that it's more than half a century ago since we so easily climbed all our well known, well loved Scottish hills, isn't it?'

Gordon sighed, 'Aye, I know. Oh how can it be over fifty years since we were in our glorious youthful climbing prime?' He suddenly grinned, 'Do you remember all the heated arguments at that time about the increasing use of ironmongery, hardware, pitons etc?'

'Aye, of course I do. What about it?'

'Och, I was just wondering if my titanium replacement hip would be classed as an artificial climbing-aid.'

'Aye,' Bob laughed, 'nae doot it would.'

'Och, but without it I'd never have managed to climb this grand wee hill. But it's certainly not always an aid, it can be a bloody pest each time I walk through airport security and it sets off their sensitive alarms. Do you know when I explained once that I had an artificial hip, the policeman asked to see it, I thought he was going to ask me to climb on the luggage belt and go through the x-ray scanner.'

Bob again laughed then plaintively asked, 'Aye, and why are my aching knees complaining about grand wee Craigower getting steeper with each passing year? And, are age's sadly narrowing horizons linked to our hardening, narrowing arteries?'

'Aye,' Gordon sighed, 'it's hard to bear that these days we can only sit and stare and no longer dare climb the good auld Buachaille.'

Bob grinned, 'Och we're getting awful sorry for ourselves. Surely that Westerly view should uplift us in song, should take us gaily striding on *The Road to the Isles* by Loch Tummel, Loch Rannoch and Lochaber, and then we'll joyously ken the tangle o' the Isles.'

Gordon laughed, 'Och I smelt more than enough o' the guff of the Isles seaweed when I worked on yon kelp-stinking Clyde Puffer, the *Glenshiel*, all these years ago.'

'Aye and you were real lucky to leave that ill-fated ship before she sank with the loss of all but one of her crew, weren't you?'

'Yes I was. Aye I was really lucky then.' This led them on to active thoughts and eager talk about good and bad luck; about grandly fulfilled long lives; about lives tragically cut short.

They were fortunate enough to have known three of Scotland's greatest post-war climbers before these three fell to their separate tragic deaths.

Robin Smith was the youngest and, despite his all too few climbing years, possibly the greatest of that great climbing trio. To Scottish climbers he had become a legendary figure even before he reached the age of twenty.

Gordon was pleased to meet Robin at Glencoe's Cameron's Barn, and at Kingshouse Hotel. He, and the other 'Lomond Tigers', and even the notoriously hard to impress tough Creagh Dhu characters, could not fail, albeit somewhat grudgingly, to admire this fresh-faced 'Boy-wonder' who in his few remarkable climbing years was to quite amazingly put up some forty new rock routes in Scotland.

To those Glasgow climbing types Robin Smith gave the impression of being something of a happily bohemian hippy adventurer (although the label 'hippy' was not yet in common use) who, while joining in the banter and their hearty laughter, did not quite seem truly at home, nor completely relaxed. Of course he was from Edinburgh and was studying philosophy; perhaps that explained a lot!

But every one of these climbers was deeply shocked to hear of Robin's tragic death when climbing in Russia. Robin Smith and Wilfrid Noyce had fallen together and died together on the Pamir Mountains. Robin was only twenty three years old when he died there in 1962.

Doctor Tom Patey was another great climber who flared to sudden glorious brightness in that grand time of post-war Scottish climbing. Then he too had his life tragically cut short.

Being from Aberdeenshire, Tom's first love was for the Cairngorms. It was there that his first great climbs were done. Then he discovered and, daringly exploring, did many first climbs on some of Scotland's sheer sea cliffs. He took an active part in the first ascent of the Old Man of Hoy.

When Tom settled as a conscientious and greatly liked doctor in Ullapool he spent much of his free time fearlessly climbing solo on the little known, almost completely un-touched fierce cliffs of Scotland's wild North West coast.

The all too frequent savage winter gales made these salt spray lashed cliffs too dangerous even for fearless Doctor Patey. He would often then look after his patients in a lively way by uplifting their weary winter souls with his accordion. He often set Ullapool's or Lochinver's village hall alive with his glorious musical sounds. Many an Assynt gamekeeper's, shepherd's and fisherman's, weather-beaten sweating faces were first kindled by whisky and then stoked by Tom's accordion playing. Were *ceilidh-furnaced fiercely ablazed* and 'MacCaiged' *to a true Rembrandt glow.*

For Robert Scott, as for all others, it was always a great pleasure to meet that cheery doctor at a lively ceilidh or on his way to climb an Assynt hill or search for fearsome new routes on remote sea cliffs.

It was terribly tragic that one simple mistake, when Tom was abseiling from a sea-stack near Whiten Head in North Sutherland in 1970, should have ended his 38 years of useful joyous life; should have resulted in him falling to an untimely death.

Many of Tom's shocked non-climbing, uncomprehending older patients plaintively asked, 'Oh why did our grand young doctor waste his life on yon mad mountain climbing?'

Johnny Cunningham was the last of that tragic trio. He was by far the brightest star in what was a truly bright group of great post-war Creagh Dhu climbers. He too had put up many new rock routes on Scottish hills, probably as many as sixty. Of course he had lived a bit longer than either Robin Smith or Tom Patey. He was aged 52 when death claimed him in 1980.

For Bob and Gordon, those two auld men sitting on Pitlochry's grand wee Craigower Hill and reminiscently rambling on, Johnny Cunningham was the one of these three great Scottish climbers they (especially Gordon) had known best. Gordon with other young 'Lomond Tigers' had climbed many of Johnny's new-rock routes; had often done them shortly after they had first been put up, on The Cobbler and The Buachaille. They had drunk with Johnny at Glencoe's Kingshouse; they had even sometimes shared the Creagh Dhu's exclusive Jacksonville Bothy with him.

They, and the entire Scottish climbing fraternity, were shocked and saddened to hear of his tragic death.

With cruel irony he had not died on those savage Scottish rock-faces he had fearlessly mastered but in that element he disliked and perhaps feared – the sea.

While he led a party of six students on sea-cliffs in North Wales, one of the students was swept into the sea and Johnny, virtually a non-swimmer, was attempting his rescue when he too was swept into the sea. He drowned. His body was never found.

After his solemn thoughts on that sad death some thirty years ago, Gordon grinned, 'Well anyway, I'm pleased that poor old Johnny never found out that it was me who accidentally set fire to the Arrochar Cave he was going to use.'

Bob said, 'I suppose if those three had not climbed they could still be alive in this 21st century.' Then he added, and Gordon agreed, 'Och, but I'm sure they would say that if they had never climbed they would never have truly lived.'

Their talk rambled on to another three great Scottish climbers they had sometimes met in their own early climbing years: three who had all lived on to a good old age. These three who had greatly helped the grand upsurge in Scottish climbing in the pre-war 1930's were: Jock Nimlin, Bill Murray and Tom Weir.

Bob and Gordon fondly remembered Jock Nimlin telling of his

frustration when stuck at his work as a crane driver on his massive crane that towered high above its Clyde shipyard and from which he could clearly see the Campsie Hills and even, weather permitting, Ben Lomond. How he longed to be out on his Scottish hills and adding to his impressive record of some thirty first ascents on challenging rock-faces.

They vividly remember the immense pleasure they had got from first reading W.H. Murray's great book *Mountaineering in Scotland*. That wonderful book had – and hopefully still does – inspired many an adventurous youngster to take to these Scottish hills he had so deeply loved. It also opened up much wider prospects than the joys of 'merely' rock-climbing.

The one they had met most often was Tom Weir. They greatly enjoyed the talks he gave, complete with colour-slides, each winter to their Lomond Climbing Club. In his first fine book, *Highland Days*, he too had pointed the way for those who aspired to capture something of the wonderful pleasures to be got from our wild Highland countryside.

They were delighted that grand auld Tom had lived on into this 21st century; had continued his useful, well-fulfilled inspiring life until his 91st year in 2006.

Yes, Bob and Gordon agreed, it was great that they had met these six great Scottish climbers and, to a greater or lesser degree, had got to know them; had been saddened by these three tragic deaths, had been uplifted by the example of these other three's well-lived long lives.

'Oh, Bob, do you remember how impressed we were by Bill Murray's first, mountaineering book? We found its philosophical, almost spiritual, outlook on climbing our loved Scottish hills really uplifting, didn't we?'

'Aye, of course I clearly remember it. That great book articulated strange thoughts and deep feelings that had been a mixed-up jumble in my young mind. Aye, I clearly remember it although it was all those years ago. Why do you ask?'

Gordon laughed, 'Och, I was just thinking that now we no longer need his spiritual uplift, but we most certainly could do with some physical uplift, like those Alpine mountain railways, to ease our way up even this grand wee hill.'

'Aye,' Bob agreed, 'I doot the only way we could ever again reach Cairngorm's high summit would be via its braw new furnicular railway.

Och but surely we shouldn't complain. We've both been fortunate enough to have, in our own different ways, lived long and good, lives.'

'Aye, and think of the many times in our young climbing days we, often quite recklessly, came within a hair's-breadth of death.'

After a solemn thoughtful silence Bob said, 'Aye, I know. Perhaps we should put some of these escapades in our book.'

'Och aye, maybe we should.'

So here are some of our, 'it was a near-thing,' stories.

# Bob's Involuntary Somersault

On this fine crisp clear March day the party of four climbers; Podge Morrice, Dave Martin, Gordon Nicol and Bob Scott had left their Ben More Farm bothy early; had sweated up the long slog to Ben More's powdery-snowed summit where Podge had taken his usual keen quota of photos.

They had joyously strode down the long smooth slope that joined on to the easy ridge that climbed up to Ben More's near neighbour, that other Munro, a mere 22 ft lower, Stobinian. They laboured up to Stobinian's snowy summit where Podge, of course, took more photos.

Bob was leading this experienced hill-walking party down this easy Munro's more Westerly slope when his vibram-soled boots suddenly slipped on a smooth, skin-thin sheet of verglas ice that the faint powdering of snow had treacherously concealed.

His halted companions watched aghast as, gathering speed, Bob slid faster and faster down the icy slope on his back.

Before he could consciously react, his boots hit a large embedded stone and he was thrown head over heels in a wild involuntary somersault.

Amazingly, he landed standing in a crouched position with both feet firmly planted. Miraculously his boots had landed on what seemed the only small, almost level, patch of ice and snow free grass on this smooth slope.

His ex-army ice-axe still hung by its web strap from his right wrist, and he expertly brought it into use and scraped at the thin ice and crabbed a cautiously slow way across the smooth icy slope to where his companions were anxiously waiting on a safer, snowy ice-free, grassy slope.

The first to express his feelings was Gordon, who with admiration in his voice said, 'That was some somersault you did there Bob, I thought you were a goner. Have you signed up for lessons in a gymnastics class at night-school?' Bob grinned and rather shakily answered, 'No, I assure you I did it quite involuntarily.'

Auld Dave also laughed his heart-felt relief at Bob's escape from that sudden desperate danger. 'We've all heard o' folk being lucky enough tae land on their feet, haven't we? But, by God, Bob, that was the most amazing demonstration I've ever seen of how you actually do it.'

'Aye, I know, Dave. I know.' As his all too vivid imagination swept his nervous gaze down that steep dangerous slope of more than 2,000 ft. of smooth thin ice to the jumble of rocks at the bottom, he could almost feel his body being savagely smashed and his life being suddenly ended.

He forced another, a more unsteady uncertain grin, 'Oh, I assure all of you that I never want to repeat that trick again.'

# Gordon's Desperate Moves on Guerdon Grooves

L ooking back through many years as he re-told this story, Gordon had absolutely no doubt that these desperate moves on – or near to – the crux of the second pitch of Guerdon Grooves were where he came closest to the terrible oblivion of sudden death.

Guerdon Grooves a route on the notorious Slime Wall of Buchaille Etive Mor's North Butress, is graded a "Hard Very Severe" rock climb.

When Johnny Cunningham and Bill Smith first climbed it in 1948 even many of their keenest climbing companions in the Creagh Dhu, looking on, thought these two were pushing their outstanding climbing skills beyond the limits of justified risk into the realms of mad folly.

As Gordon looked up and let his eyes explore this extreme route he silently agreed with that great climber, Robin Smith's often quoted description of this rock face as being, "vertical, if not overhanging". Still, smothering all trepidation, he started up with a Lomond Mountaineering Club friend, Robbie Hutchison, as second on his rope.

Moving with his usual smooth steady climbing skill, Gordon progressed up this route that, in these early 1950's, had not been often climbed. The climb's first pitch went well. The second pitch – or what Gordon thought, and desperately hoped, was the correct route on the second pitch – turned into a climb of hellish danger.

Having run out one hundred feet of his 120 ft. nylon rope without finding anywhere to hammer in a piton and place a runner for some safety or make a good belay and bring up his anxious waiting second, Gordon was tiring fast on very thin holds on this terribly exposed face.

He knew he couldn't reverse this pitch and climb back down. He had to find a way up or fall off!

Seeing Gordon's dangerous dilemma Robbie nervously shouted, 'You've only got 15ft. of rope left. And remember this belay's not great.'

Looking up this "vertical, if not overhanging" cliff, Gordon saw a desperate possibility.

He lunged upwards and found a good handhold.

He needed a higher new foothold to get some purchase on, but all he could see was a tiny wrinkle in the rock about the size of an eyebrow. He got a knee up to it, less than ideal, but it would need to do.

Ignoring the pain, that stabbed from his knee as he thrust up from that rocky 'eyebrow', his right hand rose, and blindly groped above his head for another handhold.

This was it! If he couldn't find another hold he was off. He would have a 200 ft. free fall before he'd smash onto the rocks. And when his weight violently came on the rope Robbie was almost certain to be dragged from his insecure belay.

Gordon's desperate hand found and urgently grasped a good hold. With his utmost strength he pulled up. He found slightly easier rock above. He was over the crux of this extremely dangerous climb.

Now almost at the very end of his rope, he thankfully saw a large flake of rock that would make a good belay.

With trembling fingers he looped a rope sling around the flake, clipped the climbing rope through a karabiner then shouted down to his second, 'No problems now, Robbie. I've got a good belay. Come on up when you're ready. I'll keep a tight rope on you.'

As Gordon and Robbie lay and relaxed at the top of this mind, nerve, and muscle testing climb Robbie grinned, 'You were too busy wrestling with that rock to notice it, but climbing history was repeated today. Just as when Johnny Cunningham first climbed Guerdon Grooves, so again today some of the Creagh Dhu's climbers were watching you struggle on the crux and forgot their usual mocking shouts and jeers and just stared in silence.'

'Och well,' Gordon modestly said, 'I suppose watching in silence is a back-handed kind of compliment.' He grinned, 'More like, of course, they were standing in silence waiting for me to fall off. Then they would have rushed over to 'borrow' my rope, my new boots and any more of my now un-needed climbing gear before they helped carry my dead body down the hill.'

After a thoughtful silence Robbie said, 'Anyway I know I will not be in any great hurry to do that climb again.'

Gordon again grinned, 'C'mon, Robbie, it was a piece of cake.'

★ ★ ★

Even now, after all these years, Gordon very occasionally feels little nervous shivers when he thinks back to those few terrible seconds when his life 'depended on a kneecap and a rocky wrinkle' and he was not so much a hairs-breadth away from death but more an 'eyebrow' from death.

# Bob's Slip on Tower Ridge

To save precious January daylight hours our climbing party of four bypassed the impressive mass of the Douglas boulder and aimed directly for a higher start on Ben Nevis's vastly imposing Tower Ridge.

Well plastered with soft snow this long, high, ragged ridge truly towered and seemed to proudly glow with winter's bright sunshine despite being mostly in its perpetual cool Northerly shade.

Bob Scott and Gordon Nicol led on the first rope. Lawrie Travers and Dave Martin followed on the second rope. All four thought themselves fit enough and experienced enough to take this impressive winter climb in their stride.

Looking back from this 21st century with its winter climbers equipped with all the latest climbing gear: their lightweight, front-pointed crampons, their two wee, curved, ice-axes, their safety helmets and bright glowing weather-proof clothes all festooned with multi-coloured ropes and a clanging array of pitons and ice-screws, Bob and Gordon wonder how they ever survived with their simple primitive winter climbing gear on their sometimes rather careless, casual winter climbing outings.

We had no crampons and three of us merely had vibram-soled boots, while auld Dave Martin wore his ancient pre-war tricouni-nailed boots. Our cotton, wool, or tweed clothes certainly were not waterproof. Only flat Glasgow bunnets or ex-army balaclavas protected our heads. Our long, wooden-handled ice-axes were ex-army too. At least our climbing ropes were now made of white nylon. Even auld Dave had given up his thick old hemp rope that had 'strayed' from Glasgow's Barlinnie prison and might once have belonged to that prison's hangman.

Gordon and Bob took turns to lead and the ruggedly steep climb went encouragingly quickly and exhilaratingly pleasantly.

Grand old gentlemanly Lawrie kept up with these two keen younger climbers at a good assured pace and guid auld Dave also climbed quite speedily, although with a more laboured, but uncomplaining, panting pace.

The eagerness of and the ceaseless pleasure that these two young-at-heart old-timers got as they did this wondrous, in places quite dangerous, winter climb belied their all too rapidly advancing years.

With cautious care and making good use of safe belays all four eagerly climbed the ridge's steep, imposing, snow-plastered Great Tower.

Gordon led the savagely steep way down from this tower. Bob followed him down, keeping to his guiding snow-steps.

Gordon reached and cautiously crossed the infamous Tower Gap where a giddy void fell sheer away on both sides of the awesomely narrow ridge.

Roped together, but not belayed, Bob started to cross this intimidating gap, towards the patiently waiting, Gordon.

A sudden slip of vibram boot on snow-covered ice sent Bob slithering right to the edge of the frightful void.

Just in time he thrust in his ice-axe's sharp point and halted his almost lethal slide.

With extreme caution he joined Gordon who had watched with dismay. 'Oh hell, Bob,' he gasped, 'that was a near thing. I thought you were going right over.'

Bob managed a grin, 'Aye, I know. I thought that too. Aye, and had I gone, I would have dragged you after me, wouldn't I?'

Gordon, too, now managed to grin, 'Aye you would.' He rather nervously laughed, 'Och but it would never do for the Lomonds to lose two of its fine braw young climbers.'

Steady Lawrie and labouring Dave had been so engrossed in their own slow safe descent from the Great Tower that they had not seen Bob's almost fatal slip, and so he whispered to Gordon, 'There's no point in us telling them of our brush with death, is there?'

'No,' Gordon agreed, 'there's no point at all. We don't want them to think we're incompetent, now do we?'

So those two, comparatively auld old-timers never knew of these comparatively young youngsters' hairs-breadth escape from death on that great winter climb, on Ben Nevis's Tower Ridge.

# Gordon Meets a Deer-Stalking Hermit

Already at this early post-dawn time the June sunshine was brightly shining on Gordon's wee tent, was already giving a welcome hint of the heat to come.

As he hurried through his rather frugal breakfast, Gordon thought of how wise he was to make the most of this glorious weather.

Up here in Scotland's North West Highlands, May and June were often months of wonder that could give week after week of cloudless, rainless, midge-less bliss. They made up for the other Highland months that, all too frequently, were very far from being enchanting.

Yes, Gordon resolved, I will make the most of this perfect day. I will travel light, be unencumbered by rucksack or even the lightest jacket.

So in only a white shirt and dark jeans he eagerly set out for a place to which he'd never been, but had heard glowing stories of, and had seen in pictures and in dreams – Sandwood Bay.

With his tent pitched near the crofting township of Sheigra, a few miles North of Kinlochbervie, he was perfect positioned for the four mile path that led directly to that fabled bay.

Although in his 38th year, he was still physically in good shape, and, exhilarated by the prospect of a new experience in this remote landscape, he strode along the moorland path in fine mile-devouring style while the early morning's smiling sunshine gave him its cheery, invigorating company.

This was a place of strange contrasts. In many parts of the path he encountered deep, dark, menacing peat bogs, while on higher ground he found the peat dried out, all baked and cracked under the weeks of May and June's fabulous sunshine.

Soon he stood and, amazed, gazed at Sandwood Bay.

This fine long sweep of pure sandy beach, the undulating dunes with their protective marram grass that made an uncertain barrier between the ever hungry sea and the fresh waters of Sandwood Loch, all were revealed at their golden glowing best.

The bay's sun-bright glory *did* live up to all those stories extolling its beauty.

As Gordon walked along the sand's calm, low-tidal edge and admired the gentle rippling waves he thought of how that great poet Norman MacCaig had praised another lovely Sutherland bay with its gentle rhythmic waves *playing their million-finger exercises on the keyboard of the sand.*

Then as he rambled around the sun-lit dunes it seemed that the marram grass thrust itself upright in delight at not, for a time, having to curve and cower away from the prevailing Atlantic gales.

Even some grains of dry dune sands seemed to gently whisper their delight at not being wildly blown about.

It still being quite early morning, Gordon decided to leave this glorious bay and go and 'have a look' at that unknown land Northwards towards Cape Wrath.

Although not mountainous, this uninhabited pathless tract of land was a true wilderness of heather moors, rough grassy hummocks, peat-hags, lochs and weedy lochans.

Eventually after some hot and thirsty hours, Gordon reached the narrow road which led to Cape Wrath lighthouse.

The glaring brightness of the building and its whitewashed cottages dazzled his exploring eyes. He then saw a lighthouse-keeper's wife hanging out her washing. After some pleasant talk she hospitably offered to make him a pot of tea.

Later regretting his decision, he politely declined her offer, saying, 'That's very kind of you. Thank you. But I better get started on my return journey. I've a long way to go.'

After some miles he wondered if this long way was *really* getting longer, or was he only getting thirstier and perspiringly weary?

The relentless sun endlessly blazing down, persuaded him to take off his white shirt, knot it around his waist and get a touch of that rare condition, a West Highland tan.

The numerous slippery grassy hummocks seemingly rose ever higher and got ever more difficult; the tough old heather clumps got ever rougher and snatched and scratched ever more savagely; the dark peat-bogs seemed ever darker and more menacingly deeper while he seemed to get thirstier and hotter by the minute.

Reaching a lochan a little North of Sandwood Bay, Gordon pushed through the enclosing heather then crouched on the stony shore and was about to plunge his sun-burned face into the cooling water when a loud shout stopped him.

He sprang up and turned to see a wild-looking man standing some twenty yards away.

It was startling to suddenly see another human figure in this vast uninhabited wild land.

It was much more worrying however, to see the rifle that the stranger was pointing at him!

'What the hell are you doing?' the menacing stranger demanded, in what he recognised as a strong Glasgow accent.

Giving a rather forced nervous smile, Gordon replied, 'I'm just having a wee drink, that's all.'

'You silly bloody fool, I nearly shot you. I thought you were a deer.'

Gordon did not know how to reply to that. Surely, even when crouching down, he did not really look like a deer? However, now that the rifle was no longer pointing in his direction but was being loosely held at the stranger's side, he could more calmly inspect that strange, that rather dangerous man.

He was of middle age and medium height; his sturdy body suggested powerful strength; his intense eyes stared from a rugged weather-beaten face; a thick black beard and, correspondingly dark hair. On his head he had a flat cloth cap, the skip unfastened from its stud, but incongruously, he was wearing an old, torn, thick, heavy reefer jacket in what was, a blazingly hot, June day.

As the stranger came nearer, Gordon noted that the rifle was a •303 Lee-Enfield, the standard British infantry weapon in both world wars. He presumed it was loaded, but he could not see if its safety-catch was on or not.

This weird and deluded deer-stalker now said, 'Aye, it was your red skin that made me think you were a thirsty hind and I'd an easy shot for the pot tonight. What saved you though was that white shirt. I've often seen bloody Jerry sodgers wave white flags o' surrender, but I've never seen a deer wear a white shirt o' surrender aroon' its waist afore!' He gave a roar of laughter at his own wit then said, 'So there ye go, you were bloody lucky this time. My advice to you is, if ye're ever in this part o' the world again, and I hope you're not, keep yer stupid white shirt on.'

After uttering some rather more friendly words, rather deferentially, he asked if Gordon had any whisky, beer, or food with him.

Inwardly smiling as he noted that order of priority, Gordon told him he was travelling light and unfortunately had none of these commodities with him, although in his mind's eye the glorious image of a cold pint briefly rose up before him.

Frustrated by the deprivation of his deer, his whisky and beer, the stranger quickly lost interest in Gordon. After saying 'cheerio' quite pleasantly, he strode off through the heather and out of sight around a nearby hillock.

Gordon also walked on and soon, overheated and still somewhat dehydrated, stopped for a much needed rest on the Northerly cliffs that overlooked Sandwood Bay.

Although a bit tired and more than a little thirsty and hungry, he was pleased that the great aesthetic pleasure he got from that beauty spread out before him, was in no way diminished.

As his gaze swung round to that striking sea-stack, Am Buachaille, he thought of the late, great, Scottish climber, Tom Patey, who had first climbed it.

It was hard to believe that five years had passed since the shock of Tom's tragic death on another Sutherland sea-stack in 1970.

Gordon sighed, how all too easy it was to go from glorious life to sudden oblivion. He gave a rueful smile and reflected how he had come close to death today, not by a tragic fall from a rock face, but by a trigger-happy stranger's search for his evening meal.

He made a quick resolution that if he was ever again up here in this eccentric's domain he would be sure to bring a mug in his rucksack, quickly scoop up burn or loch water and stand erect as he drank it down, surely, no danger then, of being mistaken for a deer. I mean it's not often you see a female of that species standing on her *hind* legs do you?

That evening as Gordon relaxed and 'rehydrated' in the Kinlochbervie hotel, he made discreet enquiries about the armed wild man he had met.

His name was James McRory Smith. He was better known to one and all as, 'Sandy.' It seemed he was a hermit who had lived alone for many years in Strathchailleach bothy, some distance North of Sandwood Bay. He was the only human living in that remote path-less wilderness that stretched from Cape Wrath lighthouse almost to Kinlochbervie.

According to these pub informants, Sandy was rarely welcoming to any intruders in what he thought of as his very own territory. Obviously no legendary Highland hospitality from him!

Gordon again inwardly smiled as he thought of the vast contrast between the only two humans he had met all day on his great Cape Wrath ramble: one who offered him a most hospitable pot of tea, and one, who rather inhospitably, almost put a bullet in him.

# We Still Sit on Wee Craigower Hill

As, more than thirty years later, Gordon finished telling Bob that strange story he laughed, 'Och, even now I can feel the intense pleasure I got from downing these pints at Kinlochbervie pub, replacing all the sweat I'd shed on my Cape Wrath trek.'

Bob grinning said, 'Aye, and had yon eccentric trigger-happy hermit actually shot you in error, perhaps that might have been another hind getting its mystical revenge on you, for having shot her near Staonaig bothy, remember?'

'Oh aye, I remember that well. The first deer I killed. That was my entry into the deer-hunting fraternity. Not the one you were employed by, mind you.'

This had happened more like forty years ago. This rifle too had been an ex-army, •303 Lee-Enfield. It had been secretly hidden away 'somewhere in the Scottish Highlands' only to be used against any 1940's invading German soldiers.

After the war, the rifle had been 'liberated' by some wild Glasgow characters, loosely attached to the Creag Dhu, who did their own brand of hunting and fishing on the estates of the landed gentry who owned much of the Highlands. Collectively this group were known as 'the Purvi', or 'the Corbi', after the names of two of their ring-leaders, Purvis and Corbett. Sharing many of the qualities of the Creag Dhu, they made a big thing about, 'Never having done a rock climb in their lives,' disdaining that sport as being dull and pointless compared to their own.

A while after three of these characters, who had been poaching out on the Rannoch Moor, had had enough of an unproductive morning and of getting miserably soaked through and returned to the bothy, Gordon asked if he might have a go with their un-fired rifle.

After being given a fair bit of good-natured ribbing, grudging permission was given and he set out alone.

310

At least the rain had stopped and the afternoon light was getting brighter. He checked the wind direction and strode off into the gusting breeze that would carry his scent away from any deer ahead of him.

And quite soon he *did* find deer, a group of five hinds.

With a miserable crawl through soaking heather, eventually he got within range of these grazing beasts.

The insinuating dampness was quickly forgotten as adrenaline's nerve-tingling excitement took over.

An accurate eye, a held breath, a gentle squeeze of trigger-finger, and a perfect heart-shot, the hind dropped dead.

Thank God he had remembered to bring a large sharp knife with him. But none the less, the gralloching became a bloody shambles!

He dragged the gutted beast some way towards the bothy, then went and triumphantly, got his jeering mates to help drag it the rest of the way.

If the gralloching had been a shambles, the un-skilled skinning and butchering of the poor hind was an awful bloody mess. However, after the division of the spoils was over, a strange little ceremony took place. Bert Corbett, or 'Ahab' as he was commonly known to the week-ending crowd, congratulated Gordon on his kill and, after dipping his finger into a pool of blood on the ground by the side of the carcase, touched him on the forehead, leaving a bloody mark on his brow. He was thus welcomed into the hunting fraternity, much as he had heard being done by the hated gentry to initiates into fox-hunting. Finally, the rifle was cleaned, liberally oiled, wrapped up in water-proof oil-cloth, and re-buried in its secret peaty grave.

Pleasantly burdened with their shared venison they all left the isolated bothy and made their way through the wild rugged beauty of Glen Nevis to reach the hired Lomond Climbing Club bus awaiting them at the glen's Youth Hostel.

On this return Sunday journey to Glasgow some of that crudely butchered venison quickly made its presence surprisingly and unpleasantly felt.

One of the club's more sedate middle-aged lady members was the first to complain. She loudly and indignantly shouted, 'Oh God, there's blood dripping on my hair from the luggage rack!'

A bald male climber then, much less upset, said, 'Aye, and there's blood dropping on my heid too.' He wiped it off and laughed, 'Och, I'm bloody but un-bowed!'

With his usual unflappable diplomatic skill, Lawrie Travers, the Lomond Club member in charge of hiring the club's weekend bus, got things sorted out.

Not too severely he reprimanded the deer-hunters, 'Oh, my dear fellows, I hired this bus for use by a happy crowd of mountain climbers, not for use as a mobile butcher's shop.'

The bus was stopped. The parcels of bloody-dripping meat were consigned to the rucksack-crowded luggage compartment at the rear of the bus. Lawrie was surreptitiously given a piece of deer liver which he swiftly hid away in his rucksack with a mild, whispered protest, 'Gordon, my dear fellow, I really should not accept this bloody bribe, you know.'

Hours later as Gordon walked through dark Glasgow streets on the final part of his homeward journey he knew that drops of blood were dripping from his venison-heavy rucksack. A few hungry stray dogs knew this too. They eagerly trotted behind him, licking up the bloody trail, while he hurried through the streets of Ibrox, hoping this bizarre procession would not be noticed.

After his laughter at again hearing this old tale, Bob said, 'You should think yourself lucky that you only had hungry stray Glasgow dogs following you. In future years, if certain conservationists have their way, it might well be a pack of re-introduced Scottish wolves that escort you home! Maybe that's a bit far-fetched in Ibrox, mind you.'

'But, instead of thinking forward to that possible Highland future which we'll probably never live to see, thinking back from your Cape Wrath hike, when you were almost shot, to your trek to Annapurma Sanctuary, didn't you almost come to grief there too?'

'Oh aye, I did. Close to it, I suppose. You could say I was a hairs-breadth from death there as well.'

Bob grinned, 'Och but surely at Sandwood Bay you were not so much a hairs-breadth from death as a hair-trigger from death?'

Gordon now told of his Annapurna lucky escape.

# Gordon Almost Dies on Annapurna Trek

Gordon's almost fatal slip while on his Annapurna trek has already been mentioned in this book, but he now re-told that story in much greater detail.

Having seen some alarming avalanches in the previous few days, Gordon's trekking party were acutely aware of these dangers as they made their way down from the highest point of their trek that had gone to the foot of that fabulous mountain, Annapurna.

Cautiously descending the steep, snow-covered narrow track Gordon constantly switched his anxious gaze from the huge, and menacing, snow slopes above them, in the direction of the sirdar, Ang Nuri. It was that experienced Sherpa who decided when it was safe to hurry on and just how quickly they needed to cross the most dangerous, most avalanche prone part of their journey.

The group halted when they came to a truly alarming sight: the all too obvious evidence of a recent large avalanche that had completely obliterated their track.

This avalanche's awesome debris was composed of masses of rough fresh snow and countless large rounded boulders of compacted snow and ice which, when roaring down at high speed, would have destroyed everything in its way.

Gordon hardly needed the Sherpa to tell him, 'Much danger here,' he could see that for himself. Nor was it particularly re-assuring, to have Ang Nuri tell him that seven Japanese climbers had been killed by just such an avalanche at this very place, three years previously.

After pausing for a moment listening and looking for any tell-tale signs, each person in the party made a quick dash across the jumble of snow and ice before arriving at the safety of the path at the other side.

Once the last man was safely across, Gordon congratulated them all on now being out of danger.

Soon, as they continued on down the now avalanche-free track, his cheerful confidence that the worst of the dangers were now over was suddenly proved wrong.

As Gordon stepped on to a snow-covered boulder that formed part of the narrow trail his foot skidded on the slippery surface and he slid over the edge of the path.

By exceptional luck rather than any conscious skill his six-foot long bamboo walking pole jammed deep into a jagged crack between the rocks.

Grabbing the pole with both hands he swung outwards for a moment before his scrabbling feet found a small ledge. Using the life-saving bamboo stick, which magically, had become firmly wedged, he pulled himself upwards and scrambled back, out of danger, to the safety of the track.

He stood up, covered in snow, but otherwise unhurt.

He gazed down the steep slope to the wild roaring river far below. Had it not been for that long bamboo pole Ang Nuri had given him in place of his short-handled ice-axe, he would now be a savagely battered, lifeless figure tumbling down that tempestuous cascading mountain river.

Relieved, Ang Nuri said, 'Oh, sir, you save yourself well. Oh, most well done.'

Not to be left out of this genuine display of thankful relief, Sherpa Lawry pointed down to the savage river, shook his head and said, 'Oh, sir, not cricket, no, not cricket, old boy.'

Thankful to have his feet back on solid ground again, Gordon looked at him in astonishment. Turning to Ang Nuri, he said, 'I thought Lawry didn't speak any English.'

'Oh, sometimes he says strange things like that. His grandfather was a Sherpa on British Everest expeditions a long time ago. He learned some English from him.'

'Well tell him that falling down there would have been a lot worse than cricket, and cricket's bad enough.' Ang Nuri said something in Nepalese to Lawry and the latter laughed and shook Gordon's hand warmly.

As they continued down the track Gordon was thinking about Lawry, (at least that was how he thought the name might be spelled from how it was pronounced.) It suddenly reminded him of another climber, his old friend thousands of miles away, also called Lawrie, Lawrie Travers of the Lomonds. What a coincidence that both used quaint, outdated English expressions, Himalayan Lawry with his, "not cricket, old boy," and Glasgow Lawrie's, "My dear fellow," (even to his bemused and amused, tough fellow mechanics at his workplace, a bus repair garage.)

Gordon now chuckled aloud as he thought: 'Perhaps being given that rather unusual name (however spelled) somehow inclines one to use unusual sayings.'

# Still Sitting, Still Rambling

When Gordon finished his near-death Annapurna trek story, Bob smiled and said, 'Oh surely on that almost fatal occasion you were not so much a *hairs-breadth* from death as a six-foot bamboo pole's length from death.'

'Aye, I suppose so,' Gordon agreed. Grinning, he imitated a doddery auld man, 'Aye, I...I...I remember one great benefit I got from that experience.

'That evening as I stood at our base camp waiting for dinner I stared up at Annapurna with a fabulous sunset glowing on the snow-clad summit and never before had I been so deeply moved by the great privilege of being alive to wonder at such a picture of pure awesome beauty.'

He laughed, 'Och, but when our cook shouted, "Dinner ready! ... Dinner ready!" my mind's noble emotions were quickly forgotten by the more mundane, but no less real, pleasure of filling my empty belly.'

'Aye,' Bob said thoughtfully, 'nearly dying truly makes you greatly appreciate the glorious wonder of being alive.'

It was now his turn to imitate the quavering voice of an auld man, 'Oh, do you ...do you remember? ... Oh damn, I've forgotten what I remember! ... Oh hell, all too soon there'll be no need for us to *imitate* doddery auld men, will there?

'Oh now, thank God, I remember what I'd forgot. Do you remember that weekend we spent at our secret Tyndrum Doss and we once almost came to grief on our snow and ice winter climb?'

'Oh aye, I remember that weekend clearly. The thick snow in Ben Lui's steep gully fairly slowed us down, didn't it? Then the overhanging snowy cornice at the top was really massive and took quite some time to tunnel through, remember that as well?'

'Aye, that's right. And it being early January, the few true bright daylight hours were soon swallowed up by early dusk and dark clouds storming in from the West.'

'And it was almost pitch-dark by the time we got to the Ben's deep-snowed summit, if I remember correctly.'

'Aye, that's right. Then freezing sleety rain, driven by a strong wind, battered its soaking misery at us.'

'Aye,' Gordon agreed, 'it sure turned into a night of real dark misery. Aye, we were lucky to come out of it alive.

'I remember your dropped lighted torch sliding down a steep snow slope then, flying off into space, warning us that what we thought as a safe way down was actually a place of unseen cliffs and extreme dangers.'

'And soon after that your torch batteries gave up the ghost and left us in complete sleet-battered darkness with nothing to guide us but the faintly seen gleam of Tyndrum's street lights, as for many weary hours we ploughed through Ben Lui's deep snows.

'Yes, we truly were extremely lucky to get back to our own secret Doss alive. And after all that soaking scary misery, our basic wee Doss was a place that seemed pure cosy luxury.'

Bob laughed, 'Aye, thank God for that life-saving primitive wee Tyndrum Doss of ours. In fact thank God for all the Highland bothies, dosses, caves and howffs we've both used in the distant past.'

Gordon agreed, 'You know I would drink a hearty toast to that if only we had brought something to drink with us. Och, but of course we had more than enough to do to get our auld bodies up here to grand wee Craigower's summit without carrying a load o' food and drink.'

These two bald auld men fell silent for a short time – perhaps they were dreaming of all that non-available food and drink – then Bob said, 'Aye we have been real lucky to have had the use of so many mountain bothies; to have enjoyed all their great, safe, cosy shelter.

'Och but even the safest seeming cosy wee bothy, can be a place of sudden violent tragic death.'

'Oh, I sense a story there,' Gordon said, 'one I haven't heard. On you go.'

'Aye, all right, this is not about people being a hairs-breadth from death, but people – two fine young men in fact meeting an all too real, all too sudden violent death.'

Bob gave this true story the strange title, *Fifty Two Special Trees*.

# Fifty Two Special Trees

**B**ob Scott felt sad as he stood alone among these fifty two special young trees in this small, deer-fenced enclosure and remembered what used to be here.

He solemnly though of what these trees represented – the combined years of the two fine young men who had violently died here some years ago.

One, the experienced local gamekeeper from Poolewe, had been thirty one years old. The other, only recently taken on, but passionately keen, trainee gamekeeper, had been a mere twenty one.

Bob's memory now clearly flashed back almost sixty years to the last time he, a madly keen young hiker and hill-climber, had been here and had spent some happy days in this exact place that is now home to these fifty two special trees.

Inspired by grand wee Tom Weir's first great book, *Highland Days*, Bob had decided to spend some of his fortnight's annual holiday in that vast, remote, road-less, population-free wilderness that stretched north from Loch Maree to Little Loch Broom.

Rambling unburdened by the weight of a tent, he intended to use the three bothies that were so well positioned between these contrasting fresh water and seaweedy lochs.

Discreetly keeping well clear of blimpish Colonel Whitbread's Letterewe Shooting Lodge, and avoiding that Sassenach laird's hiker-hating obsequious gamekeepers, Bob eagerly strode the stalking path that stabbed into the very heart of this vast, wildly mountainous, Letterewe Deer Forest; this 'Forest' where for rough, lonely and wild square mile after square mile hardly one tree was to be found.

This path crossed a narrow rocky causeway to that deer-stalker's house, Carn More, where, pre-war, a soaked and bedraggled youthful Tom Weir had received such true Highland hospitality from the gamekeeper, Calum MacRae, and his family.

This once so hospitable house was now securely locked and boarded up. Still, tiring after his long, greatly enjoyable hike to this remote place, Bob found the nearby, snugly dry, wooden stable to be the height of bothy luxury.

The next morning, as he stood outside the bothy surrounded by a treasure-trove of Munros, Bob's only problem was trying to decide which he should climb today and which should be left until tomorrow.

Two days and five Munros later, Bob moved on.

After striding through the narrow glen that led directly into endless, and also tree-less, Fisherfield Deer Forest, he was delighted to see the landscape open out and give more extensive views. And there, exactly as promised by his reliable old one inch to one mile O.S. map, was his next bothy.

Here, too, a gamekeeper's old house was locked up and its windows firmly shuttered. Here there also was a ghillie's comfortable wooden bothy which, thankfully, was not locked.

Bob had smiled when he'd read the name of this old house on his map –Larachantivore. Little wonder that rather than struggle with such an unpronounceable name this house's nearby bothy was known to climbers as Sheallag Bothy.

Alone, but never lonely, Bob rejoiced in having this grand accommodation for his own private use.

The views from here were grand: the large glittering loch; the lush June greenness of Sheallag Strath, with its cheery chuckling little river; the more distant mass of rugged An Teallach.

After a quick meal Bob climbed the bothy's nearest neighbour, the impressive, even, if not quite a Munro, Beinn Dearg Mhor.

After two more wonderful days and one more Munro, Bob moved on from this, what he almost thought of as *his* very own bothy, in this very special idyllic setting.

As he easily waded through the June-shrunken wee river that flowed between him and Shenavall Bothy, he again self-praised his wisdom in rambling here at this time of year when the West Highland weather is at its most glorious, driest and best. He knew that more than one hiker had been drowned when trying to wade across when this river was in the rush of autumn flood.

Bob happily shared the well-known, well-used Shenavall Bothy, with three youthfully gregarious Glasgow climbers.

Next day the four of them gloried in climbing An Teallach's jagged towering ragged ridges together.

Only the urgent need to replenish his food dragged Bob away from his convivial new friends and the homely comforts of Shenavall Bothy.

★ ★ ★

Time moved on. All too many years all too quickly passed and now Bob contentedly lived in his Pitlochry retirement flat. From there, one year he went with close friends from American on a salmon fishing holiday. They rented a homely cottage that had the salmon fishing rights on the modestly small, but most attractive and wild Little Gruinard River.

As if trying to make up for its modest size, this wee river flowed past our cottage with ceaseless noise of loud and cheery voice as, with eager haste, it rushed to meet the salty waters of beautiful Gruinard Bay.

We were delighted to hear that this glorious bay's Gruinard Island was now, at long last, free of its wartime anthrax poison. Even more delighted than ourselves were the re-introduced sea-eagles we eagerly watched as they fed on the Island's thriving colony of anthrax-free rabbits.

The great pleasure Bob's American friends got from seeing red deer stags carelessly wandering around our cottage did not lessen when he expressed his thoughts that there now seemed far too many of these greedy grazing deer about.

One morning this river's keen young ghillie told them he had to take some things to a house that was being renovated in the remote wild heart of this vast, Dutch owned sporting estate.

'Oh, and exactly where is that remote house?' Bob asked

'Och, it's right at the Eastern end of Loch Na Sealga.'

The grinning ghillie struggled to pronounce his next word, 'Larachantivore, is its name.'

That Gaelic name sparked a light in Bob's memory. He eagerly asked, 'Isn't there a wooden ghillie's bothy beside that remote house? A grand dry shelter we old-time climbers knew as Sheallag Bothy. I would love to see it and its wonderful wild surroundings once again.'

For some silent moments the young ghillie seemed strangely put-out by Bob's remarks. He quickly brightened and invited, 'You're welcome to come with me to that remote wild place and in the boat going down the loch I'll tell you all about Sheallag Bothy. Is it many years since you last used it?'

Bob laughed, 'Oh aye, it must be damn near sixty years since I last stayed there.'

After a long, wildly rough land-rover ride up the rutted track by the side of the true Gruinard River, Bob sat at ease in the sturdy estate boat while the ghillie steered with the powerful outboard engine, down the length of Loch Na Sealga.

Bob grinned, 'This is a fine easy lazy way to get into the heart of this marvellous wilderness. It's much easier than when I rambled here by myself and stayed in these remote bothies all these years ago.'

This was the young ghillie's opportunity. He solemnly said, 'I'm afraid there's one of these bothies you could not use now. That one you mentioned, Sheallag Bothy, is no longer here. There is not a trace of it left.'

He told a tragic story.

'Some years ago an experienced gamekeeper and a younger trainee gamekeeper had gone down this loch in this very boat. The boat was laden with many things to be left at the Sheallag Bothy and be used during the deer stalking season. The keepers intended to stay in that old wooden bothy for two days and give it a much needed coat of creosote. They also hoped to do some trout fishing.

Among the many things they carried from the boat to the bothy were Calor gas cylinders and jerry-cans of petrol for future use in the boat's outboard engine.

Seemingly there had been a cool breeze and heavy showers that day so doubtless these two men, after heaving in their final load, would have firmly closed the bothy's door.

They could not have noticed it, but dangerous petrol vapours must have leaked from these old jerry-cans. Perhaps there had been leaks of Calor gas too.

These deadly un-noticed vapours must have built up while the two men were busy unloading their bulky rucksacks, were throwing their sleeping-bags on the bothy's bunks, were neatly stacking their food and their fishing gear, were gently placing their frugally lonely solitary bottle of whisky on the bothy table. Then the one who was a cigarette smoker must have lit a match.

These deadly vapours ignited.

The wee wooden bothy blew apart. In the fierce explosion and engulfing flames these two young gamekeepers must have died instantaneously.'

For a time after the young ghillie told this tragic story he and Bob sat in solemn silence as their boat continued steadily down the loch.

Then Bob quietly said, 'And so that devastated wee bothy has never been re-built.'

'No it hasn't. There isn't a trace of it left. There are Scots Pines, rowans and birches growing in its place instead. The wealthy Dutch owner of this estate, Mr. Paul van Vlissingen, was shocked and deeply saddened to learn of the violent death of his two young gamekeepers. He did all he could for the bereaved families.

As a fitting living memorial to these two dead men who had loved this remote Highland wilderness he had fifty two trees, representing their combined ages, planted where the bothy had been.'

When the ghillie went into the remote house, Bob went and solemnly stood alone amongst these fifty two special trees. He again clearly remembered his pleasant stay almost sixty years ago, at that grand wee bothy which was now replaced by these memorial trees.

He felt a special strong empathy with that young trainee gamekeeper who, like Bob, had dreamt of leaving the hated city and spending a worthwhile life in the marvellous wilds of the North West Highlands. While Bob had fulfilled that dream, seemingly that young man had only been employed on the estate some few months before he so tragically died.

Bob sighed then thought, 'Oh well at least that lad *had* realized his great dream, even if for only such a terribly short time.'

Now eagerly looking around, Bob wondered if he was to come back in fifty two years time, would he see not a mere fifty two special trees but a re-introduced scattered forest of birch, rowans, hazels and rugged Scots Pines; a land that was no longer a barren, 'deer forest', but a true natural forest in which some red deer would have their rightful place.

As he left this sad place and went to the nearby house that was being renovated, his hopes rose that this dream of future years *would* come about.

322

# Still Rambling On and On

Once Bob finished telling that sad story of those special trees they sat in silence for some solemn moments then Gordon said, 'Oh, Bob, like you I can feel deep empathy for that young trainee gamekeeper who so tragically died that day.'

'I remember I felt like you in my great desire to get out of the smothering city and live a more natural, a more truly real life amongst our loved Scottish hills, just as obviously he did too, all these many years later than us.'

Gordon grinned then again imitated a doddery auld man's quavering voice, 'Oh aye ... I ... I re-mem-ber how I envied you when you left Glasgow, worked for a few years as a Youth Hostel warden at Achmelvich then, just like that tragic young man, got taken on by a large North West Highland estate as a trainee gamekeeper.'

'Aye, I clearly do remember how not only I but also two of my climbing pals, Tony and Alex, who while camping at beautiful Achmelvich Bay, saw you in your fine new job and wished we could do something similar.'

It was now Bob's turn to grin, 'Aye, I remember that too. But, if I recall correctly, the three of you in unholy chorus sang a rude song at me as you watched me clean out Assynt Estate's setters and pointers kennels at Torbreck; something like, *Oh, Bob, what a tit, you're not fit to shovel shit!*'

Gordon laughed, 'Oh aye, I seem to remember that. But seeing you at that mucky work didn't put us off. I think it was about one month later that I read about a somewhat similar job being advertised on the remote island of Rum. That island's quaintly attractive name was enough to make any possible work there seem especially interesting. So I wrote for details and a job application form.'

'The successful applicant would work for the National Trust for Scotland who owned the island. He would be not quite a gamekeeper, but more a wild-life ranger looking after and studying the island's large population of red deer. Rent-free accommodation would be provided in the large, imposing Kinloch Castle. It sounded a wonderful job. Was it too good to be true?'

'As I filled in the application form I came to a nasty snag. I needed a church minister or priest or someone in an official position to vouch for my good character.'

'I certainly knew no minister or priest and at first could think of no suitable official. Then I remembered an older member of the Lomond Mountaineering Club who would suit: Police Superintendent Calum Finlayson.'

'Calum was one of that grand band of pre-war Glasgow climbers who just as keenly still climbed in these brighter, more hopeful post-war years. Now however they climbed with a touch of more wise, more mature caution. Tom Weir and Jock Nimlin were two of his climbing friends from these precious pre-war youthful years.

'Calum's cheery friendship and sage advice were greatly appreciated by the climbing club's younger, less experienced members.

'When I asked him to vouch for my honest character and my increasing experience of the outdoor life he willingly signed. But I noticed what seemed strange suppressed amusement in him as he said, "I hope *you* get the job, Gordon."'

About two months later, while on the Lomond Club's weekend bus, Calum said, 'I'm sorry *you* did not get that job on Rum, Gordon.'

Again Gordon noted his barely concealed amusement. He asked curiously, 'Do you know something about my job application that I don't?'

Calum laughed outright, 'Och it's just that you are not the only one on this bus who applied for that job. Two of your climbing pals tried for it too.'

Hardly any need for Gordon to ask, 'which two?' The wide grins of Tony and Alex strongly suggested they were the pals in question.

Calum confirmed this, 'Aye, Alex and Tony applied for the Rum job as well as you.'

With seeming anger Gordon accused his pals, 'Oh you're a pair of sly deceitful bastards applying for that job and saying nothing about it to me.'

Tony rather grimly replied, 'Och, you were a sly and deceitful bastard yourself, not telling us you had applied.'

Alex, apparently with real anger, now said, 'Aye, Gordon that was a dirty, low down thing to do, keeping secrets from your mates.'

Calum said, 'Listen to me, when each one of you asked me to vouch for you, you requested that I kept your application secret. I did. So none of you knew what the others were doing.' 'Och, you were all equally guilty of making a big mystery out of this.' He grinned, 'So calm down, lads, or I'll be using my official police powers tae keep the peace!'

Johnny Harvey, the Lomond Club's founder and long-time president, now smilingly intervened, 'Och, I'm pleased that none of you lads got that job on the remote island of Rum. I don't want to lose any o' my club's best rock climbers.

Calum laughed, 'Aye, that's right, Johnny. Let's keep them. These lads are fairly pushing up our club's rock climbing standards, the ones that we "auld-timers" started in yon grand, free and easy pre-war years.'

Calum Finlayson later rose to the rank of Chief Superintendant. He was awarded the M.B.E. for his great bravery in facing up to, and in self-defence, shooting dead, a most dangerous armed criminal who had gone on a berserk killing spree in Glasgow.

★ ★ ★

As Bob and Gordon, these now themselves real "auld-timers", continued sitting in contented ease on Craigower's summit, Gordon said, 'Well, Bob, even if our rambling days are now truly past us, at least in memory and in happy talk we can still ramble on, can't we?

'Aye we can, we certainly can. All our talk about these times when we almost met the 'Grim Reaper' suddenly reminds me of another time when I put myself in real foolish danger of sudden violent death.'

'Oh is this something I already know about?

'No, you don't. In fact I've never revealed this incident to anyone.'

'Oh really Well you've whet my appetite now to hear more, so tell it now.'

'Aye all right, I'll call it: *The Anvil.*'

# The Anvil

This story really started when Bob read a book about St. Kilda. One of the book's photos showed *The Lovers Stone,* a smooth slab of rock that jutted out from a high sea cliff and had a man precariously standing on it on one leg with the other leg lifted and bent, with its booted foot poised near his straight knee. Both arms were held out sideways from his shoulders to keep what seemed a defiant jaunty balance.

The book explained that love-sick young St. Kilda men stood like that on *The Lovers' Stone* to prove their bravery to their nervously watching wife-to-be.

If two men were competing for the same woman the one who stood motionless on one leg the longest was proved the bravest and most worthy to have the watching woman as his wife.

★ ★ ★

As with pleasant effortless ease, Bob Scott rowed the neat, light, clinker-built wooden boat along the calm sea near the high cliffs of Ardroe Point, the boat's owner his great Achmelvich crofter friend, Donald Pollochan, also sat contentedly on the broad stern seat with his long bamboo fishing-rod firmly held in ready hand and his favourite auld pipe cheerily glowing and pleasantly drifting its aromatic wake.

They were blessed with yet another of these wonderful June evenings that up here in Scotland's Far North would endlessly linger with the sun forever clinging on before reluctantly sinking into the lulled silent sea while casually painting a glorious glowing golden Turner-like sunset.

And sometimes, not to be upstaged by chuckling sea and painted sky, Assynt's jagged landscape of timeless gneiss rock, the honed bare bones of this ancient rugged land, would – blushing at its own daring – for some fantastic minutes come unbelievably alive; would awesomely flare with sunset's final gushing flood of bright arterial blood.

Reminded by their nearness to Ardroe's sheer sea-cliffs, Bob mentioned to Donald Pollochan what he'd read about St. Kilda's, Lovers' Stone.

Donald's actual surname was MacLeod, but to distinguish him from all the other Donald MacLeod's in Assynt he was commonly known as 'Pollochan', the name of his old family croft. He did not seem greatly impressed by the bravery of these amorous St. Kilda men. He removed his pipe, pointed with its stem, smiled and said, 'Och, there's something like that Lovers' Stane up there at Ardroe Point. Do you see yon jutting anvil o' rock right at the top there?'

'Oh aye, I see it. I've noticed it before.'

'Aye well, that's 'The Anvil', the jutting rock where, not courting young men, but us brave local twelve year old boys, used to stand on one leg tae prove our great bravery.' Pollochan's remembering eyes brightly gleamed, 'Aye, and tae prove our burgeoning approach tae manhood too.'

'So you've actually stood one-legged on that rock anvil, have you?'

Pollochan nodded and grinned, 'Aye, I have. Aye, Dougie Munro from 'The Shore' and me were told about yon Anvil by 15 year old boys who endlessly boasted to us of their great manhood proving bravery. We in turn assured them we would soon stand there too. We were warned not to tell our parents, as they would greatly disapprove of such dangerous foolish behaviour.

'None of those, oh so wise brave boys, knew that their fathers, aye and their grandfathers too, had, as boys from Achmelvich, Ardroe, Rhicarn or Torbreck, stood one-legged on that Anvil long before these boys were born.'

Answering Bob's questions, Pollochan told of how Dougie Munro and he had got permission to fish for trout one thankfully school-free day (not a Sabbath of course) at Ardroe's grand hill lochs.

After fishing the highest loch they hurried to Ardroe Point and that great waiting challenge of The Anvil.

Seeing the wedge of flat rock jutting out from the cliffs like a blacksmith's actual anvil some 300 ft. above a sheer drop to the sea both boys had some second thoughts about standing one-legged out there. But, determined not to 'lose face' in front of his great schoolboy pal, one, then the other, stood on one nervous leg for a brief time that seemed an eternity.

Delighted with their great brave success, they charged all out for the loch and their fishing rods while loudly roaring wild triumphant Gaelic war-cries.

Bob was always pleased to hear Pollochan's interesting stories of his early life in his native Assynt, and as he effortlessly rowed Pollochan's immaculate wee boat into the rocky narrows of Loch Roe and then to the boat's gentle waiting moorings he decided that he'd go and have a closer look at the Anvil sometime soon.

And he did. Four days later he again happily crossed the old narrow iron foot-bridge that spans the attractive mini-ravine that links Loch Roe's salt water to the fresh water hurrying out from the Manse Loch. He smiled to see the eager haste with which the inward rushing flood-tide combed the mass of dark seaweed strands away from the sea as if indicating the way for returning salmon and sea-trout.

Soon he was happily fishing for fine plump brown trout in a narrow hill loch that was nameless on his map.

Although reluctant to leave the grand fishing, Bob forced himself to do what Pollochan and Dougie had done all those years ago. He put his fishing rod down, took the steep heather slope at a steady pace and soon was at the high cliffs of Ardroe Point, and sure enough, there was that damned jutting Anvil.

Should he really stand one-legged out there on that smooth wedge of flat, high and airy rock? The almost windless conditions were perfect. The Anvil rock was bone dry. So he had no excuse for turning away. Yet, looking down, there was a 300 ft. sheer drop, clear to the waiting glittering sea.

Standing dithering, he almost *did* walk away. Almost hurried back to these alluring trout, then he remembered a recent tragic accident when a young angler he knew had drowned while fishing a safe, easy, mostly shallow, local loch.

'Och, damn it,' Bob thought, 'I've as much chance of drowning while fishing as drowning below that nerve-testing Anvil.'

So he did stand one-legged on that airy jutting Anvil. With no one watching him, he stood there only very, very briefly.

But that brief time was truly long enough!

Safely back on glorious heathery ground he did not quite roar a triumphant war-cry, but he did rejoice with loud laughter as he raced back to the narrow loch and his impatiently waiting fishing rod.

★ ★ ★

'So, Gordon, now you know the story of Pollochan's and my Assynt Anvil.'

Gordon smiled, 'A most interesting story. Aye, Pollochan was a real grand auld character, wasn't he? Och it's a real pity there are so few of his kind left alive now.'

Bob laughed, 'Och, perhaps us, "auld-timers" might almost, in our different ways, take his place, eh?'

'Aye, perhaps, anyway I'm real impressed by your Assynt Anvil story.'

'Och, my one-legged Anvil stand was nothing compared to the many very severe rock climbs you did in your young climbing prime.'

'Aye, maybe,' Gordon said. He grinned, 'I suppose if anyone stood on that anvil now they, complying with all the latest Health and Safety regulations, would need a mass of safety gear: a helmet, a life-jacket, a harness and be firmly attached to a multi-coloured nylon rope.'

Bob laughed, 'Aye, and they would have Lochinver lifeboat standing by below the Anvil, just to be extra safe.'

Somehow this mention of modern Health and Safety regulations led their rambling talk away from Assynt and its long gone, fond remembered grand auld crofting characters to a place with no links to any sea, but strong links to old, cruel, Highland history – Glencoe.

They wonder if there is now a safe strong footbridge at a certain part of the small, but often high, fierce and dangerous, River Coe?

Between them Bob and Gordon brought back to vivid life that grand post-war time when they'd crossed that wee tumbling river to find Glencoe's Lost Glen.

# Finding the Lost Glen

Once again the Lomond Climbing Club's hired weekend bus was heading for that always popular place – Glencoe.

A few older, more affluent, club members as they got off to stay at auld, historic, unpretentious Kingshouse Hotel were assaulted with mocking laughter and boisterous cries of, 'Bloated Plutocrats!'

The next dropping off point was Cameron's Barn at Altnafeadh where the more impoverished young Glasgow climbers rushed to gain a sleeping place in one of the old, cold, concrete cow-stalls. A few members of the Creagh Dhu Climbing Club got off here as well, not to use Cameron's Barn, but to use their very own, most exclusive, Jacksonville Bothy.

The bus next stopped in the very heart of the Pass of Glencoe, this place where, hidden above Ossian's mysterious cave and coyly tucked away between Glencoe's Three Sisters, was the Lost Glen.

This Lost Glen was a place little visited by eager young climbers, all much more keen to test their skills, muscles and nerves on 'The Buachaille's' steep rock faces or on Aonach Eagach's jagged narrow ridges. But six young Lomond Club climbers, including Gordon and Bob, had decided they'd like to visit that often heard of, but never seen place for themselves. So they were going to camp in that secluded, massacre-linked glen.

After descending from the Glencoe road to the unseen fast-flowing wee river Coe, these six were pleased to find an easy place to cross. At this sun-blessed time of mid-May, and after a very dry spring, some large, man-placed stepping stones were well exposed; were effortlessly crossed.

Trying to follow an ill-defined slippery old path that climbed steeply up by the side of the plunging rushing wee burn that drained the Lost Glen they slipped, stumbled and cursed their way through an ancient wood of stunted grey birches. These desperate struggling tenacious auld trees were eerily shrouded with smothering clinging and phantom-like hanging lichens of ugly greys and solemn greens.

They often had to clamber over fungi covered horizontal trunks of fallen trees which were slowly merging with slippery mud in Nature's rejuvenating decay.

They were pleased to now and then meet, and silently greet, fine sturdy healthy rowans. These wondrous mythical trees were brightly aglow with their bridal pure white blossom which unstintingly gave out its sharp attractive scent.

A final gasping steep climb through these smothering auld trees brought them suddenly out into another world, a treeless paradise of bright green lushness neatly hidden away in the heart of wild Glencoe's savage, jaggedly inhospitable, landscape.

This Lost Glen's flattish verdant turf with its draining glittering burn seemed a perfect Shangri-La.

Soon one small tent was a glaring orange splash on the verdant green, while two ex-army tents unassumingly tried to hide themselves away with their confusion of camouflage.

Without even delaying for refreshing tea, Gordon and Bob set out to explore this wondrous place and make the most of evening's lingering light as it gleamed on the fresh snows of the steep rugged ridges that enclosed and hid this secret glen.

They soon came to a huge boulder. They explored this block of solid rock for practice mini-climbs. Then Bob saw an array of faint lettering scraped on one smooth surface. They made out a definite 'MacD's' and that fatal date, '1692'.

This confirmed what they had read. Fleeing from murderous Campbell soldiers who had merciless massacred these very Glencoe MacDonald's who had been their hospitable hosts, some MacDonald's had, struggling through February snows, reached and remained hidden in this secret Lost Glen.

For some sad shivering seconds they stare at that tragic history written here in timeless stone. They soon discover the grass covered square outline of a small building. 'I expect this was a summer shieling,' Gordon said.

'Aye,' Bob agreed. 'Once peace returned to Glencoe, the local Highlanders would be sure to graze their vital black cattle on this hidden glen's grand verdant lushness.'

Gordon grinned, 'And from what I've read, these high shielings were not only good for fattening winter-skinny cattle, but were also ideal courting grounds for the young men and women who looked after these beasts.'

'Yes, no doubt it was at this shieling, far from all disapproving auld, stern, Calvanistic eyes, that the surviving young Glencoe MacDonald's made an effort to re-populate their savagely massacred clan.'

Once these six campers' had eagerly consumed their filling evening meal, they hurried down to those auld woods to gather loads of fallen brittle firewood.

Soon their campfire's cheery blaze was reflected in a dozen gregarious gleaming eyes.

In the enjoyable warmth of this Mid-May evening the fire's extra heat was not really needed, but perhaps these six, all to different degrees, subtly felt an older deeper need; an insistent need to get in touch with their ancient fire-worshipping ancestors.

As they gazed at images in these active dancing flames, and later in these glowing red embers, they felt deep strange strong links to all those who had gathered around blazing fires here before: such pre-war climbing pioneers as Tom Weir and Jock Nimlin; these Glencoe MacDonald's at this place's Summer shieling, in use almost until early this 20th century; the ancestral MacDonald's evading the infamous massacre; their pre-historic ancestors who from what is now Ossian's Cave came up here to hunt reindeer and red deer enticed to this place's marvel of grassy lushness.

Flames die and ember's reds dull to ghost grey, obvious hints that it's time to seek cosy tents and even cosier sleeping-bags.

The surrounding mountains high steep snowy ridges brightly glow in post-dawn's cheery sunshine and urge these drowsy six to leave their shaded tents and hurry to these enticing higher slopes.

Gordon and Bob were the keenest to get going. After arranging to meet the other four on the snowy Munro summit of Bidean nam Bian, they set out in an Easterly direction and climb up Beinn Fhada's long ridge where it thrusts out to overlook the place where Glencoe's 'Three Waters Meet'.

They rejoice at getting out of the Lost Glen's early morning shade into this high bright warm paradise of sun and glittery snow. They applaud the eager grip their Commando-sole boots take on the firm crisp snow. They delight in the unfailing support of their well-used ex-army ice-axes.

All went exactly as planned. Each climbing party arrived at much the same time on Bidean nam Bian's summit. After sitting, eating, merrily chatting and congratulating one another on the glorious glowing beauty of the limitless landscape the two groups again went their separate ways. All were full of eager keenness to complete their circuit of this glorious horse-shoe ridge that kept the lost Glen so well hidden.

Later, their evening meals eaten, their tents packed, they again crossed those dry stepping-stones over the un-changed wee River Coe.

The Lomond Club's hired bus picked up its last passengers at the Kingshouse Hotel then hurried its cheery load reluctantly back to Glasgow.

The Creagh Dhu's tough few were now especially lively characters. They were on a real 'high' not just from their exploits on The Buachaille, but also from the drinks they'd celebrated with at the King's House.

When someone suggested that a footbridge over the River Coe would be a fine thing to allow more climbers to reach the unique pleasures of the Lost Glen, these tough Creagh Dhu stalwarts gave loud condemning jeers. 'Och,' one fervently declared, 'What kind of climbers are you if you need a bloody bridge?'

When the laughter died down most agree that they did not want to see their wild Scottish Highlands made too tame by too many well-meaning, but unnecessary 'improvements'.

Yes some – a stubborn few – declared they saw nothing wrong with a few footbridges where the crossing of high Highland rivers or even some tempestuous flooded mountain burns could be really downright dangerous.

One Creagh Dhu character didn't agree, 'I tell you if they try building a bridge at Jacksonville it'll end up on the fire. Wade the burn high or low, that's what week-ending's all about.'

This finished the argument. Laughter and cheery bawdy songs took over.

★ ★ ★

Many years later, as they sit on Craigower's wee summit, Bob and Gordon know that this question of 'improvements' to some of the wildest, remotest parts of the Scottish Highlands is still a matter of heated debate.

'Och well, I remember being real pleased to find a fine new footbridge across the infant River Dee when I went to stay at Corrour bothy for the first time,' Gordon said. 'The wee river, pouring down through the Lairig Ghru was in fierce spate. I would not have fancied trying to wade it.'

Bob nodded, 'Aye, that footbridge was badly needed. When I went to Corrour Bothy, a few years before you, I had to cross it on a three-wire bridge. The two hand wires were very loose, so, laden with a heavy rucksack, the crossing was alarmingly shoogly.

After two ladies were drowned trying to cross the flooded river to the bothy these unsteady wires were replaced by that grand new footbridge.'

Gordon said, 'I wonder if there's now a bridge over the River Coe to allow easy access to the Lost Glen?'

'Och,' Bob said, 'I'm sure with all the modern Health and Safety regulations there'll not only be a stout, high-railed footbridge there, but also a well made path complete with firm stone steps. Aye and at the steepest narrowest parts there will be secure hand-rails too.'

Gordon suggested, 'I suppose we could go and see these *great improvements* for ourselves?'

'Aye,' Bob agreed with no great enthusiasm 'Aye, I suppose we could. I might manage down the steep slope to Glencoe's wee river; och but I very much doot if I'd manage to climb back up!'

Gordon laughed, 'I think I'd rather no' risk either the up or the doon, I'll just keep a pint company in the Clachaig Inn.'

★ ★ ★

Bob and Gordon continue sitting on Craigower's summit seat; continue eagerly gazing beyond Loch Tummel and the only just seen Loch Rannoch and the vague dark shape of Rannoch moor to the distant peaks of rugged Glencoe.

Gordon smiled, 'Och, we just have to face it: we'll never again see the Lost Glen. I'll never again be face to face with the delights of the fabulous Rannoch Wall, I suppose.'

Bob replied with a strange question, 'Isn't there a Scottish pipe tune called, *Lochaber No More*?'

'Yes, I believe there is. Why do you ask?'

'Och, it's just that I think you should compose a tune, a lament, called *The Buachaille Etive Mor No More* and play it on your concertina.' Gordon laughed, 'Aye that would be a most appropriate title for us auld-timers, our final swan-song. Oh it's terrible that never mind the Buachaille, we could not now manage the simple scramble to go through the eye-of-the-needle on the Cobbler's easy middle peak.'

'To return to that tune I suggested,' Bob said, 'you did compose and play some tunes out in Brunei, didn't you?'

'Oh yes, one or two. I played the concertina in a ceilidh band. It was quite popular with Brunei's, at that time, quite large, and very keen St. Andrew's Society.'

'Were the Society's members all actually Scottish?'

'Oh aye, they were. As is usually the case, the further they were from Scotland the more patriotic they felt and behaved. At Brunei's annual St. Andrew's Ball the members of the Society, the men in their kilts and the ladies with tartan sashes were a brilliant sight.'

Gordon paused then said, 'But now I remember that one member of our St. Andrew's Society was not Scottish. He was Indian, a Dr. Chowdhary, assistant to Dr. Mathieson, the Chief Medical Officer in Brunei's main hospital.

'Although Dr. Chowdhary was definitely not truly Scottish he was an honorary member of our St. Andrew's Society and an honorary Scotsman.'

'Oh, how did that come about?' Bob asked.

Gordon told the following (almost) true story:

# A Wild Rush to Give Blood

To allow his wife, Jill, and him to be free to attend the Brunei St. Andrew's Ball, Dr Mathieson (who, by his skill as a surgeon, had earned the nickname, 'Chopper', a name he accepted with good grace) had arranged for Dr Chowdhary to be on duty at the hospital the evening of the dance. Unless there was an emergency, evenings were quiet times at the hospital as most local people tended to go early to bed and most cafes and restaurants were shut up by 8 p.m.

As Dr. Mathieson was about to get changed for the Ball his phone rang. 'Oh damn, he said, 'Now who can that be? Never mind, I'll get it Jill, it might be for me.'

After silently listening for a bit, he asked, 'How bad is he? Oh I see. All right Erwan, I'm on my way, I'll be there in fifteen minutes.' He put down the phone, shook his head and looked at his wife.

'That was the hospital, dear. Poor old Chowdhary, when driving there in the dark, to go on duty, hit a bloody buffalo crossing the road. They've managed to get him to the hospital. I'm going to see how bad he is. Bang goes my big night out I'm afraid. Depending on how serious his injuries are, I'll try and manage to the Ball later. 'I'm sorry, but that's life for a doctor, and of course for a doctor's wife, you know.'

'Yes, I know. I know that all too well,' Jill smiled, 'I'll phone and ask Jim and May to take me. We'll all hope you do make it to join the fun later. Get off now and let's hope your poor colleague is not too badly injured.'

'Let's pray he's not. I don't want to miss all the free drinks tonight, so I'll try to have him all patched up before you can say, Eightsome Reel!'

Medical orderly, Erwan, was waiting at the hospital door, 'Oh, hurry, sir, Dr. Chowdhary has lost consciousness.'

In the treatment room Dr. Mathieson made a quick examination of the unconscious patient. There was massive bruising on his upper body. He

336

was pale and sweating. His blood pressure was dangerously low. It seemed he had suffered a ruptured spleen.

'Right,' Dr. Mathieson said to Erwan, 'I suspect he has massive internal haemorrhaging. We'll need to operate at once. Get the nurses and all the equipment ready, and, Erwan, check his medical records to find his blood group. We'll need plasma and as much blood as we can get.'

★ ★ ★

The Ball was going with a happy noisy swing. The perspiring band was playing flat out. Jigs and reels rang out in the humid tropical air; *"the mirth and fun grew fast and furious … the dancers quick and quicker flew."*

Suddenly the music stopped. The hesitant unsteady dancers loudly roared their disapproval. A laughing voice asked, 'Why have the musicians been cut off in their prime? The poor buggers were doing their best. They weren't all that bad, were they?'

The Chieftain of the St. Andrew's Society stood in front of the puzzled crowd. He raised his hands and pleaded for silence. 'Give me your attention everybody,' he shouted, 'Please be quiet. I've just had an urgent phone call from Chopper.'

'What's happened? Has his Filipino nurse run away?' a drunken voice shouted.

'Please, this is serious. Dr. Chowdhary has had an accident. His car collided with a buffalo on the way to the hospital.'

'I didn't know they were treating buffaloes at the hospital these days,' shouted the same inebriated wag.

'Shut up!' roared the now anxious, motionless dancers. The guilty culprit gave a shame-faced grin then frowned and looked down at the dance-floor.

The Chieftain continued, 'Chopper has called for volunteer blood donors. Dr. Chowdhary is in a bad way. Anyone who's "O-positive" please get to the hospital at once to help out.'

As about twenty men starting hurrying for the ballroom door, the Chieftain shouted, 'Oh aye, and please drive carefully. We don't want any more casualties tonight.'

'I've never seen them move so fast before,' said one lady to her friend, both now left standing without partners, 'at least not when they're moving *away* from their drinks.'

'No, nor not since the last time they announced a *'Ladies' Choice,'* another lady ruefully observed.

The hospital receptionist on night duty was startled by the sudden screech of a car's brakes as it slid to a halt just outside the main door. She was further shocked as several other vehicles, lights blazing, simultaneously came swerving in to stop alongside the first car.

Her bewilderment turned to uncomprehending amazement when the door burst open and in staggered a group of large, red-faced, noisy men. Many were wearing kilts of various tartans and had bright polished daggers stuck down their stockings. The remainder were dressed in white dinner jackets and black bow ties. All were boisterously shouting and wildly laughing as if at a party.

'Is this where the bloody blood is needed?' shouted a huge man with a bald head and a compensatory large black beard. 'You can take a gallon of mine and I'll never miss it.'

'Don't take it, it's contaminated. His mother was English,' yelled another kilted giant. 'Take mine, my name is Bruce.'

'Och, get away back tae Australia,' mockingly shouted a slim young man proudly wearing a kilt of Royal Stewart tartan. 'Take my blue blood instead. Royalty flows through my veins.'

The noisy good humoured banter and jocularity continued as the boisterous mob were tested for "O-Positive" compatibility by a baffled but valiant, medical technician.

To the great disappointment of all those foiled in their noble attempt to be stalwart blood-donors, only twelve were selected. Eight pints of blood were taken and transfused to Dr. Mathieson's critically ill patient.

Soon, spleen-less, neatly stitched up, Dr. Chowdhary was resting and seemed to be out of danger.

Dr Mathieson left the operating theatre and went to give the cheery waiting mob this good news. It was greeted with hearty cheers.

Wanting to thank them all for their willingness to give blood, the doctor's gaze swept over his lively audience and summed them up: none seemed completely drunk; none seemed entirely sober. He started his speech by saying, 'Gentlemen'…He got no further than that one word. He was drowned out by their happy chorus of, 'Gentlemen? Who? Us?'

The doctor valiantly started again, 'Lads...' He was again drowned out by uproarious cheers and shouts of, 'Good auld Chopper, success with the saw again!'

'No, not so much Chopper now, more like Dracula!'

'I'm feeling weak after all this drama, Doctor I think I need a dram.'

'If you haven't any whisky, I'm willing to try your best surgical spirits, Doc.'

'Tell us some of your medical jokes and have us all again in stitches, Doctor.'

Realizing the hopelessness of attempting to give a thank you speech, Dr. Mathieson laughed, waved, and shouted, 'I give up. I'll leave you lads now. I'm going back to Dr. Chowdhary. I'll get much more sense from him than from you lot, he's unconscious.'

As he checked up on the smooth flow of blood entering his patient, the doctor wondered if the amount of whisky in the transfusion would help or hinder his patient's recovery.

He got his answer fairly soon, Doctor Chowdhary did make a speedy recovery. He was back at work a few weeks after his accident. As a token of his appreciation he offered to make a donation to the St. Andrew's Society's funds. He was thanked and informed that the Society, being self-financing, did not need any donations. However he was warmly invited to attend a special meeting of the committee.

The Indian doctor eagerly attended that mysterious meeting. He was amazed to be presented with an ornately-decorated certificate that proclaimed him to have been elected as an Honorary Member of Brunei's St. Andrew's Society and also to be recognised as an Honorary Scotsman.

Flushed, bemused, delighted, Dr. Chowdhary stammered his profound thanks, 'But why, gentlemen? Why award me this most great honour?'

The Chieftain smiled, 'This certificate is presented to you, dear Doctor, in view of the fact that as a result of your recent transfusion, the blood flowing in your body, is now approximately 50% AUTHENTIC, SCOTTISH BLOOD AND 50% GRAND AULD SCOTCH MALT WHISKY.

# Charlie Bags His First 'Macnab'

Bob laughing said, 'That's an amusing story, Gordon. Mary and you must have had a fine life during your thirty years of teaching in Brunei.'

'Yes, we did. Aye, our living standards were high.' Gordon paused, thought back through many years, then, smiled, 'Aye, we gained a life far brighter than anything to be found in a Glasgow tenement.'

'But it seems obvious that you retained something of our old Glasgow liking for alcoholic drink.'

'Yes,' Gordon said, 'I did. As my Brunei living standards rose, so too did my drinking standards. It was a far cry from the auld, often impoverished weekends when most of us youngsters in the Lomond's and the Creagh Dhu could afford nothing more than a pint or two of the cheapest beer, and aye, that only once a week too.'

'In Brunei at that time we had an abundance of cheap, duty-free malt whisky, gin and brandy plus a good selection of fine wines.

'However the wisest of us, fearing – and feeling – the effects on our livers, moderated our drinking. Therefore we confined ourselves mainly to good auld Uisge Beatha and not ruin our health with that other stuff.'

Bob again laughed, 'Aye, I gathered that from your blood donor story.' After a thoughtful short pause, he continued, 'You know, Gordon, I've just thought of a strong strange link between your Brunei story and an Assynt story of mine. A story I've never told anyone before. Two stories, that while of events 10,000 miles apart, are linked by the coincidence of them both involving great malt Scotch whisky and two quite unique certificates.'

Gordon smiled, 'Well, go on tell that story. I'm waiting. Like Prince Charles, I'm all ears.'

So Bob told the following Assynt story:

What was most unusual in mid-September, Glen Canisp Lodge would have no gentry staying in it for two full days. Only the housekeeper and some more lowly servants would be there.

Normally at this time, the height of the deer-stalking, grouse-shooting and salmon fishing season this shooting lodge was crowded every single day with ultra keen stalking, shooting and fishing Vestey gentry.

One week before this unusual sporting gap Mr Vestey, the owner of this lodge and of the surrounding vast Assynt Estate, had been delighted to bag his second 'Macnab'.

This fairly rare Scottish sporting achievement consisted of fairly and sportingly killing a red deer stag after a strenuous stalk, bagging at least one brace of red grouse, and catching a wild Atlantic salmon by means of expertly cast artificial salmon flies; and all this achieved in one day; a day of exactly twelve hours and no more.

On both notable sporting occasions when Mr. Vestey got his 'Macnab' his head-gamekeeper, Charlie Ross, had been with him and had played no small part in making sure his boss got his stag, grouse and salmon. So over celebratory drams in the lodge's gun-room, a jubilant Mr. Vestey said, 'Oh, Charlie, it's most annoying, but I'm afraid the lodge will be empty for two days next week. Mrs. Vestey and I have to attend a family wedding in London.

'I know you've never managed to bag a 'Macnab' yourself, although without your expert help I, and others of my family, would never have got our own. So why don't you go on one of these free days and try to bag one for yourself?'

'Thank you sir, aye, I would like fine tae bag a 'Macnab' before I get too auld and decrepit.'

'Oh, Charlie, surely there's no fear of you getting frail for a good number of years yet.' Mr Vestey smiled, 'I fear I might get decrepit before you. Anyway, that's your 'Macnab' chance arranged. I'm sure you'll achieve it. I'll let Major Farran know and he in turn will inform me of how you get on.'

Major Farran was Assynt Estate's factor. He, perhaps rather snobbishly, did not seem too pleased at Charlie getting that gift of this grand sporting chance. No doubt he'd much prefer one of his friends amongst the gentry to have obtained this favour. But, after all his years in the army, he knew how to obey orders.

At 8.30 a.m. on Charlie's appointed 'Macnab' day, he set out to shoot his stag. He was accompanied by trainee gamekeeper, Bob Scott, and sturdy young pony-boy, Jamie Ogston, who was leading Nell, the hardy stalking pony. The eager men and steady plodding garron swallowed up the wild Assynt miles as they penetrated ever deeper into lovely, lonely Glen Canisp.

None of the men could, nor would want to, ignore the sheer towering presence of that fantastic hill, Suilven, as it dominated the end of this long glen.

Stoic pony and keen pony-boy were left waiting while Charlie and Bob continued cautiously on to find a suitable stag and get Charlie's great day underway.

They soon did, and Charlie's usual accurate heart-shot dropped his eight-pointer 'Macnab' stag, stone dead.

To the delight of the patiently waiting familiar ravens the stag was quickly gralloched, loaded on steady auld Nell's big deer-saddle and the return journey started.

Uplifted by their stalking success the three men barely noticed a heavy rain shower that suddenly battered in from the West. They continued walking on, eager to get to Charlie's 'Macnab' grouse and salmon, their eagerness kept in check by stag-burdened auld Nell's steady plodding pace.

At last the stag was skinned and left hanging in the deer-larder. The rifle was cleaned, oiled and locked away in the Lodge's gun-room. 'Oh damn, the housekeeper's left no drams for us', Charlie complained. 'She couldn't know we were stalking today.'

'Will I see if she's in the kitchen?' Bob asked.

'Och, no, we better no' waste time, let's get on wi' my Macnab.'

They did. Charlie drove them all (excluding Nell) in his van to Torbreck. Robert MacDonald, the gamekeeper in charge of the estate kennels, welcomed them. He had two English Setters ready and impatiently waiting. 'I've decided to use Shadow and Juno they're both fine calm steady workers.'

Robert MacDonald, leading the way in his van, took them up the rough rutted track towards large Loch Crocach.

While Robert worked Juno through some lower heathery ground where he'd recently seen grouse, Bob worked his favourite setter, Shadow, over slightly higher steeper heather.

As always, it was a real pleasure to see these well-trained dogs eagerly run in controlled sweeps through what they hoped was grouse-rich heather, their keen quivering nostrils ceaselessly testing every scent the Westerly wind brought them.

After some disappointing grouse-less twenty minutes, Robert delighted, shouted, 'Juno's got a point at last.'

Then Bob excitedly waved and shouted, 'Oh, and Shadow's now got a point as well.'

Charlie laughed, 'Och, now I'm real spoilt for choice. Surely I'll have nae trouble getting at least one brace to keep my 'Macnab' quest going.'

Robert shouted, 'Oh, Bob, just keep Shadow steady at her point until Charlie attends to Juno's grouse.'

Standing beside Shadow, Bob admired her motionless statuesque pose as from quivering nostrils to tip of 'feathered' tail she was one lovely straight line accurately pointing at the scented, but unseen grouse.

Charlie's double-barrelled shotgun blasted out twice. Two of Juno's pointed grouse fell dead to the heather.

The two loud shots sent an extra quiver of excitement through Shadow's tense nerves but she still motionlessly held her steady point.

Charlie, his re-loaded gun held ready, cautiously walked beside Bob as they moved forward with Shadow leading them in her eager, unerring, stealthy way towards her still unseen grouse.

Although expected, there was the usual sudden shock as a covey of nine grouse exploded from concealing heather in wild scattering flight.

Again both Charlie's barrels blasted out. Not the expected two, but three dead birds, fluttered to the heather.

Robert MacDonald applauded and laughed, 'Och, Charlie, you've sure made certain of getting more than your needed quota of Macnab, grouse.'

'Aye, thanks tae you and your well-trained setters. Och the stag and thae grouse were the easiest part, but bagging my salmon could be quite tricky. We all too well ken just what thrawn buggers thae damn fish can be, don't we?'

They little thought how, all too soon, Charlie's wise words would prove to be all too real.

After leaving Robert and young Jamie at Torbreck, Charlie drove to his home at Inveruplan to collect his salmon-fishing rod. Bob willingly went with him. After seeing, admiring, and perhaps secretly envying the skilful expertise with which good auld Charlie had got his stag and grouse, Bob wanted to be 'in at the kill,' when he bagged his River Inver salmon and triumphantly completed his first 'Macnab'.

Bob nobly tried to banish any unworthy thoughts of any, almost certain, celebratory drams from his mind.

After meeting and warmly greeting Bob at Inveruplan's ever hospitable door, Charlie's wife, Jess, eagerly asked, 'Well, how did it go? Have you got your first 'Macnab'?'

'Och, not quite yet, I got my stag and grouse, I've still to bag my salmon. I'll grab my rod and hurry to the river.'

Jess turned to Bob, 'Of course you'll come in and have a cup o' tea and a scone before you go.' This was not a question, but a hospitable command.

Charlie replied for Bob, 'Och, wifie we've nae time for tea just now. Once I've caught my salmon there'll be plenty time for time for tea.' With anticipatory gleaming eyes he added, 'Aye, an' nae doot for a dram or twa, too.'

'Och, Charlie, Charlie, you don't really think I'll let Bob go away from Inveruplan without him getting tea and some o' my fresh-baked scones, do you?'

Charlie, experience telling him when he was defeated, grinned, 'All right, Bob, go in and have your damn tea an' scones, but don't take long over them. I'll be just a minute. There's something I must do before I come in.'

Although Bob was almost as keen as Charlie to get to the river and complete this 'Macnab,' still, as always, he was delighted to spend some time in Inveruplan's cosy wee living room and be refreshed by Jess's hospitably urged scones and tea.

During his happy years in Assynt Bob had received much true Highland hospitality in many scattered locations: Achmelvich, Inverkirkaig, Torbreck, but none of these grand places could beat the happy warmth of Inveruplan's conviviality; this small, isolated, unpretentious Assynt home was radiantly alive with Charlie and Jess's lively good humoured presence.

The congenial wonders of Inveruplan's unique all night ceilidhs, were the stuff of glowing fables.

In further confirmation of this place's genuine pre-eminence, Bob saw a slim volume of poetry on the table. He picked it up and read the familiar title: *A Man in my Position* by Norman MacCaig. It was signed by the author and inscribed to Charlie and Jess.

'I see you've got Norman's latest book,' Bob said.

'Aye,' Jess replied, 'Norman always gives us a signed copy of each new book.'

Bob laughed, 'Och, I don't know him as well as you two. I buy his books and he willingly signs them for me.'

'I think his long poem, *A Man in Assynt* is his best yet,' Charlie said as he gulped a hasty cup of tea.

Bob nodded, 'Aye, Charlie, I agree. I like his description of a keeper, (who surely must be you) *tilting his Rembrandt face in the light as he bangs the chorus round then takes up his dram and drinks it down.*'

'Aye,' Charlie laughed, 'I suppose that might be me. Aye, true enough, I've downed quite a few drams in my time.'

Jess indulgently smiled, 'Oh, Charlie, surely more, many more, than just "a few"?'

'Another short poem I really like also involves you two,' Bob said, his, *Walking to Inveruplan*, with Norman's, *miles to go and friends to meet.*

Again Charlie laughed, 'Aye, I think they're a' braw poems, right enough; at least the ones I can understand are! Och but that's enough o' this fancy poetic talk. Come on, Bob, gulp doon that cup o' tea, your third cup, I think. Och, but who's counting, let's hurry tae the river an' my waiting 'Macnab' salmon.'

They did. Soon Charlie's expert flies were enticingly swimming through the well-named Star Pool, the River Inver's best, most, productive salmon pool.

But even Charlie's greatest (and it *was* great) fishing expertise was, after one hour, still of no avail.

He tried many different bright alluring patterns and sizes of salmon flies; he hurried to many different salmon pools. Using his many years of intimate knowledge of this lovely, wildly-rushing river he skilfully fished each pool's most favoured places to hold resting salmon.

But still all to no avail.

'Oh God damn thae surly buggers, it seems their lack o' co-operation will scupper my chance o' getting my first 'Macnab', doesn't it?' Charlie plaintively asked.

'Aye, I'm afraid it does,' Bob replied. 'I'm real sorry, Charlie. It's a terrible shame after you've got your stag and grouse, too.'

'Aye, I know. It's bloody awful.'

It was extremely rare for anyone to see Charlie in a despondent mood, in fact it was almost unheard-of, so Bob was not surprised when he noticed what seemed a mischievous gleam brighten his eyes as he asked, 'What's that saying aboot desperate situations requiring desperate measures, eh? Well I'm going tae take a desperate measure now tae catch my salmon. I'm going tae dae something that's not quite posh English "cricket," so, Bob, just you walk away if you don't want tae be involved wi' me in my dastardly act.'

Bob laughed, 'Och, Charlie, I'll stick wi' you through thick and thin. What exactly do you intend doing?'

To answer this, Charlie plunged a hand into his tweed jacket's large, deep, 'poachers's pocket,' and brought out an old pipe-tobacco tin. He opened the lid and held the tin for Bob's inspection. It was packed with damp moss and a wriggling mass of large pink earth-worms.

Again Bob laughed, 'Oh, Charlie, Charlie, this most certainly isn't cricket on this strictly fly-fishing only river, is it? Och, but what the hell, go ahead and at long last get your 'Macnab' salmon.'

And Charlie quickly did. Hardly had his hook, baited with what he always called 'garden wanderers,' been dropped into the Star Pool's fast stream, before a salmon grabbed the un-needed food, was firmly hooked and dashed off in wild unstoppable flight.

Charlie allowed the strong fish to make one more tiring run before, with no gentle finesse, he guided it into Bob's waiting landing-net.

As they shook hands Bob said, 'Well done, Charlie, my sincere congratulations on you bagging your first 'Macnab.'

'Thanks Bob. Of course you ken that no one must ever learn how I caught my 'Macnab' salmon wi' the help o' thae 'garden wanderers', don't you?'

'Oh, of course, Charlie, I'll never tell a soul.' (And he never did, until now, 38 years after Charlie's tragic death.)

The following morning Major Farran made a surreptitious check that there actually was a skinned 'Macnab' stag hanging in Glen Canisp Lodge's deer larder, two brace of grouse in the grouse larder and the required 8lb. salmon in the kitchen's chill room.

He then met Charlie and said, 'I was on the phone to Mr. Vestey last night and I mentioned that you'd bagged your first 'Macnab.' He sent his congratulations and asked me to give you this from him.' He handed over a bottle of grand auld Glenlivet malt whisky.

'Oh, Charlie, and this certificate was made by my wife, who's a bit of an artist, for you.' Smiling, he gave him a large, elaborately decorated colourful certificate with Charlie's name inscribed, which stated that, having fairly and sportingly, bagged a stag, a brace of grouse and a salmon on the one day, he was now a member of the exclusive, Macnab Society.

Charlie felt his conscience give a painful stab as he read these words, "fairly and sportingly" and thought of his helpers, his, 'garden wanderers.' But he let none of this brief unease appear as he thanked the major.

★ ★ ★

'So there you are Gordon,' Bob said as they sat on Craigower Hill all these years later, 'two stories some 10,000 miles apart but linked by made-up certificates and good auld malt Scotch whisky.'

'Aye,' Gordon grinned, 'it sure is quite a coincidence that they should both involve fake certificates, but there's nothing strange about the link between whisky and Scotsmen. The two go together like conjoined twins.'

'Aye you're spot on there,' replied Bob, nodding his head.

'By the way, you met Charlie Ross, didn't you?' he then asked.

'Oh yes, I met him, but unfortunately only the once, when I was with you. I got the impression of a good warm presence.'

'And you must have met Norman MacCaig on your summer holidays at Achmelvich.'

'Oh yes. I often saw him there. Although I didn't really know him, I did once interview him with a questionnaire for my university thesis, on Assynt. He was very pleasant and helpful then.'

'Och, Gordon, even if this book we're writing doesn't bring us fame and fortune, at least we can claim to have made the acquaintance of two famous people: Norman MacCaig, one of – if not *the* – greatest Scottish poets of the 20th century, and the Duchess of Argyll who gave us that unforgettable lift in her Rolls Royce when, in all innocence, we knew nothing, at that time, of her notoriety, her scandalous behaviour.'

'Aye,' Gordon laughed, 'If only we could have featured on her list, I'm sure we would have been fast and very keen, learners.'

Bob also heartily laughed, 'Aye, maybe too fast, the way we were feeling that night.'

'Aye, and while still wearing yon fabulous three-strand pearl necklace she always wore, no matter what tricks she was getting up to.'

'You could say with us two, it might have been a case of the Duchess casting her expensive pearls before us poor common swine, eh?

'Och, but come on, Gordon, let's have no more o' this nostalgic talk and vivid thoughts of what might have been. We better make a move; not just sit here and endlessly ramble on and on. Let's get back down to the worldly delights of Pitlochry. Let's summon up the energy to stumble down to Drummond's and again get stuck into that homely wee restaurant's great food.'

'Aye, I'm looking forward to again savouring their *famous* haddock and chips! Thank God that, although we can no longer climb our still loved Scottish hills, we can, and do still greatly enjoy good food and drink.'

So, with protesting knees and aching hips, they rose and slowly, and happily, made their way down from the modest heights of grand wee Craigower Hill.